Lebanon

Lebanon

1761 * 1994

the evolution of a resilient New Hampshire city

by

Roger Carroll

Published for the

LEBANON HISTORICAL SOCIETY

by

PHOENIX PUBLISHING
West Kennebunk, Maine

The quotation on page 87 is reproduced from *Goodbye Highland Yankee* by Scott Hastings, published by the Chelsea Green Publishing Co., and used with the kind permission of Elsie Hastings who holds the copyright.

Library of Congress Cataloging-in-Publication Data

Carroll, Roger, 1959–
Lebanon, 1761–1994 : the evolution of a resilient New Hampshire city / by Roger Carroll.
  p. cm.
Includes bibliographical references and index.
ISBN 0-914659-71-5
1. Lebanon (N.H.)—History. I. Title.
F44.L4C37   1994
974.2'3—dc20   94-24652
                                                             CIP

Copyright 1994 by the Lebanon Historical Society

All rights reserved. No part of this publication may be reproduced, stored in a retrieval system or transmitted in any form or by any means without the prior written permission of the Lebanon Historical Society, except for brief quotations in a review.

Printed in the United States of America

*The Lebanon Historical Society
dedicates this book to
Governor Lane and Elizabeth Dwinell . . .
staunch advocates of this state and city . . .
without whose vision and support
this history would never have
come to fruition*

For Bozie

R. C.

Contents

Preface	xi
Introduction	xiii
Part I New Town	1
1. "Some Suitable Stream"	3
2. Churches, Etc.	17
3. The City, Secession, and Center Village	27
4. Turnpikes and Locks	36
5. About Town	42
6. District Schools	51
7. Wool Depots and Dairies	59
8. The Railroad	68
9. Westside	79
10. A Most Uncivil War	98
Part II Boomtown	107
11. Before the First Great Fire	109
12. "Where Is Up-Street Gone?"	138
13. Woolen Mills, Canadians, and Catholics	148
14. A Penny Saved	160
15. World War I	172
16. The Great Depression	181
17. World War II	193
18. Seats of Influence	201
19. Lebanon vs (West) Lebanon	207
20. Decline	221

Part III	White Collar City	237
21.	"If People Like It, We'll Build More"	239
22.	Rock and Roll	248
23.	The Hanoverization of Lebanon	255
24.	The Go-Go Eighties	261
25.	Pastimes	266
26.	New Town	280

Appendices	287
Bibliography	288
Illustrations and Credits	291
Index	293

Preface

EVEN THOUGH my wife Elizabeth and I are not natives of Lebanon and no longer live within its borders, Lebanon will always be our hometown, as it actually was for over sixty-five years. We both graduated from its high school, and it was where, among other things, my political career was launched.

We have long felt that Lebanon deserved a new chronicle of its 230 years. The only previous history, by the Reverend Charles A. Downs, stopped its account more than a century ago. A few times over the past several years we inquired of prospective authors, and for some thirty years have had a contingency plan to finance the writing of such a book. Then, when Roger Carroll became available to write the book and the Lebanon Historical Society agreed to publish it, we decided to proceed at once.

The two-year time span in which the project was completed is unusually short for a local history (although the author, no doubt, wishes he had another five years to devote to it). It stands in especially sharp contrast to the timetable in which the first Lebanon history was published. Selectmen were empowered at the 1880 town meeting to secure an author and spend such sums of money as were needed, but it was not until 1908, two years after the death of Mr. Downs, that the book was finally published. That this new history was completed in such a relatively short time is a testament to the close cooperation between the author and the historical society, especially its curator, Robert Leavitt, whose knowledge of Lebanon history, if fully recorded, would fill many volumes. In addition, the town has also benefitted from the workings of such men and women as Robert's grandfather, George U.L. Leavitt, Frank Churchill, Ethel Rock Millen, Sam Stevens, and Helen Smith, whose family published the *Granite State Free Press* for over one-hundred years.

Lebanon has, as the title states, truly been a "resilient" community. The farmers who once comprised the backbone of the town made successful transitions from sheep to dairy farming; Lebanonians rolled with the punches of the 1887 fire that destroyed the dominant woodworking and metal shops, replacing them with textile industries that were a hallmark of the local economy for several decades. By the time the last of the woolen mills died and a second major fire struck the downtown, the interstate highway was already looming on Lebanon's horizon, marking yet another evolution: The town that once had three railroad stations had become a city with four interstate exits and a budding service economy.

These changes and others are covered in Mr. Carroll's readable, well-illustrated, sometimes amusing account of Lebanon's history. Hopefully, our successors will not wait quite as long to publish another.

Lane Dwinell

Hanover, New Hampshire
July 1994

Introduction

I MAKE NO pretense about being an historian, and harbor no illusions that I have exhausted the subject of Lebanon's history. I merely tried to paint a picture that captures how the city evolved from agrarian roots, through a long period as the home to a large blue-collar population, into the place it is today: An increasingly white-collar city characterized by a mixture of malls and industry, yet retaining some of its rural flavor.

The hardest part was deciding what to leave out, and there were judgment calls over which I will surely agonize forever. Since this book is more about trends than biographies, many individuals who played a significant role in Lebanon's evolution are either not mentioned, or are noted only in passing. Their stories warrant a separate book altogether.

I also struggled with the issue of lists, and ultimately opted not to include them. The torment was especially acute when considering whether to publish a roster of war veterans. While the Historical Society has a great admiration for Lebanon's veterans, the record of who served is sketchy, and the chances were high that someone would be omitted. Therefore, lacking confidence that such a list would be comprehensive, the author and the board of the Historical Society reluctantly decided not to include one.

With a few exceptions, I also did not delve deeply into either the town's religious or political history. The Reverend Charles Downs book covered those topics in some detail, while paying little attention to the town's industrial background. Since Lebanon had defined itself as an industrial community almost since its inception, I chose to focus on the latter.

If history is any judge, there are probably some factual errors in this book. I take responsibility for those and pray they are not many.

A book of this nature does not come into being without an assist from an enormous number of people. I am indebted to Jean Mansell for giving me a key to the library, and to her very competent and dedicated staff. I also am grateful to City Clerk Dorothy Doyle and her assistant clerks. Dartmouth College records manager Raymond Cunningham provided a significant assist; the staff at Baker Library was ever-helpful, especially former archivist Ken Kramer and those in the Jones Microtext Center. The people at the state library, state archives, and the New Hampshire Historical Society also proved invaluable; Edwin Battison of the American Precision Museum in Windsor was gracious with his time and knowledge; and my old batting-practice partner, Jim Fox, let me use the *Valley News* library; a special note of thanks goes to Polly Goralski at the Grafton County Superior Court, who looked up many a long-forgotten case for me.

As I pursued a variety of dead-end leads over the course of a year and a half I kept hearing the voice of Dartmouth history professor Jere Daniell, who sagely reminded me in the beginning to be patient.

I also thank the hundreds of people who submitted to interviews, answered questions, dug up bits of small but essential information, and never once complained. This book could not have been written without them.

Olive MacGregor, Art Pease, Eliot Page, Terry Lopata, Gene Paige, Helen Smith, Jim Wechsler, and Nancy Pyer read all or parts of the manuscript and offered feedback in the most gentle but helpful way. I thank them all. This book also would not have been possible without the professional guidance of Lex Paradis and Al Morris of Phoenix Publishing, nor the tremendous support from the directors and members of the Lebanon Historical Society; especially Russell Cantlin, whose soft-spoken manner belies his willingness to roll up his sleeves.

I am especially indebted to City Historian Robert Leavitt, whose grandfather, George U.L. Leavitt, fostered his interest in Lebanon's history. As the curator of the Lebanon Historical Society, Robert guided me through the maze of files he has meticulously collected and organized over the years. Then he read, suggested, and corrected what I had written. The word "patience" is inadequate to describe what he put up with. In many important respects, I share the authorship of this book with him.

I do, in fact, share authorship with two contributors. Much of the section on the Civil War was taken from the work of Mark Leno, a Lebanon High School graduate who spent five years studying the town's role in that war. He is responsible for bringing that section to life. I merely rewrote and edited his unpublished material, and added a few details.

In addition, Jim Wechsler contributed the passage on the Lebanon Senators baseball team. Hopefully, this book will spur him to write the one he has been keeping inside himself all of these years. The literary world would be the better for it.

A word about Lane Dwinell, who, along with his elegant wife Elizabeth, made this book a reality through their generous financial contribution. If Governor Dwinell were the owner of a major league baseball team he would be in the mold of Gene Autry, rather than George Steinbrenner: Always supportive, never meddlesome, and ever patient. I am extremely grateful for the advice he provided and the faith he showed in asking me to embark on this project. It may be a long time before we again see anyone who cares as deeply about Lebanon as do the Dwinells.

Finally, I am extremely grateful to my wife, Cathleen, who read, suggested, encouraged, listened, and most of all, persevered.

Roger Carroll

Lebanon, New Hampshire
June 1994

Lebanon

I

New Town

The Dana House on Elm Street in West Lebanon constructed in 1765 stands as an example of colonial pioneer architecture.

1

"Some Suitable Stream"

THE ICE was more than a mile thick before it receded some eight-thousand years ago from the land that would one day be known as Lebanon, leaving behind a desolate, boulder-strewn landscape. The large stones were a bane to farmers who had to plant, mow, and harvest around them.

The runoff from the melting glacier created a chain of deep glacial lakes, two of which—Lake Hitchcock and Lake Upham—flooded Lebanon between seventeen- and eleven-thousand years ago, accounting for the presence of the Boston Lot Lake on the hilltop just east of Wilder Dam. When an earthen dam burst in what is now the state of Connecticut, the ensuing drainage from the lakes left a lake bed with clay and gravel deposits which ultimately proved a boon to the Densmore Brick Company and many a local road builder. As time passed, the White, Mascoma, and Connecticut rivers cut their paths through those glacial deposits and the landscape began to take its present form.

The River

Although the Connecticut is New England's largest river, it is the Mascoma to which Lebanon's fortunes have been most closely tied.

The river, though, has powered industry in three different Lebanon villages, its shad runs provided food for early settlers, and it has furnished the town's drinking water for several decades. The dam at the foot of Mascoma Lake offers excellent trout fishing, and kayakers travel from throughout the northeast each spring to test their skills against the river's rapids.

The river has been good to Lebanon, although the converse has not always been true. Three Dartmouth College students observed in 1924 that the Mascoma was serving as the town's de facto sewer: "Lebanon is extremely fortunate in being so free of scarlet fever because the Mascoma River which runs through the central part of the town is absolutely stagnant. Slightly below the town small boys go in swimming regularly, yet this part abounds with cat-tails, the water is infested with rats, and it is the village dump. Sewage enters the river above the water line. All along the river bank people throw refuse into the water and as yet the Board of Health has done nothing about it."

Despite its many uses and misuses over the years, it is unclear just how the river was named. Mascoma was a Native American whose name—with the variation Masscommah and Mascommah—appears on three property deeds in Hampstead County, Massachusetts. Unfortunately, little is known about him or how his name became connected with the waterway.

There is scant evidence of Native American activity in the town. An archeological dig at the True Farm near the Plainfield town line in West Lebanon in 1964-1965 found a hunting camp dating to before 700 A.D. on the bank of the stream known as True's Brook or Blood Brook. The excavation yielded spear points made from rock which appears to have been brought from an area of upstate New York that housed a larger Indian population with which the local group was probably marginally affiliated. The dig also concluded that the camp was probably used for only a short time and lacked evidence of agricultural development that would have indicated long-term occupation.

Although it is a modest-sized river, the United States Navy named one of its tankers after the Mascoma during World War II. The reason, however, remains a mystery, other than the fact that all tankers were named for prominent rivers.

The 524-foot *Mascoma* was launched on May 31, 1943, with the obligatory smashing of a champagne bottle on her bow. The ship was commissioned in 1944 and sent to the Pacific where, the *Granite State Free Press* later reported, she refueled over a thousand boats in the Third, Fifth, and Seventh fleets during the remaining years of World War II. One of the *Mascoma*'s sailors was Warrant Officer James Anderson, who married Lebanon resident Merilynn Gray. They live less than a quarter mile from the river.

In addition to oil, the *Mascoma* also carried food, ammunition, depth charges, medical supplies, mail, and movies. The vessel received seven battle stars for service in World War II that included conflicts in the Marshall Islands, Marianne Islands, the Philippines, Okinawa, Third Fleet operations against Japan, and liberation of the Philippines.

Norman Decato saw the ship from a distance while stationed in the South Pacific during World War II, and even fifty years later recalls the sighting. "That seemed like home to me—my God—the Mascoma River."

She was decommissioned after World War II, but reactivated as a noncommissioned ship in 1950, and provided wartime support off the coast of Korea for which she received the Korean Service Medal and the United Nations Service Medal.

The ship was dropped from the Navy's list of active ships in 1959, and the *Mascoma* sat idle in Virginia's James River until 1966, when she was sold to a civilian shipping concern and renamed.

The Charter

When the French and Indian wars ended in the late 1750s, three companies of soldiers returning from battle in Canada sliced across Maine and northern New Hampshire to the Connecticut River, which they followed home to Connecticut. One of those soldiers was William Dana, who undoubtedly passed the big river's confluence with the smaller Mascoma and White rivers.

Back in Connecticut, Mr. Dana and a group of men from Lebanon, Norwich, and Mansfield, Connecticut, pooled their money in the spring of 1761 and sent Jedediah Dana, William's cousin, to Portsmouth, New Hampshire, to buy two charters from Royal Governor Benning Wentworth—one for Lebanon and another for Enfield.

Mr. Wentworth, the only royal governor allowed to grant charters, handed them out by the score for nominal sums under the premise that increased settlements would lead to more trade, economic prosperity, and taxes. On July 4, 1761, he signed a charter for a six-mile-by-six-mile township to be known as Lebanon. The neighboring grants of Enfield, Hanover, Norwich, and Hartford were also chartered on that day. Lebanon's charter listed the following names as a majority of the town's first proprietors:

John Hanks	Joseph Dana
John Salter	John Swift
Obadiah Loomis	Daniel Allen, Jr.
Elijah Huntington	David Eldredge
Huckins Storrs, Jr.	Jesse Birchard
John Baldwin	Nathan Arnold
Robbert Barrows, Jr.	Levi Hyde
Richard Salter	John Birchard
Constant Southworth	Nathan Blodgett
Thomas Storrs	Moses Hibbard, Jr.
Hobart Estabrook	John Allen
Samuel Storrs	Robert Hyde
Charles Hill	John Hyde
Benjamin Davis	Lemuel Clark
Joshua Blodgett	Jesse Birchard
Joseph Turner	Daniel Blodgett, III
Josiah Storrs	Nehemiah Estabrook
Joseph Wood	Jonathan Martin
John Storrs	Nathaniel Porter
Jonathan Murdock	Jonathan Yeomans
Jabez Barrow	David Turner
Seth Blodgett	Daniel Blodgett
Joseph Martin	Jonathan Walcutt
Nathaniel Hall	John Birchard
Thomas Barrows, Jr.	Edward Goldstone Lutwych

Some families were represented more than once. The Storrs, for example, bought five shares and eventually settled atop the hill that bears the family name. There are five Blodgetts on the list. They settled in the Hardy Hill region, and one of the ridges to the west of Hardy Hill was once known as Blodgett Hill.

Other families with more than one grantee on the list included the Barrows with three and the Birchards with four, although the latter was an error. Jesse Birchard's name appears twice on the charter by mistake, while Amariah Storrs was omitted, although he was later given a share and its cost, four pounds, was paid for by the other proprietors.

In addition to using grants as a means of establishing settlements, Governor Wentworth also was in the habit of using them to enrich his friends, family, and political associates by including them among the list of grantees of the new townships. Thus, the charter also contains a second group of proprietors, most of them men from the New Hampshire seacoast, including two Wentworths who were relatives of the royal governor.

> Jedediah Dana
> Mark H. Wentworth
> Jonathan Blanchard
> Clement Jackson, Esq.
> Samuel Penhallow
> William Dana
> James Nevins, Esq.
> Onell Lamont
> Hugh Hall Wentworth
> William Knight

These proprietors became the means by which towns were settled. As Roy Hidemichi Akagi wrote in *Town Proprietors of the New England Colonies*, proprietors were:

The original grantees or purchasers of a tract of land, usually a township, which they and their heirs, assigns or successors, together with those whom they chose to admit to their number, held in common ownership. They enjoyed the absolute ownership and the exclusive control over such tracts of land granted to them and were responsible collectively for the improvement of the new plantation. More specifically they were responsible for inducing and enlisting settlers and new comers, for locating home lots and dwelling houses, for building highways and streets, for subdividing the arable land, and subjecting the meadow and forest, for a time at least, to common management. In other words, they constituted the nucleus of the newly settled community and at first they controlled the whole machinery of a town's life, both political and economic.

Although their domains and officers tended to overlap, the proprietors and the town were distinct political entities with separate offices and records. They operated simultaneously at least until 1806, when the proprietors' records end (probably because the group dissolved itself).

Since the purpose of the grant was to encourage development, Lebanon's charter set out incentives for proprietors to lure settlers to the wilderness: Once fifty families settled the town would be entitled to hold two trading "fairs" a year and also to hold a market on one or more days a week.

In what was standard procedure for such grants, the charter also imposed a nominal annual rent on the proprietors, reserved for the crown any white pine trees that might be suitable as masts for the royal navy, and set aside a 500-acre tract for Governor Wentworth. When Plainfield was chartered a month later, Mr. Wentworth parlayed his five-hundred acres in Lebanon into a thousand-acre parcel by reserving for himself another five-hundred acres in Plainfield that abutted his Lebanon grant.

That tract was later annexed and divided up among townspeople when the royal government was ousted from power.

Camp Meadow

With the charter in hand, the proprietors' first order of business was to explore and lay out the grant. They first met on October 6, 1761, at the Mansfield, Connecticut, inn of Amariah Storrs, where a committee was formed to survey the new township and divide it into lots. They taxed each shareholder ten shillings for laying out the town, and three committee members—Charles Hill, Levi Hyde, and William Dana—left for Lebanon within days of that first meeting to begin their survey. They returned home for the winter but came back in the spring and finished the inspection by the fall of 1762, after which the land was doled out by lottery. Each proprietor received a hundred-acre parcel and a lot next to the river, and a tract of single-acre lots in the center of town was set aside for common use.

The winter of 1762-63 marked the town's first recorded year-round habitation. William Dana (a surveyor by trade), Levi Hyde, Samuel Estabrook, and a fourth man believed to have been Charles Hill or William Downer built a lean-to on the bank of the Connecticut River just downstream from what is now Wilder Dam and stayed through the winter. They called their dwelling place Camp Meadow.

The men gathered enough hay to feed their two oxen and also enough food for themselves, although "during a severe snow storm, Mr. Dana came near perishing, while absent from his companions to feed their oxen at a place called Beaver Meadow." (This was near where Mascoma Street Extension runs into the east end of Old Pine Tree Cemetery Road).

First Things First

Although most of the proprietors were speculators who had no interest in moving to Lebanon, the charter contained a clause common in other grants that said five acres had to be planted for every fifty acres owned or the grant would revert back to the royal governor. The threat of forfeiture was a powerful mandate for settlement, and one of the proprietors' earliest concerns was providing a road for would-be residents. Thus, constructing roads to and through Lebanon took up much of their energy during the early years.

The first road north of Fort #4 in Charlestown was "The Horse Road," named after the beast it was designed to accommodate. To improve upon that, proprietors appointed a committee to lay out and clear a road and levied a tax to pay for it. Members of Lebanon's road committee worked with proprietors from Hanover, Lyme, and Norwich to share the cost of the road, which ran along the Connecticut River and was completed in 1763.

Having laid out the township and cleared a path to it, proprietors then sought to procure a minister and convince someone to build a sawmill. At their second meeting, held December 22, 1761, proprietors voted a tax of ten shillings apiece for each of the next two years, "to encourage Mr. Oliver Davison to build a saw mill upon some suitable stream within the township of Lebanon."

The money—plus first choice of hundred-acre lots—lured Mr. Davison to the grant. He chose a site on the Mascoma about a mile upstream from the Connecticut (Glen Road-Route 4 intersection, 1994), and by the fall of 1763, his mill provided the means by which felled trees were turned into lumber for framed houses.

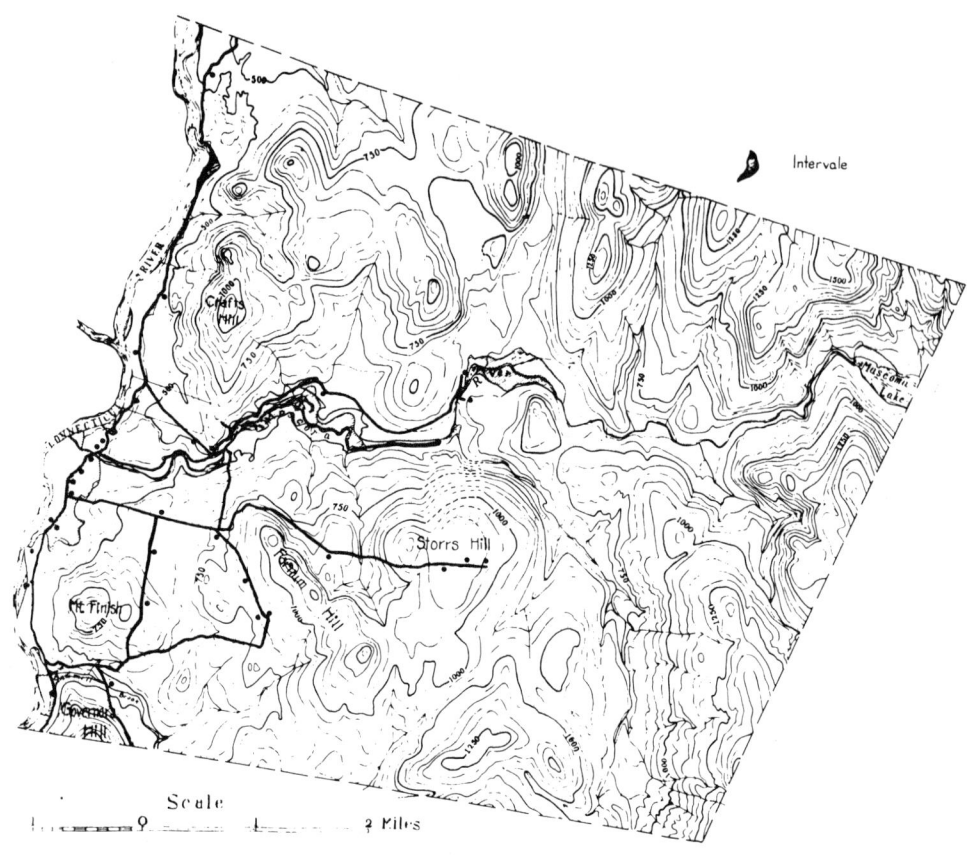

Probable roads and settlements in 1767*

Such inducements of land and money were a common way of attracting settlers and supporting industry. The town in 1779 voted a tract of land for a cloth mill in West Lebanon, and early makers of nails also were paid a subsidy.

Mr. Davison's sawmill also cut the lumber for the first bridge over the Mascoma River. The span, later known as Hubbard's bridge, was put up in 1767 and stood for many years at the Route 4-Glen Road intersection, a location that has endured as a river crossing to the present (1994). Proprietors also greased the wheels of progress for that first bridge by purchasing three gallons of rum for those who showed up to help build it.

Burying Grounds

Mr. Davison also holds the distinction of being the first resident to die in town. He thus was the first person buried in the cemetery that came out of a 1768 swap in which the town traded Charles Hill an acre of common land for an acre of his property between the top of Seminary Hill and the Mascoma River. The exchange resulted in

---

*This and the maps on the following pages are from an article by Edward N. Torbert titled "Evolution of Land Utilization in Lebanon, N.H." published in *Geographical Review* in 1935.

Lebanon, 1761-1994 / 8

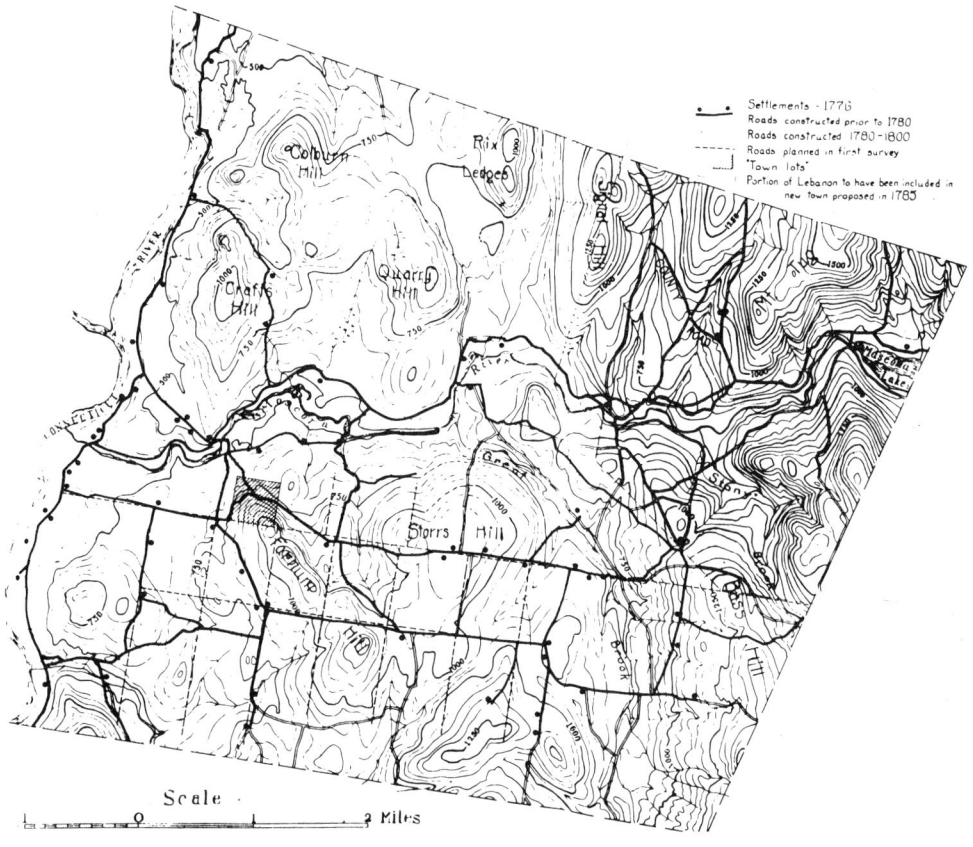

Probable roads and settlements in 1776

Lebanon's first "burying ground," the Old Pine Tree Cemetery, which was needed when Mr. Davison died the next year. He was not, however, the last to do so. The Village Cemetery was established on School Street in 1797; a small children's cemetery dating to about 1810 was discovered in some woods off Poverty Lane in 1963; the East Lebanon Cemetery was started in 1807 on a lot just east of the town line with Enfield; a graveyard at the foot of Great Brook Road near East Plainfield, known as the Cole Cemetery, dates from about 1820; the West Lebanon Cemetery near the Mount Lebanon School was opened in 1852; Glenwood Cemetery was established in 1872 just west of the present (1994) Storrs Hill ski area, and the adjacent Mount Calvary Cemetery was established in 1891; the Sacred Heart Cemetery on Mascoma Street Extension was started in July 1931, and the adjacent Valley Cemetery was first used the following year.

The Coming

The William Downer family was the first to arrive in town. Mr. Downer, his wife, and their eight children made the journey from Connecticut in 1763. The family genealogy says they came up the horse path, while other accounts say they traveled by boat.

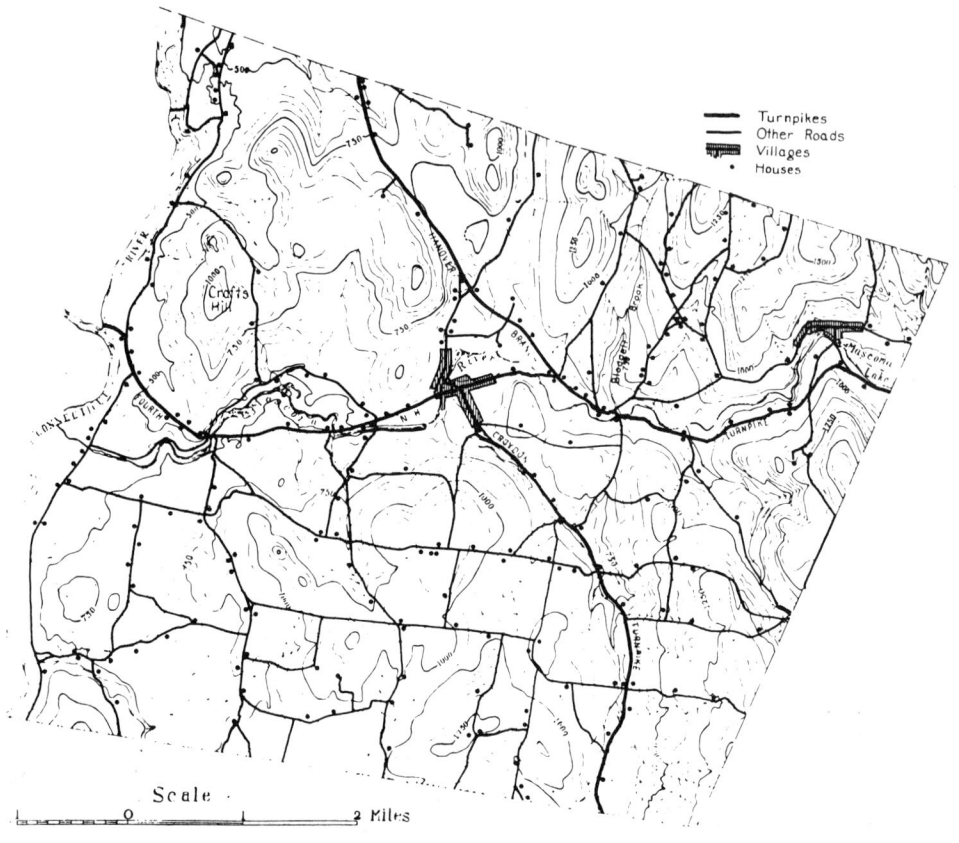

Probable roads and farmhouses in the early nineteenth century

Either way, with eight children in tow it must have been an interesting journey, and at its conclusion the Downers settled near the Plainfield line not far from the stream now known as True's Brook. As other families followed that spring, a modest settlement took root on the Connecticut River floodplain south of the Mascoma River on land now occupied by two large shopping centers on either side of Interstate 89.

Like most new settlements, early Lebanon's was a closed economy with few imports and exports. Real money meant silver and gold or Spanish coin, and such hard currency was scarce. The monetary standard was a bushel of wheat, which brought about six shillings, but barter was the primary means of exchange, and the closest trading post was in Charlestown.

As more migrants arrived, the town's population grew at the rate of about nine families per year. Many new arrivals established hilltop farms in the vicinity of Poverty Lane, Podgum Lane (now known as Slayton Hill Road), and Storrs and Daisy hills.

Joseph Wood, Sr. was an early settler in the uplands area, and he was the patriarch of the family that was the town's largest during its first one hundred years. He arrived about 1765-1766 from Mansfield, Connecticut, with his wife and some of their children, and they lived on a large tract of land on the south side of the King's Highway—near

Lebanon, 1761-1994 / 10

the present airport (1994). According to the *Grafton County Book of Biographies*, Mr. Wood's home on the King's Highway also doubled as an inn: "Like all country taverns of that time [it] was rude in its conveniences and unceremonious in its management; but nevertheless it was truly a traveler's home, where the landlord was pleased to welcome and attend to the wants of the weary traveler, who in turn was grateful to find a resting place."

Other early settlers included the families of Elisha Dewey, James Jones, Nathaniel Porter, Asa Kilbourne, Samuel Meacham, Joseph and Jonathan Dana, Silas Waterman, Jedediah Hebard, Jesse Cook, Zalmon Aspinwall, Huckins Storrs, and his distant cousin, Nathaniel Storrs.

The Jones family had the honor of giving birth to the first child in town, but Sarah Jones has long been the victim of sex discrimination. Born on December 22, 1764, she is rarely mentioned in the town's early historical writings. Instead, Thomas Waterman has received far more credit through the years for having been the first *male* born in town, even though his birth on July 11, 1766, came nineteen months after that of Sarah Jones.

Domestic Affairs

Nathaniel Storrs arrived in 1769 and bought fifty acres on a hill called Tadmor from his brother Constant, who had acquired the grant from John Hanks, a quintessential charter speculator (like the majority of those whose names appeared in the Lebanon charter) who sold his rights and never set foot in Lebanon.

Many early settlers came to Lebanon either as bachelors or without their wives and families and returned to Connecticut after they had established a clearing and built a home. Nathaniel Storrs spent two years in Lebanon alone before returning to Connecticut, where he married Ruth Hall in 1771. They set up housekeeping in Lebanon later that year, although their start was inauspicious enough. According to *The Lebanonian*, "The home of Mr. and Mrs. Nathaniel Storrs, which was only a rude shanty, was burned with their entire stock of provision during their first year in the forest, and for some time they were compelled to subsist principally upon summer squash and milk." Despite that shaky beginning, they persevered and established a two-hundred-acre homestead at the top of what is now known as Storrs Hill.

The development of a tract of land usually started with groups of men felling trees in the heavily forested uplands, handwork that both established a clearing and provided the timber needed to build a home. Wells dug close to the house provided a source of water, and trees and underbrush were hacked away and burned to provide space for crops such as corn, cabbage, peas, turnips, potatoes, squash, flax, and grain, and to give farm animals a place to graze. Typically, the stumps from the felled trees were left in the ground and the farmer planted around them until they rotted.

Oxen were the early-day equivalent of tractors, used to plow and haul; cows provided milk and beef; horses were the main means of transportation; and sheep provided wool that could be used for cloth. An abundance of game was available for the farmer who was handy with a gun, but since gunpowder and lead were scarce he also relied on snares or traps.

While the farmer and his sons culled what they could from the land, a mother and her daughters turned flax to linen and fleece to wool on spinning wheels commonly found in the home. They also churned butter and made candles and soap from a mixture of animal fat and potash. The latter was an early commodity that was made by running water through the ashes of logs, producing a liquid known as lye, which was then boiled off to produce a thick black substance known as potash. When heated in an oven the potash became a white powder known as pearlash, which was valued in England and in southern New England markets for making soap, bleaching, and glassmaking, among other uses.

Women also were often responsible for boiling down the sap acquired each spring from the bountiful maples that made up much of Lebanon's forests, and they gathered spruce moss for pillows and corn husks for mattress fillings.

As the number of families increased, so did the collection of mills that serviced them. By the close of the 1700s mills were scattered along the rivers and brooks of the town. Proprietors, who controlled water rights as well as most of the land, gave John Bennett permission in 1764 to build a gristmill on the Glen Road downstream from Oliver Davison's sawmill, and residents for the first time had a way to turn their grain into flour without going to Charlestown. John Slapp received a water right from the proprietors to operate a gristmill in 1765, and a deed from Charles Hill dated September 11, 1768, gave Mr. Slapp a grant of land to build a gristmill and sawmill on the Glen Road.

William Dana is believed to have run a mill (and a ferry in 1784) on the Connecticut River, but is better remembered for the inn he opened on the corner of what is now Main and Bridge streets, near the Connecticut River. It was widely regarded as the town's first inn, and its location was enhanced by the joining of the Fourth New Hampshire and the White River turnpikes in the early 1800s. (The bridge between White River Junction and Lebanon was built in about 1803.) Dana's inn, which was augmented by nearby stables, survived under several different owners for 150 years, and it was a common site in the 1800s to see West Lebanon's Main Street lined with teams of horses while their drivers were inside being watered.

Joseph Wood, Sr. operated a gristmill and sawmill near the mouth of the Mascoma, "doing a large business in manufacturing his stately first-growth pines into lumber to be floated on rafts down the Connecticut River," according to *The Lebanonian* magazine of the late nineteenth century. The families in West Lebanon also had the option of taking their goods to Huckins Storrs' sawmill on True's Brook, which was known as Sawmill Brook in the mid-1770s. It also was called Hinkley Brook for a while, the namesake of Daniel and David Hinkley who were given a tract of land along the brook in 1779 in exchange for operating a sawmill and a carding and fulling mill. Farmers who raised sheep brought their wool to this mill to be carded, or combed, and then took it home to be woven before bringing it back to the mill for a process known as fulling, in which the cloth was dyed and shrunk. Although the Hinkleys operated their mill until a flood wiped them out in 1829, the brook was finally named for Osgood True (a fact not to be told to Plainfield residents who have long known it as Blood Brook). Mr. True used water from the brook to power the town's first tannery in 1790, enabling residents to have leather for shoes, harnesses and saddles.

Constant Storrs, who migrated from Connecticut in 1780 and established a farm on Daisy Hill near brother Nathaniel's, was taxed for a mill operation for a few years in the late 1790s. Howard Townsend, a former state senator and agriculture commissioner, and a relative of Constant Storrs, recalls viewing the remnants of an old mill along a Daisy Hill brook on the former Constant Storrs property. If that was, in fact, the mill that Constant Storrs ran, it was probably either a modest gristmill or sawmill that serviced the hilltop farms.

Revolution

By 1775, a development was taking shape. Subsistence farming was the dominant enterprise in town, supported by several mills. The town had shoemakers and joiners, but not yet a lawyer or doctor, although both would arrive fairly soon.

The Connecticut River, which had functioned as the first highway, still served that purpose but was paralleled by the County Road that wound through Lebanon and points north. The Old King's Highway, also known as the Old Enfield Road, ran east to west over the tops of Aspinwall (now called Farnum), Storrs and Daisy hills. Another east-to-west road followed the north bank of the Mascoma River to the (as yet undeveloped) center of town, where it ran through East Lebanon to Enfield.

Settlers still traded and relied upon British currency, but the province also printed money, resulting in a counterfeiting problem with which the local committee of safety chronically struggled.

Amid this progress the Revolutionary War broke out.

Some towns in the state had a mixture of residents who supported either side, but there appeared no such division in Lebanon. The provincial assembly sent selectmen an "Association Test" to be signed by each man in town stating his loyalty to the rebellion. A man not signing it might be seen as sympathetic to the British. On the other hand, the average man had to be mindful that the British might win the war, seize those tests, and consider one's signature evidence of treason. Thus, it must have taken a fair amount of courage to sign a document which read: "We, the Subscribers, do hereby solemnly engage and promise that we will to the utmost of our power at the risque of our Lives and Fortunes, with Arms oppose the Hostile Proceedings of the British Fleets and Armies against the United American Colonies."

Despite its risks the test was endorsed by every man in Lebanon. It was dated July 4, 1776, a sheer coincidence that what amounted to a local Declaration of Independence was signed in Lebanon on the same day that the nation's Declaration of Independence was approved in Philadelphia.

The next day Nehemiah Estabrook of Lebanon moderated a joint meeting of the committees of safety from Lebanon, Hanover, Lyme, Hartford, Norwich and Thetford.

Aware that the rivers would provide the easiest means of transportation for an army (many committee members were veterans of the French and Indian wars and had come to the region by boat themselves), they expected any attacks to come via water. Therefore, they voted to send fifty men to fortify Royalton on the White River, and also established four companies totalling 250 soldiers to guard against an attack via the Connecticut River on the settlement in Newbury, Vermont.

The local committee of safety was the governing body responsible for stopping and interrogating any strangers who passed through town, and for finding and equipping men to patrol. Locating the men was relatively easy; outfitting them with something to eat and shoot with was not. In a letter to the New Hampshire Assembly dated July 6, 1776, Mr. Estabrook spelled out the fears and the hardships shared by many. It read, in part:

The . . . alarming circumstances the Inhabitants are under in these important Frontier Towns since the army have retreated to Crown Point out of Canada, leaving a Large Extent of our frontiers open to the Ravages of the Savage Indians, being almost Destitute of arms and ammunition & many of our Inhabitants Leaving their houses and fields to our Enemys;—We humbly trust your Honours will . . . afford us such Relief as you in your wisdom shall judge Necessary . . . We would inform your Honours that the Committees of several adjacent towns met together & agreed to raise three hundred men to build Garrisons and scout for our Defence . . . But as we are destitute of arms, ammunition and money, we are fearfull it will in a great measure prove abortive; and this only alternative left us; Either such as can to make escape into the Lower Towns, or fall a sacrafice to our enemies.

It was like a child at college writing home for money, except that the parents were as broke as the children who, ironically, would soon run away from home, anyhow.

Soldiers in 1777 were paid a bounty of twenty-four pounds to enlist in the army, with the money raised by subscription. Apparently the bounty was not enough to entice everyone, because a local committee was established to investigate the circumstances of those who declined to join. A man without a good excuse was fined up to ten pounds, although the town later withdrew that fine. It is doubtful, however, that there were many who opted out, for 1775 census records record 91 men in town between the ages of 16 and 50, and that is precisely the number of men listed as Revolutionary War veterans.

Although not a single Revolutionary War battle was fought on New Hampshire soil, Lebanon men were spread out among different regiments and fought in several notable battles. Nehemiah Estabrook, Jr. was said to have been a bodyguard of George Washington and wintered at Valley Forge. Thomas Blake, a joiner who took over Oliver Davison's sawmill in 1775, joined the army after the battle of Lexington and is said to have fought at Bunker Hill.

Fourteen Lebanon men are listed as having been at the historic Battle of Bennington on August 16, 1777, as members of the New Hampshire Regiment of Colonel Jonathan Chase, and Lebanon men were also said to have been present at the Battle of Saratoga in New York.

Phineas Parkhurst

Local fears of attack proved well-founded when a band of Indians acting at the direction of the British attacked Royalton, Vermont, on October 16, 1780, killing four men and taking several prisoners.

The raid brought to town a man who would be a leading citizen for the next sixty years, who was to become one of the largest landholders in Lebanon, the town's most popular physician, a successful farmer and industrialist, and the first president of the town's first bank. As if that were somehow not enough, he came to town as the local equivalent of Paul Revere.

Dr. Phineas Parkhurst was born in Royalton and was living there at the time of the Indian raid. By all accounts he jumped the nearest horse and fled down the White River valley to warn other settlements of an impending attack. Before he left, however, he was shot in the lower part of the back, the lead ball passing through his abdomen and lodging under the skin in front.

The Vermont Society of the American Revolution raised a bronze plaque in his memory in 1920 on a site near Hartford. The inscription read: "This tablet is in honor of Phineas Parkhurst who though wounded rode from Royalton, Vt., to West Lebanon, N.H., on Oct. 16, 1780, warning the settlers of the coming of Indians. He halted here at Tilden's Tavern and Stephen Tilden fired the alarm gun."

The alarm sounded and the local militia turned out, but the Indians returned to Canada while the rider continued on to West Lebanon, where he was treated for his wound by Dr. Ziba Hall, the town's first physician, who had settled on South Main Street.

Thus began the medical education of Phineas Parkhurst. "His wound preventing his usual labor [farming], he decided to study medicine and did so with . . . Dr. Hall." Such apprenticeships were the normal way of becoming a doctor in the late eighteenth century.

After completing his apprenticeship, Dr. Parkhurst married Lucy Pierce, a cousin from Royalton, in 1784. (Marrying one's cousin, it should be noted, was also a fairly common practice at the time.) They settled in the present Dana House when it was on South Main Street in West Lebanon, where Dr. Parkhurst began a successful medical practice. He also invested wisely, establishing a carding and fulling mill on the Mascoma River in West Lebanon that prepared wool for spinning, and he later ran what was described as "the best grist mill in town" in the center of town.

Dr. Phineas Parkhurst . . . Lebanon's Paul Revere, physician, banker, and raiser of mules

But it was for his mules that he was best remembered. Town records from the early 1800s show Dr. Parkhurst was taxed for more than 20 mules, which he raised and shipped south at an apparently handsome profit.

By that time the Parkhursts had moved from West Lebanon to the former Wheatley-Colburn homestead in the center of town (Marion Carter Home, 1994). A painting of the Old Meeting House in Colburn Park shows Dr. Parkhurst in front of the building and in the background were his omnipresent mules, which local residents jokingly referred to as the doctor's "chickens."

Phineas and Lucy Parkhurst had seven children, and the oldest, Phineas Parkhurst, Jr., seemed destined to follow in his father's footsteps. He attended Dartmouth College and the Dartmouth Medical School and was a physician when he died at the age of thirty-six.

Sadly, only one of Phineas and Lucy Parkhurst's children, a daughter, lived past forty. The others died of "consumption," known today as tuberculosis.

2

Churches, Etc.

The Meetinghouse Flap

THE TOWN'S first church, the Congregational, was established as a "standing order" (a town-sanctioned, tax-supported religious body set up to attract settlers and minister to their spiritual needs) on February 25, 1768. The founders were Jonathan Wheatley, Azariah Bliss, John Slapp, Jonathan Dana, Joseph Dana, and Zacheus Downer.

Although the proprietors began their search for a pastor in 1762 by assessing a gospel tax, Lebanon remained without a settled minister for its first ten years. Several men auditioned for the job on a temporary basis, and the case of a Reverend Wales seems among the oddest. He preached, was invited to stay, accepted, and was then mysteriously disinvited. Immediately following the vote to revoke his welcome, the town took another: "To see if they will think proper (as a town) to make Mr. Wales some compensation for the loss of his horfe suppofed to be Gored to Death in Levi Hyde's pafture ye last year." Having already decided that the pastor was not to their liking, it was probably a foregone conclusion that voters would decide that, no, they would not pay for the gored horse. Mr. Wales then left town, presumably on foot.

Ten years after the search started, the town welcomed its first settled minister. Yale graduate Isaiah "Priest" Potter accepted the town's invitation to stay in exchange for a tract of land (set aside in the charter for the minister), a bonus of one-hundred pounds, and a starting salary of fifty pounds, all to be paid by taxes. His ordination on August 25, 1772, was a momentous event attended by Dartmouth College President Eleazar Wheelock and by ministers from as far away as Charlestown and Cornish.

The ordination was held on the bank of the Connecticut River in West Lebanon (along South Main Street) under a great elm tree that served as the usual gathering place for religious services and town meetings in lieu of a meetinghouse. One of the Reverend Potter's first orders of business, in fact, was to settle the dispute that had been raging for four years over where to build that first meetinghouse. The town had devoted countless meetings to the matter between 1768 and 1772, but had not been able to agree, even though none of the half-dozen or so sites under consideration was more than a half-mile from one another.

A half mile, however, was not an inconsiderable distance in those days, as Charles A. Downs, author of *History of Lebanon, N.H., 1761-1887,* points out: "Let us remember that the population is scattered—an opening here and there in the primeval forest made for a home. Roads are few; none are good. For many a log cabin, there would only be a rough path. Distance under such circumstances counts. A mile or a half mile is worth a struggle to avoid, when probably the whole family must go on foot 'to meeting,' or at best in the rudest of vehicles." Mr. Potter, who had been listening to the bickering during his tryout period in 1771, provided the impetus for agreement by threatening to quit unless the dispute was settled. Rather than spend another ten years hunting for a pastor, the town put up the first meetinghouse later that year on a tract of land belonging to Charles Hill, just north of the Old Pine Tree Cemetery Road. That did not, however, bring permanent closure to the issue.

"Frolic and Vain Mirth"

The meetinghouse in colonial times was as much a religious building as political, and the church's role was as much social as religious. It functioned as the community conscience, and it was where transgressions were dealt with, especially violations of the Sabbath. Recreation and work ceased on Sunday, and some residents were punished for raking hay or gathering sap. All travel was forbidden except to attend church, to visit a sick person, or to perform some other act of charity.

People also were expected to behave themselves on other days, too, as a motion passed by the local church in 1784 spells out: "That the church view it unbecoming the profession of godliness for young people, professors, to practice frolicing and vain mirth, likewise for elderly persons, to indulge in idleness, in foolish talking and jesting; and voted that they should set a watch about themselves and in the future refrain."

Three young ladies who engaged in "frolic and vain mirth" at a wedding were censured by the congregation, as was a man who sent his children to dancing school.

In addition to the usual positions of moderator, selectmen (three), town clerk, constable, and surveyors, early residents also voted for a town-sanctioned religious officer charged with keeping the Sabbath. Church services lasted for hours in those days, and tithingmen roamed the interior of the meetinghouse with wooden rods to make sure people stayed awake. Pokes with the stick or ungentle tugs on the ear were employed to rouse someone from slumber. More serious Sabbath violations brought fines between fifty cents and six dollars. Perhaps tired of having their ears yanked, residents abolished the position in 1845.

Construction of the first meetinghouse did not settle the dispute over its location, but at least it put it to simmer until 1780, when a group of apparently disgruntled marauders took it upon themselves to dismantle the house in the middle of the night. They rebuilt it on Farnum Hill, probably not far from where the town animal pound was constructed in 1781, which put it closer to the center of town but not near enough to end the quarrel over its location.

Wrote D.H. Allen in an address delivered to the town at its centennial celebration in 1861: "The fathers and mothers of some of us used to ride on horseback and ox-cart from the extreme northeast of town to the house of worship, but some refused to go there and were accustomed to meet in the house of Mr. Robert Colburn, which stood near Mr. Carter's residence. Our records tell us that the church voted to suspend those members for the present who were active in pulling down the meeting house."

Robert Colburn's huge barn in the center of town was the de facto meetinghouse for those residents who refused to travel to the one on Farnum Hill, and he entered the dispute in 1792. Mr. Colburn, who had married John Wheatley's daughter and inherited her father's estate, offered the town a field in front of his house if they would build the meetinghouse on that spot. He received ten pounds for the land, and the structure was erected in his field later that year in what is now Colburn Park. That settled the meetinghouse location, but the early 1800s brought unrest of a different kind.

The town passed a religious milestone in 1815 when the Congregational church appointed a committee to negotiate a retirement settlement with "Priest" Potter, who was then about seventy and had ministered to his flock for more than forty years. After prolonged discussion he agreed to abdicate his pulpit and the town voted on September 19, 1816, to pay the pastor's salary until August 22, 1817. Sadly, he committed suicide on July 2, 1817, and membership waned over the next two years, during which time the congregation surrendered the use of the meetinghouse and instead gathered occasionally in schools and private homes.

The Reverend Potter was succeeded in 1819 by the Reverend John Foord, whose coming, it was predicted, would increase the value of real estate in town by 30 percent. His arrival raised the local blood pressure instead.

According to a sermon delivered by the Reverend E. C. Garfield on the one-hundredth anniversary of the building of the church, "While a brilliant and forward looking preacher, it was not long before a division sprang up in the church which resulted in Mr. Foord's withdrawal with 32 members and a subsequent attempt to found the Second Congregational church of Lebanon. Had the conduct of his personal life and affairs been above reproach it is certain that the coming of Mr. Foord to this community would have been a means of great spiritual growth rather than disagreement and division."

His old Piermont congregation charged that, among other things, the minister neglected to say grace at meals, used profanity, skipped his own prayer meetings, and was "ungovernable in his passions." He was censured on three counts, although his supporters claimed that Mr. Foord was the victim of political persecution. Just or not, the sanction lasted until 1826 and led to a fracture in the Lebanon church. Mr. Foord's faction functioned as a second, independent, Congregational church and left the original group without a pastor until 1823, when Reverend Calvin Cutler took over.

While that rift was taking place another developed regarding the tax-supported "standing order." Although the institution had helped to settle the town, it also outgrew its usefulness in that regard. "The people were no longer of the same sentiments and belief," Reverend Downs wrote of the town's seventeen-hundred residents about 1820, "and those who dissented from the Standing Order . . . began to think of it as a hardship to be taxed for the support of a form of worship with which they did not

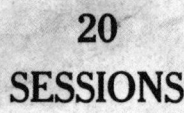

1917 poster announcing Sunday School convention shows four of the town's churches.

sympathize; to build meetinghouses in which they never worshipped, to pay for preaching which they never heard gladly, or . . . at all. There began to be complaints against the system."

Universalists/Unitarians

Some of those gripes might have come from the Universalists, who organized about 1808 and held their first meetings at the home of Thomas Packard on Sunset Rock Road, or at various schoolhouses. They were chartered by the New Hampshire Legislature in 1816 and adopted their own constitution in 1831 during a meeting at the Lafayette Hotel. In 1835, the Universalists installed a second story in the gallery of the meetinghouse and held their services there until about 1868, when the town, in order to renovate the meetinghouse, voted to buy out the sect's interest in the second-floor pews. The Universalists then merged with the Unitarian church, a society that was organized in 1865 and constructed its first church in 1880, at the corner of Elm and Green streets. The Unitarians continued in Lebanon until declining membership prompted the church to close in 1967.

Methodists

The discontent with the standing order might also have come from local Methodists, who either shared a meetinghouse with the Baptists in the Methodist Hill area or gathered on Hardy Hill, where Canaan-based itinerant preachers held services as early as 1810.

Methodism became more organized when Reverend Robert Williams preached to a gathering in the Hardy Hill schoolhouse about 1821: "He formed a 'class' of seven persons which was continued, and from which the present church sprung," according to the Downs history.

Reverend Williams also performed widely watched baptisms in the Mascoma River, and in one of its Hardy Hill tributaries, Alden Brook. Eunice Edwards and Isaac Fitch were the first in town to be baptized. Mr. Fitch was one of three men—Marlin Downer and Christopher Tone were the others—who bought a parcel of land on School Street in 1832 for construction of a church building. It was finished the following year and stood for 160 years until it was destroyed by a devastating midnight fire on February 21, 1992.

The fire occurred after two young men broke into the church and the candles they used to find their way ignited the blaze. One of the youths showed enormous courage about a year later when he attended services and admitted to his involvement in the fire. "No, I did not set the fire," he said, "But if I had not been there it would not have happened." He then apologized and asked for forgiveness. After a pause, one member of the audience clapped. Others joined in the applause, which turned into a standing ovation. "That was a gutsy thing to do," said the Reverend David Polhemus.

The fire served as a rallying point for the church, which saw an increase in its membership, and with the support of a community that raised more than $50,000 in donations a new church was dedicated on the site of the old one on March 6, 1994.

Baptists

The last of the early churches to be founded was the First Baptist Church, whose members began meeting informally in the winter of 1860 at the home of Joseph Cummings. The following year Mr. Cummings, Thomas Hough, and Charles Cobb formed a committee to look into building a house of worship, but the Civil War delayed matters until 1862, when a church was built on Green Street. In October of that year the Reverend John McKinley became the church's first settled pastor.

That Green Street structure was later sold to a private group for a high school, and the present church was put up on the corner of Green and School streets in 1869, where it stands as the city's finest example of Gothic Revival architecture.

The growth in the town's religious community in the early nineteenth century created the problem of which denomination—First Congregational, Second Congregational, Methodist, or Universalist—should have use of the meetinghouse, which was still the town's only bona fide house of worship prior to 1828.

When the new meetinghouse was built in 1792, the pews had been auctioned off to recover construction expenses. (Most people paid in wheat, livestock, or hardware, and only slightly more than seventeen pounds was paid in cash, which was still scarce.) Although the town owned the land and the building, the pews themselves belonged to the individuals who had successfully bid on them. Thus, the town apportioned use of the meetinghouse in proportion to pew ownership.

Members who had defected to the second Congregationalist society led by the Reverend Foord owned the most pews, so they were granted the use of the meetinghouse for twenty-two Sundays; those in the first Congregational order were allowed to use the meetinghouse on fourteen Sundays (increased to twenty in 1827); Universalist members owned enough pews to earn them twelve Sabbaths, while the Methodists had the meetinghouse for four.

"It was a bad arrangement for all the societies," according to the Downs history, "productive of jealousies, bitterness of feelings, each having only fragmentary services." The situation prompted Reverend Cutler to resign from the First Congregational Church in 1827, although forty new members had joined during his tenure and it was on his watch that the first Sunday school classes were established in 1825.

The arrangement, however, also led to construction of the town's first private church building when members of the first congregation turned their frustration to creation. Raising money by subscription, they purchased a lot from Timothy Kenrick on the southwest corner of Colburn Park for five-hundred dollars and built their own structure, designed by Ammi Burnham Young, a native son who went on to fame as an architect. The church frame was raised on April 24, 1828, and the building was dedicated on August thirteenth of that year at a total cost, including land, of $3,162.

Once again the wheels of progress were lubricated by rum, according to an account given to the *Granite State Free Press* by F. W. Strong, who said he hewed the timber along with Joseph Mason and John Sawyer. "Strong worked with them and the three used one quart a day of Jamaica rum. The church did not furnish the rum but that was only because it was part of the contract for the men to find their own."

Late nineteenth-century photograph of the Congregational Church with Aaron Gove's tailor shop on the front lawn. This building had previously been occupied by Gilman Whipple and, before that, Timothy Kenrick.

Church members also contributed $1,000 for an endowment to support church activities, and deacon Nathaniel Porter donated a house and land for a parsonage. A bell was added a few years later, and horse sheds, as important then as parking spaces are today, were later added to the rear of the building.

Although those early churches—along with the Catholic (see Chapter Thirteen)—formed the foundation of the town's religious community, other denominations settled in town later.

The Christian Science Society of Lebanon was established on February 8, 1910, and after meeting in several different locations members then purchased a house at the corner of Green and Union streets, which was dedicated in September 1934.

The Seventh-Day Adventists moved in 1936 from White River Junction to Maple Street in West Lebanon onto a plot of land donated by Milton Reynolds. They also opened a private school in 1935 in the present S & S Auto Parts building, and moved it into the church basement the following year. It was originally known as West Lebanon Junior Academy, but has since been renamed the Estabrook School, the town's oldest surviving private school.

The latter part of the twentieth century also saw a period of religious growth: the West Lebanon Baptist Church opened on Route 4 in 1972; the Trinity Baptist Church was constructed on Route 10 in 1986; the Lebanon Assembly of God Church opened on Buckingham Place in 1987; the Dartmouth Area Christian Fellowship (renamed Grace Outreach, 1994) moved from Hanover to Seminary Hill in 1980, and eight years later built a new school and church on Oak Ridge Road in West Lebanon; the Church of Jesus Christ of Latter-day Saints (Mormons) opened a new chapel in East Lebanon in 1990; while the New Believers' Center constructed its own church next door to the Mormons in 1994.

The Prophet and the Doctor

It seems only fitting that Lebanon should have a Mormon Church, in light of the fact that the founder of that religion, Joseph Smith, once lived in town, where he encountered another famous Smith who saved his limb if not his life.

Joseph Smith moved here with his family as a boy in 1811, the year before a great typhoid epidemic struck the region.

Typhoid, smallpox, and scarlet fever were among the diseases that kept life expectancy down and had prompted the town to build a "pest house" near Storrs Hill to quarantine the seriously ill.

"The spotted fever is still ravaging various parts of the country," wrote Dartmouth Medical School founder Dr. Nathan Smith in a letter to a friend in 1811. "I saw four persons sick of that terrible disease at Bath a few days since. Two children, who were taken the morning of the same day I was there, died before noon." The "spotted fever" was typhoid, and a strongly worded letter from Dr. Smith to a Yale professor in March 1813 indicates that the epidemic was so severe in the Lebanon area that it forced Dr. Smith to postpone a visit to New Haven:

. . . four of my children have lately been affected by the prevailing epidemic, but by the Divine Goodness have nearly recovered. I believe this country has never before been visited by sickness which has carried off so great a number of adult persons in so short a time. In some towns of this vicinity which contain perhaps from 1000 to 1500 inhabitants they have buried over 50 persons since last January. The disease has not yet much abated either in its violence or frequency of attack. We hear of new cases every day, and almost every day brings me an account of the death of some friend or acquaintance. How long this dreadful calamity will be suffered to afflict us, none can tell, but we hope and pray that when the winter is over the disease will disappear.

Nine-year-old Joseph Smith lived on South Main Street in West Lebanon (KFC, 1994) when he was stricken by typhoid in 1813. Although he recovered from his fever, he soon complained of a shoulder pain which a doctor, remembered by his mother Lucy as "Dr. Parker" (almost certainly Phineas Parkhurst), diagnosed as a sprain. Two weeks later, however, a blister that had formed between his shoulder and breast was lanced by the doctor and drained of a quart of pus. The boy was better for a short time, but when the infection and severe swelling then showed up in his lower left leg the family carried him around for three weeks before sending for the doctor again. This time "Dr. Parker" incised the front of the leg between the ankle and the knee, and the swelling subsided until the wound closed. When it returned the doctor cut again, this time to the bone, and with the same unsatisfactory result.

It is at this point that the future Mormon Church founder supposedly encountered Dr. Nathan Smith, who founded the medical school at Dartmouth and several other colleges.

House on South Main Street in West Lebanon was once occupied by Mormon Church founder Joseph Smith. He underwent a severe operation here when a boy.

Lucy Smith recalled that "a team of surgeons" from the Dartmouth Medical School visited her son, although her recollection is probably mistaken. More likely it was Dr. Parkhurst, Dr. Nathan Smith, and a group of medical students who went to the house. Because Nathan Smith never mentioned Joseph Smith by name in any of his letters, it cannot be conclusively proven that they met. However, in one letter the physician wrote that while returning from a trip he treated a young boy with a severe case of "necrosis," the same disease that Lucy Mack Smith identified as the one that afflicted her son.

Necrosis was a term for a disease in which part of the bone becomes infected and dies. The standard treatments at the time—lancing the infected area and applying warm medicated dressings and plaster—were ineffective and usually led to amputation to save the patient's life. However, Joseph Smith's parents resisted that course and instead agreed to permit Dr. Smith to try an experimental operation in which only part of the bone would be cut away.

Mrs. Smith's harrowing account of her son's operation provides a good example of what patients had to endure during an era when many cures were worse than the ailments to which they were applied. There was no such thing as anesthesia at the time and the boy declined brandy or wine to dull the pain. Instead, his father held him down as the surgeons sliced open Joseph's leg and bored holes into either end of the infected bone. Large sections of bone were snapped off and removed, and Mrs. Smith recalled hearing her son's desperate screams and seeing "the wound torn open, the blood still gushing from it, and the bed literally covered with blood."

Bad as it was, the treatment worked and Joseph began to improve shortly after the operation, although for the next three years he needed crutches to walk. With his medical ordeal in Lebanon behind him, he moved with his family to New York, where he encountered other challenges which ultimately led to the creation of a new religion.

Quarantine

Nearly a hundred years after the Smith case, diseases like typhoid and smallpox were still a major worry for the town. The board of health reacted swiftly in 1907, when it was learned that the mother of a family living in a Mechanic Street tenement had contracted smallpox. Their building and several others were immediately sealed off and a twenty-four-hour guard was posted outside the area to ensure that no one entered or left the structures. Two days after the quarantine took effect, "the woman who had smallpox, her husband and two years' old child, and a young woman to care for the patient, were removed to an isolated hospital, improvised for the occasion, about two miles out of the village," according to the town report of 1908. The husband and child caught the disease while in the hospital and the family was kept in isolation for thirty-three days, while twenty-two others from the same neighborhood were quarantined for eighteen days. The apartments were disinfected (the one in which the disease had occurred was scrubbed down twice) and all occupants were required to take an "antiseptic bath" before being released back into the community. Other diseases that year, none of them fatal, included three cases of measles, eleven instances of scarlet fever, six residents were afflicted with diphtheria, and eight contracted typhoid.

The board noted that "the sanitary condition of the town has been improved by the extension of the sewers to a number of places where the need was greatest, so now there is little excuse for the existence of surface drains or cess pools in town." Those gradual improvements, coupled with improved medical techniques and the advent of antibiotics and vaccines, did much to reduce the mortality rate of diseases whose mere names were once enough to evoke horror among residents.

3

The City, Secession, and Center Village

IF YOU had asked Lebanon residents in 1835 to forecast the location of the town's economic center in 1885, most probably would have chosen East Lebanon, which supported the town's largest array of merchants and manufacturers.

Exactly when people began to settle in East Lebanon is unclear. In March 1769 the town considered a plan to build two bridges over the Mascoma River. "One at the ford way near Benj. Fuller's (East Lebanon) and at the Other near the mills in said Lebanon." The proposal was defeated, but that record provides the earliest known reference to a settlement in East Lebanon.

The village at the foot of Mascoma Lake began in earnest with Elisha Payne, a 1750 graduate of Yale University who was one of the first settlers in the town of Cardigan, New Hampshire (later renamed Orange).

He was much in demand as an industrialist, having built mills in Cardigan and Enfield, and Lebanon's proprietors convinced Mr. Payne in 1778 to settle and build mills at the foot of the lake. They offered a tract of land "on conditions that the said Payne . . . shall build and erect a good sawmill & gristmill on the Mascomme river near the place where said river empties out of the pond." The grant contained between 500 and 600 acres, encompassing almost all of East Lebanon, and town records from 1787 show that he was the town's largest holder of uncultivated land.

It appears that he moved to East Lebanon in late 1779. Deeds from the spring of that year still give his residence as Cardigan, but deeds dated November and December list him as a Lebanon resident. His large farmhouse sat across Route 4 from what is now Payne Road, and his mills were located at the foot of the lake where he did a brisk business with customers from Enfield, Canaan, Hanover, and Lebanon. "The lumber from the extensive pine lands of Canaan and Enfield was transported through East Lebanon to the Connecticut River to be rafted to tide water for a market and much of it was sawed at Payne's mills, as well for market as for home consumption," according to the *Lebanonian*.

Details about the mills are few. In a monograph about Mr. Payne, Lebanon attorney William Cotton wrote that the records of the operation were burned in an 1840 fire that destroyed much of the mill complex. However, tradition holds that the lumber used to build the original Dartmouth Hall in Hanover was cut at the Payne sawmill, although the history of the college says that Dartmouth professor Bazaleel Woodward set up a sawmill in Hanover and then hired Mr. Payne to be the contractor.

It is clear that Elisha Payne had close ties to Dartmouth College, serving on its board of trustees and receiving an honorary degree in 1779. He was friendly with Professor Woodward, and the two of them played important roles in a movement that twice saw Lebanon and several other towns in western New Hampshire secede to the Republic of Vermont.

Secession

New Hampshire and Vermont had more in common than a boundary. They also shared a political philosophy (rooted in their Connecticut heritage) that emphasized the individual and town as the keystones of government, rather than the state. At the same time, Lebanon residents had no love for the Massachusetts-oriented state government in Exeter, which seemed a world away (a round trip, made by horseback or carriage over miles of inhospitable road, took several days). In addition, Lebanonians were dissatisfied with the perceived lack of representation they received there.

Lebanon residents voted on March 31, 1778, to join Vermont and directed Nehemiah Estabrook (another leader of the secessionist movement) and John Wheatley to attend a meeting of delegates from like-minded towns. The two men were seated as Lebanon's representatives to the Vermont assembly that October, although Vermont withdrew the welcome mat after New Hampshire officials—unhappy at losing the towns—threatened to block Vermont's bid for statehood.

Lebanon voted to withdraw from Vermont, in December 1778, but there was no eagerness to return to New Hampshire. In fact, the town seemed to consider itself something of an independent entity, voting in 1780 to abide by the laws of Connecticut, the mother state.

Deeds of the era illustrate some of the confusion about the town's status:

State of New Hampshire, Grafton County, Lebanon;
Province of N.H., Grafton County, Lebanon, on the New Hampshire Grants.
State of Vermont, Lebanon.
State of Vermont, on the Grants east of Connecticut River.
State of Vermont, territory east of Connecticut River.
State of Vermont, Windsor County, Lebanon.

And one man covered his bases by writing, "Lebanon, State of Vermont, alias New Hampshire."

The matter was further muddled on March 13, 1781, when Lebanon voted again to join Vermont, which then chose Elisha Payne as the state's lieutenant governor (he also served the state in a position equivalent to chief justice of the state supreme court).

The town's second tryst with the Green Mountain State again proved short-lived.

New Hampshire threatened to obstruct Vermont's bid for statehood and appealed to George Washington, who hinted that force might be used if Vermont did not give up its claims to the New Hampshire towns. Thus, Lebanon's delegates traveled to Windsor to join the Vermont legislature in 1781, only to be jilted again.

In August 1782, the town reluctantly sent John Wheatley to the New Hampshire Constitutional Convention, where it was agreed to give every town with more than 150 voters its own General Court representative. That addressed Lebanon's grievance over fairness of representation, and the town returned to New Hampshire.

During that same August meeting at which they sent John Wheatley to the constitutional convention, voters also rejected a motion to pay the 914 pounds that the state was demanding as the town's share of New Hampshire's Revolutionary War expenses. The town argued that since it had not been part of the state during that time, and since it had raised and paid for its own soldiers, it was not obligated for state expenses.

How much of the town's resistance was due to unwillingness to pay is hard to tell, but inability to pay may have influenced some votes. During the war, with an army to feed, the state took payment in farm goods instead of cash. After the war, however, the state demanded payment in silver, which was not widely held.

The dispute over the war bill dragged on for years and was finally resolved largely at the expense of two of its leading citizens. Lemuel Hough and Robert Colburn agreed in 1786 to pay the town's back taxes in return for wheat, pork, beef, butter, and other goods valued at one-thousand pounds. Unfortunately, they were unable to sell the goods and suffered a heavy financial loss that the town refused to cover.

The so-called Vermont controversy, however, was not the last secession movement in which Elisha Payne was involved. In 1782, he proposed the creation of a new town by joining East Lebanon with parts of Enfield, Hanover and Canaan. Supporters of the plan petitioned the legislature to create the town of New Connecticut because, ". . . their local situation is such, being in the four adjoining corners or parts of said towns, and so remote from the center of the respective towns to which they belong, and the places of holding their town and other publick meetings, that renders it very inconvenient and almost impossible for them to attend, especially on the Sabbath or Lord's day . . . that it makes it convenient for them to be a district or town by themselves and will not hurt nor injure the respective towns from which they may be taken off."

The legislature rejected the proposal, but they had not heard the last of their petitioner.

Mr. Payne was elected as Lebanon's representative to the New Hampshire legislature in 1784, the first year the town participated in state elections, and he quickly made an impact. He was chosen by his colleagues to represent the state in the Continental Congress, an appointment he accepted but for some reason did not carry out. He also served in the New Hampshire Senate in 1786-87. Or, at least, he was elected. In a letter to the Senate dated September 5, 1786, Mr. Payne cited "previous engagements" that prevented him from attending the session, and asked to be excused. Two days later the Senate responded: "Voted that the within [excuse] is not a satisfactory excuse."

In 1788, he was a delegate to the historic state convention that considered and ratified the proposed federal constitution. (The town's first choice was David Hough, who asked voters to send Mr. Payne in his stead.) New Hampshire was the ninth and decisive state to ratify the constitution, and Mr. Payne is credited with an influential role in shaping the opinions of delegates from Grafton County, who voted 10-1 in favor of ratification.

He also was elected to the convention that drafted a new state constitution in 1792-93, but "the infirmities of age made Payne inactive," according to Governor William Plummer. The record shows that he was there in September 1791, and again in February 1792, when he was appointed to several committees. However, he missed the May and June sessions, and also the one in September during which the state constitution was finalized.

"The City"

Elisha Payne's mill development at the foot of the lake spurred other economic activity in East Lebanon.

Scotsmen James Ralston and Thomas Rea set up a carding and fulling mill in the 1790s that was said to have been one of the earliest in the country. Mr. Ralston, who was appointed the town's first postmaster in 1801, eventually gave up the wool business to become a storekeeper (notice of the auction of Elisha Payne's estate was posted at James Ralston's store) and Mr. Rea moved on to operate a cloth factory near the western end of what is now known as the Miracle Mile. Clark Aldrich, meanwhile, also ran what was probably a gristmill along the river next to Mr. Payne's sawmill between 1790 and 1819.

A store ledger that begins in 1802 indicates that Mr. Ralston carried everything from eggs to axe handles and soap to silk, and he sold mighty quantities of rum, brandy, and beer by the glass or quart. Another East Lebanon businessman of the same era was German immigrant John Winnek, who had a saddle shop on what is now Payne Road and inherited the postmaster job from Mr. Ralston. When the post rider showed up, an event that happened about once a fortnight, a flag was raised to let residents know that the mail had arrived.

Other East Lebanon businesses included a blacksmith shop run by a man named Gates, a wagon and wheel shop operated by cabinetmaker Joshua Cushman, who was involved with the cotton factory, a sawmill operated by Jesse Cook, Jr., and Simon Peter Slapp's tailor shop.

In 1795, Aaron Cleveland opened the first of the several inns that sprang up in East Lebanon.

A succession of businessmen picked up where Elisha Payne and his son John left off: Jesse Cook ran a saw and gristmill starting in about 1815; Joshua Cushman, who came to East Lebanon in 1821, operated the former Thomas Rea cloth works from about 1823 to 1829; beginning in 1819 Josiah Barnes ran a store and inn on Payne Road between the present iron bridge and the wooden railroad bridge, and he also had an interest in the saw and gristmills in the village; in 1828, Halsey R. Stevens moved from Enfield to the former Elisha Payne house on the north side of Enfield Road (Route 4) at the top of Payne Road and opened a store that grew to rival the largest in town.

Our fictitious resident who bet on East Lebanon in 1835 would have seemed like a soothsayer a year later when the legislature incorporated the Mascomy Manufacturing Company, naming Amos Bugbee, Halsey R. Stevens, Caleb Plastridge, Timothy

Dam at the foot of Mascoma Lake around 1888. In the background are the Mascoma railroad station at the left, the ice-house, and a woodshed at far right.

Kenrick, and Peter Burgin as principals in the "manufacturing of cotton and woolen goods, or cotton yarns, and any or either of them in all their various branches."

Mr. Bugbee and Mr. Burgin were residents of the center village, while Halsey Stevens was an East Lebanon storekeeper (the former Ralston store) and Caleb Plastridge was a physician who practiced in the east village from 1813 until his death in 1871. Mr. Stevens, who served as a selectman and was a member of the legislature the year the Mascomy factory was chartered, was East Lebanon's postmaster from 1828-1836. He also was a wool buyer for the Middlesex Manufacturing Company of Lowell, Massachusetts, and eventually became a partner in a center village store with his son-in-law, William G. Perley.

Although there are no deeds or other records that define its exact location, it seems likely that the Mascomy Manufacturing Company was one of the mills that eventually fell under the ownership of James Willis, a man who bet heavily on East Lebanon's future and for a while reaped the benefits of that wager.

Mr. Willis was born in 1795 and resided until 1830 in Enfield, where he operated a tavern along what is now Route 4A. His acquisition of East Lebanon land began in 1823 with the purchase of a saw and gristmill from Jesse Cook, and continued until he had acquired most of the valuable land and water rights at the outlet of the lake. He bought the former James Ralston house and store on Payne Road in 1826; acquired the old Thomas Rea cloth mill—and a distillery—in 1829; he also bought a saw and gristmill in 1831 from Josiah Barnes, with whom he had a partnership.

View of "The City," as the village of East Lebanon was once known, from Mt. Tug

Tax records show Mr. Willis as the town's foremost industrialist in 1837, when the cotton factory he owned in conjunction with a Mr. Osmond Willard was assessed at seven-thousand dollars, more than the combined value of the mills owned by Mills Olcott along the River Road north of West Lebanon, and Phineas Parkhurst in the center of town, who were the second and third largest taxpayers, respectively.

Mr. Willis is said to have employed about thirty people, some of whom probably lived in the boarding houses that sprang up along the road to Enfield. The inventory of the Willis-Willard factory also was the highest in town, with a value of five-thousand dollars. Their partnership also extended to a sawmill that appears to have been a sizable operation, judging from a chattel mortgage from the mid-1830s that shows Mr. Willard lent fifteen-hundred dollars to two Claremont men whose collateral included "about 250 thousand boards and planks at James Willis' mills in East Lebanon . . ."

In addition to his factory and mills, Mr. Willis ran a blacksmith shop and storehouse, according to *The Lebanonian*. A ledger of uncertain origin that appears to be that of an East Lebanon store, sawmill, and cloth-factory operator also indicates that the owner—perhaps Mr. Willis—also had a carriage-and-horse-rental business in the late 1830s and 1840s.

James Willis also purchased a building near the intersection of Payne Road and Route 4, from which he operated a tavern and, from the basement, the largest store in the village. He later added a third story and an annex and converted the third floor of the annex into a community center known as "Union Hall." He paid for the heat and lighting, and the hall hosted religious meetings, schools for singing and dancing, and

Lebanon, 1761-1994 / 32

public lectures. A town record shows that Mr. Willis had permission to serve liquor at "Union Hall" as early as 1832.

East Lebanon also had a printing business at least as early as 1834, according to an entry in the town records that lists the firm of Benjamin Fuller and John Moore as having two printing presses and a printing contract with the Claremont Manufactary Company. One publication put out by the Fuller and Moore press was *The Watchman*, an organ of the Universalist Church, of which Mr. Moore was the pastor in Lebanon.

The East Lebanon village was known locally as "The City," but the beginning of the end came on a cold night in February 1840, when fire destroyed the mills, factories, and a two-story building that housed a stock of wool or wood. The damage was estimated at about ten-thousand dollars, a large sum for the time, and Mr. Willis had little insurance. He did not rebuild before he died in 1846, and the water rights that had powered his rise to prominence were sold to the Mascoma Improvement Company, a consortium of men from the center of town who controlled it with an eye toward their own purposes, depriving potential East Lebanon industries of a source of water power. Without that water power, the village never again gained the social and industrial prominence it enjoyed during the Willis era, although neither did it die out overnight.

William O. Haskell of Boston became a member of the Mascoma Improvement Company and started up a furniture company on the site near the old mills, manufacturing the so-called Windsor benches once found in meetinghouses and churches throughout the region, and he later (1850s) made school furniture that was shipped from the East Lebanon railroad station. The business lasted at least through about 1878, during which time its consumption of water was sometimes a source of irritation to downriver manufacturers. On several occasions the owners of woodworking and machine shops in the center of town sent letters to the furniture company, pleading for more water to turn their wheels.

Downstream from the dam a slate factory was started up on the River Road about 1867 by Doctor Dixie Crosby of Lowell, Massachusetts. Operated by Elijah Liscomb, slate was shipped from a quarry on the north side of the river to a factory that was powered by a steam engine, and one account said the quarry employed fifteen to twenty men making flagstone, table tops, sinks, and other items.

The *Free Press* of May 25, 1867, reported that there was also a quantity of sandstone nearby which "was once carted in considerable quantities to Keene, to be made into glass." The mill produced slate until about 1880, when the site was sold to Albro Emerson, who had operated a scythe shop at the foot of Slayton Hill from 1856 to 1871.

Mr. Emerson moved his Emerson Edge Tool Company to East Lebanon in 1880, and after his death in 1893 his son Frank and grandson Elmer employed about thirty people making scythes, axes, corn knives, and drag rakes. The site was sold to Edward Hambleton in 1907, and he employed about twenty-five people in the production of bobbins that were widely used in the local woolen mills. The bobbin company relocated to Mahan Flat on Spencer Street in the center of town in the early 1920s.

A hint of East Lebanon's social life is found in a flyer (printed by the Novelty Printing Co., of East Lebanon) from the 1870s that touted an oyster supper and play at Union Hall. One resident of East Lebanon in the late 1800s recalled that the hall was the

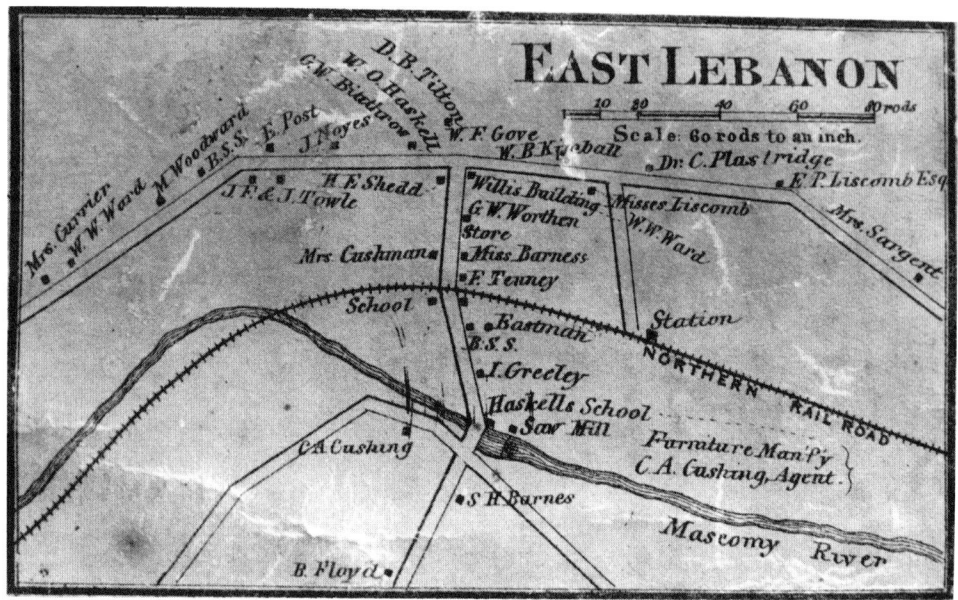

East Lebanon map of 1860 shows Haskell Furniture Company and George Worthen's store

center of the village's religious activity and residents often held Sunday dinners, "ice cream suppers," and other social events to raise money for the ministers who preached there. The village seems to have held its own into the twentieth century, probably because it continued to have at least one major employer and a place for religious and social activities.

When the building was converted into apartments and the hall closed in 1892, residents petitioned to use the B&M Railroad's old freight house at the depot, and the furnishings from the hall were moved in. One resident remembers that, "One night they gave a supper and ran a special train from W.R. Junction to Mascoma . . . We got from Mascoma a record-breaking crowd, too many moved into a corner after supper and a dowel gave way and let a cross-beam settle, causing the floor to sag. This caused a small panic but order was soon restored, the people were led downstairs quietly to safety."

That was the last time the railroad let residents use the freight house for social purposes. The women of the village, however, organized the East Lebanon Endeavor Society, which staged a letter-writing campaign, held five-cent socials in the brick schoolhouse, and ran other fundraisers to raise money to build a new religious and social center.

Albro Emerson donated land for a chapel on Payne Road, and it was constructed in 1893. When the last of the jobs moved from the village, most of the residents followed and the chapel saw little use. It was heavily damaged in the Hurricane of 1938 and was then sold and removed, with the money placed in a trust fund for the East Lebanon Cemetery.

Center Village

While West Lebanon and East Lebanon were well established by 1790, the center of town was still dormant.

One of the early arrivals was Simeon Peck, who came to Lebanon about 1774 from Norwich, Connecticut and six years later purchased a tract of land reaching from Mascoma Street (Alice Peck Day Memorial Hospital, 1994) to the Mascoma River, where he ran a sawmill and a mill for separating the seed from clover.

Although the Peck enterprises were among the first in the center of town, they were actually a bit downstream from the rapids that powered Lebanon's mills during their heyday. That part of the Mascoma, marked by a seventy-foot drop and a series of rapids, remained untapped through the town's first thirty years and was first used at about the time that the meetinghouse came to town.

Some sources cite the meetinghouse relocation as a factor in the development of the center of town, and, at the least, the events coincide. Two years after the hall was put up, Lemuel Hough and Silas Hyde built a dam near the intersection of Hanover and High streets in the area now known as Hough Square (in front of Sacred Heart Church). The following year Mr. Hough deeded a half interest in land along the river to Samuel Lathrop, on the condition that Mr. Lathrop build a gristmill, and for the next twenty years they appear on the town tax rolls as millowners. Although ownership changed countless times over the years, there was a gristmill in roughly that same location well into the twentieth century, and the street on the east side of the river was known as Mill Street.

Mr. Hough and Mr. Lathrop also were partly responsible for the appearance of two other mills in the center of town. The first was a fulling mill run by Barnabas Fay, who bought a parcel of river property in 1795 just south of the gristmill (a little upstream from the present Logan Insurance Agency). The other operation was a linseed oil mill run by James Duncan, who was a storekeeper in 1793, according to town tax files, and is generally credited with having the first store in the center of town.

While industry was a relatively new thing in the center of town, inns were not, and two of the earliest belonged to Jesse Cook on Hanover Street in the mid-1770s, and Beriah Abbot on School Street between about 1780 and 1820.

With a gristmill, a carding and fulling mill, and the meetinghouse, the center of town took on increased importance as the nineteenth century arrived, and it would be helped along by changes in transportation patterns that were soon to follow.

4

Turnpikes and Locks

The Turnpikes

THEY WERE rutted, rock-strewn, often muddy and almost always bumpy, but Lebanon's two dirt turnpikes were still an improvement to the local system of crude roads that existed shortly after the turn of the nineteenth century. "The stage from Lebanon to Meriden was a large, heavy open wagon on springs with three seats," Lebanon resident Forrest B. Cole wrote of the Croydon Turnpike in the Lebanon Historical Society's *Fourth Annual Report*. "In stormy weather the passengers used umbrellas. The horses had to be of superior quality as the road from Lebanon to top of Rowell Hill in E. Plainfield was all upgrade. The horses were changed at Meriden and fresh horses and a lighter wagon were used for the rest of the journey to Claremont."

The Croydon Turnpike, the town's second, was chartered in 1804, shortly after the Fourth New Hampshire Turnpike, linked the town with the New Hampshire seacoast and Boston. Because of its connection to those potentially lucrative markets, the Fourth New Hampshire was the more important of the town's two turnpikes.

In 1796 Elisha Payne of East Lebanon and Jonathan Freeman of Hanover petitioned the New Hampshire Legislature for permission to build a toll road from the Connecticut River in West Lebanon to the Merrimack River in Boscawen. Such a road, it was thought, would open up previously inaccessible markets in Boston, Portsmouth, and other coastal cities. That first turnpike proposal passed the House and died in the Senate, but four years later Mr. Payne—along with Constant Storrs of Lebanon and Russell Freeman of Hanover—tried again. They argued that they were being inconvenienced by the lack of good roads to the east and also noted that another turnpike was being contemplated to link the Connecticut River Valley with the Lake Champlain area.

The legislature had established the state's first turnpike between Concord and Durham in 1796, and four years later lawmakers granted permission for the petitioners to lay out, survey, and operate the Fourth New Hampshire Turnpike from the east bank of the Connecticut River, near the mouth of the White River, to Boscawen or Salisbury. They also approved construction of a spur road to Hanover.

The turnpike was privately built and much of the stock was owned by residents of Lebanon and Hanover, who undoubtedly hoped to reap the rewards of having new markets opened to them. It started just across from the mouth of the White River, went down what is now Main Street in West Lebanon, and up Seminary Hill where it made the first of five passes over the Mascoma River. It crossed Hubbard's Bridge near the present intersection with the Glen Road, and kept to the south bank of the river; it crossed again just east of what is now Exit 19 of Interstate 89; it hooked up with Mascoma Street and crossed the river again near Water Street; it then ran through the middle of what is now Colburn Park and out Bank Street, crossing the Mascoma at the entrance to Riverdale where it joined the Hanover branch of the turnpike to the foot of Hardy Hill.

It was here that a bitter battle was fought over whether the road should follow the river on the north or the south side. It was a fight not unlike the one over where to put the meetinghouse. Votes were taken and reconsidered, measurements were made, and committees were formed to report on the best route. Some of the turnpike shareholders were also innkeepers who undoubtedly saw placing the road on the other side of the river—away from their taverns—as bad for business, and lobbied accordingly. It was finally decided that the road would cross the river at Packard's mills, onto what is now Riverside Drive, and climb up Fellows Hill, away from the river.

Route 4 today makes a northward turn at the bottom of Eastman Hill Road and hooks up with Route 4A at the foot of Mascoma Lake. When the Fourth New Hampshire Turnpike was first laid out, however, it continued straight at the foot of Eastman Hill Road along the hill south of the lake, and then went past the present Shaker Bridge to Enfield Center, Springfield, and on to Boscawen.

Although the cost of building the road was estimated at $600 per mile, the finished price was more than double that, and the total exceeded $67,000. Holders of turnpike stock were billed to pay for construction costs and overruns while the road was built between 1801 and 1805. By the time the road was finished they had paid almost $190 per share.

Toll houses were set up (Lebanon had one in the Riverdale area and another on Mascoma Street) and users of the road were charged on the basis of mileage and use, according to rates set by the state. Anyone who turned off the road to avoid paying was liable for three times the amount of the toll.

A horse and rider was charged $3/4$ cents; a sulkey or chaise with two wheels and one horse was charged $1 1/2$ cents; for a wagon or stage with four wheels and two horses, the toll was three cents; 15 sheep or hogs cost a penny, while 15 horse or cattle cost two cents; charges for large freight wagons were based upon the number of wheels and horses. Exemptions were made for people traveling to and from churches, mills, on family business, or within a town's borders.

The Fourth New Hampshire was a dirt, rocky road laid out in long, straight stretches, and travelers who used it knew they had been for a ride. There were mud flats, ruts, rocks, and some parts were little more than a series of logs laid across the right of way to cover up swamps or stumps—sections known as corduroy roads.

Over time the road transformed both transportation and marketing patterns. Many goods that were once shipped down the Connecticut were now hauled overland to destinations like Portsmouth or Boston. Huge freight wagons became a common site on the turnpike, and sleighs carried loads in the winter when packed snow made traveling the smoothest.

The Fourth also spurred the local agricultural trade. Starting in the early 1800s, cattle drives to Boston became an annual autumn ritual for farmers from Lebanon and surrounding towns. The road also allowed farmers to beef up production of other products, as Edward N. Torbert noted in *The Evolution of Land Utilization in Lebanon, New Hampshire*:

The opening of good roads particularly stimulated shipment of butter and cheese. Between 1790 and 1810, although local demands for dairy products remained comparatively uniform, dairy herds more than doubled in size. To convey these goods to market there developed those annual pilgrimages in farm sleighs that seem to have been welcomed by farmers as a holiday and social event, quite apart from any extra profit involved. When the traveling was good, box sleighs, drawn by a span of horses and laden with butter, cheese, pork and poultry, were said to have 'almost filled' the Fourth New Hampshire Turnpike and connecting roads from Montpelier to Boston.

The turnpike also prompted the establishment of a stage line, one in which passengers were expected to get out and help push when the wagon came to a hill that was too steep to navigate with a full load. Despite sometimes inconveniencing its passengers, the stage did enough business to support three runs a week between Hanover and Boston in 1809. Inns also sprouted up every few miles to service travelers, and stage lines kept a fresh team of horses at stables near the inns. Josiah Barnes' inn in East Lebanon was one of the more popular local taverns, as was the Lafayette Hotel in the center village (originally named Hough's Tavern). A tavern also was located at the junction of the main road and the spur to Hanover, in a building that still stands as one of Lebanon's last surviving turnpike taverns. "Benton House," as it is known (1994), is the large brick building at the intersection of Bank Street and Heater Road.

The greatest local change for the turnpike came in 1833, when the legislature shifted the road from the top of Fellows Hill to the River Road, which ran along the south bank of the Mascoma River. The apparent purpose of the move was to avoid Fellows Hill and the ridges that run along the present Route 4-A side of Mascoma Lake. The result was that the stretch of road from the foot of Eastman Hill Road to just north of the Shaker Bridge was abandoned.

In the 1830s residents of many towns began to push for the Fourth New Hampshire Turnpike to become a free road. The westernmost end became free in 1839 and the section from West Lebanon to Enfield the year after, although the portion that ran through Springfield and Wilmot remained a toll road until 1844.

Shortly after the Fourth was established, Lebanon residents welcomed their second turnpike when the legislature chartered the Croydon Turnpike (now Route 120) in 1804, connecting Lebanon with Plainfield and points south. A stage was also opened along

Early photo of logging on the rapids known over the years as White River Falls and Olcott Falls, just above the present Wilder Dam site. Logging camps were once a common sight on the banks of the Connecticut River.

that route to carry passengers between Lebanon and Claremont or to Windsor via Cornish if they wanted to switch lines in Meriden.

"The completion of other turnpikes in New Hampshire and Vermont made Lebanon an important crossroads town," wrote Mr. Torbert, "and the way was paved for further commercial and industrial development, as well as for agricultural advance."

Locks and Gates

The Connecticut River was the other main road to Lebanon, and boat traffic was heavy in the early years. The vessels that made their way up and down the river at the start of the 1800s were propelled either by sail or, when there was no wind, by long poles driven into the riverbed that pushed the boat upstream. Either way it was a laborious trip hampered by a series of unnavigable falls along the Connecticut that required a boat's cargo to be unloaded and hauled around the rapids by teams of horses or oxen.

There was an especially impressive series of falls where Wilder Dam now sits (1994). Here, the river dropped thirty-seven feet over the course of a mile, and three ledges or "rockbars" in the middle of the channel made this part of the river especially treacher-

Suspension bridge between Wilder, Vermont, and the Lebanon village known as East Wilder connected a paper mill on the Vermont side with the West Lebanon pulp mill visible in the background. The bridge was built in 1883.

ous. It was called White River Falls, and one account says it was here that Rogers' Rangers tipped over while returning from the French and Indian wars in the mid-1700s.

In 1792 the New Hampshire legislature approved a charter for the White River Falls Bridge Company. Its principals were Lebanon lawyer Aaron Hutchinson (the town's first attorney who arrived in 1783), Hanover innkeeper Eleazar Brewster, and Rufus Graves, a Hanover merchant.

The site hosted a bridge, a small dam, and at least one sawmill when Gordon Whitmore acquired the privilege in the spring of 1806 and convinced Hanover lawyer and businessman Mills Olcott to join him in constructing a slip around the dam to help assist the log runs that were then common on the river.

Mr. Whitmore estimated the cost of building the slip at about $300. Mr. Olcott, a speculator in timber, agreed to pay two-thirds of the cost and furnish the wood, which Mr. Whitmore would saw. After a few months, however, the bill was already more than $500 and it was apparent that a slip would not suffice, so the project was upgraded to a series of locks and canals cut into the riverbank to allow boats to circumvent the rapids, as had been done previously at Bellows Falls.

There were, however, numerous delays. In September 1808 three workers drowned when heavy rain washed away a dam at the bottom of the locks. Finally, in 1810, after Mr. Olcott fired Mr. Whitmore, the job was finished. "After four years of amateur engineering, frequent disappointments and even tragedy, the dams, locks and canals were completed and ready for business," wrote Dartmouth College history professor W. R. Waterman in a 1967 edition of the journal *Historical New Hampshire*.

The final cost of $23,433.89 was a far cry from Mr. Whitmore's estimate of $4,000, but Mr. Olcott recouped his investment. Given carte blanche by the legislature to charge whatever he wanted, he set the highest tolls on the river. That first year 113 flatboats paid two dollars each to pass through the canals, and it was the most boats the operation would ever see in a single season. Lumber, merchandise, and other goods were charged at a rate of one dollar per ton.

The lumber trade was by far the most profitable. Mr. Olcott grossed more than $4,000 from lumber tolls in 1816, while the receipts from boats and merchandise was just $505. Increased competition from overland roads eventually caused boat traffic to bottom out, but Mr. Olcott operated the locks at a profit for thirty-five years, until his death in 1845.

The area then more or less languished until the late 1800s, when Charles Wilder built a pulp mill on the West Lebanon side of the Connecticut River and constructed a suspension bridge over the water to allow him to go back and forth between the pulp mill and his paper mill operation in Wilder. When Olcott, Vermont, agreed to change its name to Wilder, Mr. Wilder paid for the erection of an iron bridge for vehicle traffic which survived into the 1940s, and the area north of the present Wilder Dam took on the name East Wilder.

5

About Town

Agriculture

THE TRANSPORTATION network that would service the region for the next forty years was essentially in place by 1810. The Fourth New Hampshire and the Croydon turnpikes intersected, quite literally, in the middle of what is now Colburn Park.

Farming was still the town's principal occupation, but it was changing. Instead of operating on a subsistence level, agriculture became more of a commercial venture marked by specialization. Rather than raising a little of everything to support his family, the Lebanon farmer produced fewer items, but raised those things in surplus amounts which could be sold for cash or traded for other goods at the local store.

This change was enhanced not only by the new roads but also by new agricultural techniques, as Mr. Torbert noted in *The Evolution of Land Utilization in Lebanon, New Hampshire*: "Careful use of manure, thorough plowing, and a judicious rotation of crops were urged through books, papers and local societies concerned with farm management, and the stimulus of profitable markets may have hastened somewhat the slow adoption of these practices."

Some farmers who did not or could not adapt to the changing farm technology joined others who migrated west, where cheap land was available that was flat and easier to farm. In many cases those migrants sold their Lebanon acreage to neighboring farmers who merged the lots to make larger farms. Consequently, while the number of farms declined, the acreage of the farms that remained increased. The most notable example was Daniel Hardy, who purchased so much of the farmland in the hills between East Lebanon and the Center Village that the area came to bear his name—Hardy Hill.

Mr. Hardy bought neighboring tracts and built an agricultural empire that employed up to thirty-five men during haying season. He also raised mules in partnership with Anthony Colby of New London, who would become governor of New Hampshire in

1846-1847 (and the namesake of Colby-Sawyer College in New London). The mules were raised in Lebanon and then taken to market in Virginia, where they sold for as much as $1,500 a pair.

Mills

The water-powered grist, seed, and lumber mills that had supported subsistence farming during the town's first forty years remained important to the economy after the turn of the nineteenth century. Beginning in 1809, Joseph Amsden, David Anderson, Brackett Greenough, and Joseph Wood, Jr., ran a sawmill and gristmill at the mouth of the Mascoma River in West Lebanon on a millsite operated by Joshua Markham from 1792-1808.

The original town millsite worked by Oliver Davison continued in operation, as George Hubbard, Richard Kimball, Luther Waters, and John and Erastus Chamberlain operated a gristmill and sawmill, which later evolved into a cloth-dressing mill owned by Philip Cambridge of Lempster, New Hampshire.

Simeon and Eliel Peck continued to operate their cloverseed and sawmills on the Mascoma River along what is now Mechanic Street. Ichabod Packard did enough business to keep his sawmill viable at the foot of Hardy Hill; Howard Phelps operated a sawmill on the bank of the Connecticut River between West Lebanon and Hanover; and Phineas Parkhurst invested in mills near the Glen Road and in the center village. The community also supported a few tanneries, including Osgood True's on the West Lebanon brook that bears his name, and Paul Buswell's at the lower end of Water Street. There was also one on Great Brook near the southern end of the Meriden Road.

The early mills also played a social role, as Colbee C. Benton recalled in an article for the *Granite State Free Press* in 1872: ". . . it was something like the bar-room. There was a continual vibration of news between the two . . . Each were happy meeting places for a social class of kindred spirits, and everybody was social then. Hard labor during the day was sweetened with jovial recreation in the evening. Feats of strength, pulling sticks, telling marvelous stories, singing songs and sometimes a game of 'high-low jack' were among the amusements."

As essential as those mills were to the town's development, a greater mix of businesses also began to emerge, including two cloth factories with similar names in the center of town.

Lebanon Cotton & Woolen Factory Company

In 1814 the Legislature passed an act giving Amos A. Brewster and Henry Hutchinson permission to run the Lebanon Cotton & Woolen Factory Company. They were allowed to build a dam and factory on the Mascoma River "near the meeting house in Lebanon" for the purposes of manufacturing cotton and wool cloth. The enterprise underwent a legislative name change in 1824, when it became the Lebanon Cotton Factory Company, and was reincorporated in 1825 with Amos Bugbee, Calvin Benton, Arad Simons, Samuel Young, Ammi Burnham Young, and David Whitman, Jr. as the principals.

In 1815, the year after the Lebanon Cotton & Woolen Factory Company was established, the Legislature passed an act that allowed Jacob Putnam, Amos Bugbee, and William Harris to run the Lebanon Mechanics' Cotton and Woolen Factory, "to carry on the spinning of Cotton and woolen yard, and the manufacturing of the same into cloth." That Mechanics' factory is believed to have been situated at the corner of Water and Mascoma streets, and seems to have been a separate corporation from the one approved in 1814. In 1821 its taxes dropped sharply, which seems to give weight to an account that says that it was heavily damaged by a fire in 1820.

The "Mechanics'" factory disappeared from the town tax rolls after only a few years, but the Lebanon Cotton Factory Company was still around in 1832, when an industrial census was taken that provides some insight into the business. It had five-thousand dollars worth of real estate; its machinery and equipment was valued at fifteen-thousand dollars; the value of the inventory on hand was fifteen-hundred dollars; annual wages were listed at $3,726; and the work year was 311 days, indicating that employees had Sunday off, but only two other days during the year. Three men over the age of sixteen were employed at the rate of a dollar per day; three boys under the age of sixteen made thirty-four cents per day; and the twenty women or girls who worked there received forty-two cents per day, probably for spinning and weaving. The factory's raw materials included twenty-five-thousand pounds of Alabama and Georgia cotton from which was produced one-hundred-thousand yards of "coarse shirting" that sold for about eight cents per yard. Half went to market in Boston while the rest was sold directly from the factory.

It seems that cloth was not all that was retailed at the shop. An 1828 entry in the town records of liquor licenses gave the Lebanon Cotton Factory Company permission "to sell retail and misc any and every kind of spiritous liquor or wines in any quantity or quantities more or less than one gallon at their store in Lebanon lately occupied by Timothy Kenrick for one year from the date of this license."

Others licensed to sell liquor included Uriel Huntington on the Meriden Road, Turner Peterson on the Connecticut River Road in West Lebanon, Joel Tilden in the north end of West Lebanon at Olcott Falls, and James Ralston in East Lebanon.

Blacksmiths

Blacksmiths were as important to the age of the horse as service stations would later become in the age of the automobile. Lebanon had several early blacksmiths, including Daniel Morse in the Hardy Hill area, Alexander Grimes on School Street, and Frederick Lull on Hanover Street. It was a hard and sometimes dangerous business, and one account says that a Lebanon blacksmith was kicked to death by a horse as he tried to shoe the animal.

Hats and Bricks

Among the new products made in Lebanon in the early 1800s were hats made by Andrew Post at a factory on the Mascoma River in the center of town, and a brickmaking business that lasted for over 150 years began in about 1806 when miller Comfort Goff started making bricks from clay dug out of a pit on a site at the north end of Hanover Street. Bricks had been cast by hand in the home since the early days, and the

Aerial view of the kilns and racks of the Densmore Brick Company on Hanover Street. Lebanon High School was later constructed with Densmore brick in the field at upper right. Thompson's garage is visible in the very top of the photo which was taken before the interstate cut the street in two.

first commercial brickyard is believed to have existed between 1771-1817 near where Exit 19 of Interstate 89 is today. Samuel Barrows, who arrived in Lebanon in 1806 and went into business as a cooper (maker of casks or tubs), bought out Mr. Goff in 1810 and ran the Hanover Street brickyard through the 1820s, living in a house built (of brick, naturally) near the yard. Mr. Barrows' business was later taken over by his son and then by his son-in-law, G. N. Greeley. The brickyard was bought by Jason Densmore in 1881; it remained in his family for three generations and made what was reputed to be the hardest surface-clay brick in the world.

In 1829 the legislature granted a charter to West Lebanon residents Roswell Sartwell, Erastus Clark, and Benjamin Green, establishing the New Hampshire Salt Manufacturing Company, authorizing the men to sell stock and "purchase, construct and use such machinery and apparatus as may be necessary and useful in boring for salt water, and for the manufacture of salt, either by boiling, evaporation or otherwise." Salt was commonly used as a preservative, but it seems unlikely that the principals ever drilled for salt. A twenty-year tax exemption in the company's charter renders town tax records silent on the matter, and there is no mention of the enterprise in anything previously written about the town.

Taverns

Standing at a crossroads also meant that Lebanon was a logical location for taverns and inns, of which there were about nine in the early nineteenth century. The most

View of West Park Street where the Bank and Whipple blocks were later constructed, about 1865. From the left are Benton's store at the top of Benton Hill, the Lafayette Hotel run by William Benton and later his son Colbee, Hildreth's Hardware store, and Gilman Whipple's second store. The Benton home on Court Street is at the far right.

prominent was Hough's Tavern on West Park Street, built by Thomas Hough in 1804 on a lot near where the Whipple Block presently stands. Shortly after it opened it became the home of the village's first post office. Letters were sorted alphabetically into a series of cubbyholes in a desk that sat on the end of the bar, and residents asked the barkeep for their mail. Presumably, no purchase was necessary.

One account says that six-hundred people ate dinner at Hough's Tavern for the Fourth of July celebration in 1806 or 1807, and attended a ball afterward. The inn later passed to William Benton, who renamed it Benton's Tavern, and it continued to serve as the local gathering place. According to *The Lebanonian*, "The Benton tavern was always an interesting haven for the neighbors, as well as for travelers, a central depot for receiving and distributing the latest news; a place where men congregated for social enjoyment and the latest news. There was no railroad, no telegraph, no balloon, no nothing but the stage with its four or six horses—the great attraction of the country."

Benton's Tavern was renamed the Lafayette Hotel in 1828, in honor of Revolutionary War General Lafayette, who stayed there during a tour of the United States. The hotel was later moved down the hill on Mascoma Street, near the present junction of routes 4 and 120 (1994).

Although it was the most prominent of Lebanon's hotels, the Lafayette had plenty of competition. In 1829 another hotel went up in the center village when Wareham Morse built the Rising Sun Hotel at the corner of School and East Park streets (post office, 1994). William Dana—Senior and Junior—continued to run an inn at the junction of the

Lebanon, 1761-1994 / 46

Fourth New Hampshire and White River turnpikes in West Lebanon, and Ephraim and Benjamin Wood built Benwood, a hotel on the Croydon Turnpike along the Meriden Road. The brick house that sits at the junction of Heater Road and Bank Street Extension was also an inn, built and run in 1823 by Uriah Amsden, and Sumner Clapp kept an inn in the Hardy Hill area on what is now Stevens Road, which was then a main road from East Lebanon to Etna.

Three Boys

One of the youths who worked in Amos Bugbee's cotton factory was Benjamin Champney, who later became famous for his paintings of scenes in New Hampshire's White Mountains. Young Master Champney was Amos Bugbee's nephew, and the boy lived with the Bugbees for a few years in the late 1820s or early 1830s. Mr. Champney in his memoirs recalled the cotton factory mainly for its boredom. "I worked by myself in the picking room, tending a picker, an insatiable machine requiring constant feeding. I took the cotton from bales and pounded it with a club thus loosening it so that it could be placed in the jaws of the machine. This was not very hard work, but it was dull working all by myself, and the first few weeks I cried a good deal . . ."

Another youth who worked in the factory was William Wallace Smith Bliss, whose name is still recalled in military circles. He was a Whitehall, New York, native whose

Major William Bliss for whom Fort Bliss, Texas, was named was the son-in-law of President Zachary Taylor.

father and mother were born in Lebanon. The father, John Bliss, attended Lebanon schools and graduated in 1811 from the United States Military Academy at West Point, New York. After serving in the War of 1812 he worked as a Whitehall merchant from 1815-1818 before moving to Alabama, where he died in 1822. His widow, Olive Hall Simons Bliss, returned to Lebanon with her seven-year-old son, who attended school with young Champney.

Benjamin Champney recalled William Bliss as ". . . a noble fellow—not cast in a common mould—with high aspirations and elevated tastes. I never knew a boy like him. He cared not for boyish fun . . . His father had been an officer in the Army. He was fitted to go to West Point, and his admission was already secured."

William Bliss enrolled at West Point in 1829 and graduated ninth in the class of 1833. After serving in the infantry he taught mathematics at the academy until 1840, when he returned to field posts that took him to Florida, Indiana, Arkansas, and Louisiana.

When the Mexican War broke out in 1846, William Bliss was General Zachary Taylor's chief of staff. The former Lebanonian received medals for gallant and meritorious conduct in the Battle of Palo Alto on May 8, 1846, and also at the Battle of Buena Vista in February 1847. His heroics in the Mexican War also earned him an honorary degree from Dartmouth College in 1848, and the state of New York struck a gold medal in his honor in 1849.

When Mr. Taylor rode his own war-hero image to the White House as the Whig Party's presidential candidate in 1848, Mr. Bliss went along as his private secretary. Lebanon was abuzz later that year when Mr. Bliss became the nation's First Son-in-Law by marrying President Taylor's daughter, Mary Elizabeth, in 1848.

His White House tenure was cut short, however, when Zachary Taylor died in office in 1850. William Bliss returned to army life but died of yellow fever in Pascagoula, Mississippi, in 1853, only about three weeks after visiting New Orleans, which was in the middle of an epidemic. His body was returned to that city, and the 38-year-old hero was buried beneath a twenty-foot-high monument. The following year the U.S. Army fort near El Paso, Texas, was named Fort Bliss in his honor.

That was not, however, the end of the story, for about a hundred years after his death the army waged a successful and sometimes-heated battle with New Orleans officials to rescue Mr. Bliss' body from the condemned cemetery in New Orleans. He was then reburied at the Texas fort.

There was still a third high-powered talent in the Lebanon classroom shared by Benjamin Champney and William Bliss. Henry L. Kendrick, who graduated from West Point in 1835, served in the Mexican War, accompanied several military expeditions to the southwest, and commanded a fort for a while, is best remembered for the thirty-five years he spent as a professor at the military academy. Before he retired in 1880, his roll of former students included Ulysses S. Grant, William Tecumseh Sherman, and Stonewall Jackson.

Ammi Burnham Young

One of the first Lebanon residents to gain fame was Ammi Burnham Young, a builder who crafted a national reputation out of his self-taught architectural skills.

"To Young's early career have been attributed several buildings of modest merit to a

Buck House on High Street was designed by Lebanon's famous architect Ammi Burnham Young in his trademark Greek Revival style with Roman arches.

provincial builder," wrote Geoffrey P. Moran in the April 1967 issue of *Granite State Architect*. "His Congregational Churches in Lebanon and Norwich, Vermont [1817, believed to be his first], are typical New England white frame churches of the Asher Benjamin type. Although they display the dignity and charm associated with the best examples of these styles, these early churches lack the originality of Young's later work." Other buildings from his early period include a pair of Dartmouth College buildings, Wentworth Hall (built in 1829 and named for the late royal governor John, a college benefactor) and Thornton Hall (1828). These, Mr. Moran wrote, were "typical nineteenth century collegiate with their three stories of white-painted brick, topped with a steep gabled roof. Reed Hall, built in 1839, boasts Greek Revival detail lacking in the others. The later Shattuck Observatory of 1854 strikes a happy balance between continuity in style and the unusual function of this building."

Mr. Young's first significant commission outside of the immediate area was a contract he won in 1831 to design the Vermont State House in Montpelier, which was built between 1836-1838. With that and the Dartmouth work to his credit, he had become a successful architect but hardly one with a national reputation. That would come as a result of "a talent, a diligence for self-education and a stubborn Yankee devotion to the highest standards of practice with which Young was possessed," Mr. Moran wrote.

His rise to national prominence came when he was awarded a contract to build the million-dollar Boston Custom House, a commission he won over architects of loftier reputation. The Custom House, started in 1837 and ten years in construction, was called "the most highly developed example of the Greek Revival style in that area," according to Mr. Moran.

Mr. Young's work was noticed in Washington and by 1842 he was on the staff of the Treasury Department, which oversaw most federal construction. In 1852 he became Supervising Architect of the Treasury Department, which meant he was responsible for the design and construction of as many as eighty buildings at a time during a period of intense federal construction. During his tenure as a federal architect, he designed the Windsor, Vermont, courthouse and post office building that is still in use (1994).

He retired in 1862 and died in 1874 at the age of seventy-five. "The remarkable transformation from an unlettered journeyman builder to a true professional who was destined to occupy a position of national primacy was an accomplishment which hardly warrants the virtual anonymity in which Young remains today, even in the State of his birth," wrote Mr. Moran.

The Poor

In 1805 and 1806 the town voted "to procure a work house for the poor," but it appears that this was not done. Instead the town retained the custom by which indigent residents were "farmed out" to the lowest bidder who agreed to care for them for one year. The provider was paid by the town and also received the added benefit of having an extra pair of hands to help with labor around the farm. Apparently, however, it was not always a smooth arrangement, judging from the town meeting record of 1814 in which voters were asked "to take into consideration the case of Mr. William Payne and see if they [the voters] will in equity make to him some further compensation for the great trouble cost and loss by him sustained in consequence of his agreement to support Cuff Searle." The record is silent on what the problem was, but the town voted Mr. Payne the seventy-five dollars for his trouble.

Fire Wards

In 1824 the town took its first steps toward organizing what would eventually become the Lebanon Fire Department. Stephen Kendrick, Samuel Selden and Calvin Benton were appointed the town's first fire wards. According to a state law in effect at the time they were distinguished by: ". . . a staff five feet long, painted red, and headed with a bright brass spire six inches long. And the firewards . . . are hereby required, upon notice of the breaking out of fire in said town, to take with them the badges of their office [the staffs], and immediately repair to the place where such fire may be, and vigorously exert themselves and require and demand assistance of any inhabitants of said town to extinguish and prevent the spreading of such fire."

Fire wards were also authorized to appoint guards to prevent looting, and a person who refused to assist the fire wards was subject to a fine.

6

District Schools

The Schoolhouse

STUDENT BEHAVIOR, teacher pay and performance, and upkeep of school buildings are twentieth-century education issues that Lebanon residents also wrestled with in the nineteenth century, when the town was divided into as many as eighteen separate school districts, most with their own school buildings.

The town's first school opened in 1768 in a log cabin on a parcel of land along the King's Highway, west of the present airport. Lebanon's first public building, it stood for over one-hundred years and was last used as a sheep fold.

The first teacher, a master-of-all-trades named John Wheatley, accepted the job in return for a grant of land. According to one observer,

Were I to single out an individual to whom this town in its early days was specially indebted for his exertions in its behalf, I would name John Wheatley, Esq. He was the first town clerk; for nearly twenty years the first civil magistrate; the first schoolmaster; and the first representative under the present constitution of New Hampshire. To all his acknowledged qualifications for civil life, was added piety, and such religious gifts as made him a suitable person to lead in the meetings of the Church in the absence of a minister.

Mr. Wheatley's homestead sat on the corner of Bank Street across from the present library (Marion Carter home, 1994). From there his holdings extended east up Bank Street to the first knoll (Welch's Gun Shop, 1994); it was bounded on the west by the Mascoma River; to the south it stretched up School Street to the intersection of South Street; and to the north it ended at the river behind Eldridge Park. To reach the school Mr. Wheatley forded the Mascoma River near Hough Square and either walked or rode on horseback to the school in West Lebanon.

Lebanon's first schoolhouse was built in 1768 in the middle of what is now Airport Road. This photograph was taken about 1870, when it was used as a sheepfold, just before it was torn down.

Mr. Wheatley was an Irish immigrant who arrived in Connecticut and was indentured to a farmer at the age of fourteen. He later enlisted in the colonial militia, and it is not implausible to think that he passed through Lebanon during the French and Indian wars.

He moved to Lebanon from Connecticut in 1764 and was given the lot in the center of town. The record of the second town meeting (1765) shows him elected moderator, and he was appointed the town's first judge in 1773, a post he held until he died on July 30, 1786, at the age of sixty-seven. He was also elected selectman several times, and in 1775 and 1776, while still a teacher, was a school committee member.

Mr. Wheatley was fifty-six when the Revolutionary War started and his age kept him home, but it did not keep him idle. He was a member of the Committee of Safety which was responsible for obtaining Lebanon's share of ammunition and supplies, and which also functioned as a court and filled the governmental void that existed while Lebanon was vacillating between membership in New Hampshire and Vermont. Although John Wheatley's role was limited to the homefront, he and Submitt Wheatley lost two of their sons in the war, and the Daughters of the American Revolution named its local chapter for Submitt Wheatley.

The town was divided into four school districts in 1775, and split into eight in 1784. It was an era in which schools went to the children, rather than the other way around. If there were enough children in a neighborhood whose parents desired a formal education for them, a school was started.

The eight districts reflected the settlement patterns of the time: West Lebanon village north to the Hanover line; Route 12A south to the Plainfield line; Poverty Lane, Slayton Hill, the Meriden Road, Hardy Hill, the Center Village, and East Lebanon.

By the middle of the century there were some eighteen districts, although not all of them had their own schoolhouse. One that did was School District No. 5, which served the children of hilltop farmers along the south side of Podgum Lane (now Slayton Hill). An early record book from the district survives and provides a feel for turn-of-the-century school administration in Lebanon.

At the top of the district hierarchy was the prudential committee, usually just one man who functioned as a principal and handled the district's money, a chore that was ripe for second-guessing even then. The district in 1827 "voted not to ratify what the committee (viz) Luther Wood has done in respect to the summer school." The record gives no indication of what action Mr. Wood had taken, but it apparently cost him his position as the school committeeman, because "John Hebard was chosen Committee to the exclusion of the former committee (viz, Luther Wood) to lay out the public money."

Part of the district's annual business routine was making sure each family came up with its required proportion of the wood needed to heat the schoolhouse during the winter when class was in session, sometimes for only two or three months. To that end, residents of the district voted in 1807 "that the delinquent get their wood when called for by the committee in alphabetical order and in case of neglect he or they shall pay their proportion of money to the committee whose business it shall be to procure the same."

In 1810 the district voted to raise nine dollars to fix up the schoolhouse, but by 1812 voters decided to replace the school altogether. The project was put up for bid, and while they waited to see who the low bidder would be, voters opted "to sell the nails found where the old schoolhouse stood to the highest bidder." The nails brought a price of two dollars and twenty-two cents. On March twenty-sixth the three-man committee overseeing construction awarded the project to Edmund Freeman and gave him a subscription paper with the amounts he could collect from residents in the district, totaling $131.50. The district leased land for the new schoolhouse and directed that it "should stand a few feet north on the same Central Ground where the old school has stood."

Benjamin Champney, one of the boys who worked in the cotton factory in Lebanon, attended one of the district schools in the late twenties and early thirties when he lived with his aunt and uncle. Although it is not certain which school he attended (probably in the center village), he recalled in his memoirs that he walked a half mile with "low shoes" and no overcoat to get to school in the twelve-week winter term:

The schoolhouse was crowded with boys and girls of all ages from five to eighteen years . . . [It] was heated by a huge stove, and the little boys and girls in the small seats in front were roasted, while the larger scholars at the back were nearly frozen. The master was usually an undergraduate at Hanover. He made our quill pens when the writing hour came, and acted the tyrant at all times when he caught us whispering or doing aught against the rules. But the scholars were cute, and we had our fun in spite of him.

Apparently, whispering was also a classroom problem more than thirty years later, as the *Free Press* in 1867 published a list of "students who have not whispered," and those who were neither late nor absent.

One recurring topic of school affairs was (and continues to be) repair of the schoolhouse, and workdays were held periodically for that purpose. Perhaps to cut down on the need for such workdays, the district in 1819 "voted that every parent or guardian shall be holden to the district for any damages done to the schoolhouse or anything appertaining to the same—by their children or any other scholar sent by their direction and for every other expense arising on their account."

In the early years schoolmasters boarded with local families. Some years the teacher's board was put out to bid, and in others it was handled on a rotating basis throughout the term; the more students a family sent to the school, the longer they were required to board the teacher. These arrangements, while they lasted, helped keep school costs down. However, the 1893 school board reported that the demise of the practice, coupled with the fact that a prospective teacher could make more money in the mills and factories than in the classroom, meant that "in order to secure good teachers we shall have to pay higher wages."

Another recurring theme was teacher performance, and Andrew Chellis was publicly criticized in the school report of 1850 for not having a handle on the behavior of his thirty-seven students. The board expressed its displeasure in the typical take-no-prisoners terminology of the day. "We say it with regret, and in the spirit of kindness, for Mr. Chellis is our friend, but most truly; we think this winter's school money thrown away. Nay, take your money and throw it into the fire, and it will be thrown away. But that money, which is paid to make your children worse scholars, worse citizens, worse men and women, is more than thrown away." The report also noted that when the school committee visited his classroom, they witnessed students insulting the teacher and damaging the school.

The board kept abreast of school conditions and noted in 1850 that teacher Solon Peck did the best he could in a deplorable situation. A small building (probably on Mascoma Street) bursting with sixty students studying a range of subjects out of mismatched textbooks. Many of the students attended class only on an irregular basis, the report said.

What were students supposed to be learning? The curriculum listed in the 1847 report of the eleventh school district seems typical in its offerings of algebra, basic arithmetic, grammar, philosophy, geography, reading, writing, and spelling. The report also noted that, "This is the only school in our town, where the scholars were taught to rise when a visitor entered. This may seem to some a small matter; but, in truth, it is no small matter to have the heart so educated as that we shall pay due respect to age and wisdom."

Lebanon High School

The town's first high school was a private institution built in 1835 on a lot next to the Methodist Church on "South Street," as School Street was then known. Lebanon Academy opened in 1835 with Dr. Edmund R. Peaslee (who would go on to join the staff of the Dartmouth Medical School) as its principal, but the school failed after a few years for lack of money; and the pitched-roof building was turned over to the Universalist Church, which reopened it in 1841 under the name of Lebanon Liberal Institute. That name and "Lebanon Academy" became synonymous, and the road on which the school was located carried the name Academy Street for several years before it was called School Street. The school was run by a board of trustees that included attorney Elijah Blaisdell, farmer Roswell Sartwell, and merchants Wareham Morse and Timothy Kenrick.

It offered four eleven-week terms in which students were charged by the course, and classes were segregated by gender. (It was common at the time for boys to study math, science and philosophy, while a girl's education was primarily confined to music and other "ornamental" studies.) The Lebanon Liberal Institute's advertisement in the *Granite State Whig* gave the following prices for the fall term of 1851:

Board, including lights, wood and washing, can be readily obtained for 1.50 to 1.75 per week. Also, Rooms, at low prices, for those wishing to board themselves.

Common English Branches	$3.00
Higher " "	3.50
French Italian and Ancient Languages	4.00
Penmanship	1.00
Drawing	1.00
Music, with use of Piano	8.00
Vocal Music	1.00

The student body included local boys (when not working on the farm) as well as tuition students from Massachusetts, Vermont and New Hampshire who boarded with local families.

Like its predecessor, financial problems forced the Lebanon Liberal Institute to close about 1852, and the schoolhouse on Academy Street stood vacant until 1857, when a district school at the corner of Prospect and School streets merged with one on Summer Street to form the Union School District, which moved into the two-story Academy building. Although it would not acquire the name for several more years, the Union School District was the forerunner of Lebanon High School.

The school rules dictated that classes begin with religious exercises at 9:00 A.M. Classes apparently were let out for lunch, as the rules mention that students were required to be back by 1:00 P.M. They also attended school on Saturday mornings, and teachers were allowed to exercise control of students not only on school grounds, but also in the streets and at other public places. The last of the rules urged parents to cooperate with teachers to ensure punctual attendance and prompt completion of lessons.

The effort to create a formal public high school began about 1866, shortly after the state passed a law allowing contiguous districts to form high schools. A resolution supporting the concept stalled at town meeting, but in 1870 a group of the town's leading men formed the "Lebanon High School Association" with an aim toward opening their own school. The president of the group was postmaster Elisha Liscomb, and other backers included Dr. L. C. Bean, storekeeper Joseph Gerrish, *Free Press* editor Elias Cheney, and Charles Downs, who in 1876 was appointed the state's superintendent of public education, the equivalent of today's education commissioner.

They fitted the former Baptist chapel on Green Street with furniture from the East Lebanon factory of William Haskell and opened in April 1870 with about forty students. Attendance, however, was apparently not what organizers had hoped, and the association dissolved in 1871.

Meanwhile, the debate over whether to fund a public high school continued as a testy affair: Two members of the three-person prudential committee resigned in the summer of 1871, and a special district meeting held that fall to consider buying a high-school building was adjourned before any of the articles could be considered.

The high-school proposal was not the only school topic being considered. The *Free Press* published a column in February 1871, asking, "Shall our School District System be Abolished?" It read, in part: "Every one must see at a glance the inequality of the present arrangements, and the resulting disadvantages to our 568 different pupils whom our schools are designed to benefit.

"Some of these schools are crowded much beyond the capacity of the buildings to accommodate. Others are so small that the advantages of classification are entirely lost. And there is great inequality in the length of our schools. Some districts are able to sustain their schools, during the entire year; others one-half, and still others only one third."

Attendance at district schools ranged from five to fifty-eight students, and teachers were paid between sixteen and eighty dollars per month, including board, the newspaper said. The town, however, retained its system of district schools.

Voters in June 1872 passed a $33,000 bond issue to pay for a new school building on School Street, but could not agree on what to construct: a new wooden building, a new

The School Street School, the original Lebanon High School, before the third story and the mansard roof were removed.

The second Lebanon High School on the corner of Elm and Bank streets about 1910. It was later replaced by the New England Telephone building.

brick structure, or an addition to the existing school.

Meanwhile, the legislature in June 1871 had passed a bill requiring students to attend school for at least twelve weeks (six consecutively) if they were between the ages of eight and fourteen and lived within two miles of a school.

The divisiveness over the high-school issue carried over to the March meeting of 1873, when it took six ballots to choose the three members of the prudential committee from among eighteen candidates. Finally, on May 29, 1873, voters appropriated $20,000 for a new schoolhouse on the School Street lot and in July 1874 the old brick schoolhouse was torn down and replaced by the new brick building—the present School Street School. The three-story building was designed to house 294 students on the two lower floors. It had a mansard roof (replaced in 1951), a hall on the top floor, and a basement that could be used for play in inclement weather.

Having approved the building, district voters officially endorsed the creation of a high school in 1876, the same year that the legislature chartered the Lebanon High School District, although classes were held prior to that time.

Then, as now, school spending was an issue. The *Free Press* reported in 1883 that the Union School District in the 1860s spent $544.10 and had only three teachers, but sixteen years later was spending $3,511 and had a staff of nine. In 1884 voters approved the teaching of music in the school for the first time, and the school board passed a new policy that indicated, perhaps, that the good old days were a thing of the past: students were no longer allowed to come to school barefoot.

The high school, which had an enrollment of 51 in the 1902-03 school year, was bursting with 101 students by 1905, when a new brick building was constructed at the corner of Elm and Bank streets. That building proved inadequate within twenty years. Superintendent Caleb Niles noted in 1923 that the school, which had been designed to accommodate 125 students—150 in an emergency—had an enrollment of 173.

A new school was constructed in 1925 on Bank Street next to the lot known as "the basin" (Lebanon Junior High School, 1994), and two years later—in a move many west-side residents would come to regret—voters in the West Lebanon High School District successfully petitioned the state to merge with the Lebanon School District. The union took effect on July 1, 1927, and while West Lebanon continued to have its own high school, the merger brought all of the town's public schools under the same administrative roof.

In addition to the regular courses offered at the high school, there was a separate slate of classes held in the evening, and it was as if there existed an entirely separate school culture. Many of the students were French-Canadian mill workers, and the curriculum included courses in Americanization. There was even a night-school basketball team.

The building at the corner of Bank and Elm streets, meanwhile, was used for elementary school students from 1925 until it closed in 1952 and was sold in 1960 to the New England Telephone and Telegraph Company, which put up another brick building that is still in use.

The high-school population outgrew the second Bank Street building in the 1950s, and the present high school was constructed in 1958 next to the Hanover Street Elementary School (built in 1952). Completion of the new high school laid the groundwork for one of the town's most contentious issues—the closing of West Lebanon High.

7

Wool Depots and Dairies

The Sheep Craze

WHILE THE turnpikes allowed Lebanon to make economic inroads during the first thirty years of the nineteenth century, sheep as a cash crop provided an important economic link between the turnpike era and the arrival of the industrial age ushered in by the railroad in 1847-48.

There were sheep on Lebanon farms prior to the 1830s, raised either for their dietary value as mutton or for their wool, which wives and daughters would weave into clothing on the looms that were commonly found in homes. Just how many sheep the town had is unclear since they were not taxed until 1828, when the legislature passed a law placing sheep alongside cows, horses and oxen as taxable property. However, the fact that Calvin Benton kept a wool depot in the center village as early as 1830 indicates that wool was an important commodity even before sheep showed up on the tax rolls.

The legislation that allowed sheep to be taxed in New Hampshire also coincided with an 1828 tariff imposed by Congress that levied a forty-cents-per-pound tax on foreign wool imports which had been flooding the country. The tariff limited imports and boosted the demand for domestic wool, resulting in a price increase from thirty-six cents in 1827 to fifty-seven cents in 1835, as southern New England textile mills sought wool from the hill country.

The town's 1829 inventory shows four-thousand sheep in town under the care of forty-eight farmers who kept flocks ranging from only a few to several hundred. Lebanon was firmly in the grip of the sheep craze by 1835, when 127 men were taxed on flocks that totaled about 13,000. By 1840 the number of sheep exceeded 17,000.

Sheep quickly became such a dominant enterprise that they dwarfed the numbers of other stock, and by 1832 a square-mile of land in Lebanon supported five-hundred sheep, thirty-three hogs, ten horses and forty-two cows or oxen. More land was cleared to accommodate the increased need for pastureland and by 1855, 80 percent of the town

Left behind by the glaciers, rocks like these on the Townsend farm had to be dug up before planting.

was deforested. Photographs taken in that decade show the surrounding hills barren of trees. About half of all land in New Hampshire was cleared at the time, as compared with 10 percent in 1994.

The sheep, mostly Spanish Merinos, thrived on the rocky, scrubby hillsides where they could graze on weeds and briers that cattle would not eat, and the cold weather was said to enhance the growth of the fleece. Sheep were also less labor-intensive than cows, if for no other reason than that they did not have to be milked twice each day. As Harold F. Wilson wrote in *The Rise and Decline of the Sheep Industry in Northern New England*: "Indeed, during the summer season the latter animals required little more attention than to be salted once or twice a week."

Still, the diaries of Abel Storrs (covering a period from the mid 1860s through the 1870s) show that even with relatively low-maintenance sheep as his farm's main stock, there was plenty of work to keep Mr. Storrs and a few hired men busy through the course of the common fifteen-hour workday. Depending on the season they plowed, furrowed, planted, weeded, hoed, hauled rocks, spread manure, split rails and chopped wood, hauled more stone (a necessity if you wanted to plant anything in that rock-strewn soil), built stone walls with the rocks they hauled, mowed, mended fences, husked corn, tapped maples, boiled sap, picked apples and cut and hauled hay. There also were cows to be milked, an assortment of other animals to be fed, and harvesting to be done when the crops were ready. Planted in the Storrs' fields were wheat, corn, oats and potatoes, all in quantities large enough to yield a surplus that could be sold. Peas, cabbage, beets, carrots, parsnips, and several kinds of beans were grown for family consumption.

Sheep that were especially productive became local celebrities of sorts, such as

Charles Gates' prized Merino that earned mention in the *Granite State Free Press* for yielding twenty-six-and-a-half pounds of wool in 1863, about double the norm. Mr. Gates also had a ram that was valued at one thousand dollars, a handsome sum for the time but still far less than some other farmers fetched for their animals. Similarly, the *Free Press* saw fit to mention that Abel Storrs grossed twenty-four-hundred dollars in 1865 for his flock's wool.

After sheep were sheared the bales of wool were sold either to wool-buyers who traveled the countryside in the weeks after shearing, or to one of the local "wool depots" that sold directly to cloth manufacturers.

The relationship between the farmer and the wool-buyer seemed to be based largely on mutual distrust as they haggled over the quality and price of a bundle of wool, and each wondered whether he was the one being fleeced. An article in the *Granite State Whig* published on March 3, 1849, stated that when dealers paid a call on farmers

> *every means and artifice is resorted to by the purchaser, to obtain the wool of the farmer, at the lowest possible price. Many of the farmers, know that they frequently get horribly shaved by the speculators, and also, know, as they do, that many of the agents who are employed to buy, are fit subjects to be shaved in return, will resort to all unfair and unjust means to deceive the buyers and thus a kind of warfare is constantly carried on between the parties and not unfrequently heavy lawsuits are the result . . .*

Such an atmosphere lent itself to the creation of the wool depot, a sort of cooperative that the *Whig* described as a place where the two sides could meet on amiable terms, "neither seeking to defraud, cheat or deceive."

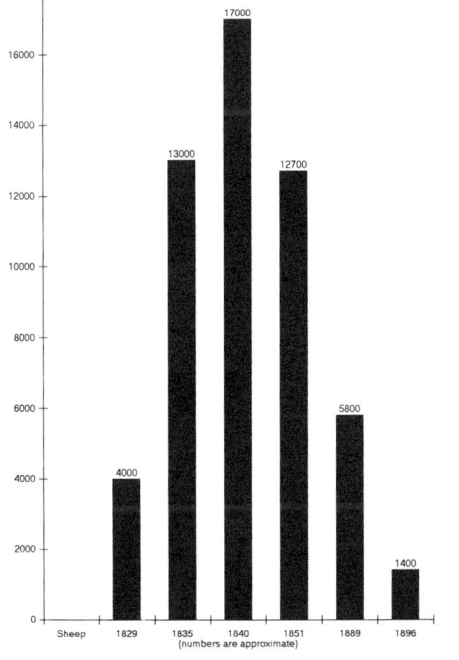

The Age of Sheep

The town had three such depots: Colbee Benton opened one in the center of town about 1830; storekeeper Abel Low, Jr. established another in East Lebanon in 1848, and a third opened in West Lebanon in 1849, backed by Lebanon farmers Abner Allen, Seth Blodgett, Zuar Eldridge, and Clark Hough, and a group of other farmers from the area.

Just two years before Mr. Low built his depot, Congress repealed the tariffs that had kept most wool imports at bay and by 1851, $3.8 million worth of wool was being imported at a time when the local shepherd and depot operator were feeling the squeeze of western competition.

Unfortunately for the local sheep farmer, a price war with his western counterpart was a losing proposition because sheep could be raised there for less than in New England. Even factoring in shipping costs, the western farmer with a virtually unlimited range of grazing land could undercut the eastern farmer's prices.

As a result of these factors prices fell; but many of Lebanon's sheep farmers toughed it out, and town records show there still were 106 men with sheep in 1851—not much of a drop from the 117 who kept flocks in 1840. However, the number of sheep in town declined during that same period from the peak of about 17,000 in 1840, to 12,696 in 1851, and just over 9,000 by 1856.

The biggest change was that the huge flocks disappeared. Although some of the decline was undoubtedly caused by farmers reducing their stock due to lower wool prices, it probably also reflected improved breeding techniques that yielded more wool from fewer sheep, thus lowering local production costs.

Greater efficiency and lower freight costs (the railroad) sustained many farmers up to the Civil War period when textile factories were forced to turn to wool to replace embargoed supplies of southern cotton. The price of wool rose to a dollar per pound in some markets and sheep farming was again in vogue, although those prices spiraled downward when the war ended.

Although the town would never again be able to boast of sheep in the numbers seen in the 1830s and 1840s, they remained in substantial numbers through the 1870s and 1880s. The town still listed more than fifty-eight hundred sheep in 1889, but by then they were being kept primarily for breeding purposes or for mutton, rather than for the value of their wool. The number of sheep continued to dwindle until by 1896 there were but fourteen-hundred sheep in town, and just over a thousand two years later.

The Milkman Cometh

"The great sheep-raising period was followed by twenty years of experimentation, of fumbling for a new and more profitable branch of agriculture," wrote Mr. Torbert. "Cattle rearing, wool growing, a combination of the two, the rearing of horses, grain farming, fruit culture—each had its advocate in 1871."

Many farmers found an answer to the post-Civil-War instability in dairy farming, which went through three primary stages in Lebanon: butter, milk, and decline.

The first era, begun in the late 1870s and continued into the early twentieth century, was one in which butter was the dominant product. The 1880 Census listed 130 farms churning out more than 68,000 pounds, and the four leading farmers each produced more than a ton: Thomas Waterman in Butmanville, Wilbur Heath and Edwin Perley on Hardy Hill, and Jerry Wood on the road between Lebanon and West Lebanon.

The dairy business moved toward commercialization when the town's first cooperative processing plant opened in West Lebanon in 1888 (probably in the area of Bridge Street, which Harrison Clapper recalled used to be known as Creamery Hill). Lebanon's second creamery (known first as the Lebanon Creamery and then as the Mascoma Creamery by about 1915) opened in 1890 on Water Street.

The West Lebanon creamery produced more than 66,000 pounds of butter in its first year, while the Lebanon plant turned out 101,474 pounds in 1892, according to the *Free Press*. The paper reported that the seventy farmers who brought their milk to the Lebanon creamery in forty-quart milk cans received about twenty-five cents per pound of butter, although not all of them made it there unscathed: The newspaper reported that Henry Noyes of East Lebanon spilled a ton of milk (literally) into the street in February 1893, when his wagon overturned on the ice just before he reached his destination. (Even had he made it to the creamery, he probably would have returned to his farm with a hefty load of skim milk, which was considered waste and fed to pigs and other livestock.)

With cream rising to the top of the agricultural field, the town's cow population nearly doubled between 1890 (878) and 1910 (when it reached a high of 1,624). Farmers increasingly turned to planting oat hay and silage corn, and between 1888 and 1898 silage production increased eightfold, from 350 tons to 2,870. To store that winter feed, twenty-five silos appeared on the local farmscape.

Since cows required less pastureland than sheep and since they ignored the seedlings and hillside brush that sheep would have wolfed down, the deforestation of the mid-1800s began to reverse itself and an assortment of white pine and birch took root, leading to the tree-covered hillsides that prevail today.

Despite the presence of the two creameries, domestic buttermaking continued on many farms. Christine Hough, who was born in 1886 and grew up on the "Hough Farm," (Walhowdon Farm, 1994) between the Meriden Road and Route 4, recalled in her memoir, *A Chip of Granite*, that churning was but one of many chores:

There were the special days of churning butter (can you still hear the plunk, plunk of chunks of sweet butter as they separated from the buttermilk as the plunger went monotonously up and down?) The soft soap making; the big round cheeses made with rennet, (Tina sat on the press to squeeze out the whey;) these cheeses had to be greased and turned every day. The sausage grinder was a formidable machine, mincing up those pink slabs of pork, seasoned with herbs to get just the right flavor, then pressed into small, long bags. The frying of lard for shortening for pies and for the beautiful brown doughnuts, the tiny centers sugared for me. The candle making, the hot tallow poured into the tiny moulds with the wicks inside. Such a fascinating sight to childish eyes.

The first decade of the twentieth century marked the start of the second phase of the dairy era in Lebanon. Midwestern imports and the introduction of margarine had softened the butter market, and milk gained favor among Lebanon farmers. It had once been impossible to ship it unspoiled to markets outside the region, but the advent of refrigeration systems—ice—allowed some locally produced milk to be carried by train to Boston and other major cities in southern New England.

Although the cow population peaked at about sixteen-hundred in 1910, the town's bovine count usually numbered more than a thousand over the next four decades. Distribution was split about evenly between a score of larger farms (more than twenty head) and a higher number of small commercial farms (perhaps as few as six cows), scattered throughout the town's several pockets of agricultural activity.

If the railroad was West Lebanon's bread and butter, then dairy farming was the mother's milk of the village. A chain of farms extended from the Plainfield line to the Hanover border, interrupted only by Butmanville and the Main Street area. There were more than a half dozen farms along Route 12A alone. The True family farm sat almost on the Plainfield line; Ross Wood's farm was just north of the present landfill (Friendly's, 1994), a farm he later sold to John Korpela and his son, Paul; then, proceeding north toward the Mascoma River, one passed the farms of the Laware, Johnson, Farnsworth, and McBain families.

North of West Lebanon village on Route 10 were some of the larger farms in town. Arthur Eastman worked the flat on Crafts Avenue; Milton Reynolds' forty-eight cows grazed the fields at the north end of Maple Street, and his homestead was on the site of the old *Valley News*/Group Habitat building, (Allards Furniture, 1994); about half-a-mile north of the present Wilder Dam site was the farm of Ira Buck, who had a milk route that served Hanover customers; John Gould had a farm about where the Campion Rink now stands (1994); and north of that farm, almost on the Hanover line, was the dairy farm of James Spencer (Pinewood Village condominium, 1994).

You also passed sizable dairy operations on either of the roads between Lebanon and West Lebanon. Joseph Wood's stood along the main road between the villages (Grand Union, 1994); and on the "Back Road" (Old Pine Tree Cemetery Road/Mascoma Street Extension, 1994) were the farms of Richard Whipple, John Sleeper, and Bill Allard. Charles LaBombard worked the Heater Road in Lebanon center, and John Hall had a 325-acre homestead on the Etna Road (New Jersey Machine, 1994).

Jerseys, Ayshires, and Holsteins also roamed the uplands. The Poverty Lane farms that dated back to the 1700s were still viable under the stewardship of men like Nathan Stearns, Austin Durocher, Edward Tourville, and Arthur Adams; Erastus Goodwin, Frank Manchester, Leonard Whipple, Maurice Benson, and Roger Farr made Hardy Hill and East Lebanon an important dairy neighborhood, and at the foot of that hill sat the Winona Farm of Alexander Pringle.

The so-called Great Brook Valley on either side of the Meriden Road proved as fertile for dairy farming as it had once been for sheep. Forrest Cole, William Stewart, and others flourished along the Meriden Road itself, and three farms sat on hills rising up from either side of the road: One of the town's leading farmers, Arthur Hough, continued the family tradition on Hough Road between the Meriden Road and Route 4 (Walhowdon Farm, 1994); from there he could see the hilltop silos of the Townsends—Harry and Hugh—located on Storrs Hill (Tadmor Farm and Tomapo Farm, 1994); and Mr. Hough could also look out on Stephen LaBombard's farm on Prospect Hill (Hillcrest Acres housing development, 1994).

Some of the milk from those farms was shipped to a nearby processing plant of the H.P. Hood Company of Boston, or to another plant in Bellows Falls, Vermont. In the 1940s Buttrick's Dairy had a facility on the Miracle Mile (Doug's Sunoco, 1994) that

Hugh Townsend plows a rocky field on his farm atop Storrs Hill in 1915.

received local cream and shipped it to the company processing plant in the Boston area.

Whereas most families had once kept a cow or two to meet their own dairy needs and perhaps those of a few neighbors, that became impractical for textile workers and others who lived in tenements or thickly settled neighborhoods. This decline of the one-cow family spurred retail demand for local milk, and dozens of large and small dairy farms offered home delivery to meet that need. The milkman thus became a morning institution eclipsed in familiarity only by the rising sun.

Honey Gardens Dairy founder Philip Townsend told his successor (and son-in-law), Arthur Clark, that there were 30 milkmen making deliveries when Mr. Townsend began his own milk route in 1916. Among the local dairies, Nathan Stearns operated the Wakema Dairy on Poverty Lane; Clarence Sleeper ran the Supertest Dairy on Mascoma Street Extension (Canteen building, 1994) before he sold it to Harvey Bassey and Hershey Packard; just north of that facility was a dairy operated by Bill Allard; and the Winona Dairy now occupied by the Winona Farms housing development was founded on Bank Street Extension by Alexander Pringle and later was operated by Volney and Barbara Slack. In the Mascoma section of Lebanon, Andre W. Fenimore operated a dairy that he later sold to Gerald Aldrich, who was bought out by Honey Gardens.

One reason for the proliferation of local dairies, aside from the sheer demand, was that milk could be delivered raw. As processing requirements tightened, however, and the equipment needed to meet them grew increasingly sophisticated, it was no longer feasible for small farms to maintain their routes, and the number of dairies dwindled.

The Honey Gardens Dairy was by far the town's largest and best-known. Mr. Townsend started the business as a beekeeping operation in 1908, and expanded into the milk-delivery business in March 1916, delivering raw milk and cream from a wagon in the summer and a sleigh in the winter. The teams of horses yielded to the Model T in the early 1920s, and by 1930 the dairy relied upon trucks to make deliveries.

Arthur Clark took the Honey Gardens business over from his father-in-law in 1942, and by 1955 Honey Gardens was processing more than two tons of milk each day, making deliveries to more than eight-hundred homes and forty commercial accounts, including local schools. The dairy also delivered chocolate milk, buttermilk, skim milk, eggs, cottage cheese, bread, and honey. By the time Mr. Clark retired in 1970, Honey Gardens had more than twelve-hundred retail accounts and more than fifty-five wholesale customers.

Mr. Clark, who had purchased the Wakema Dairy on Poverty Lane, the Mascoma Dairy in East Lebanon, and a few other smaller ones, sold the business in 1970 to Jim Austin of Daisy Hill, who in turn bought the Winona (1972) and Supertest (1973) dairies. Mr. Austin ran Honey Gardens until 1976, when he sold his two-thousand retail and seventy wholesale accounts to Billings Dairy of Wilder, Vermont, which discontinued home deliveries in the mid-1980s, according to Roger Murray, the last of the Billings' milkmen.

However, by the time Mr. Clark retired from Honey Gardens in 1970 (he still owns the property, and leases it to Dave Fuch's music store, a glass company, a storage facility, and a garage), the third stage of dairy farming in Lebanon, that of decline, was well underway. Dairy farming in Lebanon survived World War I, the Great Depression, and World War II, but a combination of factors caused the town's cow population to drop by more than half between 1956 and 1967.

One reason for the decline was a change in the economics of dairy farming that favored larger farms. Whereas the early dairy farms relied mainly upon manual labor to harvest hay, milk cows, and do assorted chores, mechanized equipment began to play an increasingly larger role, and the dairy farmer who wanted to stay competitive faced larger capital expenditures to purchase equipment like hay-balers, gutter cleaners, and milking machines. Still other farmers gave up their businesses in the early 1960s, after dairies stopped taking deliveries in forty-quart milk cans. Instead they sent bulk-tank trucks around to pick up milk, a change that required milkhouses to be remodeled to accommodate more sophisticated refrigeration equipment and stainless-steel holding tanks, which replaced the old water coolers. Such equipment outlays were especially difficult for small farmers, and in Lebanon, even the largest farms were small—no bigger than fifty cows. Therefore, rather than invest in pricey refrigeration systems and expand their herds to the scale required to justify that equipment, many farmers simply opted out.

Another factor, one that Howard Townsend said led him to discontinue dairy farming in 1972 in favor of the tree-farm operation carried on today (1994) by his son Bruce, reflected the law of supply and demand. As more efficient methods pushed milk production higher than demand, the price that farmers received for their milk dropped, and with it the profit margin upon which a dairy farm operated, presenting farmers with a choice—expand the herd to increase the margin or go out of business. Several chose the latter.

Still other farms died when younger family members who might have carried on the farming tradition opted for careers in other fields with a five- or six-day workweek and a guaranteed income.

Reuben Cole recalled that his father, like most dairy farmers, had other sources of income. Forrest Cole built houses from wood cut on the farm, and then rented out the homes. Other farmers diversified into lumber, firewood, potatoes, maple products, and poultry.

Finally, development pressures also played a role in the decline of dairy farming in Lebanon. Commercial and residential developers made lucrative offers for land that was, at best, only marginally productive farmland. Faced with ever-increasing costs for feed, taxes, and equipment, a number of cash-poor farmers living on an economic razor's edge cashed in on their only real source of wealth—their land.

The plazas of Route 12A that sprouted starting in the late 1960s (and continue through the present time) sit upon what was once the richest farm soil in town (last tilled by the Townsends of Tadmor Farm), and the businesses along either side of the "Miracle Mile" between Lebanon and West Lebanon are located on once-productive farmland.

Much farmland has also been turned over to residential use. A few of the many examples are the Hillcrest Acres housing development put up by Carl Moulton in the early 1960s on land once farmed by Stephen LaBombard, and the silo of the old Winona Farm now crowded by a cluster of homes constructed during the soaring 1980s.

As a result of these factors, the town's only two remaining dairy farms are the Tadmor Farm on Storrs Hill and Walhowdon Farm on Hough Road. In contrast with the smaller farms of yesteryear, Tadmor now milks 110 cows and keeps another 115 on hand for replacement stock, according to Robert Townsend, who owns the farm along with his wife Carolyn, son Michael, brother Eric, and mother and father, Norman and Ruth Townsend. The family members are partners in a corporation, Tadmor Farm, Inc., established in 1975 to enable the farm to be passed on to future generations. Farming is not getting any less expensive, either, said Robert Townsend, noting that a tractor purchased for $75,000 in 1989 fetched $100,000 in 1993.

Walhowdon also is significantly larger than it used to be. Whereas Arthur Hough in 1934 had only twenty-seven cows on the hilltop spread, present owners Donald and Howard Patch keep over two-hundred head on the farm, and they milk eighty-five. In addition to dairy farming and the sale of apples, cider, and maple products, the farm also has become well known as one of the premier breeders of Holsteins in New England.

Tadmor and Walhowdon are all that remain of Lebanon's dairy legacy, and they, along with Carl Adams' Ascutney View Farm on Poverty Lane (which raises beef cattle), were recognized by the U.S. Department of Agriculture as National Bicentennial Farms for remaining in the same family for more than two-hundred years.

8

The Railroad

>HOW TO READ IN A RAILROAD CAR
>
>*Hold a card or slip of paper over the line below that which you are reading; the eye being free from the disturbance caused by the motion of the train, you may then read with comfort.*
>
>—Item in the *Granite State Whig*, 1851.

"An Abominable Big Place"

IN MAY of 1982, a train derailment near Brattleboro, Vermont, prompted the B&M Railroad to break from its normal route and detour freight-train traffic onto the tracks of the old Northern Railroad between West Lebanon and Concord. On May eleventh, two light engines left White River Junction to see if the track was still usable.

On May twelfth and thirteenth, ten trains rolled warily through town at top speeds of ten miles-per-hour, making for a seven-hour journey. Even at that speed, however, the sight of the trains startled many residents who had grown accustomed to dormant tracks. Despite the hope of local railroad buffs that the detour might signal the rebirth of Lebanon as a railroad town, it proved only temporary. When the southern Vermont track was cleared of the wreckage that had forced the detour, the railroad resumed its normal route. It was, as of this writing, the last time a train passed through Lebanon.

It is hard to say how Lebanon would have developed without the railroad, but it seems clear that when the first wood-fired locomotive chugged into the depot at the center of town on November 17, 1847, it was an event that, more than any other in the first two-hundred years, shaped the town's social and industrial future. Probably the only comparable event was the arrival of the interstate highway 120 years later.

The first evidence that Lebanon residents were pondering the notion of a railroad came at the 1836 town meeting when voters approved a resolution "that the Selectmen pay the expense of the survey of the contemplated Rail Road route through the Town." It appears that the survey was not done, perhaps because there also existed substantial opposition to railroads.

As the Downs history characterized that apprehension:

The farmers opposed them because they did not want their farms divided and encumbered by the track, because their cattle were likely to be killed or mutilated. They said it would spoil the market for their horses, as there would be no call for them on stages and the big teams which carried their produce to market, and brought back groceries, dry goods and old Medford rum. What should they do with their oats.

The railroad, however, enjoyed strong support from "The Friends of Internal Improvements in New Hampshire," a group led by Dartmouth College economics professor Charles B. Haddock of West Lebanon. When the group convened in town on October 10, 1843, to whip up pro-railroad sentiment, it was Mr. Haddock who framed the arguments in favor of a railroad. He predicted that building the railroad would result in a massive public windfall through cheaper goods brought on by reduced shipping costs that would produce an economic ripple effect: the price of importing raw materials to make local goods would go down, bringing a corresponding reduction in manufacturing costs; goods could be transported to market for less than it had cost to ship them by teams of horses, and local wares would therefore be more competitively priced; and products that had not been shipped at all because of prohibitive transportation costs could be exported for the first time. In addition, the railroad would spur investment in new ventures along the rivers of the region, and the cost of passenger travel would also drop.

Mr. Haddock also sought to appeal to the local agriculturalist, arguing that "an important saving . . . would be realized in getting our beef and mutton, our poultry, our butter and cheese, to markets, in time and without injury or waste. The two former especially, beef and mutton, now driven upon the hoof with no little risk, and no little depreciation of quality, would be taken down alive in a single day, without shrinking in weight and in perfect order."

The railroad movement continued to gather steam, and voters at the 1844 town meeting instructed their state representatives to support a railroad charter and a law allowing railroads to take land by eminent domain as long as they gave the landowner "full and adequate compensation." The town seemed to be responding to an 1842 law that said property owners had to be compensated their asking price before giving up land to the railroad. Since the earlier law did not force people to sell, and some refused to do so, it effectively halted railroad expansion.

The New Hampshire Legislature succumbed to the public clamor in 1844, passed an eminent domain law, and approved a charter for the Northern Railroad to be built between Concord and the Connecticut River.

The town appropriated two-hundred dollars to help pay for a survey and construction began in thirty-four sections in 1846, using Irish immigrants as the main source of

Cutting through ledge to make way for the railroad about 1847

labor. (Some of those immigrants apparently stayed in Lebanon when the railroad construction was finished. The Federal Census of 1850 listed fifty-three Irish-born residents, most of whom were classified as "laborers." It also listed thirty-six residents of Canadian birth, ten born in England, four each who were born in Scotland and France, and eleven-year-old Austey Kinney listed as having been born "on the Atlantic.")

The laborers cut a path through ledge and forest, laid ties and rail, and on November 17, 1847, the first train arrived in Lebanon, which was the end of the line until the rail to West Lebanon was completed the following year. On June 5, 1848, the first passenger train departed West Lebanon for Boston.

The Haverhill-based *Granite State Whig* reported that more than twelve-hundred people accompanied the inaugural train to Lebanon, including guest speaker Daniel Webster and a host of stockholders and dignitaries from Boston, where most of the major investors resided.

Concord and Franklin residents also bought large shares of stock, and 74 Lebanon residents owned 834 shares, the third-most of any town on the line. One of those stockholders, Halsey Stevens, predicted at the opening ceremonies that, "Lebanon is destined to be an abominable big place."

The Enfield Shakers also owned stock in the railroad, and were at least partly responsible for track being laid on the eastern shoreline of Mascoma Lake, on the opposite side of the lake from the sect. The original layout called for the track to cut through the Shaker villages and continue along what is now the Route 4A side of the lake. The Shakers, however, opposed that plan and to coax Northern officials to take a longer

The West Lebanon railroad yard in the 1950s, with the junction of Seminary Hill, Route 12A, and Main Street at the upper left.

route that would carry the track on the other side of the lake, they are said to have donated land on that shore and also a sum of money toward the purchase of a locomotive that was named "The Shaker." Consequently, the railroad ran on the opposite side of the lake from the Shakers, who built the Shaker Bridge in 1849 to allow themselves and others access to the railroad depot in Enfield.

A train coming from Enfield entered Lebanon near the east village, and passed over the land of fifty-six different Lebanon property owners who received a total of just over eighty-four-hundred dollars in compensation from the railroad.

East Lebanon had its own depot for taking on passengers and freight, and the station serviced the extensive farming community around Mascoma Lake that shipped wool, produce, and later, dairy products. There was also an ice house on the north side of Mascoma Lake that at one time furnished all of the ice for the railroad.

The westward run from East Lebanon took the train over ten railroad bridges as it crisscrossed the Mascoma River enroute to the center of town, where the train stopped at the depot constructed in 1847 near the junction of Spencer and Taylor streets. From there it crossed the Mascoma River between High and Mill streets and proceeded along Mascoma Street to a grade crossing near Slayton Hill Road. In 1857 the railroad paid for construction of an underpass in that location, allowing carriage traffic to pass under the track.

From this arch bridge, the line continued to a similar structure that was built on the Glen Road in 1848 and placed on the National Register of Historic Places in 1985.

Tradition says that a branch of the river that ran through what is now the Riverside Circle housing development was diverted to accommodate the railroad as it neared West Lebanon village. It seems probable that it happened. A dip in the road in that spot seems consistent with the configuration of a dried-up riverbed, and although railroad records are silent on that specific location, they do indicate that rivers and streams were routinely rerouted in dozens of other places on the Northern line.

In West Lebanon the land between the west side of Main Street and the Connecticut River became a thriving railroad yard, with a 130-foot stone roundhouse built in 1848, a machine shop for repairing engines, and a freight house. There also was a shed to store some of the one-thousand cords of wood burned by the engines each month. The original roundhouse was later dismantled and replaced about 1890 by a brick structure and a four-hundred-foot-long shed to house up to ten-thousand tons of coal, which replaced wood as the principal locomotive fuel. The yard also included holding pens for cattle waiting to be shipped to market.

Railroad Village

The arrival of the railroad brought an end to most of the long, slow, bumpy stage rides over bad roads. The Northern ran four scheduled passenger trains per day—two north and two south—between Concord and West Lebanon. (The average speed for passenger trains was twenty-three miles-per-hour, increased to twenty-eight miles-per-hour in about 1879.) The railroad's annual report of 1852 shows that 76,687 passengers traveled 4,427,475 miles that year, an average of almost fifty-eight miles per trip. Most people, in other words, were traveling the entire length of the line.

The trip to Concord that had previously taken a full day by stage was reduced to mere hours at a cost of $1.75, while the trip to Boston that had taken six days in the pre-turnpike era now took less than a day at a fare of $3.25.

As railroad opponents had predicted, some of the outlying inns along the turnpike did go out of business (although hoping for a competitive edge, several Lebanon inns offered free carriage service between the depots and their hotels); but the daily slaughter of cattle on the rails that had been predicted did not occur, although it happened occasionally.

One expectation that did come to fruition was that trains almost immediately replaced teams of horses as the primry means of importing and exporting freight (although horses were still viable commodities, and teamsters were still used for local deliveries, or to areas that lacked rail service), and it all but eliminated the Connecticut River as a viable means of freight transportation. Shipping by rail was cheaper, faster, and trains were less at the mercy of the weather than turnpike teamsters had been. The railroad provided an expedient and relatively inexpensive means of shipping goods, and the railroad's annual report of 1852 shows that the Northern carried more than four-million tons of merchandise the previous year (freight trains traveled at speeds of 10 miles-per-hour, increased to twelve miles-per-hour about 1879).

In West Lebanon a bridge was constructed across the Connecticut River to link that village with White River Junction. Designed and built by Henry Campbell (who settled in what is now the Carter home on the Lebanon street that bears his name), the project was supposed to have been finished by the end of 1847. However, it was plagued by construction problems such as a collapse in April 1848 in which some workers were seriously hurt. Two months later, however, the bridge was finished.

Economically, the bridge was important because it allowed local manufacturers and those to the south to connect with the Central Vermont Railroad that began operating in 1849 between White River Junction and Burlington, and also provided a way for northern shippers to reach Boston. By 1850 a line extended from St. Johnsbury to the Vermont border, and in 1851 the network reached into Canada. Lebanon—especially West Lebanon, since it was at the end of the line—had a key spot on a railroad of economic importance, and expectations were high that the railroad would change the town from a modest agricultural/commercial center into a magnet for industry and manufacturing.

All the Live-Long Day

Railroad employees, in the beginning at least, tended to be men in their twenties and thirties who earned what was considered a good wage for the time. Depot masters were paid about one-hundred dollars a month for their work, while the railroad's annual report of 1852 shows switchmen received a monthly wage of about $30.50, gatekeepers $12.50, watchmen $34.50, conductors $44.00, and ticketmasters $27.00.

The 1850 Federal Census makes it clear that West Lebanon, by virtue of its place at the end of the line, was by far the most important railroad village in the town, with more workers than either of the other two villages combined.

Railroad employees occupied many of the homes along Main, Tracy, Dana, Elm, Pleasant, and Maple streets, as well as in the company-built tenements known collectively as the Railroad Block, located in the railroad yard itself (said to have been used as a barracks for Civil War soldiers en route to battle). The Northern paid William Ela to build four such tenements in 1848, and two others were added before the turn of the century, as the railroad became the dominant employer in West Lebanon for the next several decades.

While railroads have been romanticized over the years, in reality the tracks were often a place of tragedy from which Lebanon residents were not immune. Working for the railroad meant decent pay, but a misstep often meant the loss of a foot, leg, arm, or life. This was especially true in the era when cars were coupled manually.

The *Granite State Free Press* reported on July 7, 1869, that twenty-one-year-old John Maxwell, a brakeman from Concord with a wife and child, was killed when he was "caught between the bunters" while trying to couple cars at the West Lebanon railroad yard. Later that month Enoch Hough of Lebanon narrowly escaped harm when a derrick used to load goods onto cars on a branch track broke and fell to the ground, grazing his back. "A child had left the spot where it fell but an instant before," the paper claimed.

Baggage master Joseph Doucette was coupling air brakes at a water stop on the River Road about a mile from East Lebanon when a mail train collided with a freight train in August 1894, fatally crushing him.

Brakeman Henry Bailey of Manchester was killed instantly in West Lebanon on

December 17, 1887, when he apparently fell from the top of a boxcar and was run over by the train. "There was no evidence of carelessness on the part of any one running the train," determined the New Hampshire Board of Railroad Commissioners.

That commission, which was stacked with friends of the railroad bosses who controlled the state's political strings, was in no hurry to make the railroads safer, and discovered silver linings in the grimmest of facts. The commissioners' annual report of 1888, for example, noted that thirty-four people had been killed since the previous year's report, but emphasized what it saw as the good news: No *paying customer* had been killed *inside the doors* of a train since 1884.

However, fifteen of the dead were railroad workers. The commission concluded that while the number of workers killed was too high (it failed to state what the acceptable number would have been), several of those accidents were clearly due to the "incompetence and carelessness of fellow workmen."

As for the nonemployees who were killed, the language used by the commission in describing those deaths made it sound as if board members felt that some of the victims had it coming: "Of the seventeen not in railroad employ, one boy was stealing a ride and another was attempting to pass under a moving car, one child was at play upon the track, one man was asleep upon the track, one was unloading a car, three persons were driving and two were walking over crossings, two attempted to jump upon moving trains, and five were trespassers upon the track."

In addition to accidents in the yard and at crossings (the vast majority of which were unprotected into the twentieth century), there also were some spectacular bridge accidents and collisions. The most notable in Lebanon happened at the so-called Chandler Bridge, which crossed the Mascoma River about where the Packard Hill Covered Bridge is located (1994). When engineer Warren E. Emerson ran his sixteen-car freight train through the bridge on April 30, 1886, he felt it give way. "Under the momentum of the train and the instant opening of the throttle by the engineer, the locomotive and one car passed through the bridge, and were turned into the ditch," read the railroad commissioners' report. "No person was hurt, and the damage was light to the locomotive and cars."

The cause of the accident was simply that the bridge was old and bearing a heavier load than that for which it was constructed. When it was built in 1865, the heaviest locomotive on the Northern line weighed thirty tons; the combined weight of the Atlantic and the tender that accompanied her in 1886 was about sixty-five tons. Freight cars in use when the bridge was built were rated at ten tons, while the cars pulled by the Atlantic that day had a twenty-ton capacity. "At the inspection one month previous to the accident it had been considered as unsafe by the bridge superintendent and the report made that it should be renewed this season," the commissioners' report said.

The *Free Press* reported that while hundreds of people came to gawk at the spectacle, a construction train and large work crew arrived from Concord and a wrecking train was brought in from West Lebanon to remove the cars and rebuild the line. Within forty-eight hours of the accident a trestle was erected over the river and train service resumed.

The Chandler Bridge collapse seems to be the best-remembered and most written-about accident, but there were others. The paper in March of 1894 reported that a train

Early twentieth-century photograph of the train station in East Lebanon, after its name had been changed to Mascoma

rounding a curve in West Lebanon ran into seven cows on the track, "and there was a sickening slaughter of beef which made every person's face grow white."

And then there was this account of two trains colliding at the Lebanon Depot in September of 1893: "Fish, onions, neckties, corsets, cheese and other kinds of freight were 'hashed' together in the most approved style after the manner of wrecks."

An error by a Concord telegraph operator sent a northbound freight train careening head-on into a passenger train from Quebec, killing twenty-six people in the infamous Canaan wreck of September 15, 1907. Although the crash was not in Lebanon, four of the five-member crew on the freight train were West Lebanon men: conductor Benjamin Lawrence, engineer Elisha Shurtleff, fireman Hiram Carl, and brakeman Matthew Wallace all survived.

Westboro, Mascoma, and Other Names

There is a misconception in town that the West Lebanon railroad yard was always known as the "Westboro" station. In fact, the three depots were first known simply as West Lebanon, Lebanon, and East Lebanon, and stations elsewhere carried similar directional designations until a fatal accident a year after the Canaan crash prompted the railroad to rename two of Lebanon's three railroad stops.

On March 20, 1908, the failure of a dispatcher to include the word "East" in his instructions to a train led to a head-on collision in Haverhill, New Hampshire. Five people were killed, after which directional prefixes were eliminated in favor of one-word names that were harder to confuse. On January 10, 1909, East Lebanon became the "Mascoma" station, and the West Lebanon depot became known as Westboro the following year. Similar changes were made at other depots on the line.

In addition to numbering each locomotive, Northern officials also gave each engine a name, often one which carried some significance to a town on the line. Engine Number Five, for example, was built in 1847 and was known as the "Lebanon." Other locomotives with names of local significance included the "Mascomy," named after either the lake or the river; the "Col. Hosley," built in 1872 and named after West Lebanon resident Jewett Hosley, who supervised the building of the Northern track and then stayed on as superintendent of the western end of the line; the "A.M. Shaw," which was named after the Lebanon native who was a prominent civil engineer on the railroad.

"Not Recently Built"

By the late nineteenth century there was some grousing about the condition of the depots. In what seems to have been a recurring theme, the *Granite State Free Press* campaigned for a new depot as early as 1893, chiding railroad officials for letting the stations in Lebanon and West Lebanon deteriorate:

Out of the fullness of their treasury the Boston & Maine officials [who took over the Northern in 1890 under a long-term lease] have found money enough to pay for a coat of paint on the passenger station at the Center, and presumably—in their minds—Lebanon people have a palatial passenger station. At West Lebanon the passenger station is finely located—in a mud hole—and accommodates the patrons of the road in 'first-class style.' Lots of people would hardly stable their horses in it. The freight depot is a building about 15 feet square and looks like an outhouse, and the inward freight at West Lebanon last year was $50,000, as I was informed by competent authority. Lebanon people are kicking about their station accommodations, and the opinion among them seems to be that they can keep on kicking until they kick their shoes off and have to replace them at their own expense.

Even the railroad commissioners acknowledged in their report of 1885 that "stations are serviceable, but not recently built."

In 1921 the paper stirred up readers like Henry Knapp, who called the station "a disgrace" and wrote in a letter to the paper that, "The Chamber of Commerce's slogan, 'COME TO LEBANON, THE TOWN BEAUTIFUL' is right, but don't come by train."

That also may have been about the time that the depot caught fire one night, and "in spite of the yells of the crowd to 'let 'er burn,' the firemen saved it with a small loss," according to an article in the *Claremont Daily Eagle* that recalled the history of railroading in Lebanon.

Rust on the Tracks

The railroad began to feel the pinch from cars following World War I, but service was steady if not spectacular through World War II, when motor vehicles took a heavier toll on railroad operations. Following reported losses of $2.1 million in 1963, the Interstate Commerce Commission allowed the B&M to discontinue passenger service throughout most of the state the following year. On January 3, 1965, the last passenger train stopped in town, and the depot was razed in October of that year to create parking for the A&P store that was located at the corner of Campbell and Parkhurst streets.

Even the once-robust freight service had declined, so that by 1965 only two freights a day used the tracks of the Northern. (The last train wreck in town, incidentally, happened on September 18, 1972, when several boxcars left the track near Baker's Crossing, on Riverside Drive.) Soon, however, the regular runs ceased and the tracks sat mostly unused (although hundreds lined the tracks on April 13, 1975, to see the American Freedom Train make its way through town as part of the nation's bicentennial celebration). The demise of the railroad somehow seemed official when even the Westboro station was abandoned in the late 1970s.

The *Free Press*

The arrival of the railroad in Lebanon also coincided with the publication of the town's first weekly newspaper—the *Granite State Free Press*.

Founded in 1844 in Haverhill as the *True Democrat* and later the *Granite State Whig*, publisher George Towle moved the paper to Lebanon in 1848 after a fire destroyed the paper's Haverhill office. It became the *Granite State Free Press* on July 15, 1859.

The theory behind the early newspaper was that everyone knew what the local news was, but word from afar was harder to obtain. As Helen Smith noted in a talk before the Lebanon Historical Society in 1971, "Only the better class of people subscribed to a weekly paper, and there was no daily in the state. One weekly often served several families. State and national news were reported in great detail, but there was practically no local news." That changed over the years so that by the early 1900s local news was front-page material.

The *Free Press* also operated a job office that did contracted printing work, which was where the real money was. There also was profit to be had from running early advertisements for medicinal products that promised to cure everything from cancer to arthritis and tuberculosis.

Mr. Towle sold the paper in 1861 for one-thousand dollars to Elias H. Cheney, whose family was associated with the *Free Press* without interruption for the next 101 years. Mr. Cheney was involved for 63 of those years, and by the time he died in 1924 he was widely known as the Dean of New England Editors.

He contributed columns to the paper even after President Benjamin Harrison appointed him U.S. Consul to Cuba in January 1892, a position he held until 1894. He was then appointed U.S. Consul to the Dutch West Indies by President William McKinley in 1899, a job he maintained for fifteen years. Still, his columns showed up in the paper while his sons, Harry and Fred, took care of day-to-day operations.

Mr. Cheney's son-in-law, George H. Kelley, took over as managing editor in 1914 and ran it until his death in 1926, when it passed to his son, Richard H. Kelley. Mr. Kelley's sister and brother-in-law, Helen and William Smith, came aboard in 1941 and ran the paper until 1961, when they sold it to David Hewitt of Hanover, who also published the *Hanover Gazette*. The Smiths continued to manage the operation even after Mr. Hewitt merged the two papers in 1966 to create the *Granite State Gazette*, which was purchased in 1971 by former *Valley News* managing editor Jim Wechsler. Even though they were no longer active on the editorial side, Mrs. Smith continued the family connection by writing a weekly historical column for the paper.

Mr. Wechsler sold the *Gazette* in 1973 to the Connecticut Valley Publishing Company of Springfield, Vermont, and owner Oliver Stalter published it independently for a few years, but then merged it with the *Mascoma Week* before folding both papers in 1981, ending the 137-year-run started in 1844.

While the *Free Press* had the longest tenure of any Lebanon paper, there have been others. William Kendall, Jr. published the *N. H. News Weekly* from August 1875 to June 1876, before folding and purchasing the *Laconia Democrat*. A weekly free shopper, the *Connecticut Valley Reporter*, was published in the 1960s and 1970s. Former *Valley News* editor Sid Leavitt published the daily *Tri-Town Telegraph* for a few weeks in the mid-1970s, and former high-school teacher Thomas Bisson put out the weekly *Lebanon News* for a few months in 1990.

9

Westside

ITEM: THE arrival of a new transportation corridor turns a sleepy farming village into a viable commercial center.

It sounds like what happened to Route 12A after the interstate arrived in 1966. On the other hand, proving that history does, indeed, sometimes repeat itself, it also describes the impact that the railroad had on West Lebanon in the mid-1800s.

Although West Lebanon village had a post office as early as 1833 (William Barron was the first postmaster) and was a way station of some importance thanks to the junction of the Fourth New Hampshire and White River turnpikes, it was not much of a commercial center before the railroad arrived.

Butmanville

The most developed site on the west side of town prior to the railroad was along the Mascoma River where the Powerhouse Mall now stands (1994). The legislature in 1837 granted a charter for a cotton and woolen factory known as the West Lebanon Manufacturing Company, owned by West Lebanon sheep farmer Roswell Sartwell. This was the millsite first owned by Jonathan Dana and later by Joseph Wood, Jr. In 1836 the latter deeded a parcel of land along the river to Mr. Sartwell, who owned and operated the Dana Tavern at the corner of Bridge and Main streets before entering the manufacturing field.

The Sartwell mills included a gristmill, sawmill, and cotton mill which were bought in 1845 by William Osgood of Claremont, who brought young John Butman into his employ as a miller and bookkeeper. When the boss died in 1855, Mr. Butman bought the mills and surrounding property and the lower part of South Main Street became widely known as "Butmanville," a name that lasted well into the twentieth century.

Mr. Butman shared the gristmill business with Samuel Wood, Thomas Wood and O. S. Martin, and bought them out after about ten years. At about the same time he was selling interests in the gristmill, he also sold shares in the sawmill to Joseph Gerrish and

Thomas Waterman's saw and gristmill on the Glen Road about 1910. It is presently the site of the Powerhouse Mall.

James Hubbard. He bought them out—also after about ten years—and then sold the sawmill about 1870 to Thomas Wood, his old gristmill partner.

Thomas Wood sold the sawmill in the 1870s to Thomas Waterman (Waterman Avenue), who also ended up buying the gristmill, which was operated into the 1900s by Harry Messenger. In addition to the grist, saw and cloth mills, Butmanville was also where Edward Kelly turned out ax handles and carriage spokes in the 1870s and 1880s.

The mills were such a staple that there even was a "Mill Street" in Butmanville, probably that which is now known as the Glen Road, although a turn-of-the-century postcard also refers to Glen Road as "Lover's Lane."

The Butmanville mills also supported a modest commercial development. After giving up his interests in the mills John Butman kept a general store into the 1880s. Not far from where Longacre's Nursery was located between 1975 and 1987, the New England Nursery Company opened about 1869 under the direction of William Flanders and Elisher Kennerson. Hiram Dickinson and Thomas Maguire had blacksmith shops on Mill Street in 1882, and John Leavitt was a poultry dealer.

Also working on West Lebanon's Mill Street about 1880 was twenty-six-year-old teamster Nelson Johnson, who had not yet embarked on the career that would make him one of the largest taxpayers in town by the turn of the twentieth century. Mr. Johnson was a prolific seller of horseflesh: "His trade was essentially in western horses, and for its accommodation he built on lower Main Street extensive stables, and in a few years came to have one of the largest horse markets in New England. Going to the

Well-dressed horse traders await an auction outside Nelson Johnson's stables on South Main Street in the Butmanville section of West Lebanon about 1910.

West, mainly to trans-Mississippi points, as often as six times a year, he established monthly auction and commission sales which attracted buyers of horses from far and near," the *Granite Monthly* reported.

People flocked to Mr. Johnson's stables in a way not entirely unlike the present malls along Route 12A have enticed people to drive for an hour or more to do their shopping. As many as 2,000 horses were said to have passed through Nelson Johnson's hands in a single year. In 1904 he spun off a carriage and harness business, and also added bicycles to the mix.

The area near the present Glen Road-Route 4 intersection—as much as any place where the line between West Lebanon and Lebanon lies—also hosted pre-railroad industry. Philip C. Cambridge operated a cloth factory in the 1830s on the original Oliver Davison millsite that had passed through several partnerships over the years. The mill's previous owners included an 1810 partnership involving George Hubbard, Richard and Ebenezer Kimball, Luther Waters, and John and Erastus Chamberlain, who sold it to Samuel Tucker in 1814. Three years later Mr. Tucker sold the West Lebanon mill to Thomas Rea, who simultaneously sold Mr. Tucker his property in East Lebanon.

Mr. Rea sold the West Lebanon mill to saddlemaker Uriah Amsden and farmer Oren Hubbard in 1825, and they to Mr. Cambridge the following year. Records show that Mr. Cambridge mortgaged two carding machines from the factory in 1838, and the following year he gave a mortgage to Jonah Brown of Lebanon that provides a detailed list of some of the other items inside the factory: an oil canister and forty gallons of oil (to lubricate the machinery), three box stoves, seventy-five feet of flannel cloth, three desks, a grindstone, six augers, one large vice, fifty-four spools for the jack, several saws, two drawing knives, two pair of shears, five thousand bobbins for the jack, pails and buckets, a sink, planing tools, steel rods, a dozen spindles, a machine for rolling up cloth, scales, and two dozen lamps.

Mr. Cambridge also seems to have had a partner (probably a succession, given the business practices of the time), since in 1838 Elisha Sabin of Woodstock, Vermont, mortgaged to Hiram Simons and Horace Sessions "one spinning jack of one hundred and sixty spindles now in the factory occupied by P.C. Cambridge... and the looms now in said factory." Spinning jacks, which made their appearance in American woolen mills in the 1820s and were universally employed by about 1840, were a water-powered improvement on the old spinning-wheel or spinning-jenny concept, enabling large amounts of wool to be simultaneously spun and wound onto bobbins in preparation for weaving. A jack of 160 spindles would have been medium-sized, and probably operated by one or two men.

It also appears that the site along the Mascoma housed a brewery or distillery of some type, since the deed from Mr. Rea to Mr. Amsden and Mr. Hubbard also mentions the presence of a "malt house."

West Lebanon Village

While industrial activity predated the railroad at the western end of the present "Miracle Mile" and in Butmanville, the village at the bottom of Hubbard (Seminary) Hill was primarily a farming community before the railroad. The only commercial enterprise of note was the venerable hotel founded by William Dana in the 1700s at the corner of Main and Bridge streets. This prospered as an attraction for weary travelers on the Fourth New Hampshire and White River turnpikes, and continued to do so after the railroad arrived. A hall was added to host an assortment of balls, plays, and other entertainment in the 1870s, by which time it was owned by Edwin Southworth and known as the West Lebanon House. Mr. Southworth sold it to Dennis Sargent (a former restauranteur in Lebanon center), who named it after himself and added 38 rooms to the structure in 1888.

West Lebanon began to change as soon as the railroad arrived. The West Lebanon Congregational Church was founded in 1848 by a group of residents who had belonged to the Lebanon Congregational Church. Their desire to establish their own branch may have been motivated partly by the arrival of the railroad and a desire to enhance the development prospects of their own village, or it may have been that they were just tired of traveling the four or five miles between West Lebanon and the church in the center village. In any event, O. W. Burnap described the split as amicable in an article in the 1898 issue of *The Lebanonian*: "Consequently in just nine days after the dismissal of [Pastor] Mr. [Phineas] Cook, on the 13th of May, 1848, ten members of the parent church met at the house of O.L. Stearns, organized and voted to choose a committee to select a site for a new meeting house somewhere in West Lebanon to be improved some future time."

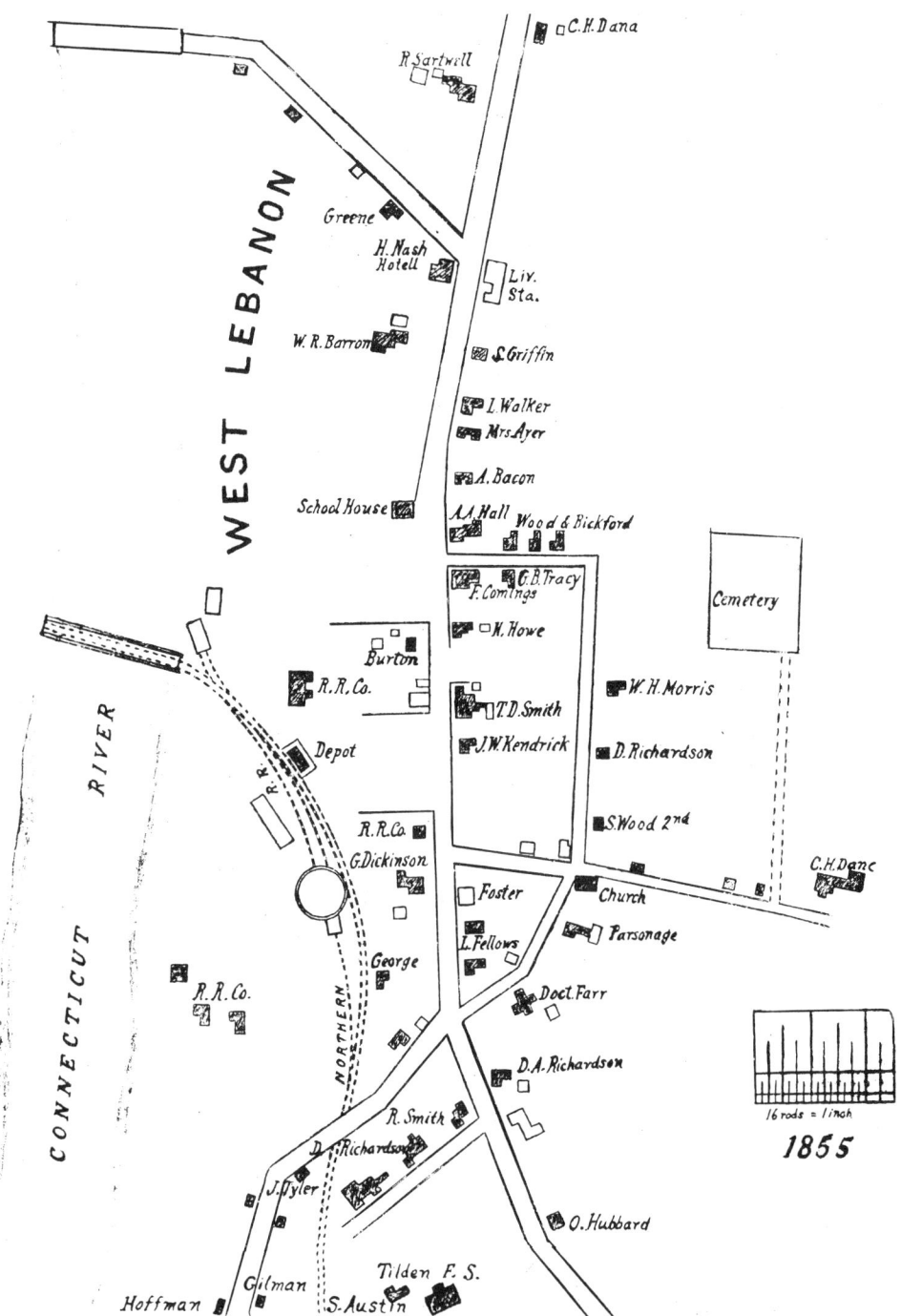

1855 map of West Lebanon from a survey drawing by W. C. Eaton

Moses Wood designed it, Oren Hubbard donated the land, money was raised for materials, and the church was built the following year, with Rufus Case installed as the first pastor.

Prior to establishment of the church, the focal point of West Lebanon's social life had been the village school which was constructed in 1826 on a lot beside the present fire station (1994). A second story added later, called Union Hall, was where school district meetings, Sunday school, singing classes, and other activities took place. The church, however, almost immediately became the preferred meeting place for such social events as concerts, suppers, and, in November 1859, a centennial birthday celebration for Joseph Wood. A month later the church's bell tolled a hundred times to mark his death.

The economic changes the railroad brought to West Lebanon were most obvious in the creation of well-paying jobs, which, in turn, changed the farming village into a modest center of commerce. Several new names began to appear on the town tax rolls under the "stock-in-trade" category, and their locations are gleaned from an 1855 map of the village.

Crossing the Connecticut River into West Lebanon over the Lyman Bridge, the first business on the Fourth New Hampshire Turnpike belonged to Henry Green, a Bridge Street resident who was listed as a chairmaker in the 1850 Census. He also kept a store that sold beekeeping equipment. Just around the corner, on North Main Street, Charles Dana worked as a farrier, although he would later become better known for manufacturing his patented ear tags that were used by farmers to keep track of sheep and cattle.

At the northern end of Main Street, between Dana and Tracy streets, was the carpenter and blacksmith shop of Abner Bacon. A little further south was the grocery of Ferris Commings, who opened his store in 1847 at the corner of Main and Tracy streets (about where the branch of the Mascoma Savings Bank stands, 1994). He appears to have been the first of the entrepreneurs to follow the railroad's money trail, as none of the other stores seem to predate his. From his store Mr. Commings also ran the town's first Civil War recruiting office in 1861, before going out of business the following year.

Just east of Commings' store, up the hill on Tracy Street, was the machine shop business of Samuel Bickford. A little south of the Commings' lot, about where the Red Cross Pharmacy stands (1994), was the Main Street store owned by Timothy D. Smith.

Moving further south, to the intersection of Main and Church streets, was the blacksmith shop of Henry Howe, and residents who needed new footwear or old boots repaired could call on Josiah George, whose shoe shop sat hard by the railroad tracks at the bottom of the hill and who probably saw a fair amount of business from the railroad workers.

On Elm Street—the first on the right as you travel up Seminary Hill—was the shop of farrier David Richardson, and between his business and the end of the street could be found John Tyler who made patented turbines that were installed in several mills in Lebanon and other New England industrial towns.

An 1860 map of the village includes several changes from the 1855 version, notably the store of William P. Burton and George Blood, which opened about 1854 across the street from where the post office now stands. This store in 1867 became the village post office (which had for years been located in the Dana Tavern). Mr. Burton was the village postmaster for more than twenty years and also a trustee of the Rockland Military

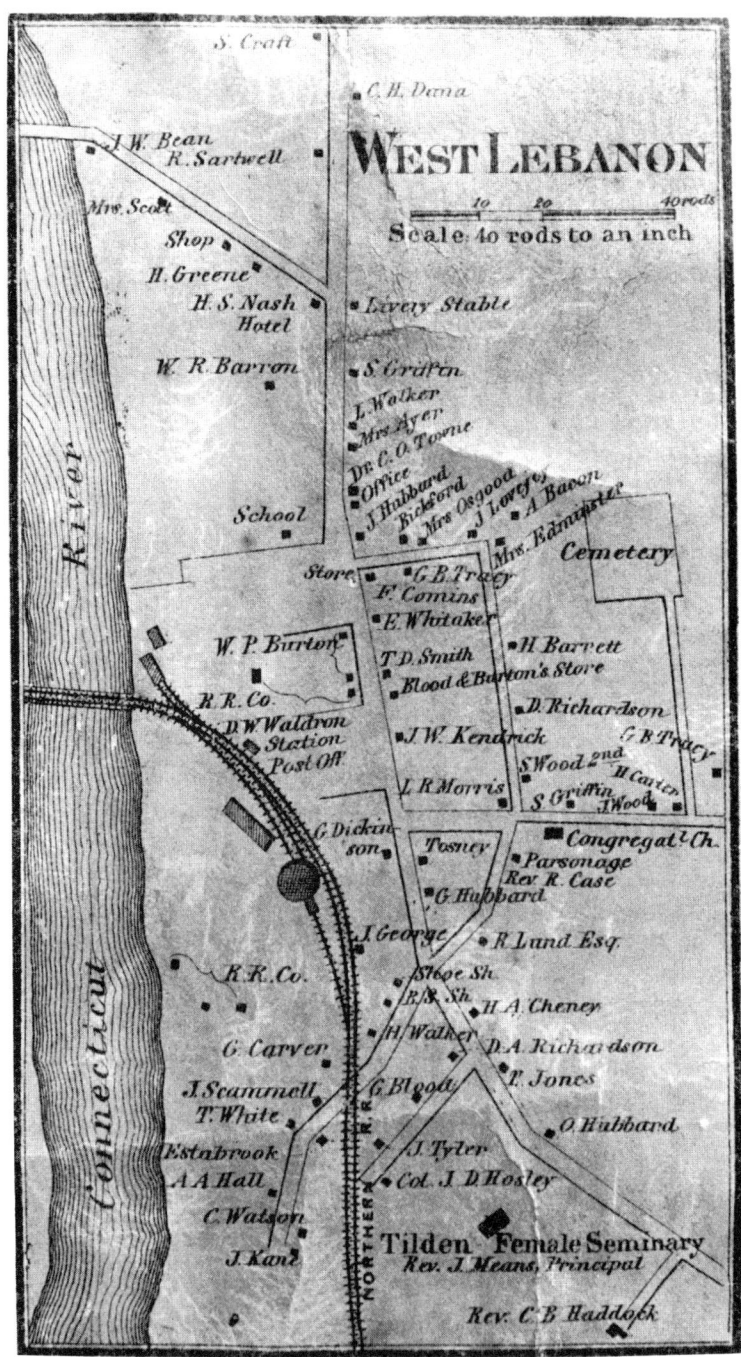

West Lebanon inset from Grafton County map of 1860 published by Smith, Mason & Co., New York

Academy, which moved to the village in the early twentieth century. He also served a dozen years as a selectman and represented the town in the legislature from 1891-1893, sponsoring the bill establishing the purple lilac as the state flower.

Added to the mix on Main Street in the 1860s were the harness shop of Elias Holt, a store run by Henry Fales in 1862, and a combination barber-and-shoe shop operated by Charles Coley in 1866 (which today would no doubt be called "Cut and Run"). W. B. Rolston & Co. had an undertaking business, and Hartford resident Whitcomb Church opened a store on Main Street in West Lebanon about 1867.

There also were a couple of budding businesses on the northern end of South Main Street in 1860. Haskell Walker made sleigh runners and carriage tops, and George Rix worked as a farrier.

Gideon Dickinson was especially well situated for the changes brought by the railroad. After selling the old William Dana tavern to William Barron in 1832, he bought a large parcel of farmland at the bottom of Seminary Hill, and the railroad was literally laid out through his back yard. He sold part of his farm to the railroad for a train yard, and during the late 1840s and the 1850s he sold house lots to railroad workers and a half dozen other parcels to men seeking to open businesses.

The passing of years brought other businesses to West Lebanon, either alongside or in place of those that came immediately after the railroad.

The census of 1880 and a directory of the town published two years after illustrates the evolution of the village economy from a place marked by a few stores and blacksmiths to one that supported a variety of trades and occupations. William Mills was a gunsmith, Albert Eaton a marble worker, and Sylvester and Charles Austin were masonry workers on Main Street. William Stearns made soap at the corner of Maple and Church streets, Elias Took is listed as a barber, Daniel Flanders and Thomas Hale as printers, and Frank King made the rounds as a sewing-machine salesman. T. F. and M. J. Bogle ran a wholesale jewelry operation on Main Street (it moved to White River Junction in 1884) for which Clarence Bogle was a traveling salesman, Lyman Gibbs, and A. J. Smith were meat dealers, while M. H. Sargent ran a fish market.

Other West Lebanon merchants in 1882 included grocers Goold and Holmes, (which became the John Goold Co. in 1898); O. B. Pierce (who was succeeded into the twentieth century by John Fulton); and George Worthen, who ran dry-goods stores in Lebanon and East Lebanon and a branch on Main Street in West Lebanon.

The 1882 directory also lists Drake and Woodman as druggists, a business that was the forerunner of the Red Cross Pharmacy presently owned by Edward McGee. Dr. Milton Woodman was a longtime surgeon for the Boston & Maine Railroad and was active in virtually every facet of village life. He came to West Lebanon in 1876 and bought a half interest in a drugstore owned by James Brown. His partner was Dr. Charles Drake, who worked at the store while putting himself through the Dartmouth Medical School (class of 1882). Dr. Drake practiced medicine in West Lebanon for more than fifty years before he retired about 1936 at the age of eighty-eight.

The Woodman and Drake pharmacy, which first shows up in an advertisement in the *Free Press* in 1877, was sold in 1905 to John McDonnell, who gave it the name Red Cross Pharmacy. James Kilton bought the business in 1930, doubled its size, and ran it until 1970, when he sold it to Edward McGee, the present owner. The drugstore, like

Aerial view of the north end of West Lebanon's Main Street in the 1950s, before the original West Lebanon High School building was torn down. The intersection of Main, Bridge, and Dana streets is located near the bottom of photo and the garage and former hotel are at the lower right.

the post office, has long been the place to meet your neighbors and catch up on the village scuttlebutt. In his book *Goodbye Highland Yankee*, author Scott E. Hastings recalled the drugstore with its soda fountain as the usual evening gathering place for an assortment of railroad men and young boys.

Mr. Hastings also observed that "except for a gasoline station and a garage, Main Street probably hadn't changed much in fifty years. Sargent's Hotel, a square, green, mansard-roofed building, marked one end, and Edson's Bakery Shop the other. In between a variety of businesses mixed with dwellings lined both sides of the road."

Edson's bakery was last located in a building that still stands on the corner of Main and South streets (Cameo Creations, 1994, but perhaps better known as Jette's Quick Stop). When George Edson started the business in 1890, however, it was on the corner of Main and Tracy streets (Mascoma Savings Bank, 1994) in a tenement building that also later housed the First National grocery store.

Mr. Edson's business was turned over to his son and daughter-in-law, Henry and Delia Edson, after George Edson died in the 1920s, and it moved to the corner of Main and South Main streets in 1925. Their son, George, operated it until his death in 1968,

The three gables of the Red Cross Pharmacy building mark the east side of West Lebanon's Main Street about 1910.

and in more recent times the building contained a store operated by the family of Robert and Betty Jette.

Just up the street from Edson's Corner Food shop was a fruit store run into the 1940s by John Panagopolous, located between what is now Jerry Hemond's Sunoco station and Cameo Creations.

North of the fruit store sat another building that was something of a village landmark—Kibling's Daylight Store (DeFelice Family Furniture, 1994). That building was constructed in 1900 by George Kibling, one of the village's best-known merchants of the early twentieth century. Mr. Kibling started his trade in 1892, and in 1900 moved into a building that became popularly known as "The Daylight Store" because of the five large windows near the ceiling that let in so much light that Mr. Kibling was obliged to cover them with shades. He sold his business in 1948 to Carroll P. Dutton, who sold dry goods, work clothes, and footwear. The building was occupied in the 1960s and 1970s by J. W. Barber, Jr.'s Discount Store, an emporium started by auctioneer Joseph Barber.

Just north of Kibling's was a large wooden tenement known as the Johnson Block, which sat at the corner of Main and Depot streets about where the post office is now located. The building housed several businesses over the years, including Thomas Heavey's restaurant, Charles Matson's barber shop (later taken over by Aime Lessard), and the Army-Navy store. In the cellar was Well's pool hall, and the rear of the structure was where illicit poker games were regularly held, according to Jim Kilton.

Pool and poker, however, were not the only diversions in the village. Just south of

Looking north on Main Street about 1910, West Lebanon's fire station, library and the twin towers of the West Lebanon High School and the Holy Redeemer Church line the west side of the street.

the big hotel on the corner of Main and Bridge streets was a large building that Mr. Kilton recalls contained a bowling alley and movie theatre operated by Henry Edson.

The west side of Main Street also contained the library over which Florence Watson presided for decades, the fire station that also housed a police precinct in its basement for several years into the 1960s, and the grammar school that was torn down to make way for the National Bank of Lebanon's first branch office in 1964. Next to the bank stood the Holy Redeemer Catholic Church.

One of the fixtures on the east side of Main Street was a hardware store started in 1890 by Elmore Plummer and Edwin Southworth, which was still going more than sixty years later just north of the Red Cross Pharmacy. Mr. Plummer bought out Mr. Southworth in 1900, the same year that Elmore's 14-year-old son, Hugh, began to work in the store. The son took over the business when his father died in 1934, and in 1947 Hugh Plummer passed it on to his son, Gordon, who ran it until 1960. Jim Hoskins' grocery store was upstairs over the hardware store for several years before moving across the street. Clement Terino also operated a grocery store from this location in the 1940s, as did Bob Gunn in the 1950s and 1960s.

Paul McNamara's enterprises were another Main Street mainstay and Mr. McNamara was a leading citizen of the village. He started in the thirties, hedging his bets by running both an insurance agency and a funeral home, and in the forties he added an automobile dealership to the mix that was sold to Philip Mans in 1982.

Bridge Street also was commercially important during that era. A 1929 directory lists the Romano Coal Company, Roy Hathorn's Garage (Foodstop, 1994), Cone Bushway auto dealers, and Williams Steam Laundry as doing business on the road between West Lebanon and White River Junction; a 1968 directory listed only the laundry as still in business.

Tilden Female Seminary

Not long after the railroad arrived in West Lebanon the village welcomed another landmark, one that visitors to the Seminary Hill School can still see subtle signs of if they look carefully. The school that stands there now is mostly made of brick, but a discerning observer notices the stone foundation, and in the rafters of the elementary school's gymnasium hangs a large gray sign with black letters spelling out the history of the building: TILDEN FEMALE SEMINARY.

Private schools were not new to Lebanon when Tilden opened in 1855. The town had supported the Lebanon Academy and its successor, the Lebanon Liberal Institute, on School Street in the 1830s and 1840s, and it was not uncommon for private classes teaching writing, music, and other skills to be held in individual homes.

There existed at the time very few schools where women could pursue serious courses of study at the secondary school level, and the fact that educating women was openly scoffed at in many circles made what happened next all the more novel, if not downright revolutionary.

On June 27, 1853, a charter granted by the state gave authority to a group of mostly West Lebanon men to "establish and maintain in the village of West Lebanon a literary and scientific institution for the instruction and education of females."

The men named in the charter were mostly the leading citizens of West Lebanon: Joseph Wood, Jr. a farmer, tavern operator, and land speculator who about 1809 purchased Joshua Markham's saw and gristmills in Butmanville, where the Powerhouse shopping center now stands; Richard Kimball, a stockholder in the Bank of Lebanon and investor in several turnpikes who also worked as a consultant in building several canals; Rufus Case, who was the first pastor of the West Lebanon Congregational Church; Daniel Richardson, a farmer, teacher, selectman, and state representative, who was one of the founders of the West Lebanon Congregational Church, as was inventor Charles H. Dana, who patented and made ear tags to help farmers keep track of their stock; mill owner and farmer Roswell Sartwell, who had once owned the Dana House tavern at the corner of Main and Bridge streets; Gideon Dickenson, who made a fortune after the railroad came to town by selling land along what is now Main Street; Nathan B. Stearns, who was a leading farmer; Oren Hubbard and William Osgood, who were both mill operators; and George Lyman, who was a merchant from White River Junction.

When the group assembled in August 1853 at Union Hall in the upstairs floor of the village school to choose a board of trustees, they were joined by a wealthy varnish manufacturer, William Tilden of New York City, who had been convinced to underwrite the effort.

Mr. Tilden was born in West Lebanon in 1796, but his family moved from town when he was only two years old. When he visited the village in 1852, he was apparently looking to memorialize himself in the town of his birth—or at least was not averse to the idea, since he became the chief benefactor of the West Lebanon school, contributing ten thousand of the fifteen-thousand dollars needed to construct a school building. The rest of the money came from local contributions, and the school was dedicated and opened in September of 1855 as the Tilden Female Seminary.

A four-story brick building was erected on Hubbard Hill, which then became known as Seminary Hill. According to the school's first prospectus: "The building has accommodations for the family of the Principal, the Assistant Teachers and some fifty boarders. It contains a bathing room, accessible to all the boarders, conveniently fitted up for cold, warm and shower baths; boarders rooms, large and well ventilated, and a school room furnished with chairs and desks from the well known establishment of S. Wales of Boston."

The school opened in 1855 with 109 girls, including 40 boarders. Twenty-nine students were from Lebanon or West Lebanon; sixteen hailed from other New Hampshire communities; twenty-four from the town of Hartford; and seventeen from other Vermont towns. There were also students from Georgia, Kentucky, Illinois, Maryland, Ohio, and three from New York City. Later classes included students from every New England state, as well as New Jersey, California, Iowa, Missouri, Minnesota, Quebec, and the District of Columbia.

Poor enrollment forced the school to close in 1864, but it was reopened the next year under Hiram Orcutt, who convinced Mr. Tilden in 1868 to contribute twenty-thousand dollars for two wings that doubled the capacity.

Mr. Orcutt turned Tilden into one of New England's finest preparatory schools for girls, and a Tilden catalog from 1882-83 stated that "The Graduates of the 'College Preparatory Course' have permission to enter Smith or Wellesley Colleges without examination, provided work is satisfactorily done here."

Portion of stereograph of Laura Dana (Hinckley) playing the guitar in her room at Tilden Female Seminary in 1870

The studies included English, composition, logic, rhetoric, and political economy as well as Latin and Greek. In the French and German courses a school catalog promised that "no English is spoken in the classroom—by the teachers or pupils . . . We guarantee pupils shall read, write, and speak fluently." Math classes covered algebra, geometry, and trigonometry, while the science curriculum covered botany, geology, chemistry, physics, and electricity. There was also a "gymnastics" class in which students were put through a series of drills not unlike modern-day aerobic exercise classes.

In addition to the liberal-arts courses the school also offered (for an additional cost) study in the traditional "ornamentals" such as music, drawing, and painting. There was also a "practical cookery" class in which a young lady would learn how to run a household and manage servants.

One Tilden brochure warned parents that "your daughters will come to you with their complaints. Lessons will appear too long and difficult, discipline too severe, teachers partial, and a thousand little difficulties arise which will find their way into letters home."

Most students belonged to upper- or upper-middle class families, the daughters of well-to-do farmers, ministers (clergymen received a 20 percent tuition discount), and successful businessmen. An 1873 issue of the school newspaper, the *Tilden Enterprise*, placed the average age of the student population at sixteen-and-a-third years, and the average expense for attending the school at somewhere between $225 and $300, depending on which electives were chosen. The boarding costs included food and laundry, but not napkins and napkin rings, which students were expected to bring with them.

"The eating is first rate, coffee excepted," twenty-year-old student Mary Parker wrote to her family in Gorham, Maine, in September of 1869. She later wrote of eating mutton and "one of the best items of news is that we once more possess a cow and hens so that we may have plenty of milk & eggs."

She described a regimented school day that started with a call for breakfast at 7:30 A.M., followed by a roll call and morning walk. The bell at eight o'clock called the girls to study until 8:45 A.M., when the hour-long prayer session began. Classes started at 9:45 A.M., broke for lunch at one, and resumed at two. Another prayer period began at four, supper was served at five-fifteen, and gymnastics were held at six. A study period started at seven-thirty, and between nine and ten the girls prepared for bed and were allowed to visit the kitchen for water.

The girls' social tether was short. They could only receive letters from parties approved by their parents or guardians, visitors had to be received in public parlors, and they could not be invited to a girl's room without permission from a school official. Outside "intimate acquaintances" could be received only with permission from a girl's parents, although that did not stop Dartmouth students from paying clandestine nocturnal visits to the school.

Although life at Tilden was not entirely a nose-to-the-grindstone affair, school officials might have wished otherwise after four girls and four young men who attended a party in 1869 took part in mock marriage ceremonies, only to learn that the man who had performed the services was a genuine justice of the peace. "Wedded in Fun, But Married in Earnest" read the headline in the *Montpelier [Vermont] Journal*. "They have searched all the law books and consulted authorities far and near, and everything only proves that the knot is still tighter," according to the paper. The *Free Press* reported that the couples wiggled out of the predicament when it was discovered that the justice of the peace was outside his jurisdiction.

Hiram Orcutt also opened a high school for boys, although little is known about it. The *Free Press* in 1876 reported that the school would open for thirteen weeks in Union Hall and be taught by Miss M. P. Brooks of Montpelier, Vermont, a Tilden graduate. A month later the paper reported that the school had opened to greater-than-expected attendance, and it appeared that it would be a profitable venture. Whether it was, and how long the school lasted, is unclear.

Hiram Orcutt, the backbone of Tilden, stayed at the girls' school until 1880, when he moved to Boston to become a partner in a publishing company. He died in 1899, and in 1920 his former students erected a tablet in his memory on the school grounds, and a stained-glass window memorializing Mr. Orcutt was installed in the West Lebanon public library.

He was succeeded by E. Hubbard Barlow, a member of the school's teaching staff who ran it until declining enrollment forced it to close in 1890.

Rockland Military Academy

They came from wealthy families in places like Mexico, Cuba, New York City, and Texas, and gave each other nicknames like Carrots, Spearhead, Waffles, and Pipeknocker. They were the students of the Rockland Military Academy, which occupied the Tilden Seminary building in West Lebanon between 1903 and 1914.

The first all-male military academy at the school was initially known as "Tilden Hall." Run by Belden Hyatt, the school offered college-prep and business classes and was soon renamed the New Hampshire Military Academy. Poor health, however, forced Mr. Hyatt to give up his school. In 1903 the trustees of the Tilden Foundation (which owned the school building) convinced Elmer and Blanche French to move their school, the Rockland Military Academy, to West Lebanon from Nyack, New York, and merge it with the New Hampshire Military Academy. As an incentive for the Frenches to make the move, foundation trustees offered Rockland a ten-year, rent-free lease.

The students of the New Hampshire Military Academy continued to go to school under the aegis of that institution, but the name was phased out after the last class graduated shortly after the merger. The roster of cadets from 1903 indicates that fifty-eight students were enrolled in Rockland, forty-eight were students of the New Hampshire Military Academy, and another thirty were enrolled in Camp Whittier, the Rockland summer camp on Mascoma Lake in Enfield.

The Rockland cadets wore military uniforms styled after those at West Point, and they led a strictly regimented life that included military drills. The school furnished the rifles, but a student had to buy his own side arm at a cost of $2.75.

Students were not, however, being groomed for the armed forces, although some graduates chose that path. Rather, the Rockland life aimed to instill in students the self-discipline required of life in the military, according to a school brochure.

Each day started with reveille at 6:25 A.M., when the boys were required to assemble within five minutes for drills, either outside or in the gymnasium. As Elmer French put it during a speech to Lebanon's Vega Club on June 10, 1904: "There are no repeated calls for Johnnie, Jimmie, or Charlie to get up. No promises of an alluring menu, if he will please come down stairs to breakfast. The shrill notes of the bugle ring out promptly through the halls, and no one but a 'beat' or 'fake' thinks of disobeying that call."

Breakfast started at seven o'clock, and the students sat down as one, ate together for precisely thirty minutes, and arose in unison. They were then given a half-hour to clean their rooms.

Eight o'clock brought a study period, and a twenty-minute chapel service that started at eight-thirty was followed by classes. Military drills ran from eleven-thirty to just after noon, and then lunch, followed by two more hours of classes.

The rules included prohibitions on leaving school grounds or dressing in civilian clothing without permission, and students were also forbidden from having "intoxicants" or visiting any place where they might be purchased. Also taboo were tobacco, swearing, gambling, card-playing, and hazing (including "teasing or nagging a cadet"). The rules also included a ban on "reading of improper literature," and "conduct unbecoming to a gentleman worthy of a place in a literary institution."

Classes were demanding. English, geography and history, algebra, geometry, and trigonometry, physics and chemistry, and several languages were required of students in the college-prep studies. The school offered one curriculum geared toward enrollment at the service academies at West Point and Annapolis, and another toward entering the business world. Students could also elect to take music lessons that were taught, for a fee, by local teachers. Maud Burton, daughter of West Lebanon storekeeper and Rockland trustee William P. Burton, taught piano. Kate Post of East Lebanon, who was renowned in the area for her abilities as a music teacher, instructed students in the violin.

To reinforce the notion of scholarship above all other pursuits, ten boys who had done exceptionally well were named at the end of the year to the "scholarship team," and their picture was published in the school's quarterly magazine, the *Rockland Review*.

The boy who had done his work and behaved himself could look forward to the end of classes at three-thirty, when a wide range of activities were available to him. In addition to sporting two football, basketball, and baseball teams that competed with other schools and local athletic clubs, Rockland was the only school in the area to field a hockey team. Other activities included drama, tennis, photography, dancing, snowshoeing, fishing, boating, and hunting. An item about the latter that appeared in a December 1911 issue of the *Rockland Review* said, "Paul W. French is to be congratulated in bringing down two buck deer and the cadets have had all the venison they could ask for."

When the activity period ended the students had supper, followed by a half-hour of free time, and then a group study hall from seven to nine. Taps was played at nine-thirty, and then the lights were turned off.

Enrollment was apparently brisk for a while as students came to Rockland from throughout the northeast, the midwest, and distant places like Mexico, Puerto Rico, Texas, and Kentucky. The school roster for 1904-05 also shows eight students who hailed from West Lebanon, and one from Lebanon.

In January 1905 a fire that destroyed the south wing of the building so heavily damaged the rest of the school that it had to be temporarily abandoned. The south wing was never rebuilt, but a White River Junction hotel served as interim headquarters for the school, which retained its students in spite of the fire.

Ironically, it was the approach of World War I that dampened public enthusiasm for military schools and brought about Rockland's demise. As Elmer French's daughter, Marion Emerson, recalled in a 1960 speech to the Lebanon Historical Society, "Parents wanted less and less to send their boys to that kind of a school which might hasten their going to war." Thus, Rockland Military Academy shut down in 1914 for lack of enrollment.

West Lebanon Institutions

West Lebanon's growth as a commercial and residential district in the latter half of the 1800s also begat other institutional changes.

On December 31, 1869, an organizational meeting held at the Main Street home of James and Sarah Hubbard marked the start of the village library. After drafting a constitution, Mrs. Hubbard was chosen the organization's first president, and the wives of some of the village's leading businessmen filled other positions. Laura Dana was vice president, Emily Burton was chosen secretary and treasurer, and the first librarian was Mrs. Charles Craft.

Money for books came from a one-dollar annual fee and fundraising events that included festivals, fairs, bake sales, and oyster suppers. The library abolished the fee about 1897, by which time the institution had led something of an itinerant existence. Union Hall, on the second floor of the old schoolhouse, was the library's first host. In later years a resident who wanted to borrow books might have to go to William Burton's home, Dr. Woodman's drugstore, or the school building on Main Street that was constructed in 1892.

A building fund was started in 1892, but it took time for the money to accumulate. By 1908 the account had reached $1,500, and a committee was established to solicit money from the businesses of the village. Ground was broken and the building was dedicated in January 1909.

Somewhere in the village there was a common, according to an 1880 article of the *Free Press* that tells of residents fencing it in and planting trees. The article does not, however, give the common's location.

The first civic organization in the village, the West Lebanon Rural Improvement Society, was formed in May 1884 out of concern that there were no sidewalks along muddy Main Street. By September, concrete walks were installed on the east side of the road from the bottom of Seminary Hill to Tracy Street.

The first firehouse was constructed in 1889, and the first waterworks were installed two years later by the Hartford Water Company from a source on the Vermont side of the river that serviced both villages. West Lebanon residents and those in White River began receiving water from West Lebanon in 1917, when the Hartford Water Company tapped into the thirty-six-acre Boston Lot reservoir on the hill east of Wilder Dam. This source was discontinued in the early 1960s. Before the waterworks were installed the village relied on underground cisterns, one of which still exists near the West Lebanon fire station, according to Harrison Clapper, the village fire chief for several years.

The earliest known photograph of West Lebanon, with White River Junction in the foreground, taken about 1866. Note the nearly bare hillside, cleared to graze sheep.

While West Lebanon's first waterworks came from the west side of the Connecticut River, the electrical feed went the other way. West Lebanon, White River Junction, and a number of other villages were powered by electricity from the dam at Olcott Falls that began generating electricity in the 1880s.

Railroad Ties

Residents of West Lebanon have long enjoyed a neighborly relationship with the people of White River Junction, and it is a tradition that goes back more than one-hundred years. Part of the reason for the alliance can be attributed to the interest the two villages shared in the railroads, which were both villages' economic mainstay for more than a century. It was not uncommon for railroad employees to live in West Lebanon and work in White River Junction, nor was it unusual for businessmen in one village to take their trade across the river. Clarence Bogle moved his wholesale jewelry business from West Lebanon to White River Junction in the early 1880s; West Lebanon carpenter Charles Bacon furnished the windows and casings for the Hartford Woolen Mill in 1886. George Edson opened a grocery store in White River Junction in 1885, and the following year opened a branch in West Lebanon at the corner of Main and South Main streets, and went on to serve as president of the Retail Grocers Association of Hartford and West Lebanon; Frank Collins moved to West Lebanon in 1893 as the general manager of the Mascoma Electric Light and Gas Company, and of the Hartford Water Company. Both companies were located in White River Junction.

There also were social ties binding West Lebanon and White River Junction, and the practice (which continues to some degree at the present time) of West Lebanon residents belonging to churches or social clubs in White River has its roots in the nineteenth century. West Lebanon was once a mission at St. Anthony's Catholic Church in White River; West Lebanon resident Charles B. Haddock was a minister at the Quechee Congregational Church; Dr. Charles Drake of West Lebanon was a charter member of the White River Methodist Church, and he also belonged to that village's Masonic and Odd Fellows lodges. When the First Universalist Society of White River Junction was established in 1878, one of the members of the executive board was Mrs. Lucy Pingree of West Lebanon.

Not only did West Lebanon residents become more closely allied with their neighbors across the river, but they also grew increasingly apart from their eastern townsmen. Furthermore, although the village always had at least one representative on the board of selectmen (as if by virtue of an unwritten agreement that reserved one of the seats for a West Lebanon person) those on the west side of town have long felt that they have been overlooked—even shortchanged—when the time came to divide town money and allocate services. In time, they would act on their resentment.

10

A Most Uncivil War

LEBANON NUMBERED only 2,300 people when the Civil War started in April 1861. Over the next four years the town contributed 281 men to the Union Army, a number equal to more than 12 percent of its population. The average age of the Lebanon soldier was 24, which included three 44-year-olds and twenty-eight who were listed as being 18. They fought in such well-known places as Bull Run, Fredericksburg, Antietam, Gettysburg, and Cold Harbor, and also engaged in many less-well-remembered conflicts.

The town's role in the war began shortly after President Lincoln ordered the War Department to prepare a list of 75,000 troops who could be called upon to respond to the Confederate attack. New Hampshire's quota was a regiment of 780 men, and recruiting stations were opened throughout the state, including one at Ferris Commings' grocery store on Main Street in West Lebanon.

Infused with the spirit of patriotism, more than two-thousand New Hampshire men volunteered for a three-month hitch with the First New Hampshire Regiment, and the state offered to form a pair of such units. The War Department declined the offer of a second three-month regiment, and soon changed its policy in favor of longer terms.

Ten Lebanon men journeyed to Concord on May 6, 1861, for the gathering of the First New Hampshire Regiment at Camp Union. After drilling for a few weeks they entrained for Washington, DC, making stops in Massachusetts and New York to let the men parade before admiring crowds.

The men of the First New Hampshire spent most of their time guarding a crossing on the banks of the Potomac River and took part in no fighting. More than half, however, re-enlisted for three-year terms when their three months were up and subsequently did see combat.

A second New Hampshire regiment was soon formed that included among its soldiers one Jesse Dewey, a Lebanon native who was working in Manchester when the war started and who took part in nineteen major battles over the next four years, winning a promotion to sergeant in December 1862 for gallantry at the Battle of Fredericksburg, Virginia.

Mr. Dewey and the Second New Hampshire pulled into Washington in June and on July sixteenth began a march through the Virginia countryside that culminated in the defeat at the first Battle of Bull Run.

Lebanon soon crawled with recruiters in response to President Lincoln's call for 300,000 more troops. Not only was Ferris Commings the town's most prolific recruiter, signing men up at his West Lebanon store, but Nathan Randlett was doing likewise from the town hall (using its grounds for drills); James Hildreth's store was the local recruiting headquarters for the U.S. Sharpshooters; and Captain S. H. Lathrop worked out of the office of attorney Aaron Cragin to find men for the Seventeenth United States Army. Other recruiters for the Fourth and Sixth New Hampshire regiments were located in the Lafayette Hotel off Colburn Park. All told, some nine regiments, the U.S. Sharpshooters and the cavalry had recruiters in town.

Throughout the course of the war recruiters from Lebanon scoured the countryside at town expense to bring in men from places like New York City, Albany, Springfield, Massachusetts, Montreal, and Toronto. Town records show that Ebenezer Cole, for instance, was paid $7.50 per day when he went on a recruiting trip to Virginia in 1864, enlisting thirteen black men who were mustered into a colored regiment on Lebanon's behalf. A few of the soldiers credited to Lebanon even came from Denmark, England, and Germany.

New Hampshire's quota of that first 300,000 troops in the summer of 1861 was set at 9,234, and the state offered a bounty of ten dollars as an incentive for men to enlist. Lebanon men who signed up received not only the state money, but also a ten-dollar reward that the town had provided at the start of the war. Voters also passed a resolution at the town meeting of May 18, 1861, instructing selectmen to "faithfully provide for and support such of the families of said volunteers as may require or need assistance." That responsibiity was later assumed by the state.

President Lincoln requested another 300,000 troops in the summer of 1862, but by then the bloom of patriotism was fading and money played a larger role in attracting soldiers to the war. Lebanon had increased its enlistment incentive from ten to fifty dollars, and the combined local, state, and federal bounties a soldier could receive for enlisting totaled about two-hundred dollars. Following the defeat at the second Battle of Bull Run on August 30, 1862, the town, in an effort to fill thirty-three slots, increased its bounty to two-hundred dollars and the quota was reached within a week. That figure was increased to three-hundred dollars just prior to the first Union draft of 1863, and the town again fulfilled its quota without having to rely on the draft. By the conscription of July 1864, the town's bounty stood at six-hundred dollars for one year's service; eight-hundred dollars for two years; and three-year soldiers received one-thousand dollars.

The bounties allowed the town to keep pace with its quotas, but at a staggering cost. The town racked up $73,842 in Civil War debt from 1861 through 1866, while the state paid more than $8,000 to support the dependents of Lebanon soldiers. The town was still paying off its debt in 1871, when it floated $40,000 worth of bonds to pay off the costs of the rebellion.

To prepare for the first draft, an office of the Provost Marshall was set up in West Lebanon in 1863, and all men between the ages of twenty and forty-five were eligible to be called. Proceeding town-by-town for each community in the third congressional district (which included Grafton and Sullivan counties), names of each town's eligible men went into a box and the prescribed number of names was pulled. Of the 229 Lebanon men whose names were said to be in the box on September 2, 1863, sixty-nine were drafted.

A draftee, however, could avoid service by paying three-hundred dollars to a substitute to take his place, and most of those drafted from Lebanon took advantage of that. Consequently, only two of the men drafted in September 1863—Edward A. Cotting and Simon Ward, Jr.—actually served.

As the size of the bounties climbed, so did the frequency with which substitutes took the money and fled. With only a small chance of being caught, some men went town-to-town and state-to-state, repeatedly selling themselves as substitutes to the highest bidder and fleeing before reporting to the regiment. When a substitute procured by Lebanon farmer Wilbur R. Heath could not be credited to Lebanon because he had previously deserted from another regiment, the town sued Mr. Heath, claiming he was responsible for the return of the $600 bounty that had been paid to the stand-in. The town won the suit but it was something of a moot point, since the verdict handed down by the New Hampshire Supreme Judicial Court came after the war.

While substitute desertions were common, the majority of the forty-two credited to Lebanon served out their terms. Three died in combat and five of disease (four while prisoners-of-war). Of the nineteen who eventually deserted, five did so only after being wounded in combat. Although there was a reward offered for deserters, only one of Lebanon's nineteen—James Cornell of the Fourth New Hampshire—was ever captured and brought to trial for desertion. He was found guilty and released at the end of the war with a dishonorable discharge.

"Less to Wake This Morning Than There Were Yesterday"

Although casualties in the war are often discussed in terms of battlefield wounds and deaths, the major killer of both armies was disease, which claimed more lives than all of the battles combined. Only three New Hampshire regiments—the Third, Fifth and Twelfth—had more deaths due to battle than disease, and the Sixteenth had the highest sickness-related death rate of any state regiment, losing more than 24 percent of its troops to illness.

Some of these deaths might have been prevented had the men not ignored written regulations that required individual companies within a regiment to dig "proper latrines" a certain distance from camp. Most companies either failed to dig the latrines or, if they did dig them, stopped using them after they became fouled. Left unburied or in poorly filled trenches, the waste attracted thousands of flies that spread diseases and contaminated rations.

A chronic lack of fresh meat, vegetables, and fruit aggravated the situation. Hardtack bread and coffee were the staples of a soldier's diet, and troops often suffered from scurvy, dysentery, and other diseases brought on by unsanitary conditions and poor nutrition.

Bad water also was a problem, as Jesse Dewey described in a letter to his mother on July 31, 1861, recounting his regiment's retreat from the first battle at Bull Run at

Lebanon Civil War veterans at a GAR encampment of unknown date. In the front row are Charles B. Cummings, Charles Messenger, Micah Howe, Freeman Gee of Etna _____ Titus, Ira Gates, Joseph DeMosh, and _____ Woodward. Standing are Charles Hunter, George Benjamin, Eben Haskell, and James Lara.

Manassas, Virginia: "All along we were troubled for want of water. The day was so very hot we would drink the water that the hogs just got up from wallowing in, and were glad to get that."

The first Lebanon resident to die of disease was eighteen-year-old John Haseltine of the Third New Hampshire, who died of "congestive fever" at his regimental hospital on December 9, 1861. About a month later, Robert Ash died in Fairfax County, Virginia, after eight weeks of sickness that saw him come down with typhoid, then the measles, mumps, another fever, and finally, dysentery. On May 3, 1862, William Miller died of disease in Alexandria, Virginia, and five days later Willis B. Hough died of disease in Newport News, Virginia. Also in 1862, Edward L. Tasker of the Seventh New Hampshire died from a fever on August ninth, and on August twenty-ninth Lucius Welch died of typhoid while serving in Louisiana.

By the close of the war in April 1865, thirteen Lebanon men (either residents or substitutes credited to Lebanon) were known to have been held in rebel POW camps at one time or another. Five were exchanged and returned alive, while three died at Andersonville, two perished at the camp in Salisbury, North Carolina, and the others died in Richmond, Tallahassee, Florida, and Glendale, Virginia.

Accidents also were a peril of war from which Lebanon men were not immune. Sharpshooter Ruel J. Walker suffered a lasting injury to his left knee after the train he was riding atop in 1862 collided with another train, throwing him to the ground. Another, Frank Flynn of the First New Hampshire Cavalry, was thrown from his horse, while William Hall of the 17th U.S. Army fell off a wagon. Still others hurt themselves moving cannons and one, Charles Balch of the 7th New Hampshire Infantry, drowned while trying to escape the heat in Beaufort, South Carolina.

There were Lebanon soldiers in thirteen of the state's seventeen regiments (along with several federal regiments such as the U.S. Sharpshooters), and they participated in most of the major battles in the war's eastern theatre. The Fifth New Hampshire—which had more battlefield casualties than any of the Union's two-thousand infantry regiments—also had more Lebanon residents in its ranks, thirty-four, than any other regiment. A member of the Fifth was the first of the town's forty-seven men to die in combat. Levi Leighton was killed at Fair Oaks, Virginia on June 1, 1862, in the Peninsular Campaign that sought to take Richmond. That effort also claimed the life of William Henry Hoffman, who was badly wounded and died in a hospital at Philadelphia on June twenty-fifth; and Ethan Dickenson, who died on September fifth of injuries he received that summer at Fair Oaks.

Shortly after the Fair Oaks battle, a clash with Confederate troops in the Seven Days Battle outside Richmond brought the deaths of two more Lebanon men. Edward Howe and George Percival were hometown chums who were wounded by the same cannonball at White Oak Swamp on June 30, 1862. Mr. Howe died that day on the battlefield and was presumably buried by the same Confederate troops who captured Mr. Percival, who died from his wounds the following day.

Lebanon men were also present for the war's single bloodiest day, September 17, 1862, at the Sharpsburg, Maryland battle known as Antietam. Among the wounded was Captain Nathan Randlett of the Fifth New Hampshire who, before shipping out from Lebanon in October 1861, had been ceremoniously presented with a revolver at a meeting of the Methodist Sewing Circle. Also wounded that day was Charles Liscomb, who three months later won a promotion to First Lieutenant for an act of bravery at the Battle of Fredericksburg, Virginia, a fight in which two Lebanon residents, James Perry and George Greeley, were killed.

Nathan Randlett recovered from his wounds at Antietam and lived to fight in the landmark battle of Gettysburg, Pennsylvania, between July 1-3, 1863. Also at Gettysburg was Jesse Dewey of the Second New Hampshire, who wrote a letter home after the second day of brutal fighting:

The night found us all exhausted and hardly able to move; the reaction after such a fight is tremendous, and to be in all day without any thing to eat, after being up at midnight and marching eight or ten miles, will take the life out of any man, and tonight we were tired, worn out and hungry. How good my cup of coffee tasted that night, and 'hard tack' too—it was a luxury. We laid ourselves down to rest and sleep as soon as possible, and we slept long and sound. What a refreshing sleep, but there were less to wake this morning than there were yesterday. How thin our ranks looked; out of 360 we had hardly 100 men left; it was so through the whole corps and today we were in reserve.

At the conclusion of the epic battle more than four-hundred New Hampshire men were dead or wounded, and Lebanon resident Lucian Gillett was among the latter.

Later that month Colonel Robert Gould Shaw led his Fifty-fourth Massachusetts Regiment on an assault against Fort Wagner, South Carolina that became the subject of the 1989 movie "Glory." About half of the men from the Fifty-fourth were killed or wounded in the attack on the Confederate fortress, and two Lebanon men who helped to storm the fort also lost their lives. Following the colored regiment on July 18, 1863 were the men of the Seventh New Hampshire, including Lebanon residents Jerome House, Andrew Lane, and Ferdinand Davis. Captain House was wounded in the hip, and although he made it back to Union lines, surgeons were unable to extract the ball. He returned to Lebanon to recuperate and died from his wound on October 7, 1863.

When Captain House went down in battle, Second Lieutenant Andrew Lane of Lebanon was in charge of the company. Mr. Lane went over the wall of the fort and was never seen alive again. Another member of Lane's company, Private Stephen D. Smith of Hanover, was captured and reported that when he was taken prisoner inside the fort he saw Mr. Lane's body.

While the fighting was horrific, soldiers who were between battles endured grueling marches or the boredom brought on by a patience-trying pattern of hurry-up-and-wait. Jesse Dewey's letters to his mother reflect that frustration. Awakened at 4:00 A.M. on Saturday, April 13, 1863, the regiment marched over a dusty Virginia road until dusk. They camped in Manassas until 8:00 P.M., the following night, when they set out again only to be halted a few minutes later to let other troops pass. Then, about midnight, they were again told to march: "At last after we had got almost ready to go to sleep we had to tramp once more, and all night too. Marching in the night is the hardest marching I ever have had, especially if the night is dark and to-night it was dark and the road uneven, so we would stumble and almost fall, perhaps bringing our gun down onto our next neighbor and causing him to break the stillness of the night with a howl or deep curses, then comes a joke, a hearty laugh from the crowd, and we tramp on again."

The routine of stop and go, wrote Jesse Dewey, ". . . is what takes the spirit and life out of a soldier, unslinging and slinging his knapsack when he is tired makes him feel almost savage, but we had not got through with our labors yet for the day, at 11 o'clock at night we were roused out of a sound sleep to go on picket."

"Appropriate Airs"

While their neighbors fought in places most Lebanonians had never heard of, those who stayed behind did not remain idle. The wheels of industry continued to turn, and as the *Free Press* noted on June 29, 1862, the town's mechanics and laborers were fully employed. "Probably few towns have suffered less than ours in a business point of view from the present unhappy condition of the country," the account said. Since most of the leading businessmen avoided the war by purchasing substitutes, they stayed behind and minded their shops and stores.

In addition to the business of industry and commerce, the men and women of Lebanon also invested large amounts of time, energy, and money for the support of the men in the field. It started in April 1861, when fifteen men donated one-hundred dollars each to start a soldiers' aid fund. In June the women of the town formed a local chapter of the New Hampshire Soldiers' Aid Society, which sent soldiers food and clothing, and in November the youth of the town formed the Young Peoples' Aid Society.

All of these groups raised money through fairs and social events such as the May 7, 1861, concert by the Lebanon Coronet Band. The money bought sheets, blankets, pillows, shirts, suspenders, socks, underwear, towels, slippers, mittens, apples, wine, jelly, soap, and various kinds of medicine. Soldiers also received supplies from their families. Albert Stearns, for one, wrote home to tell his parents that he had enjoyed the maple sugar they had tucked into his package.

Homecoming was a predictably emotional experience, as the furloughed Lebanon soldiers of the Sixteenth New Hampshire discovered when they stepped off the midnight train in August 1863: "At that late hour, the depot was crowded with the friends and neighbors of the returning soldiers," the *Free Press* reported. "The Band was present and played some appropriate airs, and for about half an hour mutual greetings and congratulations were exchanged, and the busy hum of voices was kept up. In the midst of the general joy there were a few sad hearts, friends weeping at the thought of sick ones left behind."

The farmhands were gathering sap and hauling manure when the sound of cannon fire and ringing bells wafted up to the hilltop farm of Abel Storrs on April 3, 1865. "War news probably," Mr. Storrs correctly surmised in his diary. Among the following day's entries was an account of hauling seven more loads of manure, taking in the sap-holders, and spending half the day harrowing the wheat fields. It also noted: "News that Richmond was taken."

That event sparked a spontaneous celebration in the villages of Lebanon and West Lebanon, and the festivities were duplicated on April tenth when the town received word of the previous day's surrender of Confederate General Robert E. Lee at Appomattox Courthouse in Virginia.

The war (if not the hostilities) between the northern and southern states was finally over, but the epic was not completely played out. Mr. Storrs' diary recorded that it was a bitter wind that blew across the hilltop on April 19, when his final journey entry for the day read simply: "Funeral Pres. Lincoln." Lebanon residents mourned their dead president with a memorial parade through the streets, past buildings draped in black.

Some men returned from the war to live long, productive lives in Lebanon. Jesse Dewey, for example, founded the Dewey, Peck & Co., insurance agency with Solon Peck, and it still exists today, under the banner of Degnan, Hough & Co.

Others, however, continued to suffer from their combat experiences. Many returned with diseases that hastened their death, missing limbs, and injuries to the head, abdomen, or extremities that bled openly. One man who felt the effects of the war long after it ended was Harvey Bean, who had served with the Fifth New Hampshire and was wounded at both Fredericksburg and Cold Harbor. The latter was a head wound for which he was treated at several different hospitals before being mustered out of the service when his term expired in 1864. Returning to Lebanon, Harvey Bean (according to pension papers filed by himself and his wife) suffered daily from sickness and exposure and was continually nursing his wound around the ear. On June 3, 1876, the day before the eleventh anniversary of his wounding at Cold Harbor, Mr. Bean died in Lebanon. In applying for a widow's pension in 1876, his wife, Lucinda, wrote that, "Twice during the time of our marriage I picked out pieces of bone behind his ear and know of his doing it himself different times."

Soldiers' Memorial Building

In 1881 eight influential citizens led by Frank Churchill each contributed twenty-dollars to a fund to pay for construction of a building to serve as a memorial to the town's Civil War soldiers. A campaign to raise money started and voters anteed up $3,000 at the 1882 town meeting. Civil War veteran Ferdinand Davis was the architect, and the Soldiers' Memorial Building was constructed using mostly local materials and labor. The cornerstone was laid on May 30, 1886, although when the subscription effort was still short of its $9,000 goal in 1889, the town donated another $580 to complete the structure, which was dedicated on July 4, 1890.

The first floor housed the town's first free public library, which opened on April 22, 1889. After it was moved in 1909, the walls of that floor in the Memorial building were lined with cases displaying relics from the Civil War (memorabilia from other wars were added later). The second floor served as the meetinghouse for the Grand Army of the Republic, and the funerals of Civil War veterans were often conducted there. With its stained glass windows donated by friends of soldiers and various local organizations, the building has become a shrine to soldiers of all wars.

Perhaps it was Henry Ellis of the 33rd Massachusetts Regiment who best summarized the Civil War in a letter he wrote to his family in Lebanon while stationed in the field in 1863:

I am getting tired of war. I want to have it fought out, and the clash of arms cease on all sides. But I ask not for this till right and justice prevails, and the cry of peace is sounded from the Gulf to the capital. Father and mother, you think that you know something about this war, and what the soldiers have to endure, but I can tell you that you have not seen anything about what a soldier has to endure, and still there is no complaining and no hanging back, for everyone knew and expected to see hard times before he ever made up his mind to come out here . . . Perhaps you may say when you read this that I am discouraged, but I say no, not a bit of it. I fully considered all things before I left Lowell, and my mind is just the same now as it was then . . . I came out for my countrys good and I hope that when I do return, that I may have the assurance in my own brest that I have done my duty.

Corporal Ellis was wounded in Bentonville, North Carolina, on March 21, 1865, and died of his wounds on April 13, five days after the surrender of General Lee.

II

Boomtown

The former Frank Churchill home on Campbell Street, a monument to late nineteenth-century architecture in Lebanon.

11

Before the First Great Fire

Industrial Revolution

THE BURNING of East Lebanon in 1840, combined with the arrival of the railroad seven years later, saw the town's economic torch passed to the center village. After losing five percent of its population to westward migration between 1830 and 1840, Lebanon broke the two-thousand barrier with a 14 percent increase between 1840 and 1850. The big boom, however, came between 1860 and 1870, when the population increased 26 percent.

The town's inventory—all taxable property, including farm stock, mills, and factories—climbed 47 percent between 1863-1872, while the value of real estate went up 67 percent, from $672,755 to $1.12 million. Census records show that industrial output, less than $100,000 in 1860, rocketed to more than $716,000 ten years later; and industrial employment during that same period climbed from 143 to 436, and even higher into the mid-seventies.

The bulk of that industrial activity was concentrated along five streets near the river: High and Foundry on the west side, Mill and Water on the east, and Mascoma Street where it crossed the river.

As the Foundry Street name implies, iron was an important component of the town's nineteenth-century economy. One of the earliest of the genre shows up in the town tax records of 1836 as the Iron Foundry Co., with $150 worth of stock-in-trade. Its location and ownership are unknown, but it was gone from the tax rolls by 1838, the same year that machinist Hiram A. Simons and molder Horace Sessions established a foundry on the river at the corner of Foundry and Mascoma streets. The partnership seems to have lasted only a year or two, but Mr. Simons continued in the machinery business with Martin and James Buck in 1848 and was simultaneously involved in a machinery repair business with Oliver Ticknor from about 1846 to 1852, in a building on High Street. That was also about the same time that James Bly began making lead pipe at a foundry on High Street that he later sold to the Buck brothers.

An 1849 directory of business in town also listed the firm of Tenbrook, Booth & Durant as iron founders. Mr. Durant was Edward J. Durant, who arrived in Lebanon about 1844 from Springfield, Vermont. In 1851 he went into the foundry business with Mr. Simons under the name of Simons, Durant & Co., making and selling stoves, agricultural plows, mill castings, iron water wheels, and a variety of other items until about 1858.

Mr. Durant, who served as postmaster from 1861-1866 and was town clerk for almost thirty years, went into the furniture business in 1859 and also sold insurance. He retired in 1875, leaving the furniture business to his son, who ran it into the 1880s in partnership with George Perkins under the name Perkins & Durant.

Another metal worker was Charles Baxter, who made furnaces, bandsaws, jigsaws, and planers on Water Street and later in the Slayton Hill area. He started in business about 1872, and employed twenty to thirty men in what was the forerunner of the Dulac's Building Supply business.

John Purmort also had a foundry, shown on a map of 1860 at the corner of Mill and Mascoma streets. He sold it in 1866 to three men from Lakeport, New Hampshire. Solomon Cole, Orrin Bugbee, and John B. D. Leavitt opened the Cole, Bugbee and Co. foundry on the west side of the Mascoma River in a building between the corner of Foundry Street and the river (part of which still stands, now occupied by Upper Valley Paintball, 1994). Mr. Cole was the financial backer, Mr. Bugbee the salesman, and Mr. Leavitt the superintendent in a shop that employed as many as twenty-five men making water wheels and doing machine work.

The largest and best-known foundry and machine shop in the center of town belonged to Martin and James Buck, who started in one of the buildings between High Street and the west side of the Mascoma River beginning about 1849. They supplied factories with machinery to make doors, sashes, blinds, and other woodworking products, and also manufactured iron tools, saws, portable gristmills, steam engines, mowing machines, nails, and shoe pegs (in the days before shoes had laces). By 1860, in partnership with F. A. Cushman, they had a payroll estimated at $100,000 and employed up to 150 men, some of whom undoubtedly lived in a company boarding house on the west side of High Street.

The Bucks expanded their shops to occupy most of the property between High Street and the river, and shipped machinery throughout the country, and even overseas. An 1855 report to the British House of Commons shows that the Bucks shipped $2,875 worth of woodworking machinery to the British Royal Carriage Department, which manufactured rifles.

The Bucks and Mr. Cushman dissolved their partnership in 1861, and Mr. Cushman took over the machine shop while the brothers continued to make shoe pegs until the shop burned on April 25, 1863. James Buck went into farming, but Martin was back in the metal business by 1869 with a shop on Water Street where he made machinery for blind-slats and other woodworking purposes that were sold throughout the country. Sixty years later, a letter to the Lebanon postmaster from the Osborne & Sexton Machinery Company of Columbus, Ohio, inquired whether Martin Buck's company was still in business: "The machine of their manufacture that we have is an antique, but is nevertheless good and we were wondering if we might be able to secure another one, or such spare parts as may be wanted."

Mr. Buck, who also was a partner in the Kendrick & Davis company that started in 1876, sold his machine shop to them in April of 1883, and died in December of that year. His business was then sold to A. W. Rix, who continued to manufacture woodworking machinery for a few more years.

Woodworking

Woodworking, in fact, was the town's other major industry. Henry Partridge made furniture starting about 1848 along the river near High Street, and the 1850 Census listing under his name included six others—among them two brothers—who gave their occupation as "chairmaker." When Mr. Partridge died in 1850 at the age of twenty-eight, the business was taken over by his brother, Maynard, and continued until 1855. An 1848 directory also listed Joseph Perkins as a furniture maker (later in partnership with George Durant), and he shows up on the tax rolls in 1846, the same year as Alpheus Goodwin, who made doors, sashes, and blinds.

Most significantly, however, was the appearance of Jesse Sturtevant and George Amsden, who as early as 1848 made doors, sashes, and finish work for Victorian homes in a shop near the corner of Water and Mascoma streets. In 1852 Mr. Sturtevant started J.C. Sturtevant and Co., a furniture business that turned out bureaus, desks, tables, stands, sofas, and several kinds of chairs from walnut, mahogany, pine, and other types of wood. It shipped furniture around the world and also sold it locally at a warehouse on Mascoma Street.

Some sources say it was one of the largest furniture manufacturers in the country at the time, but even if it were not, it was an expansive operation sprawled over two sites on both sides of the river. It started on Water Street in what was called the Lower Shop, and by 1865 Mr. Sturtevant was renting the former shoe-peg factory on High Street, where he moved in machinery for making bedsteads. Reflecting the lingering bitterness of the Civil War, the *Free Press* reported on November 11, 1865, that Mr. Sturtevant had contracts to provide furniture in the south, and had sent off an order of sash to Libby Prison in Richmond, "the old ones having been destroyed, probably, in shooting Yankee prisoners."

The papers also reported in 1865 that bloody encounters with the shop's saws, lathes, and other machinery were so frequent that consideration was given to building a special hospital on the Sturtevant premises to attend to the men who were hurt in accidents.

In 1867 orders for Sturtevant products were said to exceed the company's ability to keep pace, and Mr. Sturtevant doubled his capacity by constructing a four-story addition to the Water Street shop, using the upper floor for storage and the lower ones for manufacturing. The company in 1869 built a four-story warehouse and office building on the east side of Water Street and connected it to the main shops via two enclosed bridges that passed over the street at a height of forty-six feet. By 1871 the company had its own spur railroad track which crossed Mascoma Street near the foot of Benton Hill and brought the cars level to the Water Street shop. With approximately six-hundred men on the payroll at wages of about three-dollars per day, the firm was the town's single largest employer.

Lower half of the Sturtevant woodworking shop, looking north up Water Street, currently site of the Whitman Press. The upper half of the operation was located on High Street, where the tannery later stood and the Mascoma Village Apartments are now located.

The business, which soared in the fifties and sixties, soured in the depression of the mid-1870s. The employees, down to about four-hundred, took a 20-percent pay cut in the fall of 1873. By January 1875 creditors who had gathered in the bottom of the town hall to discuss the company's finances granted an extension of credit, but it was not enough to save the heavily-leveraged company. The upper shop was closed that winter, and rumors of mismanagement swirled on the streets when U.S. Marshall J. N. Patterson arrived in February of 1876 with a list of attachments that forced the company into bankruptcy with a reported 639 creditors seeking payment. The *Free Press* reported that "public excitement has been allayed, and the two questions now are what percent will the creditors get, and when will the shops start up, for it does not seem probable that they can remain idle very long."

Why the business failed is unclear. It may have been a combination of the depression, too much expansion, and too high a payroll. Town records indicate that Jesse Sturtevant was heavily mortgaged, and he left town after the failure but returned in March 1879 to a small shop on Mill Street where he carried on a small furniture business for a few years.

His bankrupt shops, meanwhile, were leased in March 1875 to Owen Mead and John Mason, principals in the Mead-Mason, Co. of Medford, Massachusetts. Little is known about Mr. Mead, but Mr. Mason had worked in town as a builder between 1855 and 1862 before moving to Warren, New Hampshire. Since the Mead-Mason Company was

Jesse Sturtevant's largest creditor, the failure brought John Mason back to Lebanon.

Mead-Mason purchased the Sturtevant mills in 1876, and although the reopening put people back to work, they employed fewer men, ran only sporadically, and paid only about a third of the Sturtevant wages.

Employment peaked at about two-hundred in the late 1870s and early 1880s, but the value of wages paid dropped from $80,000 in 1870 to $30,000 in 1880, when it operated full time for only six months. The company had a contract to make three-thousand wooden refrigerators in January 1885, but by April a column in the paper reported that "Business is very dull at Mead, Mason & Co.'s shops, and about 100 men are out of employ . . . A petition has been widely circulated and signed asking the selectmen to give the men and boys out of a job a polite invitation not to spend their spare hours sitting on the steps in front of stores, to the great annoyance of ladies passing in or by. Good idea."

Those who were out of work had three main choices: Look for a job at another establishment in town, leave Lebanon to seek employment elsewhere, or become a pauper. The town's method of providing for poor people changed in 1838 when, after decades of farming out indigent families to the lowest bidder, David Hough, James Willis, and George Lathrop were appointed a committee to purchase a farm for support of the poor. The poor farm was a 180-acre spread on the Meriden Road, just south of Great Brook Road. Residents of Lebanon and some other Grafton County towns worked the farm in exchange for living quarters in the farm's boarding house, and the resulting produce was sold to defray expenses.

The farm's animal inventory in any given year included a pair of oxen, a half-dozen cows, a horse or two, eighty sheep, and a few hogs. It sold hay, oats, corn and other grain; dairy products; beans, peas, carrots, and potatoes; and an assortment of meat and poultry.

The farm was maintained until 1864, when fire destroyed the house and other buildings on the farm, and it was never rebuilt. Instead, the town reverted to the old system of distributing the poor among the town's more prosperous families, and sending some residents to the Grafton County farm after it was erected in 1867.

Organs, Keys, and Sponges

There was, to be sure, more to industrial Lebanon than wood and iron works. Oramel Muchmore was a partner in the Shepard Organ Company, which came to Lebanon from New Hampton, New Hampshire, in 1872, locating its factory on Mill Street and its sales office in the Thompson Block next door to the town hall. President George Shepard employed about twenty men making melodeons and church and parlor organs at the rate of two per day. The company was in receivership by 1874 and was then reorganized as the Lebanon Organ Company, which employed about thirty men making fifty organs per month. A few of those instruments can still be found in town.

Another important industry in Lebanon was the Kendrick & Davis Company, which opened in 1876 in a building on Water Street and became one of the town's best-known and longest-lived businesses. Although he was one of the founders, Dr. William F. Davis was a mostly silent partner who tended to his medical practice and the drugstore

The Sponge Factory building on Foundry Street processed sponge imported from the Bahamas and sold it for various commercial uses. The lower grades and waste trimmings were sold as upholstery filling.

he kept in the Blodgett Block, at the corner of Court and North Park streets. The day-to-day operations at Kendrick & Davis were left to Frank B. Kendrick (Stephen Kendrick's grandson), who had learned the jeweler's trade from the town's first jeweler, Carlos Buswell, and opened a jewelry store in Lebanon in 1866. Ten years later he sold that business and turned to making watch keys that were used to wind watches in the days before stems. One of the shortcomings of the conventional watch key at the time was that it often became clogged with pocket lint which prevented it from fitting over the winding stem inside the watch. Kendrick and Davis, however, patented a "dustproof" watch key by drilling a hole through which the accumulated lint could be pushed or blown out, enabling the device to fit snugly over the winding mechanism. At its peak the company employed over one-hundred men producing three-hundred-thousand keys a year. When watch keys became obsolete, the factory turned to manufacturing electrical motors and by 1900 was selling them throughout the world. The plant supervisor was A. Atwater Kent, who went on to become a famous manufacturer of radios that bore his name. He never forgot his time in Lebanon, however, and whenever he came out with a new model of radio, Mr. Kent sent one to Mr. Kendrick.

The company was inherited in 1909 by Ralph Wood, one of the town's most influential businessmen before his death in 1929 at the age of forty-five. Under his guidance Kendrick & Davis began to make the tools used to construct precision timepieces in places like Switzerland and Germany, and the company also made surgical instruments for the government during World War I.

Ralph Wood's widow, Katherine, ran it after his death and then his son, Roger, took over the business. He reorganized it in 1968 by which time it employed only eighteen people on Water Street. It was reorganized again in 1971, and the name was changed to K&D. It also moved from its original location to the old American Excelsior Mill building on Bank Street Extension.

Perhaps no business, however, reflected the diversity of the downtown area more than the American Patent Sponge Factory, a one-of-a-kind operation that opened in a five-story building on Foundry Street in 1867. Although it lasted only a short time, it remains one of the most unique ever to settle in Lebanon.

Sponge that was imported to Lebanon from the Bahamas was shredded and used to stuff mattresses, pillows, cushions, and other furniture, in what might be considered a forerunner of foam rubber. The sponge was expected to replace hair and feathers as the filler of choice, and an article in an 1867 edition of the *Free Press* that compared those two products to sponge noted that a hair mattress weighed about fifty pounds and cost approximately fifty dollars, while one made of sponge weighed thirty pounds and could be sold for only thirty dollars. The factory employed about sixty men under the direction of F. A. Cushman and was successful for a while—apparently until it was discovered that among its other fine attributes, sponge was very good at retaining water, a quality which made it unsuitable as an upholstery material.

The closing of the sponge factory was yet another reason that Lebanon's industrial production fell sharply between 1870 and 1880. The factory's output in the 1870 Census was listed at about $100,000, but it was closed by 1880.

The Merchant Prince

If you live in or visit Lebanon for any significant length of time you are bound to run into the name "Carter." Although none of the original Lebanon family survives, the name carries on. The Carter Community Building has served as the headquarters for youth recreation in the center of town since 1918; the grown-up kids have played at the Carter Golf Club since it opened in 1924; local clubs meet at the elegant Marion Carter Home, which sits across Bank Street from the library; and on the traffic island in front of the Marion Carter Home is the Carter Fountain, erected by Frederick Carter in memory of his father, Henry W. Carter.

It was Henry Carter, known throughout northern New England as "The Merchant Prince," who was the first to come to town and attach his name to one of the two companies that became famous for apparel manufacturing.

"He was kind of like the P.T. Barnum of industrialists," City Historian Robert Leavitt said of Henry Carter in a 1985 *Valley News* article. His career began on a more modest note, however, when his father let the eight-year-old boy sell candy out of a corner of the family tavern in Bradford, New Hampshire, about 1830. After stints as a Concord-based traveling salesman, Mr. Carter started his own business in Chelsea, Vermont, and moved it to Lebanon in 1859, buying Henry Campbell's house on the corner of what is now Bank and Campbell streets. Although his formal residence was in Lebanon, his obituary noted that "for more than 30 years after moving here he spent but little time in town." As often as not, Henry Carter was on the road, wholesaling the wares he stored behind his house to retailers throughout the northern New England countryside.

The essence of his salesmanship was showmanship, and his wagons were an integral part of his act. In contrast to the common peddler who might have come to town with a weathered cart pulled by one or two equally weathered horses, the sides of the Carter wagons were decorated with colorful varnished oil paintings, the metal on the harnesses and wagons was plated in silver and gold, and the wagons were hauled by matching coal-black horses in teams of four. The traveling works of art were manufactured by the Abbott-Downing company of Concord, which also made the famous Concord Coach. Mr. Carter's arrival was said to have caused such a stir that schoolchildren were let out of class to see the wagons pass.

In the early years of the business Henry Carter set out from Lebanon with a dog and a hired man to look after the horses and the stock of New York- and Boston-bought goods he kept in his wagon compartments and sold to retailers for cash. An undated company catalog listed scores of items for sale, including several varieties of cigars, watches and jewelry, knives, razors, knitting needles, perfumes, leather goods, threads, silks and other types of cloth, shoe laces, stationery, brushes, and buttons. Eventually, the business reached the point where it became impractical for the four Carter wagons to carry the stock themselves, so they adopted the more modern practice of hauling only samples of the goods that storekeepers could order from the Carter warehouse on Bank Street.

What the company ultimately became most famous for, however, was its line of bib overalls, which were widely sold to railroad men, farmers, and factory workers throughout the northeast. Mr. Carter's entry into the overall business began about 1870, when he was approached by Meriden storekeeper Converse Cole about selling the overalls that Mr. Cole was having made in East Plainfield. The salesman agreed to carry a sample, and when the demand for overalls exceeded Mr. Cole's capacity to make them, Mr. Carter bought him out and within a few years moved the overall business to Lebanon, where the cut pieces of cloth were farmed out to women in the community to be sewn into a finished product. Continued demand, however, forced Henry Carter to abandon the so-called domestic system and open a factory next to his house.

Henry Carter retired in 1892 and turned the business over to his sons, Augustus and Frederick. The latter died in 1902, and although "Gus" owned the company, it was his brother-in-law, Harry Jackson, who ran it while Gus Carter was off pursuing his sporting interests. Lebanon benefited from Mr. Carter's passion for golf when he put up the land and part of the money to build a nine-hole golf course in 1923, and the Carter Country Club continues to bear his name.

When Gus Carter died in 1928, ownership of H.W. Carter & Sons fell to Mr. Jackson, who had started in 1887 as a company stockboy at the age of sixteen and became a partner in 1894.

At its peak H.W. Carter & Sons employed about 175 workers, including many who found jobs at the Bank Street factory during the Great Depression. When Harry Jackson retired, he turned the business over to his sons, Stanley and Frank. It stayed in the family until it was sold in 1967 to an out-of-town group headed by Don Penfield, and then in 1969 to the Gladding Corporation, a conglomerate based in New York whose financial problems prompted them to sell to the Maine-based Paris Industries in 1984.

On June 28, 1985, at the factory Henry Carter built next door to his home, a young woman leaned out an upper-story window and dangled a pair of white painter's pants, said to have been the last pair manufactured in Lebanon by H.W. Carter & Sons. The company closed for good that day, and its operations were moved to North Carolina, marking the end of an era that started with The Merchant Prince.

As for the Carter home—the family called the place "Lionhurst," and two lions still flank the walkway on the Campbell Street side—it remains in the same immaculate condition as when the family lived there, thanks to Marion Carter, the daughter of Gus and granddaughter of Henry. When she died in 1961 she left a trust to maintain the home, which is used as a meeting place for clubs and also houses the collection of the Lebanon Historical Society.

Profile

When Henry Carter took to the road between 1865 and 1869 he left his nephew behind to mind the store in Lebanon, and in doing so laid the groundwork for a career that provided him with competition in the overall business. A native of Warner, New Hampshire, William S. Carter left Dartmouth to join the Civil War; when he returned, he worked for his uncle as a storekeeper and traveling salesman before starting his own business in 1869, also selling notions and assorted wares.

A turning point for the business came in 1877, when he teamed up with Vermont native Frank Churchill, who also had worked as one of Henry Carter's traveling salesmen. In 1879 they opened the town's first overall factory in a building near the railroad depot that had been the first home of the Catholic Church (Parkhurst Street, 1994). That apparently did not sit well with H. W. Carter, who put up a "spite sign" on a vacant plot of land he owned not twenty feet from the front door of his rival's store. The sign, on the corner of what is now Parkhurst and Campbell streets, read:

TO MERCHANTS and PEDLARS

Don't Buy a Dollars Worth of Small Wares, Fancy Goods, Cigars, Overalls &c Before Calling and Getting Prices At H.W. Carter's Wholesale Store. Bank Street Opposite National Bank of Lebanon.

The rivalry between Carter's and Carter & Churchill's notwithstanding, the mainstay of the latter was the wholesale clothing business, and by 1882 they employed over one-hundred seamstresses, had several salesmen on the road, and were shipping goods across the country.

In addition to their clothing business, both William Carter and Frank Churchill pursued interests outside the company. Mr. Carter's diversions were community-oriented and mostly philanthropic. He was the first president of the Lebanon Electric Light and Power Company that was created in 1890, and in his lifetime he gave away about $175,000 to various organizations, including about $85,000 to create and fund the Carter Community Building, and $40,000 to Mary Hitchcock Memorial Hospital for the creation of an X-ray wing. Upon his death on July 2, 1931, William Carter left $155,000 in bequests to various organizations, making him Lebanon's greatest philanthropist to that time.

Frank Churchill's interests, meanwhile, ran to the political. He was chairman of the local Republican committee and also of the state committee in 1890-91. He was a member of Governor Natt Head's staff in 1879-80, and served on the governor's council in 1889-90. In 1890 he was elected to the legislature and helped pass bills that chartered the Mascoma Savings Bank and appropriated money for the renovation of the town hall to allow the Grafton County Superior Court to move to Lebanon. Frank Churchill also was the driving force behind construction of the Soldier's Memorial Building, the memorial to Lebanon's war veterans.

He received an appointment from the Secretary of the Interior and moved west in 1899 to take a job as revenue inspector for the Cherokee Nation of Indians in Oklahoma. He later was appointed a special agent for the Interior Department to formulate a system of public schools for half a million white children in Oklahoma, a job he later replicated in Alaska. Mr. Churchill also had an interest in Lebanon history, published several articles in *The Lebanonian* and was the author of a special 1911 supplement in the *Granie State Free Press* that marked the town's 150th anniversary.

In 1910 the business was still called Carter & Churchill, but William Carter had retired and turned the business over to Ernest Leavitt and Frank Bell. Unlike H.W. Carter & Sons, which manufactured overalls up to the time it closed, Carter & Churchill ceased most of its overall manufacturing shortly after World War I, when it still made a few for government navy yards. However, the focus shifted to other lines of apparel for both the war effort and public consumption: flannel and cotton shirts, mackinaw coats, quilted hunting jackets, and pants for men and children.

In 1923 Dean N. Dwinell came from an overall factory in Newport, Vermont, and bought out Ernest Leavitt's share in Carter & Churchill, marking the beginning of his family's forty-four-year association with the business. The company kept up its production of flannel shirts and hunting apparel, but added sportswear for women and girls. It weathered the depression with reduced profits, but lost money only in 1931-32.

Frank Bell retired in 1936, and Dean Dwinell became the company's senior executive, adding his son, Lane, as the junior partner. This was also about the time when the company issued its first complete line of clothing for skiers—parkas, gabardine ski pants, and ski suits made from the same cloth used to cover airplane wings. The company's line of skiwear would become increasingly important over time, but it would have to wait until after World War II.

Dean Dwinell retired in 1941, and Lane Dwinell became Carter & Churchill's chief executive at a time when the company focused on equipping the armed forces with field jackets and mackinaw coats. Whereas skiwear had been a sidelight prior to the war, the company responded to a post-war skiing boom by expanding its line of clothing for skiers; by 1964 the company devoted its resources exclusively to skiing.

Lane Dwinell took on two partners in 1950, Lauris Blake and J. Clayton Ramsdell, and they ran the business while Mr. Dwinell pursued a successful political career that included two terms as governor beginning in 1955. He then gained an appointment from President Eisenhower in 1959 as Assistant Secretary of State for Administration.

Lane Dwinell returned to Carter & Churchill after his political career had run its course, and remained with the business until 1967, when he sold his controlling interest to Frederick Bedford III and Stephen Chrisofulli. Mr. Blake remained with the company until 1972, and Mr. Ramsdell through 1977, times of rapid and dramatic change for the country's second-oldest manufacturer of skiwear.

With Mr. Bedford as chairman of the board and Mr. Chrisofulli as president, Carter & Churchill moved from its Parkhurst Street factory in 1968 to a building on Benning Road in West Lebanon. In 1970 the name of the company was changed to Profile Skiwear, and the Old Man of the Mountain was adopted as the company logo, although both the name and logo had been company trademarks since 1880. Profile became a publicly held corporation traded on the Boston Stock Exchange in 1970, and for a while it dominated the moderately priced segment of the skiwear market, selling $4.2 million worth of merchandise in 1970. The tide turned in the mid- and late-1970s, however, and Profile lost its niche in the market as it struggled to adapt to changing consumer tastes in skiwear.

It went out of business in 1983, selling the famous Profile name and logo to Herman's, a sporting goods chain.

Scytheville

Ask most modern-day residents of Lebanon to meet you in "Scytheville," and they are likely to respond as if you had asked them to rendezvous on the mythical lost continent of Atlantis. Yet, the town used to have a village by that name. Although the term has since dropped from use, Scytheville was important enough in its heyday to warrant its own inset on the town map of 1884.

Almost directly across Mechanic Street from the railroad underpass sits Slayton Hill Road, and it was here that the manufacture of plows, scythes and other agricultural implements during the second half of the nineteenth-century gave rise to the name "Scytheville," a term used to describe the section of town between the foot of Slayton Hill and the bridge over the Mascoma River near the present Carter Golf Club.

It seems to have begun about 1845 when Stephen Slayton moved from Woodstock to Lebanon and opened up a scythe shop at a dam on the Mascoma River, just west of the bridge at the bottom of Slayton Hill Road, which was known at the time as Podgum Lane. It is unclear how long he continued in business—the directory on the town map of 1860 listed him as a manufacturer of scythes and axes—but he eventually turned to farming and sold his business. After several changes of ownership and names (including Albro Emerson's and Messer, Colby and Company), it was purchased in 1869 by Joseph Cummings and Martin Purmort, who employed twenty to thirty men under the name of the Mascoma Edge Tool Company, which lasted into at least the mid-1880s.

The Slayton shop was joined by another scythe factory started by George and Leonard Stearns in 1852, employing twenty to thirty men making twenty-five-thousand scythes and scythe-handles, as well as sleds, shovels, and "hammock chairs." Leonard Stearns ran it by himself for about fifteen years, then in partnership with rake manufacturer Thomas Marston until the early 1880s, when it was sold to George and Milo Stearns. George then left to run a meat market in 1882, and Mr. Marston gave it up in favor of a prosperous cider mill in the center of town, leaving Milo to run the business by himself.

A residential settlement grew up in the 1850s and '60s around the lower part of what is now Mechanic Street, as Solon Peck sold off much of the family real estate for housing lots. The settlement also supported a school in what was known as the Peck District. The first school building was located on the north side of the underpass, the second was on the corner of Mechanic Street and the entrance to the railroad overpass, and the third building, still standing, was on the corner of Mascoma Street Extension and Peabody Street.

When a road from Slayton Hill to the center of town was added in 1865, Mechanic Street became the primary road to West Lebanon. The Baxter Machine Company (Baxter Court) relocated in Scytheville after the 1887 fire, making band saws, planers, and other woodworking machinery as late as 1912. Founder C. M. Baxter also sold wood and coal and operated a foundry and blacksmith shop, before selling to Martin Purmort.

That site along the river also was used to generate electricity for the forerunner of the present-day Granite State Electric Company, the Lebanon Light and Power Co., which was founded in 1890. Even after the last of the manufacturing businesses disappeared from Scytheville, the area continued to support commerce. Edmond Dulac bought the Baxter site in the 1920s and started a woodworking shop between Mechanic Street and the river that was the forerunner of the Dulac Hardware and Building Supply store, a business that later passed to his sons, Leon and Wilfred.

"Mahanville"

To walk down Spencer Street today—it is commonly called Mahan Flat—you would hardly know that it was once a place that churned out huge lots of plows, mowing machines, cultivators, rakes, and other agricultural equipment.

However, down past Eldridge Park, Emerson Gardens, the city highway garage, and Barker Steel—near the east end of the street—once sat Clarence Mahan's Granite Agricultural Works. Begun on High Street about 1866, he moved the business in 1871 onto a lot northeast of the railroad depot and built an expansive factory complex for the manufacture of agricultural equipment. There was a two-story, one-hundred-foot-long machine shop with a twenty-five-by-forty-foot ell and a seventy-foot-long foundry.

From this location Mr. Mahan entered into an ambitious marketing campaign aimed at bypassing storeowners, reducing the number of salesmen on the road, and selling directly to farmers. In an 1869 circular describing his plan he wrote that he could sell goods for less if he could avoid paying commissions to salesmen. Also, he said, "The manufacturer as a rule had much rather sell direct to the farmers for several reasons. 1st, because they are as a rule more prompt in paying for what they buy . . . 2d, because he can make a larger profit, even at twenty per cent discount . . . 3d, he would never be in danger of losing money by the failure of merchants, who often owe him large bills."

Thus was born the Granite Agricultural Implement Association, a quasi-mail-order business with offices in Lebanon and New York City that utilized traveling salesmen going farm-to-farm to drum up business. It is hard to say how well the concept worked, but the Granite Agricultural Works at one point was deemed the most prosperous business in the center of town.

Aerial view of the west end of Mahan Flat. The smokestack at the bottom of the photo marks the site of the Mahan operation, later taken over by the Spencer brothers and Ralph Millen's Hanover Ice Company. Emerson Gardens greenhouses are at the lower right, below the town highway garages and the Nabisco warehouse. The H.W. Carter shop is visible at the top of the picture and, below it on Parkhurst Street, is the rear of the Carter & Churchill factory.

Clarence Mahan also planned to divide up the eleven acres he owned between the factory and railroad depot and build homes for his workers. He hoped to call it "Mahanville," and it might have happened that way, too, except for the fires.

The first at Mr. Mahan's foundry broke out in March 1867, while he was still on High Street. It seems not to have been too serious, for the business was operating again three months later when a shell exploded in the building. In November 1873, after the business had moved to Spencer Street, fire destroyed both the foundry and machine shop.

Mr. Mahan was uninsured but was back in business by February 1874, with an operation even more impressive than the first. The main building was three-stories high, forty-by-seventy feet, with a machine shop on the ground floor powered by a steam engine housed in a separate building with a ninety-foot brick chimney that stood until 1965. About fifty people worked in the machine shop making plows, mowing machines, and other agricultural items. The second floor of the building contained a wood shop, the third floor a paint shop with an adjoining four-story elevator tower, and in the rear of the complex was an eighty-by-ninety-foot foundry and blacksmith shop.

Aerial view of the N.P. Clough lumberyard on Taylor Street, later the site of the Carter-Witherell Annex. Eldridge Park, with a wooden outfield fence and light standards, is visible at the lower left. The field has been lined for football, an indication that the picture was taken in the fall.

The *Free Press* reported in 1874 that "The most flourishing part of our village this season is in the vicinity of the Granite Agricultural Works, north east of the depot. Mr. Mahan is driving business there to the utmost, and making additions to his buildings."

In May 1875 the newspaper reported that a 120-by-40-foot wing was added to the complex, and one-hundred-fifty men worked there. A month later they were all out of work and the place was in ashes after a fire consumed the complex. Mr. Mahan, who was insured for only about $6,600 against losses of about $33,000, resolutely announced he would rebuild, and it appears he followed through on his plan but sold the business in 1877 to D. B. Emerson, who employed only ten men. From then on the complex passed through a variety of partnerships.

The ironically charred remains of an early 1880s circular listing the property as up for sale indicates that it was operated on a part-time basis after the fire. The circular also stressed that the town welcomed manufacturing, and had passed a resolution at the 1881 town meeting authorizing a ten-year tax exemption for any new enterprise investing more than five-thousand dollars in capital in Lebanon.

In 1887 William Cole bought the land and buildings and operated a foundry before selling it to William and Charles Spencer, who ran a woodworking shop that was destroyed by fire on September 2, 1920, and never rebuilt.

Caleb Niles owned the property in the 1920s, when his Lebanon Machine Company manufactured road signs, and Ralph Millen later bought the land and sold ice from a modern plant until after World War II.

Mahan Flat, as the area is now known, also contained a Nabisco warehouse that opened in 1927, and just up the road on Taylor Street stood the coal and lumber yard of C. D. Smith and later N. P. Clough & Co., which continued in existence into the 1960s.

Main Street

Along with Colburn Park, the Congregational Church, Soldiers' Memorial Building, and city hall, the Whipple Block on the corner of Hanover and West Park streets stands as one of Lebanon's premier old-time landmarks, a three-story brick structure whose steam heat and gas lighting made it all the rage at the time of its construction in 1882.

It also stands as testimony to Hanover Street's coming-of-age as Lebanon's de facto Main Street. For, just as the railroad had provided a relatively inexpensive way for Lebanon industries to ship their products to places that would have been uneconomical to reach by team, trains also afforded merchants a faster and cheaper means of importing goods. The result was a retailing boom that offered consumers a wider variety of choices about where to buy their shoes, groceries, hardware, dry goods, and specialty items like fish, oysters, fruit, and meat.

Tax records provide some indication of the size and timing of the surge. The town's 1855 stock of inventory in business and industry amounted to just over $25,000. By 1863, however, that figure had increased 64 percent, to a little over $41,000; and in the ten-year period between 1863 and 1872 it grew to $115,960, an increase of 178 percent. The growth continued through the 1870s, and by 1881 the town had $153,375 worth of stock, up 24 percent even from 1873.

That section of Hanover Street today, however, bears only a passing resemblance to the street of even thirty years ago, primarily because of alterations that followed the fire of 1964. In the pre-fire days the mall was a through street with a railroad bridge and a river bridge leading directly to Hough Square (Sacred Heart Church, 1994). It also contained a countless variety of stores, shops, and businesses.

The birth of the business district started shortly after the arrival of the turnpikes in the early nineteenth century, when a greater variety of imports and exports played an increasingly larger role in the town's formerly self-contained economy. Among the leading figures in this transformation were Stephen Kendrick and Timothy Kenrick, two relatives who spelled their last names differently but who each became prominent in the commercial, industrial and political affairs of the town. At one time in the 1830s this family owned all three of the stately homes on South Park Street. Timothy Kenrick's store stood on the front lawn of what is now the Congregational church and his home sat just to the west of the present fire station (1994); Stephen owned the home just east of the store (Degnan-Hough, 1994); and James Kendrick, who ran the bank, owned the house next to the corner of South Park and School streets.

Stephen Kendrick was a virtual one-man conglomerate. He ran a drugstore on West

Park Street, manufactured potash, made linseed oil from flax, and also exported cheese, lard, pork, hogs, grass seed, beans, and mustard seed. He sold his drugstore in 1834 to his son George, who carried it on for several decades after.

His nephew, Timothy Kenrick, arrived in town in 1809 and was town clerk from 1819-1856 while he operated a successful store in partnership with Asa Hough.

Another leading merchant, Wareham Morse, kept a general store on the corner of South Park and School streets starting in 1816. According to his purchase ledger, he bought run, wine, brandy, raisins and a bale of cotton during one trip to Boston in 1823. He also purchased razor straps, several dozen knives, hooks, an array of combs, soap, and a dozen shaving brushes. He laid in a supply of fish hooks, snuff boxes, pocketbooks, wallets, spectacles, quills and ink powder; shovels and scythes; numerous saws, and half a dozen decks of playing cards. (While that last item might not have done the tythingman any favors, Mr. Morse also bought several Bibles, prayer books, and a dozen whip thongs.)

For the ladies of the house he bought large quantities of silk, cambric (a thin linen cloth), flannel, several kinds of "fancy" cloth, ribbon and buttons, and a dozen pair of white silk gloves.

He also stocked tea, coffee, nutmeg, pepper, cloves, pimento, codfish, molasses, and buffalo skins that were used to make robes.

One of the first to open a new store after the arrival of the railroad was George Worthen, the son of an Enfield farmer who bought his freedom from his father at the age of eighteen (children were indentured to their parents until age twenty-one) and set out from home in the 1840s as a door-to-door salesman. He traveled on foot with a modest lot of goods in a tin trunk strapped to his back and was soon successful enough to graduate to a horse and peddler's cart. In 1848 he opened his first dry-goods store on a Hanover Street lot just east of the present Hildreth's store and went on to put up two Odd Fellows buildings on West Park Street that also housed his businesses. He also had branch stores on Payne Road in East Lebanon, Main Street in West Lebanon, and in Claremont. The Worthen Block on the Court Street corner was known as the Lincoln Block after the 1887 fire, when storekeeper Josiah "Ed" Lincoln rented space there for his burned-out dry-goods business. He purchased the building in 1895 and sold it two years later to the Harrison Brothers, Fred and Frank, and it was known as the Harrison Block until it was razed after the 1964 fire.

Hildreth's Hardware

The city's oldest retail establishment is Hildreth's Hardware, begun in 1855 as Ingram and Hildreth's tin shop, roughly across the street from its present location. The Hildreth end of the business was named for James, joined a year later by brother Charles M., who bought out Mr. Ingram's share of the shop. The brothers worked together in the tin and hardware business until 1862, when James sold out to his brother. Charles Hildreth worked alone until 1878, when he was joined by his son, Charles Edward (known as Ed), a founding member of the Lebanon Rotary Club who, like his father, served on the board of the National Bank of Lebanon and the Mascoma Savings Bank. The store moved to its present location in the 1880s, and the business remained in

Hildreth's Hardware and the second Whipple Block on the north side of Hanover Street after the great blizzard of 1888

the Hildreth family until 1950, when it was purchased by Francis A. Sargent and Charles McNeill. They sold it to Leo Babineau in 1965 (Mrs. Sargent and Mrs. Babineau are mother and daughter), and he to his son William—the present owner—in 1980.

McNeill's Drug Store

Another enduring business is the Lebanon Pharmacy, which has its roots in a drugstore operated for many years by Dr. Isaac N. Perley. He started on North Park Street with a pharmacy purchased in 1866 from Edward Sturtevant and, after leaving town for a year, returned in 1879 to buy a pharmacy from a Mr. Foster on the south side of Hanover Street. Dr. Perley moved into the Whipple Block in 1882, and after being burned out in 1894 he relocated to a small building on the north side of Hanover Street, where he later put up the brick structure known as the Perley Block. This building was last occupied by McNeill's drugstore before it was torn down in 1963 to make way for the expansion of Woolworth's.

Charles McNeill came to work as a pharmacist for Issac Perley in 1894 at a salary of ten dollars a week, and became a partner in the store in 1907. When Dr. Perley retired in 1912, Mr. McNeill assumed ownership under the banner of McNeill's Drug Store. His daughter and son-in-law, Mary and Francis Sargent, joined the business in 1946, and their son, Gordon, became a partner in 1957. The store moved across the street in 1963 to the Baldwin/Hunt Block and was destroyed by fire the next year, but reopened in a new building on the same site in 1965. The business continued in the same location under the McNeill's name until 1987, when Mrs. Sargent and her son sold it (retaining ownership of the building) to Steve Hochberg, who renamed it the Lebanon Pharmacy.

Whipple Block

Gilman Whipple clerked for George Worthen from 1853 until the early 1860s before opening a store of his own in front of the Congregational church on South Park Street. He moved to the north side of Hanover Street about 1870, and remained there until he built the block bearing his name in 1882 (Cowan's, 1994).

In its earliest years the Whipple Block contained not only Mr. Whipple's business, but several others, and the third story was dedicated to (and constructed for) the Masonic hall. Mr. Whipple sold the building and his dry-goods business to Clayton Richardson and Frederick Emerson in 1888, and it went through various names reflecting several ownership changes. It was known as Richardson & Emerson until 1914, when former stockboy Nelson Langlois joined the partnership and the store was known as Richardson, Emerson, & Co. When Mr. Emerson retired in 1916 it carried on under the banner of Richardson & Langlois until 1937, when Mr. Richardson died and the store was known as N.O. Langlois and Sons.

Stanley Currier came aboard as a partner a year later and the store had another new name, Currier & Langlois; that lasted until 1942, when Mr. Currier bought out Mr. Langlois and the business was called Currier & Co., the name it retained until 1985, when it went out of business.

The last owner of Currier & Co. was Frederick Cushing, Jr., who joined the business as its general manager in 1953, after stints at R.H. Macy's in New York City and R.H. White's in Boston. Mr. Cushing's father, Frederick, Sr., operated the Lebanon Drug Store just across the street, the last place in town where, until his death in 1963, you could still buy a five-cent cup of coffee.

After more than a hundred years in business Currier & Co. held its final sale in July 1985, when a line of twenty or thirty bargain hunters queued up outside the store before the doors opened. It was as if part of the town's history—from Gilman Whipple through Fred Cushing—was being liquidated.

Within a few months of the sale a new store was opened by Hanover businessman Ronald Cowan, in partnership with his son, Jeff who ran it there until 1994. The Whipple Block is presently owned by New London developer Daniel Wolfe, who also bought the abutting Pulsifer Block and renovated both structures, installing an elevator and clock tower on the western exterior of the Whipple building.

On the west side of the Pulsifer Block was the first building erected in 1873 by grocer Oscar Baldwin. The structure was destroyed in the 1887 fire, and the building he put up in its place was well known in later years as the home of Hunt's Department Store. Started in 1892 by Ancil Hunt, it was operated in later years by his son, Harold, one of the founders of the Lebanon Lions Club in 1928. This was the building McNeill's Drug Store moved to in 1963, a year before it was destroyed by fire.

Another longtime downtown merchant was Alfred J. Plamondon, one of the first presidents of the Lebanon Chamber of Commerce after its founding in 1916. Mr. Plamondon sold shoes, cars, and virtually everything else from a building he constructed about 1910, where Woolworth opened in 1911. Upstairs in the building was the Park Theatre, which was converted to bowling lanes in the 1930s.

Just as the 1964 fire changed the layout of Hanover Street, it also altered Mascoma Street, which now joins South Park in front of the fire station. Before the fire, however,

Detail of birds-eye view of Lebanon published in 1884 showing downtown landmarks

1. Congregational Church
2. Methodist Church
3. Catholic Church*
4. Baptist Church
5. Unitarian Church
6. Town Hall and Post Office
7. Memorial Building
8. Schools
9. Depot, Northern Division, Lowell R. R.
10. Sayre's Hotel and Livery
11. Chiron Spring House*
12. National and Savings Banks
13. Granite State Free Press Office
    Free Press Job Office, Freeman & Richardson
14. Mead, Mason & Co., Mfrs. Furniture and Builders' Materials
15. Mascoma Flannel Co.*
16. Kendrick & Davis, Watch Key Mfy.
    The Union Cabinet & Paper Co.
17. Lebanon Woolen Co.
18. C. M. Baxter, Mfr. Woodworking Machinery
    The Concord Paint Co.
19. S. Cole & Son, Foundry & Machine Shop
20. Mascoma Edge Tool Co., Mfrs., Scythes*
21. G. W. and M. L. Stearns, Mfrs., Scythes, Snaths, Sleds and Hammock Chairs*
22. E. F. Emerson, Mfr. Wagon Felloes
23. G. A. Elliott, Carriage Shop
24. Joseph Mace, Flour and Grist Mill
    A.W. Rix, Mfr. Patent Woodworking Machinery
25. Muchmore & Whipple, Contractors and Builders
    N. B. Marston, Rake Mfy.
    L. N. Miner, Furniture and General Repair Shop
26. C. E. Marston, Mfr. Coffins and Caskets
27. H. G. Billings, Marble Works and Livery
28. H. W. Carter, Mfr. Overalls, Coats, Vests, Pants
    Wholesale Jobber, Small Wares and Cigars
29. Carter & Churchill, Overalls & Shirt Mfrs.
    Wholesale Jobbers, Small Wares
30. G. C. Whipple, Dry Goods and Clothing
    J. N. Perley, M.D., Drugs and Fancy Goods
    Frank C. Sturtevant, Insurance
    F. Davis, Architect
    W. S. Hough, Dentist
31. Pulsifer Bros., Groceries and Crockery
32. O. W. Baldwin, Groceries and Crockery
33. J. E. Lincoln, Dry Goods and Clothing
34. G. Bennett, Groceries
35. Brown Bros., Hardware and Agricultural Tools
36. C. M. Hildreth & Son, Hardware, Iron and Steel
37. Simmons Bros., Groceries and Crockery
    G. H. Stearns, Meat Market
38. J. L. Spring, Attorney
39. T. A. Morgan, Jeweler
    C. E. Lewis, Photographer
    Cragin & Sturtevant, Boots and Shoes
    G. S. Joslin, Boots and Shoes
40. C. J. Dow, Jeweler
    F. E. Bugbee, Hair Dressing Rooms
    E. Ticknor, Harness Shop
41. Currie & Clough, Dentists
    G. W. Houghton, Dry Goods and Variety Store

*Not shown

Mascoma Street ran nearly flush against the Bank building, forming a "T" with West Park Street.

The Bank building, put up in 1893 by the now-defunct Lebanon Savings Bank, has hosted scores of commercial tenants over the years, including Fifield and Stearns men's store, Hapgood and Howard's shoe store, Niblock's clothing store, Bridgman's furniture, Pond's millinery, and C.H. Davis Jeweler in the Whipple Block.

Several structures once stood between the Bank building and the present fire station, including the Durant and Perkins furniture store on the corner next to the Bank building, and two Odd Fellows' halls put up by Mr. Worthen. The second Odd Fellows building replaced the first after an 1879 fire, and was itself destroyed along with the Park Hotel in 1931. Both of these lots were last occupied by the gas station of Alfred King, who was forced to give up his business in the reconstruction of Route 120 that followed the 1964 fire.

North Park Street

There were four major blocks on North Park Street between Court and Campbell streets. The first, at the corner of Court and North Park, was constructed by Daniel, Pringle, and Lewis Hinkley about 1853. The building, taken over in the early 1860s by Seth and George Blodgett, was known as the Blodgett Block until it was torn down to make way for the Mascoma Savings Bank building, which also housed the offices of the Granite State Electric Company for more than thirty years. While it stood, however, the Blodgett Block contained about every kind of commercial enterprise that Lebanon had to offer over the years: several restaurants, barbers, tailors, shoe shops, jewelry stores, professional offices, a broom manufacturer, a stock market brokerage, photography studios, and it even functioned as a musical studio for Hough's Band.

Just east of the Blodgett Block was a three-story duplex constructed in 1869 by a Mr. Clark on a site now corresponding to Philip Dutille's jewelry store (since taken over by his son, Jude). Although Mr. Clark put up the building, he soon sold it to Frank B. Kendrick, who owned the land and ran a jewelry store that he later sold to A. J. Potter.

Between the Kendrick Block and the town hall was the building constructed by carriage-maker Ira Thompson about 1865 for his son Elbridge, whose sixty-eight years as a milliner probably gives him the town record for consecutive years in business. The younger Thompson started about 1861 and continued in business until he became ill in 1929, two years before his death. He also had a brother, John Milton Thompson, who began his military career in 1861 and rose through the ranks to become a brigadier general.

The Thompson and Kendrick blocks were both destroyed in the same 1923 fire that claimed the town hall. The Thompson Block was replaced by the structure Carl Richards built after the fire (Dutille's Jewelers, Bruce Johnson Real Estate, 1994). For many years it was the location of Mr. Richards' shoe store, a business he sold to Tony Derrigo in 1957. Harold Blodgett was the last to run it before his retirement in 1985.

Behind the Thompson Block were the so-called city stables, owned for a time by Henry Billings, and just east of the Thompson Block was the town hall itself. On the east side of the town hall was Howe Street, which was notable as the local taxi stand into the

North Park Street in 1904. From left to right are the first Worthen (Lincoln, Harrison) Block on the corner of Court and Hanover streets, and the Blodgett, Kendrick and Thompson blocks on North Park.

1970s. Cabbies parked on Howe Street and waited to answer the phones that were mounted on the outside of the town hall. Howe Street was discontinued in the early 1970s to allow for handicapped access to city hall.

The Pavillion

On the east side of Howe Street was Bonardi's fruit stand, which was connected to the store of George Houghton, a sharp-witted, salty-tongued character who moved to Lebanon in 1851 from Boston, where he had operated a dry-goods store on Hanover Street for about four years. His first Lebanon store also was built on Hanover Street, on the south side of the present mall area (1994).

Mr. Houghton moved to North Park Street in 1871, on the lot where the Rogers House senior-citizen apartment building stands (1994). He renamed the building The Pavillion, and in it he operated the town's first full-blown department store. In 1878 it had the fancy title of Houghton & Macy's Ladies' Pavillion and Housekeeper's Emporium. Mr. Macy was Rowland H. Macy, Jr., George Houghton's nephew and the son of the founder of Macy's, the New York City department store that was once the world's largest. Mr. Macy later left Lebanon and went to work for his father.

Mr. Houghton was a successful merchant, if a somewhat cantankerous personality. A customer who complained about goods bought at the Pavillion was likely to be told never to set foot in the store again. Carrie Lowe, who worked for Mr. Houghton before taking over his business in 1890, recalled that a customer who died owing money at the Pavillion was recorded in George Houghton's store ledger as "Settled by death." An uncollectable debt from a living patron, on the other hand, prompted Mr. Houghton to write it off with the notation, "Gone to Hell." Mark Converse, a former clerk at the Pavillion, bought out Mr. Houghton in 1888, and he sold the store in 1890 to Carrie Lowe, the first woman in town to run a business other than a dressmaking shop. She lasted until 1934, by which time the store was located in the Hotel Rogers.

Hough Square

The area where Hanover Street intersects with High Street—just across the Mascoma River from the pedestrian mall—is known as Hough Square.

The name derives from the family of Enoch Hough, who owned the home that stood on the lot occupied by the Sacred Heart church. The designation of the area as a "square" is a misnomer, although "Hough Triangle" comes closer to describing the rotary that channeled traffic to Hanover and High streets.

The grassy triangle was once marked by an iron fountain in the middle and was flanked by businesses on both sides of Hanover Street.

On the west side of Hanover Street next to the river was the Densmore Block, a tenement building that housed a butcher shop in the late 1800s and a bakery in the early 1900s. Next to the Densmore Block was Knight's garage on the corner of High and Hanover streets, later operated by Jimmy Decato until the street was moved in the urban renewal that followed the 1964 fire.

Another landmark on west side of Hanover Street was Harry's White Owl Diner, operated by Harry Annuccilli, who was well known for the one day each year he gave a free ice-cream cone to every kid in town who showed up.

Further up the street on the west side was Brown's furniture store, which was torn down in the late sixties after Brown's moved to Route 12A. The structure was then replaced by the Veterans of Foreign Wars building (Lebanon Graphics, 1994). The VFW remained there until the treasurer absconded with the club's money in the late seventies, and it was forced to close.

The east side of Hough Square is much the same as it was in 1922, when the Jette and Plamondon blocks were erected. Napoleon Jette ran his cobbler business from a narrow room flush against the riverbank (Brad & Co., 1994); Leo Desparte had a drugstore in the same area; and Howard Brothers grocery also operated out of Jette Block.

In the nearby Plamondon Block (Hirsch's, 1994) was Moody's furniture store, Scannell's Cut Rate store, and the First National store before it moved up the street across from the Sacred Heart convent (U-Haul, 1994).

New Streets

Although Lebanon's industries made her a magnet for people seeking jobs and resulted in a flourishing industrial and retail trade, it also presented a series of social challenges.

Fueled by the arrival of more than 350 Canadian immigrants between 1860 and 1880, the town's population ballooned from 2,332 in 1860 to 3,198 in 1870, and housing was at

The west end of the Lebanon business district before the 1964 fire showing location of the old bridge. The Howard block (in shadow) and Landers' Restaurant are on the left. On the right side of the street Suburban Gas stands next to the taller Lindsay Block containing Hirsch's Army-Navy store. In the background, across the bridge, is Hough Square and Jimmy Decato's Mobil station.

a premium. In a scenario not altogether unlike the cry for affordable housing that went up in the boom of the 1980s, the *Free Press* in 1865 criticized the town's business barons for investing in distant railroads, banks, and mines, but not in housing for the town's workers: "There is need at the present time of twenty-five new tenements in this village, and the new factory will create a necessity for as many more."

Two years later the paper estimated that the number of apartment buildings and single-family homes built in the previous year was equal to about twenty tenements, as new neighborhoods were laid out and others expanded.

Some of the changes actually preceded the paper's call-to-hammers. The village map of 1853 shows virtually no houses in the wedge of side streets now located between School and Bank streets, an area known at the time as the village muster field. Neither Shaw, Elm or Union streets were laid out, and Green Street extended only a hundred feet or so off School Street. By 1860, however, Green Street had reached its full length to intersect with the first leg of Shaw Street, and Elm Street ran from Bank Street to Green, and even a little beyond. By 1870 the side streets in the wedge between School and Bank streets were beginning to fill up, as the *Free Press* listed about thirty new houses being constructed, including four on Elm Street by Amos Jones, who had plans for an additional ten homes on Elm and Union.

On October 28, 1865, the newspaper reported that a new, as-yet-unnamed street was to be laid out through Joseph Gerrish's garden toward "Slaytonville," and that it would be the new road to West Lebanon. Two weeks later the paper reported that the new street would be called "Mechanic Street." Joseph Gerrish owned some of the property along the east end of the street, and he sold much of it for building lots, as did Solon Peck, who also owned a large stretch of land along the new road.

Parkhurst Street was laid out in 1866 between the railroad depot and Bank Street, which it paralleled and was connected to by two side streets—the north part of Elm, and the one now called Allen Street, although that was first named Parkhurst, too.

The *Free Press* also noted that six small houses were built in 1870 on two new streets—Eldridge and Summer—running from the west side of Hanover Street. By the end of the century that ridge to the west of Hanover Street would teem with a French-Canadian population that, drawn by the mills along the Mascoma, already had grown from a mere fifty in 1860, to more than two-hundred in 1870, and double that by 1880.

Riverdale

Just over the Mascoma River on Bank Street Extension stands the development known as "Riverdale," a village whose name dates from 1874, when a group of ladies adopted it as a genteel way to describe what used to be known as The Alden Place, The Benton Farm, and "out to Mary Ann Storrs."

A fixture of the neighborhood is the Riverdale Store, dating to the 1930s, when it was Ernest Gove's garage.

The 1960s saw the closing of the American Excelsior Company, the only industry of any size located in Riverdale. It opened on the Mascoma River about 1915, and at one time employed about thirty people.

Riverdale also was home to the veterinary practice of Dr. Lawrence MacLeod, who arrived in Lebanon in 1946. He retired in 1984, but for the bulk of his career had the community's only animal hospital.

Riverdale had a race track starting in 1897 in the wedge of land—now covered by the interstate—between Bank Street and the Heater Road. The *Free Press* account of the opening described a circus-like atmosphere featuring an orchestra and vendors selling wares to more than nine-hundred people who paid to watch trotters run on a half-mile track. The oval also sometimes doubled as a fairground, but was dormant by the time it was buried by the interstate in the 1960s.

Law and Order

The late eighteenth century was not a good time to be a criminal—at least not if you were caught. Thomas Powers, described in court records as a "laborer and mulatto" was accused in 1795 of "not having the fear of God before his eyes, but being moved & seduced by the instigator of the devil" when he raped spinster Sally Messer on December seventh of that year. Mr. Powers pleaded not guilty, and at a trial held in May of the following year at the county court in Plymouth he was convicted and sentenced to be hanged. Mr. Powers petitioned Governor John Taylor Gilman to postpone the execution to allow the condemned man "to prepare for death." The governor put off the hanging, but only for two weeks, and Thomas Powers went to the gallows on July 28, becoming the first and only Lebanon resident to be executed.

The penalties meted out by the Plymouth court for lesser crimes were none too

Aerial view of the American Excelsior Company on the Bank Street Extension in the Riverdale section of town

pleasant, either. When John Putnam was found guilty of stealing $158.06 from West Lebanon resident Joshua Markham in 1802, he was sentenced to receive twenty lashes on his naked back and to pay Mr. Markham $415.60, nearly three times the value of the stolen money. James Quigley, who was convicted of stealing a horse in 1797, was ordered to pay a fine of eighty dollars and wear a mark of India ink extending in a line across his forehead, from temple-to-temple and down to the tip of his nose. The record is unclear about just what crime Glazier Wheeler committed, but he was ordered to "be set in the pillory one hour & have one of his ears cut off on Fryday the 24th Day of Oct. A.D. 1783." Mr. Wheeler also received a year in jail and was required to post a surety bond for two years to make certain that he did not repeat that or any other crime, a common condition.

Lebanon is said to have had a whipping post located about where the Whipple Block now stands, near the northwest corner of the park.

A shortage of counsel may not have enhanced an accused man's chances for acquittal. Lebanon attorney Aaron Hutchinson, who served the town as a selectman and state representative, was the town's first and one of only a few lawyers in the county. His name is found on virtually every page of the early county court records.

While the town had constables to keep the peace dating back to the 1700s, the Lebanon Police Department as it exists today began in 1860 when the town appointed Enoch F. Hough as a police officer at an annual salary of $1.50. The following year the town paid four officers. In addition to Mr. Hough, James Bly was on duty in the center of town, Herman Rix in West Lebanon, and J. W. Cleveland in East Lebanon.

A small building on Howe Street housed the first police headquarters, which moved to the town hall about 1871, the same year two jail cells were added to the building. The department remained at that location until 1992, although the 1930s saw the establishment of a West Lebanon police station in the basement of the fire house that was in use until 1967.

Clarence Wright's thirty-three-year tenure (1931-1964) is the longest of any police chief in Lebanon, topping the thirteen years (1972-1985) served by Neal Wooley. When Mr. Wooley was forced to resign he was succeeded by Donald Vittum, a disciplinarian who changed the department into a force that placed a premium on professionalism and community service. He also hired Susan LaFlamme, the department's first woman officer, who left in 1989 to join the United States Secret Service. Perhaps the officers working under Mr. Vittum were not necessarily better cops, but the public's perception of the department changed. It was a transformation not lost on the city council, which noted in a private memo that the fire department had been eclipsed as a source of civic fancy by the police department. When Mr. Vittum departed in 1991 he was replaced by Edward Laurie, who continued to emphasize professionalism and community-based policing.

The first police court was established in 1875, with James Ticknor as the first justice. The court regularly heard a variety of offenses ranging from adultery (Hutchins Moulton was sentenced to a year and a day's hard labor following his conviction in March 1881) to vagrancy (Eva Hutchins pleaded guilty in 1881 and was sentenced to six months of hard labor at the Grafton County farm in North Haverhill), to cruelty to a horse (N. W. Pierce pleaded not guilty, was found guilty, and fined a total of $8.90).

Juvenile cases were also handled by the local court (as they are now), and the judge was apparently none too bashful about handing out tickets to the state "industrial school." George Bennett, a youth convicted of larceny in 1882, was slapped with a five-year term, while later that same year Winnie Porter was given a one-year sentence for the same offense. Another minor, Charles Alden, found no sympathy at home; his father recommended (and the judge concurred) that the boy serve a one-year term in the reform school for an offense unspecified in the court records.

The Poisoning Case and Other Homicides

The headlines called it simply, The Poisoning Case, but the arrest of Sarah Willison in April 1875 was the town's biggest crime up to that time.

The details were sensational enough in their own right: Maid spikes tea with arsenic, killing family matron. Adding to the intrigue for the Lebanon commoner, however, was the fact that it was no ordinary family that Mrs. Willison was accused of poisoning. Her employers were Edward and Sarah Kendrick, one of the town's most prominent families. Edward was the assistant cashier at the National Bank of Lebanon and the son of James Kendrick, who was then in his forty-seventh year as the bank's president.

Edward's mother, Clarissa, lived with Edward and Sarah on South Park Street (James may have, too, although his name does not appear in newspaper accounts of the crime), and although James and Sarah recovered from the poisoning, Clarissa Kendrick died a few days after ingesting the tea. Sarah Willison was arrested, found not guilty by reason of insanity, and was given an indefinite sentence in the state insane asylum.

Another homicide occurred on December 31, 1923, when a man named Dement Honchuck shot and killed Densmore Brick Company worker Eddy Leah, who had married Mr. Honchuck's ex-wife. Mr. Honchuck pleaded guilty.

Equally stunning was the Beauty Shop Murder of twenty-eight-year-old Freda Lathrop on January 7, 1939, in which the dapper Henry Begin shot his estranged lover to death at his beauty salon in Hough Square and then attempted to cut up her body and flush it down the toilet. He received a life sentence after pleading guilty to murder.

The next homicide occurred in September 1972, when fifty-seven-year-old school music teacher Katherine Robb was bludgeoned to death by her son Harlan in the home they shared on Mascoma Street. Two months after they both disappeared from their bloody home Mr. Robb was apprehended in Nevada and his mother's body was found buried in a shallow grave in White River Junction. Defense psychiatrists attributed Mr. Robb's actions to brain damage acquired from a childhood bout with meningitis, while the prosecution said he was schizophrenic. He was found not guilty by reason of insanity and sentenced to the state hospital. Mr. Robb married in 1981 and by 1984 was living outside the state hospital six days a week.

Drifter William Beede was convicted in December 1975 for the death of Anita Lemay, who was strangled on June fifth of that year in a Hanover Street apartment building. Mr. Beede was given a thirty-year-to-life prison term.

The most bizarre and stunning crime in the town's history occurred March 4, 1986, when firefighters were summoned to a middle-of-the-night house fire on Brook Road in West Lebanon. In the rubble they discovered the bodies of three young children—ages four, six, and eleven—who had been shot to death as part of a murder-suicide pact involving the children's mother, Caroline Lowery Hull, and her boyfriend, Michael Frank Dean. According to letters the couple mailed to media outlets and political figures, Ms. Hull and her children were given large doses of sleeping pills and then shot to death by Mr. Dean, a mentally disabled Vietnam veteran who expressed frustration with the way the country treated—or mistreated—veterans. After killing the others, Mr. Dean set the kerosene-soaked house afire and then shot himself.

Wired

The nation's first phone exchange opened in Hartford, Connecticut in 1878, and Lebanon's first telephone line was a private connection installed in early 1881 between the home of Howard Benton and his son-in-law, George Kelly. Widespread hookups arrived two years later when residents were able to buy telephone service for $2.50 per month. The original exchange consisted of Jesse Dewey and two other employees servicing forty-seven subscribers. By July 1883 those residents who were wired could talk to residents in Enfield, and also to the Goold and Holmes store in West Lebanon, but only after having their calls routed by one of the town's two operators. Isa Emerson was the day operator in 1885, and night calls were handled by Bertrand Smalley.

The practice of placing calls through the operator continued until November 1961, when several area towns simultaneously converted to rotary-dial service, allowing them to dial direct to any place in the country. Residents of West Lebanon, in the 298 exchange, were tied in to the 295 exchange in White River Junction (yet another connection between the two villages); and even into the 1970s, when Lebanon residents had to dial a minimum of seven digits to make local calls, West Lebanon residents could ring up their neighbors across the river merely by dialing the number five (the last digit of the Hartford exchange) and then the last four digits of their party's number. That, however, is a thing of the past, as New England Telephone in 1993 began requiring anyone calling out-of-state to dial eleven digits.

Long distance service arrived in late 1884, the year after phone service itself. The *Free Press* reported in January 1885, "We talked with Concord Wednesday morning by the new telephone line, via Newport, and could hear as distinctly as anywhere about town."

There was a time when 10 P.M. meant "lights out" for the whole town, and anyone who wanted to stay up at home past that hour had to provide their own illumination.

Limited electrical service arrived in 1890 when a group of leading businessmen incorporated the Lebanon Electric Light and Power Company, one of two predecessors of the present-day Granite State Electric Company. The board of directors of Lebanon Electric was comprised of some of the town's most influential men: William S. Carter and Frank Churchill of Carter & Churchill; attorney William Cotton; storekeepers Gilman Whipple and Josiah Lincoln; and textile entrepreneur George Rogers.

The company leased land and buildings from Scytheville resident Martin Purmort at the bottom of Slayton Hill and began the generation of electricity for its first customer, the town of Lebanon, which turned on 120 new electric street lights for the first time on December 12, 1890. Prior to that time the streets had been lit with lamps fueled by whale oil and, later, by kerosene.

The first electric lights lit only the streets until 10 P.M., and even then not at all if the moon was bright. Even after homes were added to the system, electricity was still only generated at night and then only until 10 P.M. If the Mascoma River was running low, the electricity was turned off even earlier. Unscheduled outages were frequent, but most people seemed not to mind too much, judging from this January 2, 1891, passage in the *Free Press*: "The happiest people we meet these days are the ones who have got the electric lights in their houses. It is a great comfort and luxury, which is destined to be more widely used in the future. It is one of the improvements that have come to stay."

The invention of the electric iron led to limited daylight electricity so that women could press clothes on Tuesday mornings. According to local tradition, Monday was the day on which most everyone washed and hung out their laundry to dry, and Tuesday was ironing day. When a rainy Monday postponed wash day to Tuesday, the generators would be fired up on Wednesday to allow women to iron.

Lebanon's second electric company, the Mascoma Light, Heat and Power Company, was incorporated in 1891 to generate and distribute electricity in Grafton County and in Windsor County, Vermont, and also to sell gas. The company's first generating station was built in 1892 on the Mascoma River site at the western end of the Miracle Mile, and it later bought the generating site on the Glen Road.

Lebanon, 1761-1994 / 136

The company was called the Mascoma Electric Light and Gas Company in 1912, when the process began that would lead to the merger of Mascoma Electric and Lebanon Electric.

Another utility, the Grafton County Electric Light and Power Company, was incorporated in 1912 for the purpose of buying both Lebanon utilities, but state regulators held up the transactions until 1917 because of concerns about competition. When the deal finally went through, there was only Grafton County Electric, which owned and operated all three generating stations on the Mascoma River—the one in Scytheville, the station on the Miracle Mile, and the one on the Glen Road. In addition, the company opened its most powerful facility in 1922 in the West Lebanon village of Butmanville—where the Powerhouse shopping center now stands.

According to a history of the company, "As early as 1925, the distribution system of Grafton County Light and Power was tied into a system about one-half mile north of what is presently New England Power's Wilder Station. Over time, the small dams and water wheels [used to run industry] on the Mascoma River were abandoned in favor of purchasing electricity from Grafton County Electric Light and Power. The industries along the river found this to be more economical than running their own stations."

The Scytheville and Miracle Mile plants were operated until 1960, and the opening of the Butmanville facility in 1922 closed the one on the Glen Road. The Butmanville station, meanwhile, provided power to West Lebanon village as late as 1969. In fact, the station even operated during the great Northeast Blackout of 1965, and West Lebanon may have been the only village in the northeast that had power during that outage.

The end of local ownership for the Lebanon utility came in 1925, when the New England Company (the forerunner of the present-day New England Electric System) bought all of the Grafton County Electric stock (retaining the local name until 1934, when it was changed to Granite State Electric). The company also operated the Boston Lot Reservoir in West Lebanon which supplied water to both West Lebanon and White River Junction.

Grafton County Electric's first headquarters were not in Grafton County at all, but in the Hotel Coolidge building in White River Junction. They moved to the Hotel Rogers in Lebanon in the 1930s, and then to the new Mascoma Savings Bank building on North Park Street in 1952. They later moved all operations to the buiding on the Miracle Mile that they share with the New England Power Corp., which operates the 30,000 kilowatt Wilder Dam.

Completed in 1950 at a cost of $16 million, Wilder Dam was the largest construction project in Lebanon's history until the Dartmouth-Hitchcock Medical Center opened in 1991. The dam reaches about three-thousand feet across the Connecticut River and stands fifty-nine feet high. While it powers homes in Lebanon and elsewhere as part of a regional power grid, its equally important local function has been to anchor the city's tax base. New England Power in 1993 paid $1.06 million in taxes on its Wilder Dam holdings, making the company the city's largest single taxpayer.

12

"Where Is Up-Street Gone?"

> *"What with the Hanover fire, the Lyme murder and suicide, and the Hartford holocaust, '87, young as she is, has furnished us with an abundance of local sensations. It is enough; spare us anything more of the same sort, please."*
>
> —Item in the *Granite State Free Press*, February 11, 1887.

THERE WAS plenty of year left when those words appeared in the paper, and much sensation yet to come. The start of 1887 saw temperatures below zero, an outbreak of chicken pox making the rounds, fundraising for the Soldiers' Memorial Building about a thousand-dollars short of its goal, and specifications being readied for waterworks that would bring running water to the village.

At about three o'clock on the morning of January 4, 1887, a fire broke out on the third floor of the Dartmouth Hotel in downtown Hanover. On February 11, 1887, the *Free Press* carried a story on an inside page telling of a case in which seventy-two-year-old pauper Stephen Lamphere, who was boarding with a Lyme family at that town's expense, shot the lady of the house and then himself. It was sensational stuff, but was dwarfed by the headline that dominated the front page of that day's paper:

The Hartford Calamity
One of the
Most Awful
Accidents
in the History of Railroads
—and—

So Near Home

— — —-

*Nearly Half a Hundred Slain
And As Many Injured*

— — —-

Thousands Flock to the Scene

— — —-

When a Central Vermont express bound for Montreal derailed on a bridge over the White River early in the morning of Saturday, February fifth, the cars fell to the ice and about 30 people died, making it the third-worst accident in railroading history to that point. It was not so much the fall that killed them, but the ensuing fires started by the stoves that were used to heat the cars; officials were still trying to identify remains from the wreck two weeks later, as many of the dead were burned beyond recognition.

On March 25 the *Free Press* announced that a Burlington, Vermont, company had been awarded a contract to build a water system in Lebanon that would connect pipes to a reservoir on top of Prospect Street and provide running water to the village for the first time. "When the works are completed," the paper reported, "no town or city will have a better system of waterworks for fire or general purposes. Hip Hip Hurrah."

The waterworks that were under construction in the spring of 1887 marked the end of a period of collective hemming and hawing dating back to the 1860s, when several articles in the local paper campaigned for increased fire protection to safeguard the manufacturing district that had taken off after the railroad arrived and the Civil War ended. The paper's "Hip Hip Hurrah," however, was premature, and completion of the waterworks turned out to be a classic case of closing the barn door after the horse—indeed, most of the herd—had been stolen.

With its grass and walkways obscured by store and household goods on the morning of May 10, 1887, Colburn Park looked like a hastily arranged flea market, which is more than could be said for the heart of the town's manufacturing district along the Mascoma River.

That area resembled a war zone. Who could blame residents for feeling shellshocked as eighty buildings, more than six-hundred jobs, and the homes of forty families fell victim to what remains the greatest fire in town history, eclipsing even the blaze of 1964 in area burned.

The tragedy was bad enough, but the shame was that the 1887 fire might have been better contained had residents not passed up opportunities to fund a reservoir and village-wide waterworks several years earlier.

The foundation for the 1887 disaster was partially laid in 1870, when the town all but ignored a study to determine the best means of providing a reliable water supply to the village. The report by engineer J. B. Sawyer contained four recommendations, three of which entailed construction of a reservoir (although a few homes were supplied by a private water system operated by Kendrick & Davis, which was fed by wells on Storrs Hill). Residents, however, balked at the cost of a reservoir, and none of the proposals was even brought to a vote.

Photo taken from Mechanic Street looking east across Foundry and Water streets and up Benton Hill after the Great Fire of 1887. The lower shop of the Sturtevant furniture factory and the Kendrick & Davis key shop located along Water Street were destroyed as well as buildings along Benton Hill. The old sponge factory building on Foundry Street in the foreground was also leveled.

The fourth and cheapest recommendation was to install a water-powered pump in one of the downtown mills and pump water to a series of hydrants scattered throughout the town. The precinct purchased one of the pumps and installed it in Philander Hall's gristmill along the Mascoma, strictly for use in fighting fires. The town, however, remained without running water.

The precinct also entered into an agreement with Jesse Sturtevant in 1872—and Mead-Mason after they took over the business—to allow the town the use of the company's steam pump in the High Street shop if a major fire broke out.

One such blaze on February 10, 1879, wiped out six buildings near the corner of Mascoma and West Park streets, on the lot south of where the First NH Bank now stands (1994). Because the water pipes were kept empty in the winter to prevent them from freezing, it took eight-to-ten minutes to pump water from the river to the hydrants and the flames had time to spread and "clean out" West Park Street.

The one on the corner of West Park and Mascoma streets was an 1809 building occupied by the Durant & Perkins furniture company. Here the fire found a rich source of combustibles like paint, oil, varnish, furniture, and caskets. South of this building was the first so-called Odd Fellows Block owned by George Worthen, and it contained a store run by his son, Arthur, the Odd Fellows hall, and the armory of the local militia, Shaw's Rifles. South of that structure was a dwelling owned by P. E. Davis.

The trio of other buildings that were destroyed were small apartment dwellings—all owned by P. E. Davis—located in a row behind the three structures on West Park Street. The cause of the fire, which originated in the Worthen store, was undetermined.

Lebanon, 1761-1994 / 140

Before the fire there was a gristmill on the east side of the river where the four people are standing along Mill Street. The buildings that stood along the south side of Hanover Street were also destroyed by the fast-moving blaze. Brown Brothers hardware store, just west of the railroad bridge, was one of the few structures on the north side of Hanover Street that escaped damage. The Whipple Block stands in the upper right, and in the distance the Rising Sun Hotel. This view is looking east from High Street, with ruins of the Marston sawmill in the foreground.

The *Free Press* opined that, "The precinct pump is a big thing, but there ought to be a reservoir on the common large enough for both engines to pump from for several hours. It would be invaluable in case the pump . . . was out of order, and would help at any rate."

No such reservoir was constructed, but in March of 1884 the town established a committee to "procure" running water for the village, and at a meeting in May it recommended construction of a reservoir on a hill east of the center village, to be fed by a pumping station. The report was tabled, and when a motion was made to take it off the table, that motion was superseded by one calling for adjournment, which passed.

The adjournment, in hindsight, was critical, for the issue was not considered again until September 1886, when it was approved, but too late to be of service when disaster struck.

"Water Enough in the River, But No Hose"

There was, then, only the precinct pump and the one in the Mead-Mason Company's High Street shop when a watchman in the old Foundry Street sponge factory was awakened by a light coming through the window at about 12:45 A.M. on May 10, 1887. Looking out the window, the sentry saw two fires coming from the Water Street shop of Mead-Mason, on the opposite side of the river. Almost simultaneously the glow was spotted by a watchman at the Kendrick & Davis factory on Water Street, and by Noble

Photo taken from top of the Whipple Block looking west, with High Street at the top and Mascoma Street running up at the left. The space along the river where the men are standing was packed with buildings before the fire struck, and was rebuilt, only to be destroyed again by the 1964 fire. The building on the left with the chimney still stands in the same location just west of the bridge between Water and Foundry streets.

Webster, a guard at the Mead-Mason Company's lower shop whose house on Mechanic Street was to burn within hours. The Kendrick & Davis guard rang the company bell, while Mr. Webster pushed an electric buzzer connected to the fire gong at the upper shop and then rang the bell in the building where the fire had broken out.

By the time help arrived minutes later the fire had feasted on the wood shavings littered beneath and throughout the shop, and it seemed clear that the building would be a total loss. Firefighters, therefore, focused on preventing the fire from spreading, a job plagued by an inadequate water system and too few people for too much fire. A hydrant on Water Street could not be opened. Although Enfield firefighters were contacted by telephone at about 2:00 A.M. and arrived by train an hour or so later, attempts to reach the Hanover Fire Department via telephone were unsuccessful. (A virtual replay of what had transpired when Hanover had sought Lebanon's help in January.) A call to Concord also failed, and had to be routed to Bellows Falls, which notified Concord firefighters of the conflagration by telegraph. They loaded a steam fire engine onto a flatbed railroad car and hurried to town by rail, but arrived too late to help. As for the two pumps along the river, they were fine until the buildings they were housed in also burned. The first of these was the woodworking mill of Fire Chief Lyman Whipple, which held the precinct pump that had originally been in the gristmill. When the building burned the valve on the pump remained open and served to reduce the water pressure produced by the still-working (for a while, anyhow) steam pump in Mead-Mason's upper shop.

Feeding on the wood and probably fueled by the paint, varnish, and other chemicals

Residents and merchants raced against time during the fire of 1887 using Colburn Park and the streets around it as a repository for the goods they could save. This photo was taken some time after the fire was over when most of the goods saved had been removed from the park.

used to finish furniture, the fire spread almost simultaneously in every direction from its point of origin.

The flames traveled south to the key shop of Kendrick & Davis, and also devoured C. M. Baxter's machine shop, a sawmill, and part of the massive Mead-Mason lumber yard that was located just north of where Valley Street connects Water and Church streets.

Across the river from the Kendrick & Davis building was the old sponge factory building, which had only recently been sold by former Governor Samuel Hale to Albert Carter and George Rogers. That building caught fire, as did four others on Foundry Street, and three buildings on Mechanic Street, including the Mascoma House hotel.

The fire also moved eastward, thanks in part to one of the overhead bridges that connected the building on the west side of Water Street—where the fire started—to the three-story warehouse on the street's east side. The warehouse was packed with furniture awaiting shipment, and when the fire in its search for oxygen consumed one of the bridges and reached the warehouse, the wood and upholstery stored inside were just so much tinder. Flames shot an estimated two-hundred feet into the night sky, and firefighters were looking catastrophe in the eye. Catastrophe did not blink.

The fire destroyed a Mead-Mason tenement at the corner of Mascoma and Water streets, consumed the lower bridge over the Mascoma, and moved up the south side of Mascoma Street toward Colburn Park, claiming a lumber shed and three apartment buildings along the way.

Along the north side of Mascoma Street, from the corner of Mill Street, the fire consumed the livery stable and dwelling owned by Dan Scott, the Lafayette Hotel (which had moved only a few years before from its original venue on West Park Street), and a marble works and attached livery building operated by Henry Billings.

On the eastern side of Mill Street the destruction was total: a storehouse owned by O. T. Purmort, the sheds of the gristmill across the street, an apartment building that housed two families, a single-family home, and on the corner of Hanover and Mill streets, the pool hall and restaurant of P. W. Lemay.

As it worked its way along the west side of Mill Street, it destroyed Chief Whipple's woodworking shop (and the precinct pump), the Northern Railroad bridge over the river, a multi-story gristmill owned by William Shaw (which also housed Albert Rix's machine shop and doubled as the armory), the *Granite State Free Press* building, and most of a blacksmith shop near the intersection of Hanover and Mill streets.

The *Free Press* reported that the flames crossed the river to the High Street shops of the Mead-Mason Company, "the river side of which was covered with wood dust from the blower, and it went like tinder. Nothing could oppose it, and nothing tried to oppose it. Not a stream of water was put on, not a line of hose was laid on the west side until everything was flat. There was water enough in the river, but no hose."

This was the shop that housed the all-important steam pump that was such an integral part of the town's firefighting strategy. When the shop burned the pump went with it, leaving the fire free to gorge itself on another three-story warehouse full of furniture and large stacks of hardwood kept on the grounds. The sawmill of T. D. Marston, and five buildings on the east side of High Street were destroyed, but the chemical wagon prevented the fire from spreading to the west side of High Street, where it might have overtaken the thickly settled homes in the West Street area.

The flames also extended their reach to Hanover Street, along the densely packed south side of what is now the Lebanon Mall, and enveloped every building west of the Whipple Block, consuming a multitude of businesses. The Pulsifer Block owned by C. E. Pulsifer, who ran a grocery from the first floor and rented the second story to the local athletic club; on the lower floors of the Baldwin Block were the dry-goods store of J. E. Lincoln, C. E. Marston's undertaker's shop, and C. E. Colburn's grocery, while the top story was occupied by C. N. Walker's sewing machine and piano store (and his apartment), and the photography studio and residence of H. P. Granger; a building containing the cobbler shop of Anthony Rock (the second story of which served as a residence for a man and his mother), and the brick home and harness shop of W. P. McFee.

Once the fire had ripped through those buildings there was great anxiety about the flames jumping to the north side of Hanover Street, where a row of wooden blocks stood between Court Street and the Mascoma River. These buildings, however, survived when the fire was stopped by the brick of the Whipple Block.

The fire was out by morning, partly because it ran out of things to burn, and partly due to the efforts of the local firefighters and those who came from West Lebanon, Concord, Enfield, Hanover, and White River Junction. Nobody was killed in the inferno (which was attributed to a watchman's lantern being overturned in the Mead-Mason shop), but the Lebanon that greeted the dawn bore little resemblance to the one that had done so the day before. Thousands came to view the twelve-acres of ashes, and a child who had slept through the night reportedly inquired of his mother, "Where is up-street gone?"

One of the strangest sites was the clutter in Colburn Park. "There was not a spot ten feet square but what was piled with store or household goods, machinery, and property of almost every conceivable kind. Every dooryard deemed far enough away to be safe, on both sides of the river, was similarly occupied," the *Free Press* reported three days after the fire. (A no-press *Free Press* relied upon the equipment of the *Canaan Reporter* to publish its regular Friday edition, limited though it was to just four pages.) The paper's account of the story also included a reminder: "Alas! Alas! As we have twenty times expressed a fear, prophesying what has now occurred as only a question of time—the waterworks, though put under contract and to be completed by September, have come one year too late. How we have plead for them through all these years. They would have saved at least eight times their cost. But, alas, three months too late, and the burden increased upon the taxable property left in the precinct by the wiping out of one-fifth or one-sixth of it. O Folly, thy name is Humanity, and thou art everywhere."

It may have been salt in the wound, but the paper had a right to an I-told-you-so after its repeated pleas for improved fire protection were ignored. As early as April of 1870, in an article about George Worthen's plan to construct a new building in town (the one that burned in 1879), the *Free Press* expressed the hope that it would be a brick structure, reasoning that, "We must begin sometime to stop this tinder box business, or all burn up together."

In fact, because most of the buildings were wooden and closely situated, it seems doubtful that even a reservoir-fed water system would have prevented the 1887 fire from becoming a monster.

On the other hand, given the failure of the two pumps, it seems probable that a reliable source of water would have at least allowed firefighters to contain the scope of the damage, which was estimated at $300,000.

Perhaps the best perspective on the blaze came from none other than Jesse Sturtevant himself, whose furniture company had once been the linchpin of the industries along the river. "A vast amount of property, time and money gone," he said with a sigh. Then, just four days after the leveling of the shops that were once his empire, Jesse Sturtevant died.

The Aftermath

A week after the fire the town's churches established a multi-denominational relief committee to help those who were burned out of their homes, and the fire was the subject of sermons in village churches, as the local clergy trotted out biblical passages that drew connections between fire and sin, or preached the need for faith in the face of tribulation.

Rebuilding, which began while the ruins were still warm and followed much the same pattern that had existed before the fire, started with Thomas Marston's sawmill. The lower bridge was reconstructed, most of the merchants reopened in temporary quarters throughout the village, and manufacturers set up interim offices while waiting for their insurance to be adjusted.

Many of those who were thrown out of work did not wait for reconstruction. "Quite

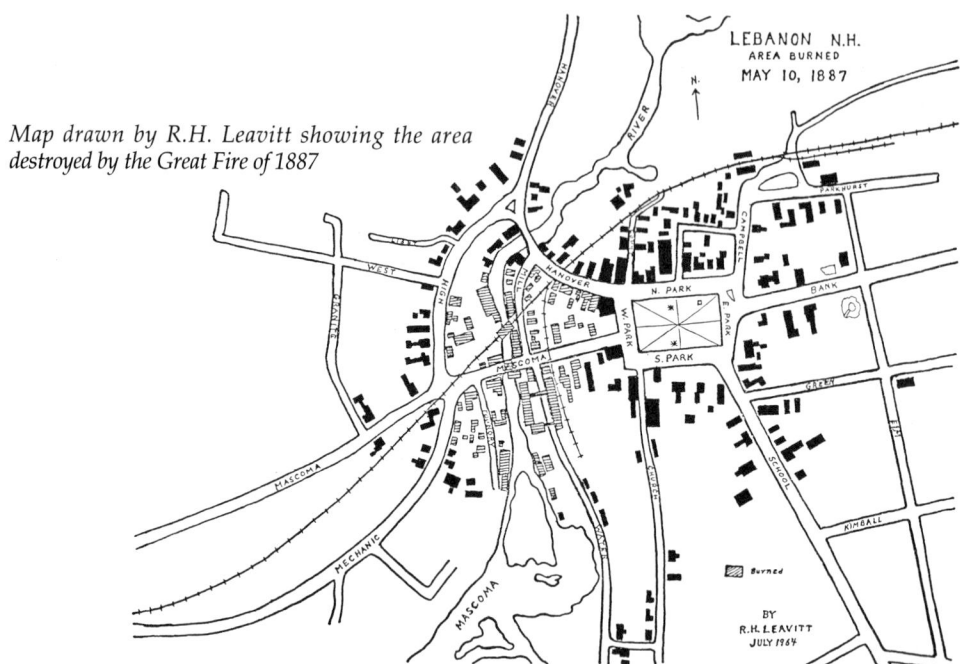

Map drawn by R.H. Leavitt showing the area destroyed by the Great Fire of 1887

a number of skilled mechanics [machinists] have left town, having offers of situations elsewhere," the paper reported. "On the other hand, house carpenters, masons and stone workers are coming to town."

The fire sparked a run on insurance policies, and within two weeks of the fire West Lebanon residents were petitioning for the creation of their own fire precinct, an idea that had been under consideration for some time.

To help facilitate redevelopment the railroad agreed to ship construction materials to burned-out businesses at a 90 percent discount, and a special town meeting approved a tax-exemption for Kendrick & Davis, Solomon and William Cole, A.W. Rix, Carter & Rogers, Byron Tilden, A.W. or W.F. Shaw, Mead-Mason, Muchmore and Whipple, Thomas Marston, N.B. Marston, T.P. Waterman, G.A. Elliott, and Ira Bucklin. (Mead-Mason & Co. did not reopen, although John Mason operated a vastly reduced lumber and woodworking business out of a small shop on Mascoma Street, just up Benton Hill from the lot that once housed the lower shop.)

The age of woodworking, however, was about to yield to the era of textiles, and one harbinger of that change came in 1890, when the site of the old upper shop was sold to the Everett Knitting Company of Manchester, which received a ten-year tax break to relocate in Lebanon. By 1892 the Everett works employed more than two hundred people, most of them women.

Although too late to help with the fire, the waterworks arrived on schedule. A sample of the water rates was published in September of 1887:

Each family not exceeding six persons.	$5.00
For each additional member of family.	.50

Lebanon, 1761-1994 / 146

For each additional family in same house.	4.00
For each private bath tub.	3.00
Each additional bath tub.	1.50
Each private water closet.	2.00
Each additional water closet.	1.50
For 40 gals. per day through gauge.	5.00
For each private stable in connection with house supply—for each horse.	1.00
For each cow.	.50
For each public bath tub.	5.00
For each urinal.	3.00
Barber shop, one chair.	3.00
Each additional chair.	1.50
Livery and boarding stable, including washing carriages—for each horse.	1.00
Livery stable for washing carriages.	5.00

The *Free Press* reported that water rates were set below those found in other communities in order to encourage quick and widespread hookups. The waterworks did not, however, render the town immune from disastrous fires.

Lebanon had a fine brickyard on Hanover Street that Jason Densmore had purchased from the Greeley family in 1881, but it did not play much of a role in the rebuilding process. The company reportedly had no bricks on hand after the Lebanon fire because their supply had been sent to Randolph, Vermont, which had suffered a disastrous fire the previous fall. Since the Densmore company only operated from April to October (anyone who has tried to dig through the frost can understand why), it had not had time to replenish its supply.

This, however, only partially explains why most of the buildings that grew out of the 1887 fire were built of wood, since bricks could easily have been shipped to town by rail. It also seems likely that in their haste to rebuild, those who were burned turned to wood as the construction material of choice, setting the stage for the disaster of 1964.

13

Woolen Mills, Canadians, and Catholics

L EBANON'S RECOVERY from the Great Fire of 1887 was so quick that, "neither the population record . . . nor the map of 1892 . . . gives any indication of the catastrophe," Edward N. Torbert wrote in *The Evolution of Land Utilization in Lebanon, New Hampshire*.

The town's population, in fact, increased 48 percent between 1880 (3,347) and 1900 (4,965), and the lots along the Mascoma River continued to carry most of the manufacturing load.

The nature of industry changed dramatically after the fire, however. When Mead-Mason officials decided by the end of 1887 not to reopen their shop, woodworking was essentially finished as a major industry in Lebanon. Into that vacuum stepped the woolen mills, which drove the town's economy for the next seventy-five years.

The era of large-scale woolen manufacturing in Lebanon actually predated the fire. In 1882, a year after voters approved a tax exemption for any company investing more than $5,000 in capital in town, Samuel W. Hale bought the old sponge factory building on Foundry Street and opened what was known as the shoddy mill, so called because it produced a cloth made from reclaimed woolen fabric.

Mr. Hale, an absentee owner who had been elected governor of New Hampshire from Keene in 1883, closed the mill in 1884 and sold the idle building in early 1887 to Albert Carter of Lowell, Massachusetts, and George Rogers of Ashland, New Hampshire. Before they could have the shop fitted up and reopened, however, the building was destroyed in the fire of 1887.

The other textile mill in Lebanon that predated the fire was Mascoma Flannel Company, which opened in 1883 on the Mechanic Street site known in modern times as the Rockdale or Rivermill complex. Frank Kendrick (Kendrick & Davis) and G. G. Kennedy lured the woolen operation from Manchester, and by 1886 it employed about fifty women who turned out more than twenty-thousand yards of woolen flannel each year. Because this mill was situated a few hundred yards downstream from the heart of the manufacturing district, it escaped the destruction of the 1887 fire.

Textiles came on in earnest after the fire, and no one played a larger role in their rise to prominence than George Rogers, who stands as the town's foremost entrepreneur of the late-nineteenth and early-twentieth centuries.

Immediately after the 1887 fire Mr. Rogers and Mr. Carter constructed a new shoddy mill on the west side of the river from the ruins of the old sponge factory and Hale mill. This factory, known as the Carter & Rogers mill and later the Lebanon Woolen Company, was built on the Foundry Street side of the Mascoma River where Kleen Laundry is now located (1994).

George Rogers was also a director of the Everett Knitting Works, which moved to Lebanon in 1892, after the town voted the company a ten-year exemption on its taxes. The Everett mill had been established in Manchester in 1888 by George A. Leighton and Rowland B. Jacobs, the latter later becoming judge of the Lebanon Municipal Court. The Everett was located on the High Street site where the Mead-Mason Company's upper shop had stood before the fire, and at its peak in 1928, the company employed about 300 people, mostly women who knitted and sewed together pieces of cloth to make union suits and underwear for customers that included Sears, Roebuck & Co. and the federal government. The complex also included a shop that made boxes used to ship the clothing, an on-site retail store that sold irregular garments to local customers, and a boarding house for workers (KindleNook, 1994) constructed in 1897.

In the early 1920s the Norfolk Knitting Mills of Norfolk, Virginia, moved to Littleton, New Hampshire, and it was combined with Lebanon's Everett Knitting operation in 1925 to form the Everett-Norfolk mill, a consolidation of two businesses owned by William Iselin & Company of New York.

In addition to his interests in the Carter & Rogers and Everett mills, George Rogers also was the founder and first president of the last of the big woolen mills to be established on the Mascoma. The Riverside Woolen Company, later known as the Lebandale Mills, opened in 1893 near the corner of Water Street (Whitman Press, 1994).

George Rogers' influence also extended beyond the mills. He was a co-founder of the Lebanon Electric Light and Power Company in 1890, serving as its first vice president and later as president. He was a director of the National Bank of Lebanon, helped to establish the Mascoma Savings Bank in 1899, and sat in the state legislature from 1897-98, and the senate from 1911-12. He also poured thousands of dollars into construction of the Lebanon Public Library building on East Park Street, and was said to have helped several young men through college.

His crowning achievement, however, still stands on North Park Street. In 1911 Mr. Rogers challenged the town to put up $25,000 toward construction of a magnificent hotel, and claimed he would put up $50,000. The public came up with its share of the money, and Mr. Rogers is said to have spent more than $100,000 to build and furnish the Hotel Rogers, which was constructed on the site once occupied by George Houghton's Pavillion store and home. The hotel, considered one of northern New England's finest during its heyday, was later owned by woolen magnate Bernard Goldfine. When his financial empire collapsed, Carl Witherell bought the hotel for $45,000 at a bankruptcy auction in 1963. By then, however, the hotel held but a shadow of its former glory. It was never full, and the dining room with its white-linen napkins had closed to the public after World War II. Some observers thought Mr. Witherell's

Built in 1882, the original "Mascoma Mill" on Mechanic Street in Lebanon was purchased by the American Woolen Company and later during the Depression, by Bernard Goldfine. It was occupied in the 1960s by the Rockdale Department Store.

investment was folly until he sold it at a handsome profit in the late 1960s to the federal government, which converted the building into apartments for the elderly. The structure still retains the name of its original benefactor: Rogers House.

George Rogers' death in December 1914 prompted a ceremony that was like the local equivalent of a state funeral. The *Free Press* reported that the display of flowers at the Congregational Church was unprecedented, the Carter & Rogers and Everett mills were both closed, and all businesses were closed from 1:30 to 5:30 P.M. Even school was only in session for half the day, and the question on everyone's mind, the newspaper said, was, "Who will take George Rogers' place?"

His wife Mary with her brother Charles Davis continued to operate the shoddy mill after his death, and the large, New Jersey-based, American Woolen Company purchased the Riverside (Water Street) and Mascoma Flannel (Mechanic Street) mills in 1899.

The factories flourished during the 1920s, but the Great Depression brought changes to the mill scene in Lebanon. The Everett-Norfolk mill cut its payroll in half shortly after the stock market crash of 1929, and those who still had jobs worked only part time until December 1, 1931, when the company closed for good. Its shop on High Street remained vacant until 1939, when the Lebanon Improvement Society convinced the E. Cummings Leather Co. to move its tannery to town from Woburn, Massachusetts.

Lebanon's other textile mills also shut down at various times during the depression.

Interior of the Everett Knitting Works factory on High Street, where women often labored twelve-hour days, six days a week

American Woolen reopened the Mascoma mill in the early 1930s, and when Bernard Goldfine purchased the idle Carter and Rogers shop on Foundry Street and restarted it in August 1932 under the name of the Lebanon Woolen Company, he was hailed as the town's economic savior for creating 120 new jobs in the teeth of the depression.

Mr. Goldfine also acquired the Riverside mill on Water Street in the late 1930s, and the idle shop was reopened under the name of Lebandale Mills.

It was common for husbands and wives to work in the same mill, and a family's economic status was often determined by which of the dozens of possible jobs its members held. Management was at the top of the scale, and some lived in houses owned by the company; weavers and spinners, who were paid according to their rate of production and were unionized, also held coveted jobs; at the bottom of the ladder were low-paying positions such as carders and dyers. (The color of the river often varied according to the color of the cloth being dyed in the mill.)

Teenagers often worked in the mills to supplement the family income. Lillian Dulac said she was the only one of the seven children in her family to complete high school. Her siblings all quit to work in the mills, some because they disliked school, but most because the family needed the extra income.

Olivine Lambert, who spent decades in the Lebanon woolen mills, recalled that her parents required both her and her brother to quit school prior to 1920 at the age of fourteen and work in the Mascoma mill. Her first job, as a spooler, paid slightly more than three-dollars for six days of work that normally consumed up to sixty hours. The factory bell summoned workers to the shop as early as 5:00 or 6:00 A.M., and they remained there until evening.

A 1924 look at the Mascoma Mill found that conditions on the top floor of the four-story building were far superior to the other floors because there was an ample supply of sunlight. The basement, on the other hand, was dark and damp, and the pots of dye gave off nauseating odors. "Many men were forced to wear rubber boots because of the water and chemicals on the floor . . . In going through the building we all felt slightly nauseated; this must have been due to either poor ventilation or else the unfamiliar smell of dyes."

By the mid-twenties, forty-eight hours was the weekly working standard, and the average weekly pay was about forty dollars for skilled labor and a little more than twenty dollars for unskilled employees. Workers did, however, begin to enjoy certain benefits as observed by three Dartmouth students who visited the mill:

> *No provision is made for recreation, rest rooms or any other social welfare. All personnel work is left to the foremen who of course, take very little interest in their subordinates. The company takes out a form of workman's compensation insurance; this is distinctly for the company's benefit because it frees them almost entirely from law-suits arising from personal injuries, etc. However, instead of paying for this themselves, it is deducted from the worker's wages at stated intervals. Certain specified sums up to $1500 are paid for injuries. In case of sickness two-thirds of the employee's weekly wage is paid to him. The company makes no provisions for housing their employees, but under certain conditions will help finance new homes.*

The mills' labor problems were infrequent, and one of the few strikes occurred shortly after American Woolen reopened the Mascoma mill on Mechanic Street in 1934. Unionized workers there picketed their non-union counterparts at the neighboring Lebanon Woolen Mill, prompting the 170 Lebanon Woolen employees to walk off the job. Lebanon Woolen workers told the *Free Press* that they had no qualms about working conditions, "but they did not like the embarassment of walking thru the lane of Mascoma mill strikers . . ." Both actions were quickly settled.

Only a month before, employees of the two companies had competed against one another in a tug-of-war, climbed a greased pole, and chased after a greased pig during a field day sponsored by the Mascoma mill.

There is no question that the lifeblood of the Lebanon economy was firmly rooted in the textile business, and while some residents have estimated that as many as 1,500 people worked in the woolen mills, that figure seems inflated even for those periods when the three mills were running three full shifts per day. Precise statistics are hard to come by because employment varied over the years, and the Riverside mill, especially, was prone to sporadic operation. However, somewhere around a thousand workers seems a reasonable peak number: A 1924 article about the American Woolen Company stated that the Riverside Mill employed about 200 workers, and the Mascoma mill another 290; during World War II, when more than 80 percent of their orders were related to the war effort, the Lebanon Woolen Company reportedly employed up to 400 people.

The fifteen-hundred figure may have come from combining the employees of the woolen mills with those who worked in one of the town's three garment factories. The Everett-Norfolk knitting mill was said to have employed about 300 workers—mostly women—prior to the time it closed in the depression; as many as 175 people worked in the Carter overall factory; and employment at the Carter & Churchill shop topped out at about 100.

In any event, there is no disputing that most of Lebanon's economic eggs were in one basket, and they were golden while Bernard Goldfine was laying them. That is, until the federal government caught up with him in the late 1950s and charged him with not paying several years' worth of income taxes. When that happened, the mills closed and the town's economy suffered badly.

The Second Migration

The clack of the looms not only altered the economics of the town, but it also spawned demographic changes. What had once been a largely homogenous, Yankee-Protestant community became one with a blend of immigrants from Italy, Ireland, Finland, Russia, Poland, England and, especially, the French-speaking Canadian province of Quebec.

Although the French-Canadian migration is closely linked in the public mind with the establishment of woolen mills in Lebanon, the first wave of immigrants actually preceded the first large-scale woolen mill. The federal census of 1850 recorded thirty-six residents of the town who were born in Canada, and the census of 1860 listed fifty-two. By 1870 that number had jumped to 211, as significant numbers of Canadians left the stagnant agrarian economy of their native land to search for better financial opportunities.

The textile industry had not yet settled in town, but there were jobs to be had on farms and in the Sturtevant/Mead-Mason woodworking factory, and the town was accessible from the north by virtue of its position on the railroad network that connected the town with Montreal and other Canadian cities.

The town's population of French-Canadians exceeded 400 by the dawn of the local textile era in the early 1880s; in 1900 it was more than 630, or about 13 percent of the town's residents, and a quarter of the town's 4,900 residents had at least one Canadian-born parent. By 1910 about 930 of the town's approximately 5,500 residents were immigrants, a figure equal to about 17 percent of the total population, and more than 700 of those 930 newcomers were from Canada. The French-Canadians were the town's single largest ethnic group, although Lebanon's numbers pale next to those of some other New England towns, where more than half of the residents were French-Canadian.

Still, Lebanon's Canadian numbers were substantial, and most of the town's immigrants settled to the north and west of the Mascoma River in a neighborhood extending from Mechanic Street at its southern end to the Mount Support Road on the north. The *Free Press* reported in 1883 that all but three of the thirty-five students in the Mount Support Road's neighborhood school (District No. 12) were French.

The tenements of Mechanic, High, and Hanover streets formed the spine of Lebanon's "Le Petit Canada," but one of the principal features of the neighborhood was the slope on the west side of High and Hanover streets. Up this hill ran a series of side streets that held the bulk of the French-Canadian population: West, Light, Mason, Eldridge, Summer, Winter, and Barrows streets all went uphill in a westerly direction and most were either bisected or connected by Granite, Ela, and Colburn streets, which ran on a north-south axis. (Not to put too fine a point on it, but there were even distinct neighborhoods within this larger neighborhood, and a kid growing up on West Street would rarely venture to, say, Eldridge Street.)

West Street, extending from High Street up to Young Street, provides a useful example of a French-Canadian neighborhood in the heart of the mill district. Only four of the forty-three households on the street in 1910 had no Canadian heritage, and two-thirds of the families had at least one spouse who was born in Canada.

One study of the Mascoma mill pegged the number of French employees at nearly 75 percent of the 270 who worked there, and only three of the households on West Street were without at least one person employed either in a woolen mill or apparel factory. Frequently, it was teenage offspring, non-nuclear family members, or a boarder who worked in the mill. Half the street's households included at least one person who was not a member of the nuclear family, an arrangement that in large part reflected the immigration process itself.

Typically, one or two male family members left the farm in Canada to find work in the United States, and those new arrivals often boarded with the established immigrants until they were able to secure work and financial stability. An immigrant then usually either sent for his wife and children or returned to Canada to retrieve them, spreading the word while he was there about the opportunities available to immigrants, and encouraging others to follow. If they did, the cycle repeated itself.

Living with extended family members or lodgers probably made for tight quarters, but it also allowed the millworkers to save money to buy homes, and about half the West Street families owned their dwellings in 1910. Perhaps not surprisingly, most of those were older immigrants who had come to America (if not directly to Lebanon) prior to the 1887 fire.

Although there was economic opportunity in Lebanon, the immigrant also encountered some obstacles, not the least of which was language. Since many immigrants planned to return to Canada after making money in the mills, they made no effort to learn English, nor did they necessarily need to. A distinct French-Canadian culture existed within which an immigrant could survive apart from the English-speaking population by working in the French climate of the woolen mill, doing business only with French-Canadian businessmen (like grocers Joseph Lemieux and Gideon Bennett), and attending French-language masses at the Sacred Heart Church.

Fostering this separatism in the early years was "L'Union St. Jean Baptiste," a club established in Lebanon in 1876 for the purpose of "rendering aid to our members and their families" and to help immigrants with their transition to American life. Such societies commonly existed in other New England towns with heavy French-Canadian populations, and they helped preserve the language and culture of the immigrants and regularly held social gatherings among their membership.

Writing about other textile towns with heavy French-Canadian populations in *The French-Canadian Heritage in New England*, Gerard J. Brault observes that many bluebloods "felt threatened by [the immigrants'] attachment to their own language and religion, and resented that many had no intention of settling permanently in New England." He also notes that there was sometimes resentment toward the newcomers on the part of working-class residents who felt that their wages were being undermined by the arrival of immigrants willing to work for cheaper pay.

The tendency to cling to the old language and resist assimilation probably contributed to some of the early antipathy that existed between the largely Catholic French-Canadian immigrants and some of the old-time Protestant Yankees in Lebanon. "There was a definite line," said Earle Burke in an opinion shared by several others, including Francis Dulac, who believes his father experienced such enmity in his woodworking business at the turn of the century. However, whether that feeling had its roots in religion, ethnicity, or both, was not clear, said Mr. Dulac. What is clear is that the Mascoma River was the point of demarcation between the turf of the Yankees and that of the French-Canadian immigrants.

The resentment toward the immigrants may also explain, in part, why some French-Canadians bucked the pressure to hold fast to the customs of the old country and chose to Americanize their names. In Lebanon, for example, some members of the Boisvert family changed their names to Greenwood, some of the LeBlancs became Whites, and some of the LeBruns adopted the name Brown.

Sacred Heart Church

There also was friction between the French-Canadians and the local Irish population over control of the Catholic church. Segregated from the Yankees by education, language, geography, and economics, the church was the focal point of French-Canadian life.

"Although early parish records reflect relatively equal Irish and French Canadian distribution (as well as others) in the population, in later years the Franco-American influence would be predominant," the church's history says.

Madeline Townsend, who attended the Sacred Heart School in the 1920s, sums up the division said to have existed within the church between the French-Canadian parishioners and those of Irish descent: "It was because the Irish had built the church and then the French were overtaking them in numbers and beginning to rule in the church, and there was great animosity there."

With its mixed population, the parish saw an alternating succession of Irish and French priests. The Sacred Heart Church moved from Parkhurst Street to a lot on School Street (Ricker Funeral Home parking lot, 1994) in 1878, the same year that Patrick J. Flanagan was appointed to succeed Francis Trudel, who had been appointed the first full-time parish priest in 1875. The immigrants' influence was clearly in effect by 1881, when Father Flanagan was succeeded by Moses Laplante, a French-Canadian priest who took night classes to improve his English, as did a number of immigrants who found a friend in instructor Oliver Burnap.

One of the most popular Irish priests was James Hogan, who served from 1913 until his death in 1937, the longest tenure of any Sacred Heart priest. It was on his watch that the local Knights of Columbus group was established in 1927, the Catholic Daughters organized in 1928, and the brick convent on Hanover Street was built in 1932, two years after a fire destroyed one of two wooden convent buildings.

An early twentieth-century postcard depicts a sign welcoming the Bishop to the old Sacred Heart Church on School Street. Befitting the town's French-Canadian heritage, it is in both English and French.

By then, the immigrant population had swelled the church's ranks to make it the largest single denomination in town, a fact reflected in a 1931 survey conducted by the New Hampshire Bible Association to determine religious affiliations in town:

FAMILIES BY DENOMINATION	LEBANON	WEST LEBANON
Advent	7	3
Baptist	177	20
Catholics	540	106
Christian	9	5
Christian Science	14	2
Congregational	180	217
Episcopal	29	41
Friends	3	2
Presbyterian	5	3
Methodist	219	31
Unitarian	72	12
Universalist	21	7
Others	147	13

Next to the church, the second-most important institution to French-Canadians was the school, and in 1889 the Sacred Heart parish established a parochial school in a two-room building near the corner of Granite and West streets. That school building, which still stands, housed fifty-eight students in that first year, more than one-hundred by 1890, and more than double that number by 1894.

Faced with a space crunch, church officials in 1909 constructed a new school on Eldridge Street and replaced most of the lay teachers with an order of nuns, the Sisters of Mercy, whose arrival and journey from the train station to the convent on Hanover Street was something of a spectacle, according to the history of the church: "From the station down Hanover Street all business was suspended while the sisters passed. Proprietors and clerks were at their doors to enjoy the sight. Windows were opened and every inch of space filled."

Sacred Heart, like most parochial schools, was long on discipline. Students were taught to stand when a nun or priest entered the classroom. Lillian Dulac recalled that when the children went outside for recess while she was a student there in the 1920s, boys played together on one side of the playground, and girls did likewise on the other.

Like all parochial schools, religious education played a large role at Sacred Heart, where students had most of the same holidays off as students in the public school system, but also certain religious holidays unique to Sacred Heart. Classes were cancelled on Good Friday, for instance, when students were required to attend mass.

Tuition in the early years was fifty-cents per month, recalls Robert Emery, a student at the school in the mid-1930s, and Mrs. Dulac says that a family sending more than one child to the school paid for the first child to attend, but not for the others.

The nuns, meanwhile, led strictly regimented lives: As late as the 1960s they could

The original Sacred Heart School building today sits to the left of another Lebanon landmark, Frank and Muriel Maville's donut shop on Granite Street.

only leave the convent in pairs and were not allowed to drive, eat in public, or stay overnight at someone else's house.

One of the church's enduring characters joined Sacred Heart in 1957, when the imperious Frank J. Crowley was named pastor of the church. "Father Crowley often had to remind people that his name was Frank, but obvious to all was the frankness of his personality," the church history states. Actually, someone who did not know his first name probably could have guessed it without much effort. Father Crowley stories are legion within the parish, where the standing joke was that the diocese sent maverick priests to Father Crowley to be straightened out. Whether is was true or not, many of the priests who worked under him felt that they were being punished, and they considered their stay in Lebanon no laughing matter. Father Crowley imposed curfews for the curates and locked the rectory doors at 11 P.M., a practice that prompted one frustrated priest to check into the Hotel Rogers late one night at the expense of the parish.

A group of local men incurred the Wrath of Crowley one night in 1960 while returning dozens of metal folding chairs to the basement of the church. In the middle of the noisy undertaking a window of the rectory flew open and out popped the imposing white-haired head of Father Crowley for what the volunteers presumed would be a word of thanks. Instead, they received a blunt admonishment to keep the noise down so he could sleep.

Among Father Crowley's strengths, however, was raising money for the church. "Everybody gave because they felt they'd better," recalls Norman Decato.

Assimilation

Although a large number of French-Canadians spoke French in their homes well into the twentieth century, many also made efforts to integrate themselves into the larger community. Night classes in English and American culture, begun as early as the 1890s, continued to be taught to millworkers into at least the 1920s, offering classes in Americanization as well as basic skills.

By the time the Sacred Heart Church moved in 1942 from School Street into a new building at the junction of High and Hanover streets (Hough Square, smack in the middle of the French-Canadian neighborhood), the barriers between the Catholics and the Protestants had fallen. The second- and third-generation French-Canadians were better assimilated into the culture (although many still rightfully cling to their heritage with fierce pride), and by World War II the ill will between the groups was largely confined to memory. Yet another sign that integration was complete came in the late 1950s, when French masses were discontinued at Sacred Heart Church. Odore Gendron, who was a Sacred Heart priest at the time and who later became Bishop for the diocese of Manchester (comprising the entire state of New Hampshire), said French masses were no longer necessary by the late 1950s because everyone in the parish either spoke or understood English.

Although the ethnicity of residents on the hill behind the Sacred Heart Church has been somewhat diluted over the years, the neighborhood retains some of the old French-Canadian flavor. Enough so that when Robert Boisvert was re-elected to the city council from Ward II in 1982 by a margin of only five votes over local blue-blood Roger

Wood, Mr. Boisvert's assessment of the victory was that it was no victory at all. "Winning by five votes in the French-Canadian ward is to lose," he told the *Valley News*.

Holy Redeemer

While Catholics in Lebanon attended the Sacred Heart Church, West Lebanon also had a sizeable Catholic population, most of whom usually crossed the river to attend mass at Saint Anthony's Church in White River Junction, a practice that continued until 1901. That year, however, West Lebanon was made a mission of the Lebanon parish and construction of the Holy Redeemer Church on Main Street in West Lebanon was completed in the fall.

In 1907 Holy Redeemer joined with St. Denis in Hanover to form a new parish under the guidance of Reverend James McCooey. He was succeeded about 1918 by Father John Sliney, who remained with the church for nearly thirty years before he was transferred to Laconia and succeeded in West Lebanon by his brother, Father Francis Sliney.

Holy Redeemer became its own parish in 1953, and Bishop Matthew F. Brady appointed Father Joseph Shields as the first pastor. The church bought the house at Eight Maple Street for use as a rectory, and a garage adjoining the church was converted into a parish hall and religious education center.

The original wooden, mission-style church seated 180, and the 200 families who belonged to the parish in 1960 encountered a standing-room-only situation at all three of Father Edward J. MacDonald's Sunday-morning masses. By November of that year ground was broken on a new church building at the junction of Maple and Tracy streets, and Paul McNamara led a fund drive in which parishioners were asked to pledge a day's pay each month for thirty-six months to help finance the building. The new facility, built at a cost of $132,342, seats 400 and was dedicated on September 10, 1961, by Bishop Ernest J. Primeau.

14

A Penny Saved

NBL

On October 6, 1829—in the middle of a depression—architect Ammi Burnham Young walked into a building of his own design on the corner of what was then called Pleasant Street and deposited $223 in the Bank of Lebanon. The bank, which was granted a twenty-year charter by the state in 1828, had opened only the day before, and at the present time it continues in operation as the city's oldest business and one of the oldest banks in the state.

It started with one-hundred-thousand dollars in capital raised by selling a thousand shares of stock at one-hundred dollars each. A hundred-thousand dollars was a large sum in those days, especially considering that the nation's 329 banks only had about fifteen-million dollars in cash reserves among them.

A list of the charter members reads like a Who's Who of the town in the early nineteenth century and provides some indication of who had money to invest and what ventures were profitable at that time. Among the charter members who either owned or had interests in local mills were Phineas Parkhurst, who also had his medical practice and raised mules, Thomas Waterman of West Lebanon, tanner Richard Buswell, John Ticknor, and woolen mill operator Amos Bugbee. Men listed on the bank charter who kept taverns and/or stores were Timothy Kenrick, Stephen Kendrick, Wareham Morse, and postmaster Calvin Benton, who also ran the Lafayette Hotel after the death of his father, William Benton. The latter, while a charter member of the bank, died before it opened in 1829. Roswell Sartwell owned the inn along the Fourth New Hampshire Turnpike at the corner of Main and Bridge streets in West Lebanon, selling it sometime around 1829 to Gideon Dickinson, who was also a charter member. Samuel Barrows was in the brick manufacturing business, Alpheus Baker was a mason and prominent builder who also served as a selectman, Uriah Amsden was a carpenter and cabinet-maker, George Lathrop was town moderator for over forty years, and Samuel Selden

The original National Bank of Lebanon building on the Bank Street lot where the library currently stands

was a lawyer. David Hough, Jr., was a sometime-selectman and state representative, as was farmer Diarca Allen. Richard Kimball lived in West Lebanon, had interests in the Fourth New Hampshire and White River turnpikes, and had worked on construction of the Erie and other canals. His brother Robert, who moved to Lebanon from Plainfield in 1835, was a charter member who was president of the bank from 1840-1865.

The Bank of Lebanon was not only the bank of Lebanon—it was also the region's bank, and the only one in the immediate area for about the next thirty years. The charter contained the names of storekeepers Elias Lyman of Hartford and John Bryant of Plainfield, and the list of non-Lebanon stockholders in the late 1830s included the community of Shakers in Enfield (sixty-eight shares), Dartmouth College President Nathan Lord, and residents of Hanover, Cornish, Windsor, and Thetford. The charter even required notices of directors' meetings to be posted in not only Lebanon, but also Hanover, Plainfield, and Enfield.

The 1830s were hardly the salad days of the banking industry. In fact, at least one local newspaper of that period ran a regular column that handicapped the relative health of banks in the New England states and New York, and not all of the ratings were encouraging. Putting money in a bank was widely seen—not entirely without justification—as a risky venture. The Bank of Lebanon, however, seems to have been fairly stable for its time.

In its annual report to the state banking commission made in 1830, the bank listed $141,000 in assets, including $127,374 in collectibles (probably most of that from loans) and $10,983 in cash. Its liabilities totaled $139,805, which included $100,000 in capital stock and $35,705 in circulated bank notes that could be redeemed for cash.

The bank, like others, issued its own notes, and except for the words "Bank of Lebanon" written in block letters across the front, they closely resembled dollar bills, right down to the portraits of George Washington and Benjamin Franklin on the front. However, the bank's charter stated that the corporation could not issue more in bank notes than it had received in stock payments, and records show the Lebanon bank started with twenty-thousand dollars worth of bank notes in various denominational values, only one-fifth of its total capitalization.

The charter also contained other provisions designed to protect depositors. The chief executive officer was required to place a twenty-five-thousand-dollar bond to guard against mismanagement; no stockholder could borrow from the bank until they paid for their stock in full, and then not more than 50 percent of the amount of stock they owned; the bank also was prohibited from lending more than ten-thousand dollars to any one person or business. Even into the 1960s the bank had a twenty-thousand-dollar federal limit on how much it could lend to any one borrower.

To paraphrase President Calvin Coolidge, the business of the bank was business, and many of the loans recorded in its early years went to people who were well-established operators of mills, stores and inns, or to people looking to set up machine shops or other commercial enterprises. It also offered checking (but paid no interest on deposits), and like most commercial banks of the age did not add savings accounts until the 1960s. It did, however, take care of its stockholders with annual dividends, continued without interruption until the stock was redeemed by the Bank of Ireland in 1987.

Interest on loans was the bank's chief source of profits, and money was lent with

James Kendrick, first cashier of the Bank of Lebanon, served for forty-seven years and guarded the bank's money as if it were his own.

great care. A bank examiner's report from 1849 stated that, "The total loss of the bank by bad debts during the twenty years of its existence under its former charter was $200 only—a fact which shows at once a well-managed institution and a solvent community around it."

There was, to be sure, continuity in personnel. The bank had only three managers in its first ninety-four years, and the first set the tone for both longevity and caution. He was James H. Kendrick, Stephen Kendrick's son, who had cut his financial teeth clerking in his father's store. As the bank's "cashier," he ran the day-to-day operations for forty-six years—from 1829 until his death in 1875, when he was succeeded by his son Edward. James Kendrick lasted so long, in fact, that his son served only thirteen years as cashier before his own death in 1887, at the age of sixty. Charles E. Cooper then took over for a thirty-six-year run that ended in 1923.

James Kendrick could see the bank from his home on South Park Street, and he seems to have guarded the bank's money as if it were his own. He had a crude alarm system with liquid batteries rigged up to his house to discourage any intruders who might have been inclined to make clandestine withdrawals during non-business hours. Furthrmore, "to protect himself from possible kidnappers [Mr. Kendrick] had double doors and barred windows installed on his bedroom," according to the Lebanon Historical Society's *6th Annual Report*.

Phineas Parkhurst, the bank's first president (a position like chairman-of-the-board that he held without pay until his death in 1844), was no stranger to banking, having functioned as a de facto town bank before there was one. He was a perennial lender in the days when wealthy private citizens were a main source of loans, and mortgage records indicate that he continued to lend money on a private basis even after the bank opened. In at least one case, a loan he had made privately was transferred into a bank mortgage, an indication, perhaps, that he also functioned as a loan officer.

The state renewed the bank's charter in 1848, and it remained under state domain until 1865, when it received federal charter number 808, and its name was changed to the National Bank of Lebanon. It carried that name for more than a century, changing little until the mid-1960s, when it became the first bank in the state to open a branch office under the 1963 state law that allowed branch banking for the first time.

West Lebanon was a logical location for the first branch, because a 1964 study on the feasibility of branch banking found that: ". . . the bank's share of the West Lebanon business is poor because of the proximity of White River Junction banks and the superior shopping facilities of the White River area. Conversely, the draw of the Bank into such isolated communities as Enfield and Canaan points up the lack of banking facilities near these towns."

The bank opened a branch on Main Street in West Lebanon in 1965, and in the early 1970s added a second West Lebanon branch on Route 12A. Branches were later extended to Enfield, Meriden, and Plainfield in an attempt to capitalize on the lack of banking in those smaller towns.

In September 1966, the bank installed drive-up service at its headquarters in downtown Lebanon, becoming the first in the area to do so. The 1960s also saw the addition of saving accounts, and the 1980s brought automatic-teller banking to NBL.

From 1964-1979, the bank's assets climbed from six-million to forty-million dollars, making it an attractive investment opportunity for a larger bank looking to gain entry into the thriving Lebanon-Hanover market. That happened in 1985, when NBL directors sold out to the Manchester-based First NH Bancorp in the banking craze of the 1980s. The National Bank of Lebanon was renamed the First New Hampshire Bank of Lebanon, then just First NH Bank, and became part of the First NH Bancorp system now owned by the Bank of Ireland. Although the parent company's financial difficulties in the late 1980s and early 1990s led to the closing of the smaller branches, the three Lebanon locations—the West Park Street site and the two branches in West Lebanon—were kept open.

Lebanon Savings Bank

To meet the demand for home mortgages and savings accounts, the directors of the Bank of Lebanon received a state charter in 1870 for the Lebanon Savings Bank. Although technically a separate bank, the two shared office space, directors, and staff (such arrangements were common statewide). The National Bank of Lebanon handled the commercial loans and checking accounts, while the savings bank offered passbook savings accounts and home mortgages.

When they outgrew their headquarters on the corner of Bank and East Park streets, it was the savings bank's profits that paid for construction of the four-story Bank Building on West Park Street in 1893.

How much strain the cost of that construction placed on the resources of the bank is hard to say, but it failed two years later in the middle of a long and severe depression.

The bank still had more assets than liabilities on September 1, 1896, when Judge Alonzo P. Carpenter issued an injunction that prevented savings bank officers from receiving or paying out deposits. Bank officials had asked the state to seek the injunction, even though the bank's assets at the time exceeded its liabilities by fifty-six-thousand dollars.

One explanation for the failure may be found in the *Granite State Free Press* account of September 4, 1896, which reported that some large depositors made a run on the bank in order to invest in the securities market, and bank officials would have had to sell their investments at a loss to cover those withdrawals. Rather than do that, officials opted to close the bank and freeze its assets, according to the paper.

A year later the bank's trustees voted to liquidate its assets. Again, the plight of the 2,960 depositors who had banked just under $900,000 was not atypical. Of the seventy-five savings banks in the state in 1896, twenty-five were in various stages of what would today be called bankruptcy. Lebanon depositors, however, were repaid in full over the nine-year period in which the bank liquidated its assets. The victims of Lebanon's next bank failure, in 1924, would not be so fortunate.

The People's Mistrust

The Peoples Trust Company was organized in July 1913, with Thomas P. Waterman of West Lebanon as its president, Lebanon insurance agent Thomas Dwyer as vice president, and Arthur Hough of White River Junction as the treasurer and chief executive. It opened on October first of that year in the Baldwin Block on Hanover Street (Lebanon

Hanover Street looking toward Colburn Park in 1922. The second structure from the right is the second Baldwin Block, now the site of the Lebanon Pharmacy.

Pharmacy, 1994) with $50,000 in capital, and by 1925 had more than a million dollars in deposits, thanks largely to Mr. Hough. An aggressive banker, one source from the period said, "He is unusually liked by everyone and enjoys the universal confidence of all. He takes a leading interest in all Civic undertakings and always has Lebanon foremost in his mind." Indeed, Mr. Hough was a gregarious personality who was a founder and president of the Lebanon Chamber of Commerce, and who also led the local war-bond effort during World War I.

The motto of his bank was "We Teach Thrift," but the failure of Mr. Hough to practice what his bank preached resulted in one of the biggest scandals in the town's history.

The Peoples Trust Company was closed by court order on January 13, 1925, and Mr. Hough was arrested and indicted on twenty-six criminal charges. In June of that year, he pleaded guilty to two of the counts: making a $25,000 loan to the president of the Rutland Marble Company without authorization from the bank's board of directors; and making a similarly unauthorized $20,000 loan to the Lebanon Machine Company, which was placed in receivership a month after the bank closed its doors. The bank's total loans to those two companies also violated a state law that prohibited a bank from lending more than 10 percent of its deposits to any one company. The *Free Press* reported that the Lebanon Machine Company had borrowed more than $200,000 from Peoples Trust.

Mr. Hough received concurrent five-to-eight-year sentences for the two counts to which he pleaded guilty, and he was not prosecuted for the other charges which accused him of criminal conduct both large and small. One alleged that he fraudulently siphoned off more than $431,000 from the bank, while several other charges claimed that he stole the war bonds that depositors had entrusted to the bank. He also falsified bank records to throw off bank commission investigators, according to another indictment. Mr. Hough was released from prison in 1930, having served the minimum of his sentence.

The betrayal felt by the community was palpable. Although savings depositors received about 75 percent of their money as the assets of the bank were sold off, the tens of thousands of dollars in checking accounts was lost forever. Many families lost their life savings.

Mascoma Savings Bank

The failure of the Peoples Trust Company haunted the Mascoma Savings Bank for years, even though Mascoma Savings officials had nothing to do with Mr. Hough's misdeeds.

Mascoma Savings was chartered by the legislature in 1899 to fill the savings void created by the failure of the Lebanon Savings Bank three years earlier. Frank Churchill was the bank's first president when it opened on April eighth of that year in quarters it shared with the National Bank of Lebanon on West Park Street.

It remained in that location until 1928, when it moved to the vacant Baldwin Block—the quarters formerly occupied by the Peoples Trust. The teller windows and the vault remained conveniently intact, but it was hardly a move that engendered public confidence in Mascoma Savings. "Many, many people associated that location with where it was that they lost some money," and were wary of doing business there again, says Reuben Cole, a former Mascoma Savings president. Some residents even went so far as to ask Mr. Cole's predecessor, Burton Whittier, to recommend a good out-of-town savings bank where they could keep their money.

Despite the negative public perception about the bank's new home, the Mascoma Savings Bank weathered the period and had $5.7 million in assets by the end of 1951, when the bank prepared to move again. This time, however, the bank moved to its own building on the lot formerly occupied by the Blodgett Block on the corner of North Park and Court streets.

The bank opened its new quarters in 1952. Other tenants on the ground floor included the Granite State Electric Company, the state liquor store, R. Thibault's jewelry store, and LaCroix's taxi stand. Upstairs were nine offices, three apartments, the law office of Fred and Robert Jones, and the Sun Life Assurance Company.

Although the venue was different, the bank's methodology remained the same. As Reuben Cole described it:

When I came to work for the Mascoma Savings Bank [in 1948], Bob Cratchit of A Christmas Carol *fame would have been very comfortable to work at the Mascoma Savings Bank . . . because nothing had changed in the way banking was done from the time Dickens was writing that story and 1948. Everything was done by hand. The high-tech objective was to buy stick pens that wrote well. You were always seeking a stick pen that would not drop a big blob of ink down on your ledger.*

One thing that had not changed much was Burton Whittier, a former World War I pilot who took over as head man in 1923 and remained for forty-two years.

Just as the National Bank of Lebanon was limited to checking accounts and prohibited from offering savings accounts into the 1960s, Mascoma Savings was limited to savings accounts and loans until the same period, when savings banks were first allowed to offer checking accounts.

Reuben Cole replaced Burton Whittier as bank president following Mr. Whittier's retirement on December 31, 1965, and Mr. Cole oversaw a period of growth over the ensuing twenty years that saw deposits jump from $9.6 million in 1966 to more than $100 million by the time he stepped down at the end of 1985. Much of that growth mirrored that of Lebanon itself in the wake of the arrival of Interstate 89.

The bank branched out for the first time in 1970 with a new building on Interchange Drive in West Lebanon. The new location was not a success, however, and the building was sold to McDonald's and razed for parking. Another office, on Main Street in West Lebanon, opened in 1980, the same year that the bank first offered automatic-teller service.

By then, Mascoma Savings Bank had expanded to Enfield and Canaan.

Although the Mascoma Savings Bank and National Bank of Lebanon competed with one another after both institutions began to offer checking and savings services in the mid-1960s, Mascoma Savings had invested in NBL stock over the years and owned 14 percent of its rival by 1987. (It was common for savings banks to own large shares of stocks in commercial banks, a practice that dated back to the days when they shared quarters, directors, and officers.)

When First NH was purchased by the Bank of Ireland in 1987 and First NH stockholders had to redeem their shares for cash, Mascoma Savings faced the prospect of paying tens of thousands of dollars in capital gains taxes for NBL stock that had grown from $16,500 to about $3.5 million. Instead, trustees reduced their tax liability and kept some of that money working in the area by establishing the Mascoma Savings Bank Foundation in 1987. The bank endowed the trust with a million dollars in 1988, and the interest earned has since been used to fund various charitable projects in the Upper Valley.

Lebanon Library

A receipt dated 1793 from Nathaniel Jewett to Nathaniel Storrs for "one share Lebanon Lybray" seems to be the earliest record of any library activity in town. Mr. Storrs may have been purchasing a subscription to the Lebanon Social Library, which was established in 1802 by Constant Storrs (Nathaniel's brother), Isaiah Potter, and David Hough. That library is believed to have been the town's earliest and is thought to have survived until possibly as late as 1832.

The town seems to have been without a library until 1874, when the *Free Press* editorialized on the need for such an institution. "If nothing more can be done," the paper said, "let's at least have a dictionary in the front entrance of the Town Hall."

Something more was done, however. Specifically, the Lebanon Agricultural and Mechanical Association opened a library in October of the following year in the

Thompson Block on North Park Street. The newspaper reported that the library had eight-hundred books, mostly related to farming and mechanical topics, and patrons paid a dollar per year for the privilege of borrowing two of them each Saturday. Circulation averaged about one-hundred books per month.

This collection was absorbed in 1880 by the Lebanon Library Association, the forerunner of the Lebanon public library which opened in 1889 on the first floor of the Soldiers Memorial Building.

The library quickly outgrew its space, however, and in 1908 the town received a twelve-thousand-dollar grant from philanthropist Andrew Carnegie to build a new facility. With a big financial assist from George Rogers and other leading businessmen, the town raised an equal amount and put up a new structure on the corner of Bank and East Park streets in 1909.

The two-story building, with a children's room in the basement, served the needs of the town until the 1980s, when a local committee headed by Theresa Lopata and librarian Jean Mansell launched an expansion drive that culminated in a two-story addition to the library that was dedicated in 1985. The annex, consisting of a new children's room on the ground floor and periodical, historical, and reading rooms on the second floor, was named after longtime Lebanon resident and former governor Lane Dwinell, who raised and donated substantial sums of money for the project.

A New Mobility

To the Auto Driving Public:
We may be a little slow and old fashioned, but don't you think we need to be considered a little?
There are so few of us left and we require so little it seems to us that it is very piggish and inconsiderate when you arrange it so that we can not even have a drink of cold water or a place to stand . . . [W]e have long been friends to man until he turned us down the for swifter automobile.
We are
THE FAITHFUL HORSE
—*Item in the* Granite State Free Press, *1930.*

There were, indeed, relatively few horses left in town when those words appeared in the paper. Lebanon residents, like those everywhere, wholeheartedly embraced the automobile.

When George Rogers ordered a Haynes-Apperson automobile from a factory in Kokomo, Indiana, in 1897 he became the first Lebanon resident to buy a car, although he was not the first person in town to actually have one. Rather than take delivery immediately, Mr. Rogers had the manufacturer store the vehicle until after the brutal New England mud season. During the period between payment and delivery Gilman Whipple and Mary Kimball jointly purchased a Stanley Steamer, which was delivered immediately and thus became the first car to arrive in town.

As George Rogers' brother-in-law, Charles Davis, remembered the Haynes-Apperson that arrived the following spring:

[It] was styled after the horse drawn buggy only much larger and heavier built. It had a straight up buggy dash (but no whip socket), full eliptic springs and a regular buggy seat which

The last parking space for horses in the 1950s occupied by Fred Manchester's horse and wagon

was deeply cushioned. Steering was done with a tiller which was fastened to an upright rod just back of the dash. It was powered by a two-cylinder horizontal motor beneath the body, which was connected with the rear axle by sprocket and chain. . . . Starting was by a crank about two feet long which connected with the motor through a hole in the side of the body. . . . The tires were pneumatics, about 30 x 3, smooth tread and if we got in to a mud hole we hired a horse or a yoke of oxen. The lights were two oil lamps with a candle power fully equal to two white beams. Instead of a horn there was a large gong under the floor which was worked by stamping on a button, like the gong on a trolley car.

 The town had fifty-two registered cars in 1907 (the first year the state began to register motor vehicles), and they were the exclusive province of the town's wealthiest residents. Six could boast of owning two automobiles: industrialist George Rogers, Carter & Churchill's Frank Bell, Rowland Jacobs of the Everett Knitting Mill, H.W. Carter & Son's namesake Augustus Carter, Doctor Frank Smith, and merchant Gilman Whipple.

 The number of cars in town grew to seventy-four by 1910, the year the Knapp Motor Car Company was established by Henry Knapp, who sold Overland-model cars from a garage on Parkhurst Street. What really set him apart, however, was his patent for a pair of skis that attached to the front wheels of a car to enable it to travel through snow in the days before decent roads, snow tires, and road salt. To demonstrate his invention, he drove through the snow to the 1916 Boston Auto Show in a Cole Eight automobile outfitted with his Napco Auto Skis. The *Boston Sunday Herald* reported that the skis on the front of the car made a track for the rear tires and predicted that, "This invention will undoubtedly prove a revelation to owners of automobiles in those sections of New England where the snow is so deep that motoring is practically forgotten and will allow the owner to use his car throughout the winter with absolute success."

Although the number of cars in town continued to grow through the rest of the century's second decade, the Lebanonians' love affair with the horseless carriage blossomed in earnest after the first world war, and the government began to pay attention to road conditions. Lebanon received its first hard-surfaced road when the town experimented with concrete slabs on Court Street in 1921. Still, most roads were dirt until the 1930s, and many people stored their cars from Thanksgiving to the end of mud season and relied on sleighs to travel over snow that was packed with the town's snow roller.

To meet the increasing demand for cars, the town had at least a half dozen auto dealers in the 1920s, of which two remain.

Smith Auto Sales, established by Frank A. Smith in 1907 as the Lebanon Auto Company, is the oldest surviving dealership of the dozens the town has seen over the years. Dr. Smith was a physician who believed cars could make it easier for him to call on patients at their homes. While that undoubtedly might have been the case, he caught the automobile bug and gave up his medical practice to sell cars full time from a garage on Mascoma Street (IGA parking lot, 1994). Smith Auto Sales became New England's first Buick dealer in 1912, and also held a variety of other franchises over the years.

Frank Smith's sons, Paul and Wade, joined their father in the dealership, and the business has been handed down through subsequent generations. Kenneth Smith, Paul's son, joined the company following his service in World War II, and took over the business in the 1950s. His son, Douglas, entered the business following his return from Vietnam in 1973.

The Mascoma Street building put up by Frank Smith was owned by the company until it was razed in the urban renewal of 1967. Smith Auto also sold used cars from a lot at 175 Mechanic Street until the company opened its showroom on Evans Drive in 1969.

The other enduring dealership from the early period is Flanders & Patch, which was founded in 1921 on Mechanic Street by George Langdon Flanders and his daughter and son-in-law, Edith and Robert Patch. In a 1990 history of the company, Robert Flanders Patch (son of Robert Patch, a founder) noted that the early cars came in just one color—black—and closing the deal often required the salesman to teach the prospective buyer how to drive.

In 1948 Flanders & Patch relocated to its present home at the western end of the so-called Miracle Mile, on a tract of farmland purchased from Ross Wood. That same year Robert Patch became the second generation of his family to enter the family business, and in 1950 his brother Richard came aboard.

Richard eventually served as president and Robert as treasurer, but the family's involvement in the company ended in 1985 when present owner Thomas Thayer purchased the dealership.

According to one account, trading in old cars for newer models was common in the 1920s, and prospective buyers shopped around for the best deal, although sometimes even that was not so great:

People buy whether they can afford it or not, even mortgaging their homes; 95% of almost every sale is 'on paper'. Local banks hesitate about lending money for this purpose so that a good many of the sales are made through investment houses, who charge 12% or 13% interest on the money. On a $1500 car the buyer must pay usually about 33 1/3 down and $136 per month for a year . . . Under these conditions the garage man [auto dealer] is lucky if he makes ends meet. One of his main sources of profit comes through accessories; these he sells at from 20% to 40% gain. Although the automobile is a great social benefit to the people, yet to many people it has meant financial ruin, because they buy cars which are far too expensive for their limited means.

As the fever took hold the landscape filled up with full-service gas stations that—unlike the self-service convenience stores which have become the modern automobile oasis—also offered car-repair service. Eighteen such garages were listed in a business survey taken in 1940, but only a handful of full-service stations remain.

The car craze also sprouted a host of ancilliary businesses selling auto parts, tires, and doing auto-body repair. The oldest of the former is Bailey Brothers auto parts on North Main Street in West Lebanon, founded in 1932 by Clifton and Hugh Bailey and now owned by Paul Bond, who has been with the company from the start.

The automobile also meant that people no longer had to live in the town where they worked, and as early as the twenties a few Lebanon residents began to motor to work at Dartmouth College and Mary Hitchcock Memorial Hospital in Hanover.

While the widespread use of the automobile sent the horse the way of the dinosaur (at least as a means of transportation) it also cut into the railroad's business. The Boston & Maine Railroad in 1932 dropped its round-trip fare to Boston to a dollar "in an effort to determine whether lower rates will attract to the railroad week end passenger traffic now moving over congested highways."

15

World War I

"One Moves We All Have To"

LIKE MOST communities, Lebanon was swept up in the patriotic fever when the United States declared war on Germany on the sixth of April, 1917. Even before that formal declaration of war, the collective town pulse had quickened in anticipation of the event. The Lebanon Chamber of Commerce enlisted one-hundred-sixty residents into the National Defense League following the chamber's annual banquet in late March. Attorney Fred Jones was credited with signing up over one-hundred volunteers for the league, which the newspaper described as an organization for "arousing, educating and directing the public sentiment of the state on the lines of true and sufficient preparedness for state and national defense, with especial regard to universal military training and service."

A crowd estimated at thirteen-hundred crammed into the town hall on April fifth for a patriotic lecture, and a week later the town was gearing up its victory-garden campaign that urged everyone to grow as much of their own food as possible to prevent a wartime shortage. By 1918 seven plots of land between eighteen and twenty acres were under cultivation. Two of the sites, covering a total of about thirty acres, were rented by the Chamber of Commerce, which offered prizes as an incentive to participate.

Local residents could not, however, grow sugar and coal, two items that were chronically in short supply. The *Free Press* reported in January 1918 that the coal shortage "was becoming a very serious matter," and said the Grafton County Electric Light and Power Company barely had enough coal on hand to fuel its plant for a week. Residents were urged to conserve a shovelful of coal each day, to heat with wood whenever possible, and to burn kerosene lanterns instead of electric lights. One unfortunate result was that the pipes in the Whipple Block froze and burst, causing water damage to the inventory of Richardson & Langlois' store on the floor below. The newspaper attributed the cause of the Sunday mishap to "a too extreme effort to conserve coal."

As for sugar, the *Free Press* noted that same year that, "During Lebanon's two big sugar days recently Pulsifer's grocery sold 7,580 lbs. of this commodity to their patrons. It was put up in two-pound bags and one was delivered to a customer... At times during the sale it was necessary to station a policeman at the door to keep the crowd from filling the store with a jam which hindered the work of dealing out the precious sweet stuff."

Residents were given cards at the town clerk's office that entitled them to two pounds of sugar each month, and the federal Food Administration also ordered cutbacks of wheat, meat, and butter.

By May 1917, the federal government had begun its campaign to pay for the war by issuing Liberty Bonds through local banks, and social pressure made it every family's patriotic duty to purchase the notes. The names of the buyers were published in the *Free Press*, and residents, clubs, and businesses bought them by the hundreds, raising almost $190,000 for the first bond issue. Like many communities Lebanon exceeded its quota for all four Liberty Bond campaigns, and news that the town was over the top was met with ringing bells and blowing whistles.

Congress passed the Selective Service Act in May 1917, and federal officials urged local leaders to make "Registration Day" a major celebration. Lebanon, never a town to pass up a parade opportunity, dutifully complied on June 5, 1917, when every man between the ages of twenty-one and thirty-one was required to sign up for the draft. As the *Free Press* reported the event:

On Registration day in Lebanon was held one of the largest parades seen here in years. Hundreds of school children with flags, as well as many adults, including Grand Army Veterans and many of the men who registered. A band concert was given in the evening by Hough's Band, but unfortunately a rain set in and marred the pleasure of the listeners. Four-hundred and sixty-five men registered during the day, and nearly twenty enlisted in the national guard.

Notable among the enlistees were two men who were exempt from service. The Reverend J. K. Miller of the Baptist church resigned his position to go overseas and work at a YMCA post, while Harry Farnham waived his postal-worker exemption and enlisted for military duty.

Much of Lebanon's business and social life revolved around the war. The mills turned out material that was used by the army, and the women who worked at Carter & Churchill and Carter & Sons toiled overtime to make hospital garments. The Everett Knitting Works employed as many as two-hundred and fifty workers who knitted more than a million undergarments for the army and navy.

Lebanon had two Red Cross branches—one in Lebanon and another in West Lebanon with over three-hundred members—and carnivals, pageants, lectures, balls, and other events raised money for the cause. The box of supplies shipped by the Lebanon Red Cross chapter in January 1918 contained more than twelve-hundred surgical dressings and bandages, seventy-five shirts, a dozen convalescent robes, and nine shoulder wraps. In May 1918, the West Lebanon branch sent a package containing an outfit for six soldiers as well as forty-nine-hundred surgical dressings, forty pair of socks, sixteen pair of "wristers," twelve handkerchiefs, ten sweaters, twenty "surgical shirts," and three sets of pajamas. In addition to separate Red Cross agencies, Lebanon and West Lebanon also supported their own Special Aid societies—relief agencies comprised of women who prepared "comfort bags" for the men overseas.

Lebanon sent 372 residents to the trenches of France, Belgium, and other World War I battlefields. Most Lebanon soldiers were given big sendoffs, such as the one in late May 1918, when the firemen presented the "boys" with wristwatches.

One soldier, Branch Campbell, wrote to his aunt in Lebanon and described his new home in France as a six-foot-wide ditch with a "scanty" roof of sheet iron and a few rocks piled on top. The ends of the trench were blocked up with corrugated sheets of iron and bags of sand, and there was little chance that the soldier would ever confuse it with the Hotel Rogers. Built for eight, the trench was occupied by twenty soldiers, which made sleeping a challenge: "Packed in like sardines," soldier Campbell wrote. "One moves we all have to."

About the food he had no major complaints as he recounted the previous night's meal of bean soup, steak, bread, and coffee; and that day's breakfast of salmon, bread, butter, and coffee. The only thing they craved, he said, was cigarettes and tobacco, and the YMCA periodically provided a modest supply of that.

Byron Clark wrote to his family in 1918 and urged them to "tell everyone you see to send every magazine they can get over here. A one-cent stamp will bring one and they are worth so much here."

Some families, to their despair, received German postcards with the briefest of messages. One such missive arrived in the autumn of 1918 at the Carlisle family home at 23 Eldridge Street. It was from Raymond Carlisle, who informed his family that "I am in a hospital in the German's hands. Got three wounds—two in the leg and one in the face. They got me July 18th." He eventually recovered from his wounds and returned home.

Bad as it was, a postcard was still more welcome than a telegram, which was the federal government's way of delivering news that a soldier had died. The first Lebanon resident to receive one was Mrs. Ranile Guyer, who learned that her son, Arthur, had been killed in the landmark Battle of Belleau Wood.

The Arthur Guyer American Legion Post in Lebanon was named for him as the first Lebanon man to die in World War I. Also, Guyer Street—between High and Granite streets—was named for Arthur. Following World War II, the American Legion Post added the name of Pat Carignan to create the Guyer-Carignan Post #22.

Besides Arthur Guyer, ten other Lebanon soldiers died in the war, some from fighting and others from disease.

A cable arrived on October 14, 1918, at the home of Frederick Emerson, informing them that spinal meningitis had claimed their son, Lloyd, in a French hospital on September twenty-fifth. With his Dartmouth education, talent for drama, and ceaseless optimism that had won him a wide circle of friends, he was, the *Free Press* reported, "a young man of great promise."

Only the day before Lloyd Emerson's death, Lebanon soldier Robert Pease Snow of the 103rd Infantry was killed by a shell in the Battle of Saint Mihiel, another of the war's major campaigns. Later that fall, a letter from Company Chaplain A. G. Butzer arrived at the home of Robert's father, John W. Snow:

One of the many floats in Lebanon's World War I victory parade

Robert was killed in action with four of his pals by an enemy shell, dying the death of a soldier. He had no pain or drawn out suffering, for he passed away immediately.

We took his body a good way back of the line to a quiet spot, and there with his four comrades laid him to rest. A large number of the boys were present for the services.

The flag he gave his life for, was spread over him while the funeral service was being read. A gun salute was then fired in his honor, and at the close the bugler blew 'taps,' the call in the army which signifies that the day is done and the soldier's work ended. Taken all together, it was a beautiful service.

The grave, wrote the chaplain, was marked with a cross and metal nameplate and surrounded with a small fence. Robert Snow also was honored by a local veterans group, as the Lebanon chapter of the Veterans of Foreign Wars was named after him.

News of a German surrender sent residents to the streets on November 7, 1919. The fire gong rang, bells clanged, people broke out their flags and horns, and a parade broke out. When darkness fell, oil-soaked bricks blazed from the fenceposts around the park, the Kaiser was hung and burned in effigy, and bonfires were torched at the east and west ends of the park. The band, Hough's, played on.

Problem was, the rumored surrender had not yet taken place. This "false armistice," as it was known, was played out in towns up and down the east coast.

No matter. When bugles signaled the formal cease-fire on November eleventh, the town did it all again. The ringing of the fire gong at 4:45 A.M. brought hundreds from the streets to prepare for the big celebration. At an early-morning meeting it was decided that mills, banks, stores, and schools would be closed. At 2:00 P.M. scores of cars—all decorated—were in line, headed by a truck with the Hough's Band, and followed by a fire truck, and private cars. The route was to West Lebanon, where a hundred or more cars from White River Junction, West Lebanon and Hanover, fell in, making over 300 cars in line.

After parading through White River Junction and back through West Lebanon the procession returned to Lebanon and broke up.

Another parade marched through the streets that night bearing a coffin meant to symbolize the Kaiser. Hundreds gathered at Rogers and Whitney Park (Eldridge Park, 1994) for a bonfire, and the night wound up with a dance at the town hall.

A more formal observance of Lebanon's role in the war was held in the fall of 1919, featuring a parade, address by Governor John H. Bartlett, band concert, baseball games, banquet, fireworks, and a ball for the servicemen.

The town was not without its war heroes. Isreal J. Chamberlain won the Distinguished Service Medal for a year and a half of service in France, and Chester McArthur, a former Lebanon resident, won the Distinguished Service Cross for evacuating wounded soldiers from front-line-trenches in the Battle of Somme in July 1918.

The war's legacy continued even into 1921, when the bodies of Lebanon soldiers began to be shipped home. The first was that of William Longever, who died of pneumonia in a Red Cross hospital in France in July 1918.

The body of Harold Goodell also was laid to rest in 1921, and "as the funeral cortege passed up School Street pupils of the grammar and parochial schools lined either side of the street, carrying flags. The stores were closed during the service."

It would be interesting to know the identities of those children who watched the procession that day, if only to be able to tell whether any of them were honored with similar services in the next war.

New Town Hall

North Park Street received an unwelcome facelift when the town hall and two other buildings were destroyed by fire on February 2, 1923.

After it was constructed on the common in 1792, a bell was added to the town hall in 1807. Town records for the following year show that James Howe was paid seventeen-dollars for ringing the bell and sweeping out the meetinghouse. "This last named operation was somewhat laborious on account of the tobacco quid deposits in some of the pews," wrote former bellringer Colbee C. Benton.

Although the type and size of Lebanon's first bell are not known, it was purchased with donations and was rung at nine in the morning, noon, nine at night, and sometimes in the summer to call men to work at five in the morning. It also rang out on the Sabbath, for funerals and on town meeting days, and he who ventured out to toll the bell in the evening found himself fair game for local youths in search of sport, according to Mr. Benton's account in *The Free Press*:

> *. . . Deacon Davis . . . did the duty and received particular attention on account of his meekness. One night he pulled the rope and heard a muffled sound, that seemed to be many miles away; with fear and trembling he examined the bell and found a stocking drawn over the tongue.*

Baseball on the common was taboo, but croquet was permissible. The Blodgett and Thompson blocks appear to the left in this pre-1870 photo, and part of the old town hall is at the right.

Once, when Mr. Davis pulled the rope and the bell let out just a solitary clang, an examination found that small boys had stuck a clump of tar onto the clapper, which adhered to the shell after the first tug on the rope.

Residents at the 1826 town meeting voted to add a clock to the meetinghouse tower, although a drive to pay for it via private subscription apparently fell a little short and the 1827 town meeting voted thirty-five-dollars to round out the clock campaign.

The building was moved from the common to North Park Street in 1851, the same year that a new spire and lightning rod were added. The bell was recast in 1853. Horse sheds were built in the rear in 1855 to accommodate the Universalist church, which met in the upper story until about 1866, when the Universalists merged with the Unitarian church. Gas lights were added to the meetinghouse in 1870, kerosene lamps were introduced in 1889, and two years later the building was lit by electricity.

With the town hall gone, the common was fenced in for the first time in 1860, and roads were rerouted around the green.

The meetinghouse anchored much of the town's social and political life, hosting town and school district meetings, plays, concerts, operas, recitals, spelling bees, dances, and political rallies. The town hall also greeted such notables as Henry Ward Beecher, Susan B. Anthony, Frederick Douglas, Tom Thumb, and John Philip Sousa. A bicycle rink was even built in the basement in 1869.

Police Chief Leon Copp was making his rounds at about three-thirty on the morning of February 2, 1923, when he discovered flames coming from the building. The fire spread quickly from the furnace where it apparently started to the stage and scenery area, and then reached the timbers and clock tower, which the *Free Press* said, "when burning was a handsome sight. It seemed loath to fall, and for quite a long time held grimly on." Finally, the clock and bell fell straight down to the ashes below. Fortunately, a brick vault protected the town's records from the flames.

Pushed along by the wind the fire jumped westward to the nearby Thompson Block and destroyed the dental offices of Dr. R. J. Couillard, Carl Richards' shoe store, and Elbridge Thompson's millinery shop. It also damaged the Adnabrown Garage in the rear of the building, and then moved west to the Kendrick Block, claiming A. J. Potter's jewelry store and the meeting rooms of the Sunset Club for young men.

To the east of the town hall, the window frames and cornices of the Hotel Rogers caught fire, sending guests scurrying into the night before firefighters brought the conflagration under control.

The process of replacing the historic landmark was swift. A special town meeting convened at the Park Theatre on February twenty-third and appointed a committee to come up with a rebuilding plan. The town met again on March thirty-first and, with attorney Fred Jones leading the charge, approved a bond issue for a new quarter-million-dollar structure.

With that done, a building committee headed by T. J. McNamara worked with the Hanover architectural firm of Larson & Wells and came up with the design of the present City Hall building, which was dedicated in October 1925.

The new building included town offices, the Grafton County Superior Court, and a theater complete with dressing rooms. The basement of the building contained a gymnasium used for meetings, dances, and athletic events, a banquet room capable of seating 250, a fully-equipped kitchen, and coat rooms and bathrooms for men and women were located in the front of the basement. The rear of the building also housed three new jail cells for the police department, which remained there until the new police station opened on Poverty Lane in 1992.

The *Free Press*, in a special edition commemorating the dedication of the new town hall, noted that: "The exterior walls are of Densmore Brick Company sand struck brick laid in flemish bond with random black headers. The outside walls are trimmed with Lebanon granite and with granite composite bush-hammered cast stone . . . The building is surmounted by a Colonial tower which houses a 2000 pound Meneely bell and a Seth Thomas electric wind clock of the latest type, presented to the town by Mr. [Ralph] Wood of Lebanon."

A renovation in 1975 relocated town offices from the front of the building just off the lobby to space formerly occupied by the gymnasium and banquet room. Howe Street, which ran between city hall and the Rogers House, was closed to accommodate access ramps for the handicapped.

To help pay for the new structure, the Lebanon Improvement Society was formed in 1925 and began to show movies in the town-hall theater during an era when having a license to show movies was like having one to print money.

It was a controversial practice, however, since it effectively put the town in competition with the Park Theatre. The matter turned bitter in 1925, when selectmen refused to grant the Park a license to show movies. A lawsuit ensued, and it was settled when the Improvement Society bought out the Park and closed it. Movies continued to be shown in the Opera House through 1970, when the Lebanon Cinema opened in the Upper Valley Plaza in West Lebanon (Cherry, Webb, Touraine, 1994).

"The Rum Trade"

Lebanon was no stranger to prohibition and the temperance movement when the Volstead Act passed Congress in 1920. Although liberal quantities of rum had long been used to entice people to bridge-buildings, church raisings, and other efforts, the issue of alcohol abuse was one that dated back to at least the late 1700s. Since alcoholic beverages were legal, available, and in demand, there was little the selectmen could do.

Voters, however, addressed the issue at the 1843 town meeting by passing a resolution that forbade selectmen to grant liquor licenses except for medicinal purposes. The vote was reaffirmed in 1848 and 1849, when the anti-alcohol sentiment was fueled by the formation of the Mount Lebanon Sons of Temperance and the Union of the Daughters of Temperance.

The groups held lectures and staged rallies in the town hall that featured prayers, songs, and orations, and culminated in people marching to the stage to take pledges of sobriety.

Despite the ban on liquor licenses and the efforts of temperance groups, the town's liquor trade continued to flourish, sometimes with tragic results. In 1851 a man was stabbed to death in the Lafayette Hotel on West Park Street. The *Whig* reported that the Mount Lebanon Sons of Temperance blamed the tragedy on "the legitimate fruit of the rum traffic" and said the town could expect repeat performances unless alcohol use was curbed.

The closest person Lebanon had to a Carrie Nation-type was Harvey Murch, a blacksmith and maker of mop handles whose name became synonymous with the temperance cause in Lebanon, although his efforts apparently made him something of a target for those with opposing views. A resolution passed by Mr. Murch's anti-alcohol allies in 1867 stated that, "An attempt has recently been made to heap undeserved obloquy upon the head of our fellow citizen and brother, Harvey Murch, Esq., because of his undaunted courage and zeal in the suppression of the rum traffic."

The temperance movement caught on at the state level in 1855, when the legislature passed a law that prohibited the sale of liquor in taverns and stores, although that did little to dampen the collective thirst for spirits. Liquor agent C. L. Buswell reported that hundreds of gallons were sold in 1855-56, every drop in the name of medicine and most of it through local drugstores, of which Lebanon boasted several.

Those unable to convince a doctor to write a prescription had the option of distilling their own liquor or buying from local bootleggers, who made regular appearances in the Lebanon Police Court.

The location of those illicit liquor sources seems to have been no secret. The *Free Press* reported on February 27, 1891, that, "The saloon kept by Leander Bordo, better known about town as 'Bumblebee,' was raided by officers and assistants early last Saturday morning. A careful search failed to reveal anything but a few bottles of champaign [sic] cider and some hop beer of doubtful quality." The Bumblebee sat at the intersection of South Main Street and Seminary Hill in West Lebanon.

It was big news when police staged several simultaneous raids in April 1901, seizing malt liquor from both the Sargent Hotel and another West Lebanon hostelry called the Elm House, and seven barrels of liquor from Joseph Lynch's drug store, also in West Lebanon. In Lebanon, meanwhile, police confiscated alcohol from druggists I. N. Perley and F. H. Willard, innkeeper Charles Williamson, and four other men. All told, the ten men were fined $820.

Not surprisingly, some illegal bartenders may have been diluting their product. One such story holds that when hotel owner Frank Sayre (Sayre's Hotel on Parkhurst Street) was arrested for selling liquor to Dartmouth College students in the 1880s, he admitted his deed to police, but also told them that he had been gradually adulterating his liquor. "If you had let me alone," he is supposed to have said, "I would have had them drinking all water."

Passage of the Volstead Act also made little difference. As was the case in towns everywhere, the illegal liquor trade in Lebanon continued through Prohibition, with much of the locally consumed alcohol coming from Canada. The fact that the town was a stopping point on the Boston-to-Montreal railroad run made it that much more convenient, and the town's strong French-Canadian population probably fostered that trade, too. Conductors sometimes smuggled liquor from the north, remembers Earle Burke, who was born in Lebanon in 1911 and was a young man during the tail-end of the Prohibition period. Virtually anyone could buy alcohol if they knew where to go, he said, and everyone knew, including the police, who cracked down periodically.

After the federal taboo on alcohol consumption was repealed in 1932, New Hampshire voters overturned the state ban on alcohol the following year by a 2-to-1 margin, with Lebanon voting 834-249 in favor of repeal. (They also voted in 1933 to do away with some of their blue laws. For the first time in the town's history, sporting events could be held on Sunday as long as they started after one o'clock in the afternoon, and movies, vaudeville acts, and theatrical performances could play on Sundays if they started after six in the evening.)

"Beer Vote Wins," declared the *Free Press* in March 1934. And how. A year after voting overwhelmingly in favor of overturning the state law, voters considered the issue of scrapping local prohibition. An article to allow the sale of beer containing 6 percent alcohol passed 1,193 to 327, and beer garnered more support than any candidate seeking a contested political seat. By the end of the year the town's first state liquor store had opened in the Plamondon Block on Hanover Street (Hirsch's, 1994).

Another temperance milestone was reached less than twenty years later when a local branch of Alcoholics Anonymous (AA) was established on January 17, 1951. The organization initially met at the home of one of its members, but opened a headquarters at 24 High Street in 1954, when there were about twenty in the group. In more recent times, however, local churches have often provided the setting for AA meetings.

16

The Great Depression

Tramps

BECAUSE OF her position on a railroad line and at the intersection of two turnpikes, Lebanon was no stranger to strangers when the stock market crashed in October 1929, signaling the onset of the Great Depression.

As early as 1875 the *Free Press* had noted that "tramps are getting thick," and called for a night watch to be established after West Lebanon residents were startled by "an advanced guard of the Tramp Army from Vermont, about to invade our territory."

In 1894 selectmen issued a warning to residents not to feed the hobos, nor to invite them in, and the newspaper reprinted the state "tramp law." It prohibited begging, and offered a ten-dollar bounty to any resident who captured and turned in a tramp—not including females, minors, or the blind—to police.

The economic hardship that had settled over the nation in both 1875 and 1894 undoubtedly brought some of those itinerants to town, but in nowhere near the numbers that arrived in the 1930s.

They came by train or on foot, and once in town they knocked on doors to ask for food, clothing, and other assistance. Many residents sought to accommodate them, and the town usually allowed transients to spend a night in the town jail or arranged for other shelter. At first their numbers were manageable. In 1925, for example, the town put up 388 people, and 514 in 1929. In 1930—the year following the stock-market crash—the town hosteled 809 wanderers. By 1931 their presence in Lebanon had increased to more than 1,200, and to 1,500 in 1932.

Clearly, the town was not prepared for the magnitude of the influx, and it strained town finances. For example, the 1932 local budget earmarked ten-thousand-dollars for welfare expenses, but by the end of the budget year the town had spent $25,000 on the poor, both domestic and itinerant.

The town cared for vagabonds until 1933, when the state stepped in and established a "transient camp," providing federally funded food and shelter for the homeless. Located off Mascoma Street Extension in the rear of the present Hannah's Mobile Home Park, (1994), it provided accommodations for itinerants through at least 1936. It was not, however, a free-lunch deal. Those who were lodged in the one-story, barracks-type quarters were required to chop wood or do other work in exchange for their food, shelter, and clothing. Billy Hubbard, who grew up in the neighborhood near the camp, recalls that residents cut brush, worked on one of the town's ski jumps, and did other public-sector work.

At least one cynical county official believed that the work requirement kept some of the most eligible candidates away from the camp. Unambitious transients would continue to seek handouts from roadside homes and avoid work as long as they could get away with it, said Grafton County Commissioner George A. Pushee, who warned housewives that continuing to feed the beggars would undermine government attempts to help them: "Because they do not want to work and refuse to cooperate with the plan they have kept away from the shelters and instead have increased their demands on the individuals and local communities . . . Each meal given by a housewife is a blow at the whole program and a direct method of sabotaging this plan which is designed to eliminate this burden on the local communities."

Mr. Hubbard recalls that the camp housed men of varying backgrounds in a large T-shaped, barracks-type building. The structure contained a kitchen, dining area, and a series of partitioned-off bedrooms that housed about a hundred men, Mr. Hubbard estimated. "There were men of all kinds of trades but there just plain wasn't any work.

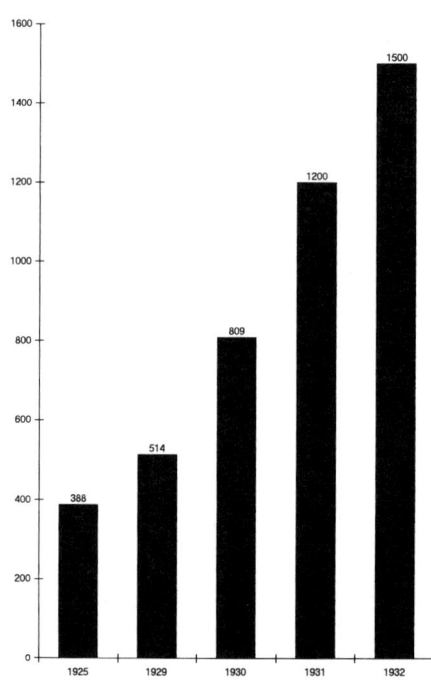

Transients housed by the town during the Depression

Lebanon, 1761-1994 / 182

Some of them were well-trained men who just lost their jobs."

When the state and federal governments stepped in to handle the transients, that left the town free to deal with its own considerable unemployment picture. In his 1930 report to the town, Overseer of the Poor John Barker wrote that his department furnished aid to forty-five families and seventeen individuals in 1929, mostly due to layoffs in the mills. Still, within a few years, 1929 would be considered the "good old days."

"Everett on Five-day Schedule," read the *Free Press* headline of April 11, 1930:

The lessening of production at this factory, which now employs more help than any other in Lebanon and is just finishing a large government order, comes as a result of the general depression throughout the industry.

Coupled with the fact that there is little production in the Carter & Rogers' [Lebanon Woolen Company] factory and the Riverside Mill of the American Woolen Co., business conditions in Lebanon are far from ideal at present, though several factories are running full time and the Mascoma Mill is operating overtime.

In addition to the welfare that came from state and local tax dollars, a group called Associated Charities was formed in 1930 by the wives of prominent businessmen and churches in town. The group reportedly distributed more than three-thousand articles of clothing, some of which may have been purchased with the proceeds from the "Unemployment Ball" held on Saint Patrick's Day in 1932.

The local Red Cross chapters also tried to help, although a collection box in the lobby of the post office was ransacked in 1931, a year when the town and county provided aid for 858 Lebanon residents.

Many of those people, wrote Mr. Barker, "are thrifty and good citizens and had saved sufficient money to meet an ordinary period of unemployment, but with the depression lasting so long they were obliged to draw on their resources until the last of their savings was used." Underemployment also was a problem, he said.

The Everett-Norfolk Knitting Company closed its High Street plant for good at the end of 1931, putting the rest of its approximately three-hundred employees out of work. When the town's textile mills shut down at the start of 1932, newly elected selectman Joe Perley predicted that the town would be feeding about fifteen-hundred residents by December first. He was not so far off, as the town ended up providing welfare services for 982 residents that year.

With up to 20 percent of the town's residents on some type of public assistance, those who were not scrambled for work. Harrison "Red" Clapper, a 1926 graduate of West Lebanon High School, recalls doing "anything to make a dollar." He picked and sold berries, moved furniture, chopped wood, and shoveled snow. He and his wife, Bessie, always had enough to eat; "But we didn't go anywhere," said Mrs. Clapper, "and we didn't spend any money."

"We didn't have it to spend," her husband added.

Families receiving support from the "Poor Department" usually did so in exchange for work. Men who were able to chop their own wood were required to do so, and those who refused were denied fuel assistance. The town furnished transportation to woodlots, since families on welfare were not allowed to own cars. "The Poor Department and gasoline do not mix well together," wrote Mr. Barker, adding that owning a radio, a dog, or a cat would also render a family ineligible for public assistance, since those items were not considered "necessities."

The hardship experienced in 1932 also was reflected in the statistics of the town. The assessed valuation dropped from the 1931 level of just over nine million dollars, to $8.1 million. The value of mills and machinery—placed at more than a million dollars as recently as 1928—was only $667,636 in 1932, and the worth of stock-in-trade fell from $1.14 million in 1931, to $729,965 in 1932. In 1933 that category was reduced to just $536,101, as production dwindled and merchants opted not to make wholesale purchases of goods they could not sell.

New car registrations were off 60 percent, according to the *Free Press*, which said the town had registered as many cars as in past years, but not as many new ones. That led to a shakeout in the auto industry, and only four dealers—Smith Auto, Flanders & Patch, Abe Caplan, and the Lewis Motor Company—were listed in the 1936 tax rolls as selling cars.

One of the town's more spectacular arsons also occurred during this period, when the Park Hotel and the Odd Fellows Block on West Park Street burned on February 10, 1931. The fire was started shortly after midnight by hotel owner James Vanetsanos, whose charred body was discovered in the basement of the building. He had apparently planned to make a swift getaway, as his car was found idling on the street outside. The fire destroyed the *Free Press* offices, those of the Singer Sewing Machine agency, the Army-Navy store, Frank Cory's printing operation, George Leavitt's upholstery business, and the Economy restaurant.

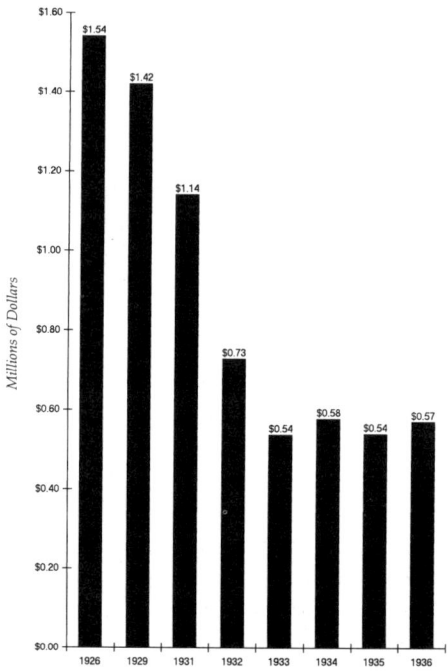

Stock in trade assessments during the Depression

The fire set by Park Hotel manager James Vanetsanos destroyed the hotel and the adjacent Odd Fellows' Block in 1931. Vanetsanos's remains were found in the basement of the hotel, and his car was idling in front of the building. The garage at left is about where the fire station now stands, and the cars to the right are parked in front of the Bank Building. Benton Hill ran between the Bank and Odd Fellows' Block.

Arson in the face of hard times is not uncommon, and the Park Hotel blaze may not have been the first to result from the Depression. In April and May 1930, the *Free Press* reported, the town experienced thirteen fires on nine consecutive Sundays. Although it is not clear whether any were set, it seems likely that some were.

The town in 1932 instructed selectmen to hire Lebanon residents for town work whenever possible, and to require outside contractors hired by the town to do likewise. Voters also established a budget committee to meet with selectmen once a month and review town finances. To cut town expenses, the town discontinued the daytime police officer in West Lebanon, and cut the pay of all officers by fifty-cents per day. Chief Clarence Wright's daily wages were lowered to five-dollars, while those of regular officers were reduced to four-dollars.

The school budget was slashed by thirteen-thousand-dollars—eleven-thousand of it in teacher salaries—to stand at $101,000, and four elementary school teachers were laid off. One teacher was added to the high school's industrial arts staff, and Superintendent William English explained that, "on account of the scarcity of industrial work a considerable number of boys are in the high school who would otherwise be working and they have elected the Mechanical Arts course." An effort to cut the superintendent's salary failed, but the board eliminated the only kindergarten class.

The town held an "unemployment drive" in 1932 in which more than 200 people signed up for jobs at the Soldiers Memorial building during a three-day period in April. Ninety-five of them were assigned work.

By 1933, with President Roosevelt's New Deal apparatus in place, public works jobs began to surface, especially in the fields of highways, forestry, and waterworks. Having the county's largest population and its largest unemployment totals, Lebanon was given thirty-five of Grafton County's fifty slots in a state public works reforestation program. The *Free Press* reported that the more important projects included "the reservoir job at Hanover, the building of an artificial pond also at Hanover, and the work on the Mt. Support Road from Hanover to Lebanon." Other construction projects took place along Route 12A, on the Heater Road between Riverdale and Mount Support Road, and on Route 4 from East Lebanon to the Enfield town line.

Women who had been thrown out of work by the closing of the Everett-Norfolk Knitting Company also found temporary employment. The local Red Cross took advantage of the ample supply of idle seamstresses and established a program in which women worked part time sewing clothes for the newly named Welfare Department, which distributed the goods to the needy.

A class war of sorts broke out in 1933, when the town's unemployed went on strike against the town, demanding improved benefits. Two men were arrested after they refused to continue working on a piece of unfinished road in West Lebanon. "There have been several meetings among the men regarding their desire to be paid in money rather than in provision slips," the *Free Press* reported, "and so much agitation resulted that practically all the men refused to work, but later gave in with the exception of the two who were arrested."

One of those meetings of aid recipients also produced several other demands, including a daily allowance of ten-cents per meal while on the job; a guarantee of four working days per week at a rate of forty-cents per hour; restoration of their right to vote; and that families in the LaBombard Block on High Street whose electricity was turned off for nonpayment have their power restored. The group also sought assurances that, in the future, unemployed families would not have their power discontinued. Their financial requests were denied.

Meanwhile, the *Free Press* reported in late 1933 that "under the CWA project 300 Lebanon men have been put to work, half of them being from the Welfare and half from the Re-employment lists . . . About a year ago almost 1000 people were being supported by the town and now there are less than 150."

It was, however, a false spring, as the Depression continued until World War II arrived to put an entirely different spin on the economy.

APD

Alice Peck Day Memorial Hospital, in which thousands of babies have been born during the past sixty years, was itself born in the era of the Depression, and it was not the smoothest of deliveries.

Alice Peck Day was born and raised on the family homestead established on Mascoma Street in 1780. Her father, Solon Peck, was a longtime selectman who co-founded the Dewey-Peck insurance agency with Jesse Dewey shortly after the Civil War. Her husband, Henry Day, also joined this agency.

When Mrs. Day died on December 5, 1927, her will provided that the Peck homestead be converted into a cottage hospital within three years of her death. Billy Hubbard, a relative of Mrs. Day, said she initially wanted to turn her home into quarters for the elderly, but changed her mind after Dr. Arthur Burnham, one of the town's leading physicians, convinced her that the town would be better served by a cottage hospital.

Even that almost did not happen, for the will included a clause that revoked the offer if the hospital was not established within three years of her death, and the initial meetings held to create the hospital generated underwhelming public interest. Finally, only three weeks before the three-year deadline that would have transferred the property for other uses, a hospital corporation was set up. The Peck home was refurbished, and refurnished (largely through public donations) over the next two years, and it opened with nine beds, a day nurse, and a night nurse, all under the direction of Superintendent Minnie Lang.

Despite its sluggish beginning the hospital quickly engendered a strong base of community support which has enabled it to expand several times and weather one particularly difficult financial period. One APD tradition was its annual "Donation Day" on which residents contributed food, bathrobes, towels, and other necessities. The haul from 1935 included an assortment of jam, pickles, vegetables, fruits, berries, and groceries. The *Free Press* also noted that "this is the second year that the school children, through the Lions Club, have given enough potatoes for the winter supply."

The specialties of the house during the hospital's first thirty years were births, tonsils, and minor medical procedures. APD admitted 122 patients between its opening on February 1, 1932, and October first of that year, including twenty-four births and twenty-one tonsillectomies. One of those births was Helen and William Smith's son, Kenneth, and Mrs. Smith recalls the charge for a corner room was five-dollars per day, while a bed in the maternity ward was three-dollars. In 1933, the first full year of operation, admissions grew to 217, with sixty-six births and 43 sets of tonsils being removed.

APD continued its modest existence in the old Peck residence for more than twenty years, but by 1960 it was evident that the old quarters were inadequate. (An "old firetrap," one physician called it.) With Dr. Arthur Burnham leading the fund drive and Francis Sargent heading the board of trustees, the hospital expanded into a new brick facility on the hillside behind the original hospital building. The new thirty-four-bed structure cost $880,000 when it opened in 1964, and the old homestead was converted into a nursing home. (Billy Hubbard points out that there is some irony in that, since a nursing home was what Mrs. Day had wanted in the first place.)

Nineteen-sixty-five was remarkable as the year of the twins. Among the 359 births were 11 sets, including four pairs born between January twelfth and February third. (By contrast, hospital officials in 1994 say APD normally delivers about three sets of twins per year.) The per-diem cost of a room in a multi-bed ward that year was twenty-four-dollars, and the charges for semi-private and private rooms were twenty-eight and thir-

The Alice Peck Day homestead shortly after it was converted into a cottage hospital

ty-eight dollars, respectively. (Gloria Green, a longtime nurse at APD, recalled that when she started at the hospital in 1945, the fee for a doctor who delivered a baby was twenty-five-dollars, and payment sometimes was made, and accepted, in the form of chickens, groceries or other goods. In contrast, a semi-private room in 1994 cost $451 per day, no groceries or chickens accepted.)

APD grew again in 1976, moving the nursing home from the Peck home into a $1.5 million wing constructed onto the main hospital building. Even with a waiting list, however, declining federal reimbursements for nursing home patients made the extended-care facility, as it is now known, a drain on the hospital's finances. The nursing home ran a deficit from 1980 to 1983, and the shortfall exceeded six figures in three of those four years. To boost sagging revenues, part of the nursing home section was dedicated to an alcohol rehabilitation center in 1983.

The emphasis on health care in the early 1980s favored outpatient treatment over hospitalization, and two physicians who had for years done their business at APD retired. Those factors added up to empty beds, and the combined deficit of the nursing home and the hospital exceeded $200,000 in 1983, when the total budget was about $3.5 million. To attract new physicians and patients, a family-care-physicians' center was constructed on the hospital's front lawn. Later that year, over the objections of a substantial portion of its corporate membership, APD joined Mary Hitchcock Memorial Hospital in Hanover in a joint holding company known as the Hitchcock Alliance.

APD was still pretty much a "cottage hospital" devoted to family medical care, while Hitchcock was a teaching hospital that emphasized high-priced specialty care at the expense of the personal treatment that Lebanonians believed made APD unique. The new coalition gave corporate control of APD to the Hitchcock-dominated alliance, and despite assurances from both sides that the two hospitals would retain their separate identities some APD incorporators saw the move as akin to making a deal with the devil. Furthermore, they said so during several meetings held to discuss the plan. "It sounds like a hand puppet," attorney James Laffan told trustees at a meeting on June 29, 1983. "It would still have a face but something else would be behind it."

APD trustees, however, said the hospital was facing financial ruin and would not be able to survive without joining Hitchcock. The APD corporation approved the merger by a margin of 80-56, but as marriages go, it was a short one.

In February 1986 APD's financial director gave the hospital six months to live. President Claire Bowen told him to get a second opinion, and by the time an outside group of auditors had finished reviewing the situation, the prognosis was down to ninety days. Hitchcock officials proposed converting APD to a nursing home, an idea trustees rejected.

It was about this time that the patient again began to breathe without the aid of the alliance. Surgeon David Kroner had been recruited to APD late in 1985, and hospital officials say it was his practice that allowed the hospital to show a modest $73,000 profit at the end of 1986. Still, a profit was a profit, and by 1987 APD was nearly $360,000 in the black and looking to leave the Hitchcock Alliance.

The hospital once again turned to its biggest asset—community support—for $750,000 to upgrade the emergency room, add a second operating room, and do other things to allow it to remain solvent outside the alliance. The campaign stood at $900,000 by the fall, when the hospital split from the alliance and regained its independence.

On its own once again and under the leadership of President Robert Mesropian, APD continued its expansion, constructing physicians' offices in the rear of the hospital in 1990, and adding a new lobby and emergency-care facility in 1992.

For all of the new construction that has taken place at APD over the years, the hospital still owns the original Peck residence that fronts on Mascoma Street. Part of it houses APD's computer and financial services, and some of it is rented to tenants.

In 1994 the hospital had 50 nursing-home beds, 32 acute-care beds, 250 full- and part-time employees, and 56 physicians with admitting privileges.

Not bad for a facility that was nearly stillborn.

"The Smallest Ball Bearing in the World"

When the pocketwatch of Winslow "Bill" Pierce, Jr. stopped in 1936, it hatched a multi-billion-dollar industry that became a mainstay of Lebanon's economy.

A jeweler diagnosed the problem as a broken jewel and suggested Mr. Pierce purchase a new watch to replace the one his father had given him. Determined to keep his timepiece, Mr. Pierce went back to the wooden building on Mascoma Street that housed the Split Ballbearing Company and made history. As Evan Hill described the moment in *Beanstalk*, a history of the MPB Corporation: "He went upstairs to a small lathe on the second floor, dropped his coat, loosened his tie, and went to work to make what was to be at that time the smallest ball bearing in the world."

Thus was born an industry—the manufacture of miniature precision bearings that have been used around the world in the aerospace, defense, and a multitude of other industries.

Ballbearings had long been used to reduce friction on the shafts of their machinery, but a failed bearing meant removing the entire shaft from its housing to replace the part, a procedure that translated into extensive downtime for a company. A bearing which could be replaced without removing the shaft would be a time saver, and Mr. Pierce applied for a patent in 1921. By making two fractures in the circular inner casing—splitting the bearing—Mr. Pierce created a bearing with two halves that could be easily removed from a shaft by pulling the two pieces apart.

Arthur Niles of the Niles Machine Company on Mascoma Street also was experimenting with split ballbearings in 1926, and in 1927 he changed the name of the company to the Split Ballbearing Corporation. By any name, it was not a company with a record to make you eager to invest your life savings.

Mr. Pierce visited Splitball in 1929, and moved to Lebanon soon thereafter to work for the company. He gave the firm three of his patents and arranged for his father to finance the business, which continued to tread water—barely—for the next several years.

Describing conditions at the conclusion of 1936, Evan Hill wrote that, "At year's end SBB had only $94.75 in cash. Roy E. Lewis, Lebanon hardware merchant and then president of the company, reported that SBB owed $35,867.79, and had exactly $24,251.20 in assets. Accounts receivable were less than $1700; the inventory a little more than $3500. If the company had liquidated at that moment, it would still owe $10,616.59. It was perfectly clear that something had to be done."

The company was dissolved in 1939, and a new corporation was established under the same name with Winslow Pierce as the sole stockholder and a board of directors that included the Lewis brothers, Roy and John. Later that year, the directors established a subsidiary known as Miniature Precision Ballbearing (MPB) that was devoted exclusively to manufacturing the tiny bearings.

The SBB-MPB financial picture started to turn, thanks to orders related to World War II. The company produced just over three-hundred miniature bearings in 1939, and by 1940 half a dozen women were hired to help assemble the more than twelve-hundred bearings produced that year. SBB's biggest problem was turning out the bearings fast enough to keep up with orders. By the end of 1941, the company employed more than eighty workers and there was an amiable split, so to speak, in the relationship between the parent (SBB) and the child (MPB). Because selectmen refused to rent only part of the dormant Lebandale Mill building to MPB, the company moved to Keene in 1941.

Winslow Pierce spent most of his time with MPB, although he continued to own SBB, which remained behind in the Mascoma Street headquarters and flourished as war-related contracts poured in. By the end of 1943, the company employed almost two-hundred workers in two shifts, and had rented additional space in other buildings.

The end of the war, however, hit SBB hard. Orders dropped, and Winslow Pierce sought contracts in the private sector. The company lost $12,000 in 1946, and the payroll was cut back to a pre-war level of fifteen workers; by the end of 1947, only eight people worked at Splitball.

the surrounding area; and until the Dartmouth-Hitchcock Medical Center moved to town in 1991, Splitball was the town's largest private-sector employer. Splitball employees tend to be a tight-knit group, a camaraderie probably fostered by the company's hiring pattern. Many daughters and sons have followed their mothers and fathers into the plant, and it is common for nieces and nephews to work alongside aunts and uncles.

And to think that the company might have failed had Winslow Pierce's watch not broken in 1936.

17

World War II

LEBANON IN 1940 boasted 113 retail establishments with sales of $4.36 million. The stores, with a payroll of $419,000, supported 403 employees. They included: twenty-seven grocery stores; five outlets dealing in general merchandise; eight apparel shops; four each dealing in furniture, household goods and radios; nine automobile dealers; eighteen gasoline filling stations; seven building, lumber and hardware stores; thirteen eating and drinking establishments; and four drug stores. The town's population was 7,564, an increase of 7 percent over the 1930 figure.

The worst of the Depression was over, but like residents everywhere, Lebanonians were attuned to events in Europe, where only the year before, Hitler's Germany had invaded Poland.

Lebanon residents Norman Decato and Jean-Paul Tanguay were standing on the deck of the *U.S.S. Argonne*, waiting to go on watch, when they first saw the planes.

"What a time to have maneuvers—on a Sunday morning," Mr. Decato said to his hometown friend.

Both men, however, quickly realized that they were not witnessing U.S. airplanes on maneuvers, but Japanese bombers on a mission of destruction. "It didn't take damn long [to conclude it was not an exercise], after I saw the battleships go up in the air," Mr. Decato recalled more than fifty years after the Japanese bombing of Pearl Harbor. "And the fires—my God—and the bodies in the oil."

It is said that the bombing of Pearl Harbor is one of those events, like the assassination of President Kennedy and the explosion of the space shuttle *Challenger*, which is so indelibly chiseled on the psyche that people can recall exactly where they were and whom they were with when when they learned of it.

About two-hundred Lebanon residents were gathered in the town hall on the afternoon of December 7, 1941, for a defense rally featuring U.S. Senator Styles Bridges. As *The Union* of Manchester recalled the event: "There was shocked silence in the Town

Hall when Judge Norris Cotton, chairman of the rally, announced, after the citizens had seen a messenger talk to Senator Bridges and call him to the telephone to answer an 'urgent return' appeal from Washington, that Japan had committed acts of aggression 'even as we meet here in New Hampshire to prepare for just such an eventuality.'"

The band broke into "The Star-Spangled Banner", which had suddenly taken on a new meaning.

Before departing the town hall, Senator Bridges predicted that the attack would mean "... new obligations and responsibilities, with contributions of every kind and every sacrifice necessary for us all."

Chief of Police Clarence Wright immediately sent officers to guard the West Lebanon railroad depot and the Mascoma mill, which manufactured cloth for the navy. The war, in fact, proved a windfall for the town's woolen mills and garment shops over the next four years, as military-related orders kept the looms in motion around the clock. The American Woolen Company, with its Mascoma mill in Lebanon and other factories in Enfield and Dover, received more war-related contracts than any other manufacturer in the state.

The E. Cummings Leather Company, which the Lebanon Improvement Society had recruited to the former Everett Knitting Works site on High Street in 1938, turned out half of all of the leather used by the Navy to line shoes.

Lebanon residents undertook the same kind of sacrifices common to villages everywhere during World War II, and in some respects it was not so different from the effort put forth in World War I. A shortage of gasoline and tires all but brought an end to the tradition of Sunday drives in the automobile. Rationing of coal and heating fuel meant that residents again had to be careful about heating their homes, and the rationing of meat, butter, and sugar altered diets.

With virtually everything in short supply the federal government implemented ceilings on the prices of many goods, including used cars, which the *Free Press* reported were "almost impossible to secure in some communities ... [and] mighty scarce in others." Regulations that took effect in 1944 required ceiling prices to be posted for forty basic items in restaurants and set the price for a cup of coffee at five cents.

The allocation of resources and enforcement of price controls was coordinated by the local rationing board, which was located in the Whipple Block and chaired by Alfred Densmore. The board was broken down into four committees: Stuart B. Emerson, Frank Morgan, and William Dubuque oversaw the sale of gasoline; Lane Dwinell, Stanley Currier, and Paul McNamara sat on the price committee; Theodore Bacon, Charles Foster, and Maynard Langlois supervised food rationing; and the members of the fuel committee were George Moore, Andrew Truxal, and Guy Demag. On September 30, 1945—a month after the war ended—the board dissolved itself.

As in World War I, the town raised money for the war through the sale of bonds and with contributions to the local Red Cross and the War Chest. To kick off the latter, the town staged a huge parade in June 1942, featuring an estimated two-thousand marchers and an assortment of horses, fire engines, floats, and bands representing the town's industries, businesses, social clubs, and schools. A crowd estimated at five-thousand witnessed the spectacle. Money from the War Chest supported the families of soldiers, while the Red Cross again sent packages overseas and prepared surgical dressings.

Almost immediately after Pearl Harbor, Governor Robert Blood appointed Norris Cotton the chairman of the local public safety committee, and the town's civil defense apparatus swung into gear. Classes were held to train air-raid wardens, and an observation tower was constructed next to the reservoir on Prospect Hill to keep a lookout for enemy aircraft. Although the air raid never materialized, the town conducted periodic drills just in case.

The induction of about a thousand Lebanon men into the military created a shortage of labor that was filled by housewives, retirees, and high-school students who were let out of school early to work on farms and in factories.

West Lebanon High School headmaster George Currier noted that

a great unrest . . . prevails among the boys, especially in the junior and senior classes. For those physically fit the immediate job which is in view is military service. The normal boy sees this ahead and wants to get at it. School life in the ordinary sense of learning is irksome against the thought of the glamour of military service. The opportunities for work for boys of this age have been numerous and the lure of money keeps children on the ragged edge of wanting to quit school either completely or partially or get out early for work.

Although some undergraduates left to join the service, there was not a mass exodus. There was, however, a 48-percent turnover in the school staff, as several members left to join the service or to work in war-related industries; among them was high-school headmaster Munro Grandy, who was granted a leave-of-absence to enter the army.

Mr. Currier noted that high-school boys worked on the railroad, in baggage rooms, and "in some instances the boys are going eighteen to twenty hours without sleep. The

Residents keep an eye out for enemy planes on the observation tower constructed during World War II on Reservoir Hill.

need for their help is very urgent and they are cooperating very well. There is a great shortage of farm help. Several farmers in this area are without sufficient help. Twenty girls and twenty-two boys have helped farmers harvest crops and some will help this spring and summer."

The curriculum of West Lebanon High also changed, as students could sign up for "pre-induction courses" in aeronautics, electricity, and physical education. The federal government provided money for additional machines to be purchased for the shop class, which produced nightsticks and stretcher poles, among other items. Children in the grade schools, meanwhile, collected milkweed floss (for use in life preservers), paper, and scrap metal. Collection points were established in Lebanon and West Lebanon to accumulate scrap metal that could be recycled and used in rifles, tanks, planes, and shops. Residents were urged to contribute garden tools, stoves, picture frames, tire chains, pots and pans, washboards, door knobs, gutters, and even—if it happened to be cast iron—the kitchen sink.

The scrap metal from the schools was collected by Bennie Goodman, patriarch of perhaps the town's most unique family. Bennie and Anna Goodman were both Russian immigrants who lacked a high-school diploma, but they raised thirteen children on the money Bennie made selling scrap metal from his Hanover Street junkyard. As son Richard wrote in 1954, "they were constantly in an economic stress, but my mother (and Dad) saw to it that essential food was provided, although minus luxuries—clothing, enough to get through some of our state's most terrible winters—and plenty of love and understanding, perhaps most important of all."

Each of the Goodman children graduated from Lebanon High School in an era when it was not unusual for the children of working-class families to drop out of school, and each child attended college. They matriculated, either as undergraduate or graduate students, at prestigious schools like Harvard, MIT, Dartmouth, the University of Chicago, Michigan, Brandeis, and several attended UNH. The siblings then entered the fields of education, business, nursing, psychology, and engineering, among others, and a few received honorary degrees. In 1954 Mrs. Goodman was named New Hampshire Mother of the Year by the American Mothers Committee of the Golden Rule Foundation.

Harry, Harvey, Joe, Louis, Robert, and Lillian Goodman were all in the service during World War II, the latter as a cadet nurse. The Goodmans, however, were just one of several Lebanon families with several siblings in the service. In fact, there were seven families with at least four members in the military.

Five brothers from the Boutin family enlisted. Lionel, killed in action, served at the same time as Arthur, Francis, Emile, and Rudolph.

Among the Creightons were brothers Crandell, Clarence, Donald, and Wendell, and two brothers-in-law, Edmond August, and Melvin MacKinnon.

The town report of 1943 noted that Florence Adams Whipple had four sons in the war, and three of them bore names befitting the patriotism of the times: John Quincy Adams, Joseph William Adams, Benjamin Franklin Adams, and Daniel Webster Adams.

Felix McGonis of Hanover Street also had four sons in the war: Albert J., who was killed, and brothers Richard, Joseph, and Francis.

The Burke family sent two brothers into the service—Roland in the navy and Earle in

Lebanon, 1761-1994 / 196

the army—and two sisters, Nina and Marion, who enlisted together in the navy on February 1, 1943.

Mr. and Mrs. Joseph Landry also sent four sons into the service—Joseph, Arthur, William, and Maurice.

Fifteen families in the state lost more than one sibling. Fortunately, no local family was included in that group, and it does not appear that any brothers from the town served together aboard the same ship or in the same company. However, Timothy and Francis Woodward belonged to the same battalion stationed on the island of Okinawa. When Francis was killed by a mortar shell, his parents learned of his death in a letter from Timothy that arrived before the official government notification.

Late in 1944, after D-Day had turned the tide in Europe, the local American Legion Post passed a resolution opposing any celebration for a victory over Germany, since the fight against Japan was still going on. Instead, the legionnaires recommended that V-E Day be observed as a day of prayer and thanksgiving on which residents should redouble their effort to bring the war against Japan to a hasty conclusion.

Once that happened—after the dropping of atomic bombs on Hiroshima and Nagasaki, bedlam prevailed as "Lebanon residents by the hundreds turned out . . . in celebration of the long-awaited word that the Japanese had accepted the terms of the Potsdam ultimatum, thus bringing to a close the deadliest war in history."

The end of the war saw Lebanon awash in Purple Hearts, Bronze and Silver stars, and an assortment of other medals earned by her infantrymen, aviators, and seamen. Some of those medals, unfortunately, were awarded posthumously, as more than thirty Lebanon residents died in Europe and the Pacific.

With the victory over Japan, the fire and mill whistles that had signaled the air-raid drills now summoned residents to celebration. "Everybody met up in the park," recalls Leonard Decato, "and everybody was hugging everybody." Schools, mills, and businesses were closed for the celebration, which started with a parade. West Park Street was closed as residents danced in the streets before adjourning later in the evening to the lower town hall, where the festivities continued well into the next morning.

The end of World War II saw hundreds of veterans return to town. New houses were added to old neighborhoods like Riverdale, but the homes were different. Increasingly, they contained televisions in addition to radios, and iceboxes yielded to electric refrigerators.

*The United States went to war again in 1950 to defend the Republic of South Korea. According to the New Hampshire Adjutant General's office, about three-hundred Lebanon and West Lebanon soldiers took part in that action, and Francis Ashey and Benjiman Griggs, Jr. were killed in the conflict. It was, however, a war with a decidedly different ring to it. The scrap drives, the rationing—**the urgency**—that had characterized World War II were missing, although it also lacked the protests that would later distinguish the war in Vietnam.*

Taking Wing

There was a foggy drizzle in the air as pilot Jack Rapsis banked Northeast Airlines Flight 946 to the left, following a course to the airport in Lebanon. "We're SIA," he radioed to the control tower, using the common pilot acronym for Standard Instrument Approach.

The so-called "Yellowbird" carried forty-two people—thirty-nine passengers and three crew members—who had departed Boston's Logan Airport shortly after five o'clock. Seventeen of the passengers were scheduled to get off in Lebanon, while twenty-two had tickets to fly on to Montpelier.

Lebanon Building Inspector Parmly Wills was bow hunting on Moose Mountain in Enfield shortly after six o'clock on October 25, 1968, when he heard the plane. Bright lights suddenly pierced the wilderness. "Then the lights, the fog, the sound of the plane and the mountain all came together, and I realized the plane was going to hit . . . There was a terrific crash, and then the plane exploded into flames, and ignited the area around."

The plane struck the area of the mountain known as North Peak, a half mile from where Mr. Wills was standing. Thirty-two people died, including two Lebanon residents: thirty-year-old Robert McLaughland of Bixby Street, and twenty-six-year-old Richard Watson of Birch Terrace in West Lebanon. The Moose Mountain crash remains the worst air disaster in New Hampshire history (1994) and is the event that many older residents most strongly associate with the airport. The National Transportation Safety Board cited pilot error and a flawed instrument guidance system as factors in the crash.

The Lebanon airport was a child of World War II, born in an era when the federal government created a network of emergency runways throughout the country that could be used for defense purposes. Engineers with the state of New Hampshire laid out the airport in 1937, and in 1940 the federal government allocated $335,000 for runway construction, which began in 1941. The first military plane to land at the airport touched down in November of that year and was piloted by Captain Robert S. Fogg, a former West Lebanon resident who had attended Rockland Military Academy (Seminary Hill School, 1994).

By 1944 the federal government deemed the Lebanon airport no longer necessary to defense needs and turned it over to the local government, which dubbed it the Lebanon Municipal Airport. The town in 1946 entered into an agreement with Sumner "Cooney" Atherton, Jr., a West Lebanon High School graduate and navy fighter pilot who had earned the Distinguished Flying Cross in World War II. He received a twenty-year lease from the town and, in conjunction with Jerry Winston of New York City, ran a charter business and flight school under the banner of Connecticut Valley Airways, the first fixed-base operator at the airport.

The lease gave Mr. Atherton the exclusive right to sell fuel at the airport, and allowed the town "a maximum 4 percent of gross receipts" from the sale of that fuel. That fuel-sales agreement ultimately led to a much-publicized lawsuit. The town in 1956 accused CV of paying on the lower net receipts, rather than the gross, and tried unsuccessfully to evict Mr. Atherton, who filed libel suits against several town officials and the *Valley News*, and accused the town of not maintaining the facilities. The case was settled out of court after a week of testimony, and the parties agreed that CV had, in fact, been paying the proper amount.

Mr. Atherton's widow, Martha Fleetwood, recalls that the first terminal was a wooden building moved from Plainfield that housed the Connecticut Valley Airways' offices, a snack bar, and the airport's first commercial carrier, Northeast Airlines, which commenced regularly scheduled service on May 29, 1948.

The Lebanon airport in the mid-1960s, before the air-traffic-control tower was constructed

By 1954 the airport was handling fifteen-thousand passengers, and the *Valley News* reported the following year that, "Dartmouth Carnival weekend passengers waiting to purchase tickets were standing two abreast in a 40-foot line outside the terminal. The temperature was two above zero. Carnival weekend was not a fluke. It merely served to highlight a steadily deteriorating situation."

A quarter of the passengers who flew in and out of Lebanon in 1954 were booked by Dartmouth Travel in Hanover, reflecting the facility's status as an airport that served the region, especially Dartmouth College.

In that vein, management underwent a major restructuring in 1960, the same year that the runway was extended to accommodate Northeast Airways' switch to larger planes. Senator Norris Cotton sponsored federal legislation that ratified an interstate commission known as the Lebanon Regional Airport Authority, which assumed responsibility for running and maintaining the airport.

The authority survived on a shoestring budget of landing and rental fees coupled with contributions from area towns. The theory behind the authority was that it would give residents of communities like Hanover and Woodstock—two of the facility's largest users—a voice in running the airport and at the same time distribute the costs throughout the region. Better yet, from Lebanon's point of view, the town would not have to bear the full burden of operating the airport at a loss.

The theory, however, broke down in practice as an increasing number of towns refused to allocate money for airport costs. "Every year the airport authority would be going around to outlying towns begging for their share," recalled former authority member Vernon Clark. As more towns refused to appropriate the money at town meeting, Lebanon, Hanover, and part-time Woodstock resident Laurence Rockefeller ended up as the biggest contributors. Finally, on July 1, 1978, the authority was dissolved and the airport reverted to municipal control.

There had been several improvements at the airport in the interim, and more to come. Instrument landing systems were installed, the Federal Aviation Administration control tower was put up in 1974, and a new terminal building was completed in the summer of 1980 to replace the outdated buildings. A variety of outbuildings also were constructed to house snow-removal and other maintenance equipment.

Northeast Airlines gave way to Air New England in 1972, and the airport has seen a variety of carriers since: Mohawk and Delta Executive Airlines in the 1970s; Command and Precision competed in the 1980s; they gave way in turn to Delta's Business Express, Northwest Airlink, and USAir Express.

The increase in traffic at the airport through the 1980s attracted car rental agencies and a newsstand; it has also supported (somewhat) a succession of restaurants—the old Skyline Lounge survived into the 1970s, when it gave way in 1981 to the Safari. Most recently, Kim Laware (whose family has operated the venerable Riverside Grill for many years) opened the Tailwind Restaurant (1994).

Although the Moose Mountain crash remains the only major commercial disaster affiliated with the Lebanon airport, there have been a number of fatal accidents involving private planes. In July 1993 two people died during an airshow watched by thousands. A parachutist died when he was struck by a plane, which then went out of control and crashed near the Connecticut River next to the town's sewage treatment plant, killing the pilot.

Throughout it all, Sumner Atherton's old Connecticut Valley Airways still survives, although under a different name. The business was sold in 1968 to Paul Moore, who changed the name of the operation to Lebanon Airport Development Corporation, known by the acronym LADCO, which was then bought out by the current fixed-base operator, the Lebanon Jet Center.

18

Seats of Influence

Norris Cotton

AT NO TIME in the town's history did more political power rest in Lebanon than in the mid-to-late 1950s, when the state's governor and one of its U.S. senators both resided in town.

The latter was Norris Henry Cotton, a native of Warren, New Hampshire, who was educated at the Tilton School, Phillips Exeter Academy, Wesleyan University, and George Washington University Law School. Having worked as a lawyer in Concord, he came to Lebanon in 1933 and opened a law office in the Whipple Block with Charles Tesreau and Jack Stebbins, Sr. as partners. He served as county attorney from 1933-1939, when he gave up that position to become judge of the Lebanon Municipal Court. He held that job until 1943, when he was elected to the New Hampshire House.

Mr. Cotton was already well established in Republican party circles when he arrived in Lebanon. He had represented Warren in the house from 1923-1925, and also held several party positions while working as a lawyer in Concord in the late twenties and early thirties.

After his election to the New Hampshire House in 1943, he was chosen speaker in 1945, becoming the third Lebanon resident to hold that position (Harry Cheney sat in the speaker's chair from 1903-05, and Fred Jones from 1921-23.) Under Norris Cotton's leadership, lawmakers adopted "Live Free or Die" as the state motto, chose the Old Man of the Mountain as the official state logo, and established a pension fund for state employees.

Tradition at the time limited a member to just one term as speaker, and Norris Cotton made the most of his tenure, using it as a springboard to help jump to the U.S. House of Representatives, defeating five primary opponents on the way to claiming the state's second-district seat in 1946. Norris Cotton became only the third Lebanon resident elected to Congress, after David Hough (1803-1807) and Aaron Cragin (1855-1859).

In Washington Mr. Cotton won a seat on the House Appropriations Committee and also joined a weekly Republican discussion group known as the Chowder and Marching Society, through which he developed a close relationship with another freshman representative, Richard M. Nixon. In 1954 he became only the second Lebanon resident to serve in the U.S. Senate when he won a special election to fill the vacancy created by the death of Senator Charles W. Tobey.

In moving to the upper chamber, he followed in the footsteps of Aaron Cragin, the only other Lebanon resident to serve in the Senate. A lawyer and native of Weston, Vermont, who arrived in Lebanon in 1847, Mr. Cragin was elected to the New Hampshire House in 1852. He then served two terms in Congress and, after returning to Lebanon to practice law, was again elected to the New Hampshire legislature. He won election to the U.S. Senate in 1864 and again in 1870, and was a member of the committees on Naval Affairs, Territories, and Pacific Railroads. He also chaired the committee of arrangements for the inauguration of Ulysses S. Grant.

Following his defeat in 1876, Mr. Cragin remained in Washington and tried desperately without success to gain appointment to a high-level government position. He lobbied hard in 1883 to win the job of Commissioner of Patents and was bitterly disappointed when it went to someone else. "I suppose the jig is up, and the fates continue against me," he wrote to a friend. "I infer that the thing was predetermined, and I regret that I could not have known this months ago, and I would not have annoyed my friends . . . I am no novice in this business, and I did not calculate with certainty on success, but truth compels me to admit that I am sadly disappointed."

Frozen out of the world of politics, Mr. Cragin settled for practicing patent law until his death in 1898.

Norris Cotton, on the other hand, never had to return to his law practice once he entered federal politics. He won re-election to the Senate in 1956, 1962, and 1968.

Norris Cotton's influence can be seen throughout Lebanon and the Upper Valley, as his position on the Senate Appropriations Committee helped secure federal money for a legion of projects back home: runway extensions, an instrument landing system, and an FAA control tower at the Lebanon airport; a new wing for Alice Peck Day Memorial Hospital; the establishment of the Cold Regions Research and Engineering Laboratory in Hanover; and urban renewal funds that flowed to Lebanon after the disastrous downtown fire of 1964. His crowning achievement, however, was the establishment in 1974 of the cancer center that bears his name. Through his work on the Senate Appropriations Committee, he was able to secure six-million dollars for a first-rate cancer-research facility affiliated with the Dartmouth-Hitchcock Medical Center.

Norris Cotton was a devout conservative in matters both fiscal and social: He voted against the 1964 Civil Rights Act, mostly supported the war in Vietnam, and remained loyal to old friend Richard Nixon through the worst of the Watergate era. In fact, it was said that Mr. Nixon knew the time had come to resign after he lost the support of Senator Cotton in June 1974. Wrote the senator in his memoirs:

After he became president, I became chairman of the Republican Conference in the Senate and, accordingly, I was one of the five Republican leaders who went to the White House regularly to meet with the president. In that capacity I went through those harrowing hours and days that led to his resignation and departure. With others who had been his friends through the years, I went at his invitation to the Cabinet Room the last night he was in the White House, when he desired to bid us farewell, and I saw him break down in tears at the end. That night, at two o'clock in the morning, he called me at my apartment, as doubtless he did others of his long-time associates, for a personal goodbye. He was then in command of himself, and the conversation was extremely personal—to be remembered, but not repeated.

Senator Cotton capped his own political career in 1975 when he became the first New Hampshire senator to voluntarily relinquish his seat since Franklin Pierce in 1842. As one of his last acts, he won passage of a resolution giving New Hampshire's senior senator the honor of always sitting at the desk once occupied by the great Daniel Webster.

Actually, there was one more chapter in Norris Cotton's senate career. The election to replace him turned out to be the closest in the history of the Senate, and there was a period when the seat was declared vacant and the state had only one U.S. Senator. While awaiting the outcome of a special election to resolve the single-digit contest between John Durkin and Louis Wyman, Mr. Cotton was returned to the Senate on an interim basis on August 8, 1975, until a special election could be held to decide the matter. Finally, on September 18, 1975, he called it quits for good and gave way to Mr. Durkin, who had bested Mr. Wyman in the special election.

One of the speakers at Senator Cotton's funeral in March 1989 was none other than his old friend from the Chowder and Marching Society, former President Richard Nixon.

U.S. Senator Norris Cotton makes a point.

Lane Dwinell

The other Lebanon resident to rise to political prominence during this period was S. Lane Dwinell, who in 1954 became the only resident of the town elected governor, completing an unprecedented political ascension not likely to be repeated.

Lane Dwinell's father, Dean, was in the shoe business in Lebanon with Carl Richards during the early part of the century before he married Ruth Lane and moved to Newport, Vermont. Lane was born there in 1906, and after a stop in Pasadena, California, the family returned to Lebanon when the senior Dwinell acquired an interest in Carter & Churchill Co. The move was just in time for the son's senior year of high school, where he excelled as a snowshoe racer on the ski team and captained the 1924 track team.

After graduating from Dartmouth College and the Amos Tuck School of Business at Dartmouth, the younger Dwinell worked in New York as a financial analyst in the treasurer's office of General Motors. His heart, however, kept him in touch with Lebanon, and in 1932 he married Elizabeth Cushman, a 1927 graduate of Lebanon High School who attended Emerson College and was well known in town as a teacher of dancing and acting classes. The couple lived in New York until 1936, when Mr. Dwinell joined his father in business back in Lebanon.

Not long after his return the son began his political career by winning election to the town budget committee, serving as its chairman. He also presided over the Lebanon Rotary Club and, as a special justice, the Lebanon Municipal Court.

His entry into politics at the state level began in 1948, when he was chosen a delegate to the state constitutional convention and also was elected to the New Hampshire House of Representatives. By then he had already served as president of the New Hampshire Manufacturers Association, and also had put in four years on the state board of education.

He was selected chairman of the House Ways and Means Committee in his freshman term, and in his second was elected speaker. Since tradition dictated that no member of the house hold the speaker's job for more than one term, he ran for and was elected to the state Senate in 1952, and was immediately elected Senate President. In doing so, he became only the second Lebanonian to preside over the Senate—*Free Press* founder George Towle had held the job in 1860-1861. Only one person from Lebanon, Ralph Degnan Hough, has held the position since. The liberal Republican has served eight terms in the Senate and won the presidency in 1992 by coaxing one other liberal Republican and all of the Democrats to support his bid, thus putting virtual control of the body in Democratic hands for the first time in eighty years.

Lane Dwinell's opportunity to run for governor came when Hugh Gregg announced that he would forego re-election in 1954 and return to the family business after just one term. Looking to preempt most serious challengers, Mr. Dwinell immediately became a candidate and defeated Rochester Mayor John Shaw in the general election, 107,227 to 87,334; and he was re-elected in 1956.

With his elevation to the governor's office, Lane Dwinell became the only man in state history to serve consecutive terms as House Speaker, Senate President, and Governor. The magazine *New Hampshire Profiles* noted that, "Other politicians of the Granite State had climbed the same ladder, but none so far in such little time."

Given the fact that present house speakers and Senate presidents now cling to their

Governor Lane Dwinell presiding over a meeting of the New Hampshire Executive Council

leadership positions for long periods of time (tradition no longer dictates that they step down after two years), the speed of his ascension seems not likely to be repeated anytime soon, if ever.

Lane Dwinell, was a moderate conservative who preached and practiced fiscal restraint, urging legislators to distinguish "between that which is necessary and that which is merely desirable."

He was a businessman first and foremost, and he campaigned on a theme of applying private-sector management principles to government operations. Once elected, he tightened accounting procedures, gave underpaid state employees hefty raises to reduce excess turnover in their ranks, and established a forty-hour work week for state police and employees of state institutions who regularly worked sixty hours or more with no overtime.

He also signed a bill that initiated state aid for school building construction, and another that allowed groups of small towns to band together into cooperative school districts. Under the law he signed, districts that took the path to regionalization were given extra building-aid money.

When Mr. Dwinell left office in 1959, he was appointed U.S. Assistant Secretary of State for administration, a position that saw him responsible for the department's budget, personnel and operations, and construction and operation of U.S. Embassies abroad.

His final foray into elective politics came in 1966, when he was an unsuccessful candidate for the U.S. Senate, losing in the Republican primary. In 1969 the former governor was appointed an administrator for the Agency for International Development, a position he held until 1971.

Following his retirement, Mr. Dwinell continued to be active in the Republican party. He chaired Richard Nixon's 1972 re-election campaign in New Hampshire and the president chose to make his formal re-election announcement through a letter to Mr. Dwinell, who was given permission from the White House to release it to the media, providing the Lebanon resident with national exposure.

The former governor remained active in the Republican party well after his retirement, and he attended the Republican national conventions of 1952, 1956, 1968, 1972, 1980, 1984, and 1988, and four times chaired the state's convention delegation.

Aside from the obvious matter of bragging rights, having a sitting governor and senator residing in town may have come in handy in one respect. Lane Dwinell says that it undoubtedly gave the town leverage in securing an extra interstate exit next to the Split Ballbearing plant on Route 4 (Exit 19). Given the notorious recalcitrance of state and federal highway officials—and the substantial costs they had to approve for building extra ramps and a bridge—that appears to have been no mean accomplishment.

Having a governor in town also made a difference in the placement of Interstate 89, which was originally slated to traverse Storrs Hill on the south side of town. As governor, Mr. Dwinell had a voice in laying out the interstate (even though it was not built until 1966) and was instrumental in choosing the route it eventually took north of Lebanon village.

The Dwinells have also shown themselves to be an immensely public-spirited couple in the old-fashioned vein of a George Rogers or William Carter, having donated tens of thousands of dollars for a variety of causes, including a new wing for the Lebanon library and a swimming pool at the Carl Witherell Center (and, in the interests of full disclosure, this book.)

While the late fifties undoubtedly marked the pinnacle of political influence for Lebanon, another benchmark was established in the 1993-94 session of the legislature. Not only did Ralph Hough win election as president of the New Hampshire Senate, but incredibly, three of the town's four representatives (not counting the one shared with Enfield) chaired committees in the House. Channing Brown presided over the all-important Appropriations Committee, Karen Wadsworth headed the Committee on Municipal and County Government, and Pamela Bean chaired the Committee on Children, Youth, and Juvenile Justice.

19

Lebanon vs (West) Lebanon

Secession

WHILE LEBANON had political clout in 1957, it was also a town at war with itself over three dominant issues, two of them involving the relationship between the town's two main villages.

"West Lebanon is a separate community, socially, economically, and except for political ties is a part of White River Junction, even if the state legislature doesn't know it," selectman George Edson told a meeting of the West Lebanon Civic Association in 1957. Many West Lebanon residents had long felt like ill-treated stepchildren in their relations with Lebanon, and Mr. Edson, who owned a bakery on West Lebanon's Main Street, was a proponent of creating a separate municipality for residents of the west side of town.

In many ways West Lebanon closely resembled a separate town. It had its own fire and police headquarters, water precinct, business district, and high school, and its residents were much more likely to socialize in White River Junction than in Lebanon. The reasons for the strong bond between the two villages were rooted in proximity (White River was closer than Lebanon), economics (the two villages shared a railroad heritage), and politics (many West Lebanon residents had long felt—probably with justification—that they were shortchanged when it came time to dole out town resources.) When the West Lebanon elementary school on Main Street found itself overflowing one year in the early 1950s, students were sent across the river to attend classes, rather than over Seminary Hill to Lebanon. Likewise, when the White River Elementary School was short of space a few years later, West Lebanon residents welcomed those Vermont students for a year.

The West Lebanon Civic Association was serious about breaking away from Lebanon and creating a separate town in 1957, and established a committee to explore the matter. The committee was comprised of chairman Irvin Davis, John Fontana,

Harvey Fellows, Paul McNamara, and Carroll Dutton, and a meeting on February twenty-fifth was attended by about three-hundred people who approved an advisory motion to secede by a margin of 193 to 17. Committee members even drafted a town budget that proposed spending $75,000 for town expenses, $150,000 to support the schools, and $18,000 for the water and fire precincts.

When no members of the town's legislative delegation would sponsor such a measure, the association convinced former house speaker Richard Upton to act on their behalf, and he took a proposed bill to the Senate Rules Committee.

The senate bill, which named Paul McNamara, Harvey Fellows, and Carroll Dutton as the would-be founding fathers of the town of West Lebanon, was referred to the Judiciary Committee, which held a two-hour hearing on May twenty-second.

Four West Lebanon residents spoke in favor of the bill, while eleven people opposed it, including four from West Lebanon. Selectman George Edson led the separationists, and was followed by Paul McNamara, businessman Robert Craig, and civic association member Irvin Davis, all of whom contended that West Lebanon was chronically short-changed by the town.

Lebanon Municipal Court Judge Mark W. Powers, speaking for the opposition, told the panel that the proposed legislation was a "spite bill" put forth by those who opposed closing West Lebanon High School and converting Lebanon into a city. He submitted a petition signed by two-hundred West Lebanon residents who opposed secession, and he was followed to the podium by West Lebanon residents Roy Hathorn, Frank Hough, and Jerold Ashley, all of whom urged the committee to reject the separation.

The committee recommended the bill be defeated as "inexpedient to legislate," and sent the measure to the senate floor. After debating whether residents of the town were entitled to hold a referendum on the issue the bill was recommitted to the Judiciary Committee for further study and reported back to the senate on June fourth, when Senator Edward Bennett—whose district included both villages—spoke against the proposal. Lebanon, he said, stood to lose about a third of its tax base under the plan, including revenue from Wilder Dam (the town's largest taxpayer), the airport, and the railroad. Taxes in Lebanon would soar, while those in West Lebanon would go down. "I don't believe it is any solution to help West Lebanon and crucify Lebanon," said Mr. Bennett.

Wilder Dam may have been the key. Initially, recalls Jim Wechsler, some Lebanon residents took a good-riddance attitude until they learned that their taxes would rise substantially when the dam was removed from the Lebanon tax base.

Meanwhile, Governor Lane Dwinell spoke out on the dispute. "I am definitely opposed to any separation of Lebanon or West Lebanon," he said. "It would remove a substantial part of taxable property from the town of Lebanon by a minority action."

Knowing it would be vetoed if it reached the governor's desk, the senate killed West Lebanon's effort to separate. While that ended the movement for a formal political division of the two villages, another rift lurked just around the corner.

Joe Perley, The *Valley News*, and WTSL

Concurrent with the discussion over whether West Lebanon should break away from the township, state representative Gladys Whipple submitted a bill to change the

Front cover and last page of a 1938 campaign brochure promoting the candidacy of Joe Perley

town into a city by adopting a council-manager form of government. The measure passed the legislature and was signed by Lebanon's own Governor Lane Dwinell on July 17, 1957, setting the stage for a referendum.

Opponents of the change argued that it would be more expensive and that doing away with the traditional town meeting and turning control of town affairs over to a nine-member city council "cuts the heart out of the democratic process of government," as selectman George Edson put it. Besides, they reasoned, Lebanon was small enough—about nine-thousand residents—to still be run efficiently by a board of selectmen.

That last claim might have been true enough, but the problem, as supporters of the city government saw it, was with the selectmen, especially Joseph "Uncle Joe" Perley.

Elected to the board in 1932, the Hardy Hill sheep farmer had served in the legislature and state senate and had won his share of ardent supporters by shepherding the town through the difficult periods of the Depression and World War II.

By 1957, however, there was a widespread feeling that Lebanon had become an autocracy and Joe Perley its de facto king, a sentiment Earl Burby captured in a letter to the *Valley News*:

A lot of people are sick of living in a town that's run by one man . . . As far as I can see decisions are made and money is spent without too much regard to the budget. In fact, the Budget Committee is often bypassed and there's darn little they can do about it. Often as not if the approval of the Committee is obtained, Joe gets it after the money is spent . . . Under this new

[city] charter the manager has to play by the rules of the game. But the game that is being played now has no rules.

If Joe Perley was running the town as he always had—and it seems likely that he was—then the town itself had changed, especially with the arrival of the *Valley News* in 1952.

The paper that debuted on June 9, 1952, was the brainchild of Plainfield residents Alan Butler and James Farley, two former *Claremont Daily Eagle* reporters who rented space in a building on Route 10 north of West Lebanon village (Peter Allard's Furniture Finders, 1994). Mr. Butler was the owner and publisher and the man with the money, while Mr. Farley was the paper's editor. The men bought the publishing rights and the subscription list to Alfred Wright's *Landmark* newspaper in White River Junction, and proceeded to do battle with their former employer.

Claremont in those days was in its heyday as a machine-tool town and served as the hub of the region in much the same way that Lebanon does in 1994. Convoys of cars left Lebanon every Friday night (Friday was payday in the mills) and headed down Route 120 to do their shopping in Claremont.

That city's influence over the region also was reflected in the *Claremont Daily Eagle*, which was the dominant daily from Lyme to Bellows Falls and boasted bureaus in Lebanon, Hanover, White River Junction, and Woodstock. Mr. Butler and Mr. Farley had plans to annex the northernmost portion of the paper's circulation area, a region Mr. Farley dubbed the "Upper Valley."

As former *Valley News* managing editor Steve Taylor recalled in a retrospective on the paper's thirty-fifth anniversary: "From the first day the valley region was witness to a real newspaper war, as the fledgling *Valley News* sought through aggressive coverage of local news and frequent creation of controversy to draw attention to itself and woo readers away from the *Daily Eagle*, which doggedly fought back with beefed-up coverage of its own."

Mr. Butler sold the paper in 1954 to Walter Paine and James Ewing, the owners of the *Keene Evening Sentinel*. Although the *Valley News* was losing money, Mr. Paine could afford the losses while continuing the aggressive news course set by the paper's founders.

While the paper went on a crusade against Joe Perley and advocated adoption of the city charter and the hiring of a professional town manager, Mr. Perley held himself out as just that. "When I came into office this town was in sad shape," he told the *Valley News*. "It was head over heels in debt... Few people were working and I doubt if Lebanon has ever seen worse days."

Mr. Perley took credit for a variety of town projects, including the resurgence of the woolen industry and the acquisition of federal and state money that had gone to build roads and bridges. That brought a sharp rebuttal from Dr. R. J. Couillard, a dentist who was a major landowner in Lebanon and its largest residential taxpayer. "Perley has done more harm than good to Lebanon," he said, claiming that it was he, as president of the Lebanon Chamber of Commerce, who had played a major role in attracting Bernard Goldfine's interest in the Lebanon woolen mills during the Depression.

Aside from the issue of who received credit for helping the town out of the Depression, there was a widespread public perception by 1957 that Mr. Perley engaged in a system of cronyism that rewarded his friends with lower tax assessments and other favors. (Mr. Perley's supporters—and there are still some around in 1994—maintain that he unilaterally lowered assessments for people who would otherwise have been forced to sell their homes had their tax bills been higher.)

Another story holds that Mr. Perley regularly compensated himself by taking advantage of his location as a resident on the Lebanon-Hanover town line. One version says that he charged the town of Lebanon for damage done to his sheep by dogs; and when the Lebanon dog-damage account was depleted, he moved his sheep to the Hanover side of his property and then charged that town accordingly. Lebanon's dog-damage budget in 1956 was a thousand dollars, of which $570 went to Mr. Perley as compensation for nineteen sheep and goats killed by dogs. In 1956 and 1957 the selectman received just over $1600 from both Lebanon and Hanover in sheep money.

Mr. Perley's claim that he could run the town in a fair, efficient, and open manner did not quite square with the eruption that took place on October 4, 1957, when newspaper staffers Arthur C. Roane, Jr. and Terri Dudley (later a city councilor) went to the town offices to copy records that the newspaper planned to publish to demonstrate inequities in the town's property assessments.

"Where do you think you're going?" Mr. Perley asked harshly. Informed that the visitors wanted to see the town's assessments for 1956-1957, the selectman replied, "You're not going to look at any books. Now get out of here."

Words were exchanged, and according to the *Valley News* account written by Mr. Roane, Mr. Perley pushed the reporter, called police and slammed shut the door of the vault that held the records.

The commotion attracted a crowd that included Earle Burke and waterworks superintendent Harry Manson, who screamed at the reporters: "*Valley News* go home. Go back to Boston. Go back to Beacon Street. You'll never run this town."

He also added a prediction: "The city of Lebanon, ha! That's a laugh. You'll never see the day."

The town released the records a few days later, and the following week the newspaper began publishing each resident's assessment. It even made a game out of it, running several side-by-side photographs of houses and inviting readers to choose the correct value from an accompanying list. The game demonstrated in graphic terms that property was assessed unevenly.

The debate took another nasty turn on the day before the referendum. Charter opponent John Brown suggested on a WTSL radio program that voters could defeat the charter change by staying away from the polls, since the referendum required 25 percent of voters to participate for the results to be valid. The *Valley News* called the effort to keep the turnout below that threshold, "a new low in disrespect for a voter's intelligence."

WTSL had arrived on the scene in 1950, although it was not "The Upper Valley's First Station," as it has claimed in a 1993-1994 promotional campaign. There were short-lived stations in Hanover in the mid-1920s, and the *Granite State Free Press* reported in 1931 that, "Next Sunday morning, May 17th, will take place the final broadcast from the local radio station WLEB, until a license is obtained from the Federal Radio Commission." The station had apparently been broadcasting for several weeks without a license.

The final broadcast, according to the newspaper, included Dr. Arthur Burnham's program on health, Alfred Densmore's discussion of elementary education, and a program by superintendent of schools William English about high-school education.

The following July the *Free Press* reported that, "Saturday evening marked the opening of the local radio broadcast and the radio placed on the bandstand in the Park drew a large and appreciative audience who received the program with interest." The article went on to say that the studio was located in the Lebanon Radio Shop on Hanover Street, which was founded in the early twenties by D. R. Houle; and before it went bankrupt in the early thirties, the business was owned by Philip Mann, Jr.

WTSL came along in 1950 as part of the Granite Broadcasting chain owned by William Rust and Ralph Gottlieb. The station signed on the air on December twenty-third of that year, operating from a trailer in the middle of a cornfield off Route 10 until a permanent building was completed on Oak Ridge Road. Norman Knight purchased the station in 1959, the same year that WTSL began live broadcasts of city council meetings.

The station almost from its inception established a niche as an important source of local morning news, weather, and sports in the region, so much so that before it became a morning paper in 1993, the *Valley News* regularly monitored WTSL's morning newscast to see what stories they might have missed.

Thousands of people wake up each weekday morning to the dependable voice of WTSL's Dave Rohde, who started at the station in 1971 when it was owned by Boston-area advertising executives Joseph Steinberg and Mark Wilcox. They brought Jim Canto aboard as general manager, and in 1980 he owned the station in its entirety.

Mr. Canto hired Darrel Clark as sales manager from a Keene radio station, and Mr. Clark became the station manager in the early 1980s while Mr. Canto pursued other interests. It was during this period that the station graduated its most famous alumnus. Gary Cohen started his radio career as WTSL's news director in 1981-1982, before landing behind the microphone as a baseball broadcaster for the New York Mets. He also announced Olympic hockey games and NCAA basketball tournament games for the CBS radio network.

Mr. Clark oversaw the addition of WTSL-FM in January 1987, and in July 1988 he and Philip Mans purchased the station from Mr. Canto and operated it under the banner of CM Communications. They moved the station into the former Tom's Toggery building on the Lebanon mall in 1989, just as a recession was enveloping the region. Heavily leveraged and having paid far more than the station was worth as a going concern, CM filed for bankruptcy protection in 1991. The Clark-Mans partnership sold the station in November 1992 to Scott Roberts' RJ Communications Inc., and in July 1993 the company changed the call letters of WTSL-FM to WGXL.

October 15, 1957, was a gorgeous day that brought out 44 percent of the 5,304 voters on the checklist. They rendered a decisive verdict against town government, approving the city charter 1,521 to 805, a margin of almost two-to-one. Town meetings were histo-

As the town's legislative delegation watches in July 1957, Governor Lane Dwinell signs the bill establishing Lebanon as a city. Behind the Governor from left to right are Fred Jones, Arthur Adams, Gladys Whipple, Forrest Cole, Harry Townsend, and J. Daniel Porter.

ry, and from then on the city council approved budgets, zoning changes, and other issues that had previously been decided by voters.

"WOW!" exclaimed the *Valley News* in a one-word front-page editorial that said as much about the *Valley News*' victory over the Claremont competition as it did about the vote itself. The West Lebanon paper had won the newspaper battle by waging war on the status quo in Lebanon, and the *Daily Eagle* eventually retracted its coverage to the Claremont area.

The paper staged a sizable coup in the publishing world in 1965 by becoming the smallest paper ever to capture the Ayer Cup for typographical excellence. (Previous winners of the now-defunct competition included the *Wall Street Journal*, *Christian Science Monitor*, and *New York Herald-Tribune*).

The *Valley News* went corporate in 1980, when Mr. Paine and Mr. Ewing sold out to Newspapers of New England, the parent company of the *Concord Monitor* and several other publications. The new owners cleaned out the newsroom shortly after they took over, summarily firing several staffers, including popular photographer Larry McDonald and reporter Eliot Page—the same Eliot Page whose firing by WTSL in 1979 had been lamented in a *Valley News* editorial.

The new ownership brought in professional newspaper people, held workshops on writing and layout, and upgraded the reporting, writing, and appearance of the paper. The scope of its coverage also changed. What was once primarily a community paper became a regional one, as it expanded its reporting in outlying towns and reduced coverage of lesser events in the traditional core towns. Regular stories on fender-benders, youth baseball games, and minor meetings became a thing of the past, as did "grip-and-grin" photographs of check passings, ribbon cuttings, and building dedications. The *Valley News* even soaked up a little reflected glory in 1992 when former staff writer Eric Lipton shared a Pulitzer Prize for explanatory journalism for his reporting of the flawed Hubble space telescope for the *Hartford Courant*. Mr. Lipton, only twenty-six at the time, was less than three years removed from his first newspaper job as the Lebanon reporter for the *Valley News*.

For a small paper, it has an admirable record for accuracy and timely reporting and has proven especially adept at covering major stories, such as the 1964 fire that leveled much of downtown Lebanon. Although it rarely mounts the kind of crusade anymore that led to the downfall of the Perley regime, it remains something of a burr under the valley's saddle and, accordingly, is an institution that readers love to hate. That feeling was reinforced somewhat when the paper changed from afternoon to morning delivery in 1993, and then added a Sunday paper. A decision to force subscribers to take all seven editions—or none at all—prompted some readers to cry extortion and cancel their orders.

Writing in 1980 about the simultaneous evolution of the paper and the region, former owner and publisher Walter Paine wrote that: "If the paper played a constructive role in this cooperative process, it was largely because a struggling daily and an evolving regional community needed each other; indeed, they still do."

There is no question the *Valley News* played an important role in Lebanon's becoming a city. Dr. Harry Savage, the dean of the Dartmouth Medical School and one of the town's most respected residents, said after the vote that, "There is no doubt that the inequalities in the tax assessments was the major factor in the change of government."

The first city council elections, held on December tenth of that year, brought more than 2,200 people to the polls to choose from thirty candidates for the nine positions. Dr. Savage, Theodore Minard, and Howard Townsend were elected to at-large seats; Roy Hathorn and Nelson Crawford were chosen from West Lebanon's Ward I; Robert Evans and Ernest Coutermarsh won the two seats in Ward II; and Harold Bond and Donald Taber claimed the seats in Ward III.

Joe Perley never sought election as a city council candidate, but two incumbent selectmen were turned out of office in the council elections. Although they were often at odds with Mr. Perley while the three served as selectmen, neither Daniel Brown nor George Edson was seated in that first council election. Both served in later years.

When the first city council was seated in January, councilors voted Dr. Savage to lead them in the largely ceremonial post of mayor. (He resigned his seat within a few months to take over as the judge of Lebanon's municipal court.) Shortly after being seated, councilors hired thirty-two-year-old Jacob Dumelle from Peoria, Illinois, as the first city manager. Predictably enough, his first recommendation to the council was for a city-wide property reappraisal.

Was the conversion to a council-manager system a change for the better? It seems to have been a mixed bag, and one that is still hotly debated in some quarters.

There are those who would argue that it is at least partially responsible for an exponential increase in the cost of municipal government. The budget in 1960 was $640,000 for a population of 9,299, and in 1990, with a population of 12,183, the municipal budget was $8.37 million, a sum that supports a network of bureaucrats and specialists, many of whom drive around in city-owned vehicles and have a cadre of secretaries and assistants to manage their paperwork.

Opponents of the council-manager setup who argue that it is less democratic than the old town-meeting system may have a point. Although supporters of city government would point to the several hundred people who turn out for a municipal election as an example of democracy in action, the council still tends to operate in something of a vacuum. Its meetings are poorly attended (except when the populace is riled up about something, which is not often), and a good chunk of the voting public probably could not name a majoirty of the council at any given time. The council has also, on occasion, gone against the will of the public as expressed in non-binding referendums, the most prominent example being the installation of a pedestrian mall after the 1964 fire.

On the other hand, several factors may justify the growth in the city budget. Commercial and industrial growth has skyrocketed since the town became a city, placing demands on municipal services that were not there in the 1950s; and those services are also required to be much more sophisticated than they had to be thirty-five years ago.

However, insofar as a major objective of adopting the council-manager system was

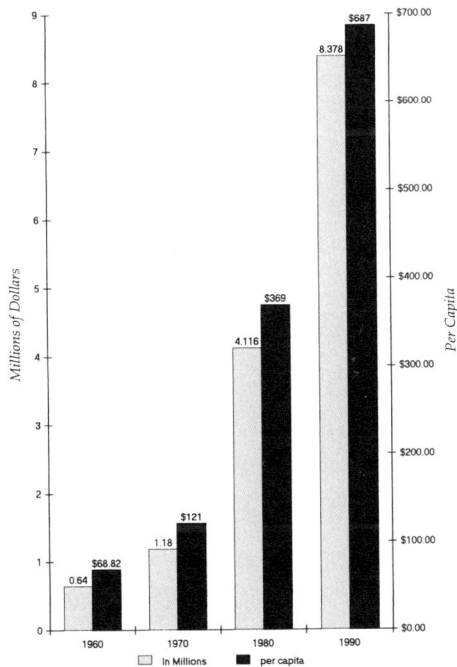

Total and per capita city expenditures 1960 through 1990

to eliminate cronyism and favoritism, the conversion seems to have been a success (although for several years temporary summer jobs often went to the children of city employees). No longer does your property assessment depend on your last name or who your friends are. In that respect, the change seems to have been for the better.

Which is not to say that the council-manager form of government has been problem-free. The relationship between the two branches of city government has been marked by periodic clashes and power struggles. City manager Kenneth D. Boehner abruptly resigned in June 1970 after butting heads with Mayor Shirley Merrill over whether he had kept the council properly informed about city matters. (Cooler heads prevailed a few weeks later and Mr. Boehner rescinded his resignation after meeting with Mrs. Merrill and other councilors.)

Shirley Merrill was a pioneer for women in both local and state politics. The town had sent women to the legislature as early as 1932, when East Lebanon resident Florence W. Hoyt was elected to the first of four terms. Furthermore, women had run for the school board as early as the 1870s. However, voters never elected a female selectman in the 196 years that Lebanon operated under the town form of government.

Mrs. Merrill ran for the council during that first city election in 1957, but finished far back among the Ward III candidates. After winning election to the legislature in 1967, she and Mary Demers became the first women to serve on the city council in 1968. Two years later Mrs. Merrill was elected Lebanon's first woman mayor.

The story of her ascension to the town's political throne was big news. Never mind that the post was largely ceremonial. Women mayors were still a rarity and the story received play in the *Los Angeles Times* and other metropolitan dailies. The mayor even declined an invitation to appear on NBC's The Today Show to talk about her election.

After two years as mayor, Mrs. Merrill left city government in 1972 and was appointed to the state Public Utilities Commission in 1973, becoming the first woman to serve on that board.

Lebanon has had several women mayors since Shirley Merrill—Pam Bean in 1977, Karen Wadsworth in 1979 and again in the 1980s, and Nancy Esquivel was elected in 1990. Mrs. Esquivel is the daughter of Shirley Merrill, and her election marked only the second time in state history that a mother and daughter had both served as mayor in the same city.

The conversion to city government did not mark the end of the debate over the charter. There have been several changes to the charter since it was first adopted. Councilors are now elected in March instead of November, the elections are staggered so that not everyone is up for renewal at the same time, and the council no longer approves the school budget as it did until the mid-sixties.

The town-city question remains a prickly one. It resurfaced in 1981 and 1982 when a group of residents led by Philip Mans and Frederick Aldrich sought a return to town government, this time with a town manager to run the day-to-day operations. A commission proposed a new charter that supporters argued was more democratic because, while reestablishing Lebanon as a town, it would have given residents a direct vote on the budget and other ballot items.

Attorney R. Peter Decato and city councilor Karen Wadsworth led opponents of the change under an umbrella group known as KEEP (Keep Efficiency, Effectiveness and

Professionalism in Lebanon Government). The group argued that the effort to reform the charter was misguided, unwieldy, and although the city would revert to a town, the proposed charter would not return the town meeting to Lebanon, since the budget would be decided by Australian ballot.

The matter was put to a vote in March 1982, and 67 percent of the town's registered voters overwhelmingly rejected the new charter by a margin of 1,752-856.

That debate occurred at about the same time that another city manager and city council were at loggerheads, and again the clash brought about the resignation of a city manager—John Wheeler—who stepped down in 1981 after a five-member conservative majority of councilors gutted his proposed budget.

Unlike Mr. Boehner, Mr. Wheeler did not withdraw his resignation; and in a final speech before a packed house in the city hall courtroom, he accused Mr. Mans and Mr. Mans' father-in-law, Wilfred "Bin" Dulac, of running a shadow government from Dulac's Hardware Store. Shadow government might have been stretching the point a bit, but the store—where both Mr. Mans and Mr. Dulac worked—was unquestionably the center of conservative politics in Lebanon. A hand-lettered sign on the front door proclaimed Dulac's to be "Lower City Hall," and informed the reader that, "If you didn't hear it here, it isn't worth repeating." Although the sign was an irritant to some, it also contained more than a grain of truth.

The School on the Hill

The third major issue debated in 1957 was a plan to close West Lebanon High School and send students to a proposed central school that would serve both sides of town. What was perhaps the first step in that direction was taken in 1954, when the school board voted to allow West Lebanon High School students to attend either of the town's high schools. "This allows pupils to take such subjects as agriculture and machine shop," the *Free Press* reported. "Pupils may shift to get academic subjects such as Latin which is offered only at Lebanon High."

Nancy Pyer, a 1949 graduate of West Lebanon High School, says some college-prep classes at West Lebanon were eliminated to force many college-bound students to attend school on the other side of town. This was especially true of Latin, which was needed to pursue a career in nursing and which was dropped from the West Lebanon curriculum in later years. "Parents were called traitors if they sent their kids to Lebanon to get the courses they needed for college," Mrs. Pyer said.

Daniel Webster's famous quote about Dartmouth College being a small school—"yet there are those who love it"—was equally applicable to West Lebanon High School in the late fifties. Feelings for the institution ran deep in the community—probably more so than on the other side of town, where Lebanon High competed for local affections with a broad industrial and commercial base, the Carter Community Building, and the seat of local government. The school was much more of a focal point for West Lebanon residents, who were loath to close their prize institution. It was, recalls Mrs. Pyer, the place where the Halloween parties, social gatherings, and virtually all other village functions were held.

For most of the nineteenth century, West Lebanon residents who wanted to attend

The first West Lebanon High School, located on Main Street next door to the Holy Redeemer Church

high school were required to do so outside the village, which had no public high school. That changed when the legislature created the West Lebanon School District in 1890, and voters approved spending ten-thousand-dollars to construct a new brick school building on Main Street where a wooden one had previously stood (First NH Bank, 1994).

The new building came in under budget, and West Lebanon High School opened in the fall of 1891 with one class and one teacher on the second floor of the building which also housed the village clock and bell. The headmaster was Joseph Dunbar, who stayed through 1893, and he was succeeded by a procession of men most remarkable for the frequency with which they departed. The headmaster parade ended in 1928, with the arrival of George W. Currier, who remained on the job until his death in 1958.

West Lebanon High School remained on Main Street until 1915, when overcrowding forced it to move out of the Main Street building (which was turned over to the New York Knitting Mill corporation). The school relocated in the old Tilden building on Seminary Hill, which the Rockland Military Academy had given up the year before. The West Lebanon School District merged with Lebanon in 1927, an auditorium was added to the building in 1934 and a gymnasium in 1940. The school over the years offered students a variety of courses, and extracurricular activities ranging from prize-speaking contests to football, hockey, music, a ski team, a rifle club, newspaper and yearbook, and track.

"They were very proud of this end of town, they were very proud of this little dinky high school, and they were very proud of what they had accomplished," said Jerome Damren, a longtime West Lebanon resident who taught at the school from 1949-1961. The size of the school—a little over two-hundred students—contributed to the sense of

Lebanon, 1761-1994 / 218

closeness. Mr. Damren said that unity was typified in many ways by the basketball team, which regularly competed against schools that were significantly larger. In fact, the West Lebanon Lions won the state Class C basketball championship in 1948, and wore the Class S crown in 1960. Mr. Damren recalled that about everyone in the village made the trip to Durham for that last championship game.

Against that backdrop of intense village pride, the proposal to merge the town's two high schools by closing the one in West Lebanon came to its first vote in 1957. The annual school district meeting started at eight o'clock, but by six-thirty the line of people extended out the town hall and blocked traffic on North Park Street. By the time the assembly convened the balcony and orchestra sections of the opera house were jammed and the crowd spilled over into the lower town hall and the banquet room in the basement.

Ironically, West Lebanon High School graduate Sumner Atherton, Jr., whose father had long managed the old General Ice Cream plant on Main Street, was the board member who did much of the speaking in favor of the plan to close the school. Proponents of the merger said that the new school was necessary because the population of Lebanon High School had outgrown the building on Bank Street, and the same would be true of West Lebanon within a few years. At the same time, they argued, it would be more economical to close West Lebanon High and send its students to Lebanon, eliminating much duplication.

Rose Putnam and Alberta Wells carried the torch for those West Lebanon residents who wanted to maintain separate high schools, arguing that the merger would actually *cost* money.

The vote was tied to a $700,000 bond issue to pay for the proposed central school to be built on thirty-two acres next to the Hanover Street elementary school. Although a majority of voters supported the measure, 827-532, it failed to carry the two-thirds majority needed for passage, and the merger plan was defeated. Voters approved a bond issue later in 1957, and the new high school was constructed the next year.

Fire at the Seminary Hill School on February 19, 1940 when it was occupied by West Lebanon High. While the building was being repaired students attended Lebanon High which held double sessions.

The consolidation movement resurfaced in 1961, and West Lebanon residents again resisted the effort to close their high school. Sixty students signed a petition opposing the merger, and letters and signs appeared throughout town urging defeat of the proposal. Superintendent Hammond Young, a West Lebanon resident who urged voters to approve the union, was a target of some criticism, and the fact that he lived on that side of town made his position on the closing even harder for many West Lebanon residents to swallow.

Again, supporters argued that a single high school would save the district money and, as if consolidation were a foregone conclusion, the school board presented only one high-school budget at the March sixth district meeting.

As she had in 1957, Rose Putnam led the charge to keep West Lebanon High School open. The school, she said, had proven itself since its inception and was worthy of continued support. "Would you from Lebanon want your children to be forced to go to school in West Lebanon?" she asked rhetorically. "We feel sentimental about our high school. Our kids are heartsick, and they don't want to leave. You are forcing it upon them."

Sentiment, however, was not enough to carry the day. The turnout was much smaller than in 1957, but 66 percent of voters approved the consolidation plan, 412-189. The school board immediately petitioned the Grafton County Superior Court for permission to close the school, and Judge William Grimes granted permission to do so in May 1961. Many West Lebanon residents felt as if they had been slugged in the gut. "It was very bitter," recalled Mrs. Pyer.

A month after the judge's ruling, twenty-seven seniors marched into a packed school auditorium and became the last class to graduate from West Lebanon High School.

When school resumed the following September, all students in grades ten, eleven, and twelve attended Lebanon High School on Hanover Street, and the old high school housed junior-high students (it was later converted into an elementary school). Carl van de Bogart, who had taken over as principal in 1958 (after Mr. Damren finished out the year as interim principal following George Currier's death in the spring of that year) remained at the West Lebanon school through the 1986-1987 school year.

Many West Lebanon residents still believe that Hammond Young was hired for the express purpose of closing the school, although Mr. Young says that was not the case and he maintains that the closing was the best thing for education in Lebanon. Still, he left for another position within a few months of the court order to close the school.

While the consolidation undoubtedly robbed West Lebanon of a major portion of its identity and engendered enormous amounts of resentment toward those in the center of town, in the long run it probably also brought the community closer together. No longer were students from Lebanon and West Lebanon virtual strangers.

The shutdown of West Lebanon High School, however, still evokes strong emotions among many longtime residents on that side of town. Even though the high school closed more than thirty years ago, you could probably still start a pretty good fight by going to downtown West Lebanon and talking about what a good idea it was to close it. Meanwhile, the loyalty behind those emotions—the very thing that prompted West Lebanon residents to fight so hard to keep their school open—is evident in 1994, in the six-hundred-member alumni association that still holds parades and banquets.

20

Decline

THE END OF the textile era in Lebanon began with the closing of the Mascoma Mill in 1953, and it culminated in 1962 after a scandal that shook official Washington and tainted two Lebanon political figures. The scandal—involving Lebanon mill owner Bernard Goldfine—no doubt hastened the closing of the town's textile factories, although they had about run their course, anyhow.

The New England textile industry—which was prone to seasonal fits and starts in the first place—was fading in the years following World War II. The rise of the synthetics industry was offering stiff competition, and cheaper labor in the south made it hard for companies like American Woolen, which closed its Mascoma Mill operation on Mechanic Street in 1953. Bernard Goldfine, the Boston industrialist who had reopened the Lebanon Woolen and Lebandale mills in the Depression, purchased the Mascoma Mill in 1955 and promised that it would reopen.

Not only did that not happen, but his two other woolen mills also closed after Mr. Goldfine's financial empire unraveled like so much cheap cloth.

Richard Wood's association with the Lebanon Woolen Mill dates to the early 1930s, when his father, Chester, ran the shop as part-owner in conjunction with Mr. Goldfine. Richard, who was part of the mill's management from the late 1940s until it closed, remembers Mr. Goldfine as an able salesman and with a magnanimous personality. "He liked to keep his finger in the political pie," said Mr. Wood. "He could be a Republican in New Hampshire and a Democrat in Massachusetts."

Mr. Goldfine also had a penchant for giving gifts, which proved his downfall. It began in 1958, when it was disclosed that former New Hampshire Governor Sherman Adams had accepted a vicuna coat and other gifts from Mr. Goldfine. Mr. Adams was President Eisenhower's chief of staff at the time, and the news forced Mr. Adams to resign and triggered congressional investigations. Caught up in the whirlwind were two Lebanon men—Norris Cotton and Joe Perley.

A 1959 *LOOK* magazine article detailed a variety of ties between Mr. Goldfine and Senator Cotton dating back to the 1930s, when Mr. Cotton had helped bring Mr.

Enter Frank Stearns, who took a job at SBB in 1947 as a designer and salesman and drummed up enough business for the company to show a modest profit in 1948. The company also caught a break that year when Mr. Stearns and toolroom foreman Bill Tucker stumbled upon a bearing that was even easier to replace than the original. It was a better mousetrap and a valuable addition to the Splitball repertoire, but the company still lost money—a reported $30,000 in 1949, as the workweek was cut back to three days.

The start of the Korean War in 1950 signaled the beginning of another profitable period for Splitball. Sales doubled, employment peaked at about sixty, and the company was ready to move out of the old wooden building on Mascoma Street. It was not the kind of place to which Splitball management was eager to invite clients, and Frank Stearns recalled the condition of the building during a visit by officials of the Sperry Gyroscope in the early fifties: "Cobwebs hung from the beams; it was dark and jammed with equipment; it was poorly organized for a flow of work. The head Sperry man almost smashed his shins out against Ray Gardner's desk as he walked along."

The question was, would management decide to continue in Lebanon? Not wanting to lose a major employer, members of the Lebanon Industrial Development Association went to SBB management with an offer to help finance a new factory building. The association put up $15,000, local banks matched that, a private individual kicked in $10,000, and the company pledged $30,000. Splitball moved into the new LIDA building on lower Mechanic Street (the old Mike's-Owl's Nest-Legacy restaurant building) in 1952.

Five years later Splitball merged with and became a subsidiary of its old satellite company, MPB, and moved to new quarters on a fifteen-acre lot at the bottom of Poverty Lane. The new factory was dedicated on December 19, 1958, with Governor Lane Dwinell—a Splitball booster and fellow Lebanon industrialist—doing the honors as one of his final acts before leaving office early in the following year. The 30,000 square-foot building (since expanded several times) stood in sharp contrast to the humble beginnings on Mascoma Street, and in 1959 *Factory* magazine named it one of the ten best new factories in the country.

Splitball struggled for a while, but showed a profit in the early sixties when it filled contracts for NASA. A high point occurred in 1962, when the company's bearings were installed in the Mercury spacecraft in which astronaut Wally Schirra orbited the earth.

Like the military and aerospace industries it has served, Splitball has seen its ups and downs over the years, and employment levels have fluctuated in response to changing economic conditions, especially in those two industries. The defense buildup of the mid-1980s saw almost a thousand people on the payroll, but the recession of the late eighties and early nineties saw that number drop to about eight hundred. Said one employee in 1989: "It's like the election: something major happens every two to four years."

It also has operated under several different corporate umbrellas since 1976, when MPB and Splitball were acquired by Wheelabrator-Frye Incorporated. Most recently, in 1990, The Timken Company of Canton, Ohio, purchased MPB and Splitball.

Despite the roller-coaster payroll numbers and changes in corporate ownership, the company has provided a steady core of well-paying jobs for residents of Lebanon and

Goldfine to town. It was clear that the Senator and the industrialist had a relationship that was something less than arm's length. According to the article:

Senator Cotton owned stock and was an officer in Mr. Goldfine's Lebanon Woolen Mill Corporation until 1957, and also lived in a Goldfine house on Abbot Street. Whether he paid rent has always been a source of speculation in town.

He continued to receive at least an indirect financial benefit from Mr. Goldfine even after he was seated in Congress. The mill owner testified before a congressional committee that Mr. Cotton had stopped representing him as an attorney in 1947, when voters sent Mr. Cotton to Congress. However, even after that time, Mr. Goldfine continued to be represented by the Lebanon firm of Cotton, Tesreau, & Stebbins, while Senator Cotton continued to draw a salary from the partnership.

Mr. Cotton intervened with the Securities and Exchange Commission in an effort to influence a suit brought by the SEC against one of Mr. Goldfine's holding companies.

While Mr. Goldfine paid property taxes on the Hotel Rogers and kept the owner's suite well-stocked with liquor and meat, the owner of record for nearly fifteen years was none other than Norris Cotton. In other words, it appears that Mr. Cotton fronted for the industrialist, although he quickly signed the hotel over to a Goldfine holding company once Congress began to investigate Mr. Goldfine. In an interview years later, Mr. Cotton maintained that a team of IRS agents had gone over his books and found him "clean as a whistle." Moreover, his relationship with the Boston-area industrialist did not seem to affect his standing with voters, who elected him to the Senate on two subsequent occasions.

The same Goldfine company that ended up with the Hotel Rogers also did business with Lebanon selectman Joe Perley. In an arrangement similar to the one involving Mr. Cotton, Mr. Goldfine, and the Hotel Rogers, Mr. Perley was the owner of record for the Mascoma Mill for a short period in 1955 before turning it over to a Goldfine holding company.

Selectman Daniel Brown told *LOOK* that Mr. Perley called a secret selectman's meeting shortly after transferring the property to Mr. Goldfine. The aim of the meeting, he recalled, was to reduce the assessment on the property from $100,000 to $25,000, which would have dropped the tax bill from $6,000 to $1,500.

"I protested that this was too low, and, after a bitter fight, we compromised at a $50,000 assessment," said Mr. Brown. "I wish I had known then what I know now. When things are done in secret, it's hard to talk, and an awful lot here was done in secret." His relationship with Norris Cotton and Joe Perley was the least of Mr. Goldfine's concerns when the Internal Revenue Service began pouring over his personal and business records in 1958. He held off a posse of government lawyers and agents for three years, but ultimately pleaded guilty to personal income-tax evasion and was sentenced to a year in jail on June 6, 1961.

Then, on January 16, 1962, teams of federal agents swooped down and slapped more than three-million-dollars in liens on Mr. Goldfine's holdings for failure to pay income taxes. In a memorandum to New Hampshire Governor Wesley Powell, acting U.S. Attorney General Byron R. White (a future U.S. Supreme Court justice) wrote that "Lebanon Woolen owes the United States [$1.2 million] in taxes and interest and Lebandale owes $150,000."

The court appointed as receiver of the mills John Cone of Hanover, whose family had been in the textile business for five generations. He arrived in Lebanon to find that there was no money to meet the $25,000 payroll, and some 360 employees were sent home and the factory was closed on Friday, February sixteenth.

While Mr. Cone scrambled for court permission to borrow money to meet the payroll, more than one-hundred mill workers applied for unemployment benefits in lower city hall, where eight representatives from the state Department of Employment Security set up shop to deal with the closing of the city's largest employer. The closing was a double-whammy for those families—and there were more than a few—that had more than one member working in the textile factories.

After Mr Cone received court approval to borrow money to pay back wages and complete the orders that were in hand when the axe fell, a consortium of six banks led by the National Bank of Lebanon agreed to lend the mill up to $200,000. The National Bank of Lebanon also set up a special teller window for mill workers to pick up their back pay, and the bank stayed open Saturday afternoon to accommodate the mill employees.

With a loan in hand, the Lebanon Woolen Company re-opened briefly in March 1962 with a skeleton crew assembled to complete an unfinished order of blankets for the military. Once that was finished, however, the mill closed for good on April twenty-sixth. Bernard Goldfine, meanwhile, agreed in 1963 to allow the government to sell his assets and pay off creditors. Said Mr. Goldfine at the time: "My deepest sorrow is that the termination of these court proceedings did not come in time to save the mills in Lebanon where 360 employees, many of whom spent their entire lives at my mills, were permanently thrown on the unemployment rolls."

The mill buildings and their contents were auctioned off in 1963, and are in use again after several years of dormancy. The old Lebanon Woolen Mill houses the dry-cleaning facility of Kleen Laundry, run by the Gosselin family; the Lebandale mill, meanwhile, is the headquarters for Whitman Communications and the Whitman Press, owned by Steve Whitman. The Mascoma Mill was home to the Rockdale Discount Department Store between 1961 and 1972, and after standing idle for several years was refurbished in the 1980s under the name of the Rivermill Commercial Center. Converted to small-business uses, it houses Systems Plus Computers, the Blacksmith Bakery, and United Developmental Services, among others (1994).

As for Mr. Goldfine's creditors, they did not fare well. Those holding liens on his properties were able to negotiate settlements with the government, but unsecured lenders received only 8 percent of the money they were owed after the property was sold. Finally, in 1965, after four years of overseeing the liquidation, Mr. Cone completed his work as receiver of the mills and the legal proceedings involving the mills ended. By then, however, Lebanon had other irons in the fire.

Although the mills were the town's largest employer and the closing *was* a major blow to the economy, Lebanon's labor force was beginning to diversify by the time the Lebanon Woolen and Lebandale mills shut down. A town labor survey published in 1953 showed that although textiles were the single largest employer in the community, there were other significant fields of work. The *Valley News* reported that: "Nearly 9 percent, or 293 of the 3,299 workers, are paid by taxation. Of this 9 percent, 65 work for the town or state, 40 for the Veterans Administration at the Veterans Hospital in White River Junction, and 87 for the local school district. The federal employment in Lebanon is about double the national average, but the larger figure is due to the proximity of the VA hospital."

The story also noted that about 10 percent of the town's work force commuted to jobs outside the town. In addition to those at the VA hospital, another 30 people were employed at the Goodyear rubber factory in Windsor, 221 worked at Mary Hitchcock Memorial Hospital, and 162 residents crossed the Connecticut River to jobs with the railroads in White River Junction.

While some of the displaced mill workers migrated to the Baltic mill in Enfield, or the Dorr mill in Newport, others left the textile industry altogether for places like Split Ballbearing or Dartmouth College. However, Richard Wood and others agree that most of the new jobs paid less than the union wages to which the mill workers had become accustomed.

Lebanon College

Nobody took Daniel Brown seriously when he suggested in a letter to the *Valley News* that opening a girls' college in Lebanon—just five miles away from all-male Dartmouth—might be a successful venture.

"Would you settle for an evening or day school for adults, using high-school facilities, old factory buildings, part-time teachers, and volunteers so that costs can be controlled?" asked Charles Dudley, Jr.

Out of that conversation the two men met with Albert Carlson of the Dartmouth-Lake Sunapee Region Association over coffee at Fred Cushing, Sr.'s Lebanon Drug Company and hatched the idea for Lebanon College.

With the mills hurting and unemployment high, Lebanon College was born on February 13, 1957. Seventy-five students enrolled in six classes that were held at the old Lebanon High School on Bank Street. Three of the courses were in business, an area that served as the school's foundation as it expanded over the years into liberal arts and assorted hobbies and crafts.

While Mr. Carlson was the first president, Mr. Dudley was the school's dean for more than thirty years. During this time, the college granted its first associate degrees in 1978, and its enrollment soared to an average of more than 1,800 in the 1980s when it offered courses catering to adults wishing to catch the computer wave.

The 1964 Fire

The mills were history and the interstate highway was just around the corner on Friday, June 19, 1964, when twenty-one-year-old Albert Healey and sixteen-year-old Joseph Thibideau left their perch on the city hall steps and headed down Hanover Street in search of something to break up their boredom.

The pair walked between the mostly wooden buildings that made up the core of the downtown area (now the mall) and turned onto Mill Street, the shabby side road that connected Hanover and Mascoma streets. Crossing the railroad tracks they entered an abandoned blacksmith shop that had become a haven for vagrants, planning to throw a

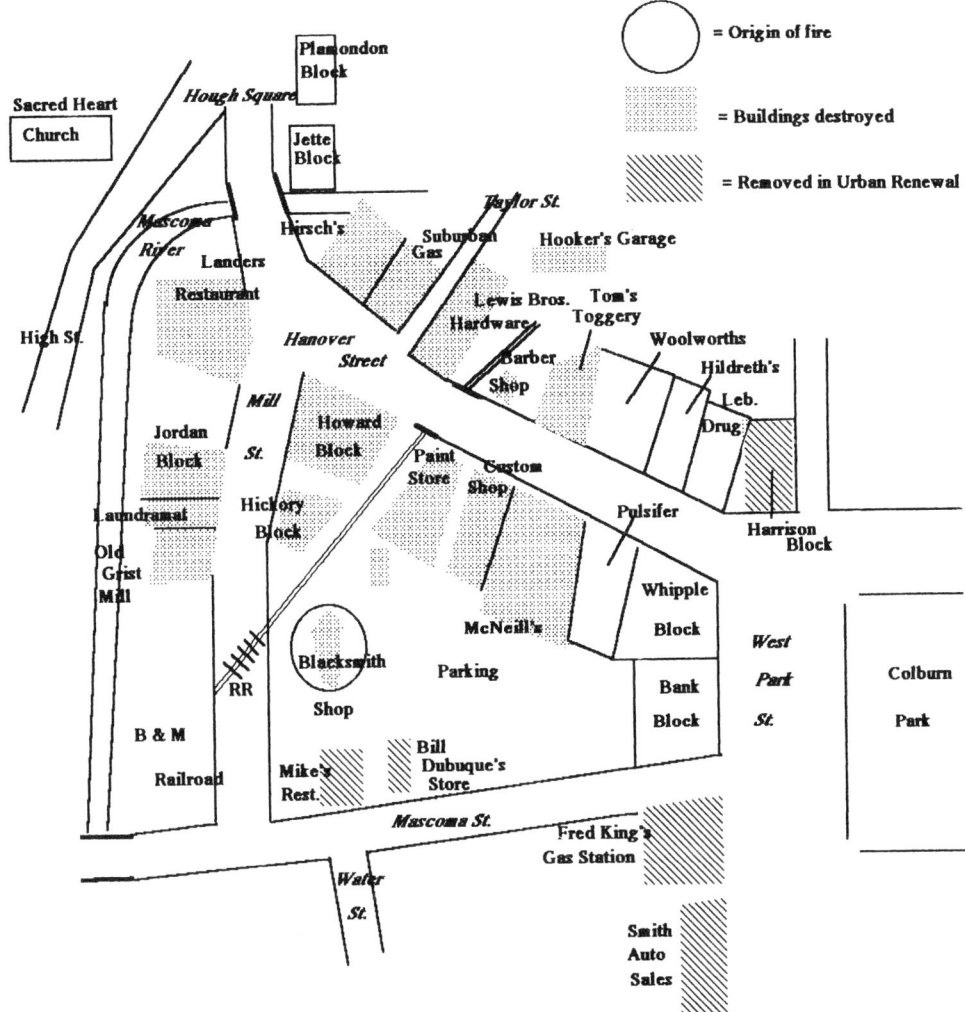

Schematic drawing of downtown Lebanon showing the buildings destroyed by the 1964 fire and those subsequently removed in the urban renewal program

scare into the winos who often slept there.

Mr. Healey leaned a rolled-up green rug against the wall and lit it. The two then went outside to witness the exodus they were sure would follow. Standing on Mascoma Street, Mr. Healey turned to Mr. Thibideau and said, "If you ever tell anyone what I did, I'll kill you."

As smoke began to show, fifteen-year-old Charles Blair ran up the street to report it to the fire station. The time was 4:08 P.M., and Lebanon was about to experience its worst fire of the twentieth century.

There were only two firefighters in the station when the call came in, but several volunteers quickly responded, including Harold Blodgett, who was one of the first to reach the fire. "I took one look at it and I said, 'We're not going to save this.' It was really going.... Those first two or three buildings down there were old, old, dry buildings—they were bone dry."

Talk to anyone who was there that day and conversation invariably shifts to the wind—gusts in excess of twenty miles-per-hour that pushed the flames from building to building to building.

Fire Chief Herman Courtermarsh put out the call for help at 4:15; but within an hour the fire was raging on three fronts, defying the efforts of more than one-hundred-and-fifty firefighters. They came from as far away as Claremont, Woodstock, Fairlee, and Sunapee, and were hampered by the lack of a common radio frequency over which they could all communicate.

Not that it would have made much difference. The fire quickly consumed the blacksmith shop and then moved north to a nearby building on Mill Street known as the Hickory Block, a four-story structure with a pool hall on the ground floor and apartments upstairs. One of those dwellings was occupied by sixty-seven-year-old George Lemay, who was trapped and managed to attract the attention of firefighters to his third-floor window.

A ladder was placed in front of one of the windows and firefighter Albert "Gabby" Herrin climbed up to rescue Mr. Lemay. According to the account in the *Valley News*, "Herrin said that the rooms behind the trapped man were a sheet of flame, giving off little smoke but such intense heat that the screen in front of him was red hot ... Herrin pushed the screen inward before him and seized Lemay's arm, though he was so badly burned that he could only repeat, 'I can't make it; I can't make it.' "

Mr. Herrin pulled Mr. Lemay through the window and, although the man's fiery clothes seared the fireman's hands and arms, he carried him down the ladder and held him as they rode to the hospital in Roger Therrien's police cruiser. Mr. Lemay died about twelve hours later. Another body, that of Henry LeBlonde, was found in the rubble of the Hickory Block the next day.

It was not Gabby Herrin's last brush with heroism. On July 11, 1969, the brakes failed on the oil truck he was driving down a hill in Etna, and a witness reported that Mr. Herrin remained behind the wheel until the last possible second to make sure that the vehicle did not strike a nearby home. The truck went off the road a split second after he jumped from the cab, missing the house by less than thirty feet. Tragically, the thirty-eight-year-old father of three was killed in the accident.

Other heros included Bruce Johnson, who worked at Lewis Brothers Hardware, and Jack Taber, whose father, Donald, owned that store. They rescued a family of three, and two women from second-floor apartments in the Howard (LeMay) Block which was located on the western corner of Mill and Hanover streets. Those residents were among an estimated one-hundred people left homeless by the fire.

From the Hickory Block the fire continued up Mill Street to the Howard Block, containing Brown's Bike Shop, Creighton's Taxi Stand, The Modern Record Shop, Lora's Beauty Shop, and the Valley Yarn Shop. Sparks from the Howard Block ignited the building across Mill Street that housed Landers' Restaurant. Michael and Beth Alafat stood on the lawn of the Sacred Heart Church as their popular business burned.

Although John Landers had operated a restaurant bearing his name as early as 1916, he was no longer in business by 1933, when he set up Michael Alafat, Sr. and his brother George in Landers' Restaurant and Sea Grill. By the time it burned thirty-one years later, Landers' was "the essence of a small-town, downtown restaurant," recalls Jim Wechsler. "Everybody stopped in and everybody knew everybody," said Mr. Wechsler. "When Mike and his wife Beth presided from behind the counter, it was a lively local gathering place. There was a lot of talk, a lot of gossip, a lot of local decisions made there."

After the fire destroyed Landers', it spread south on the west side of Mill Street to an apartment building known as the Jordan Block, containing a laundromat, and then to a building known as the old gristmill.

Just across the river, firemen hosed down the roof of the tannery to stop the fire from jumping the Mascoma River, as it had in 1887. A timely shift in the wind helped.

Within an hour of the first alarm the fire also was raging up Hanover Street. The Howard Block had given the flames a position to jump to the north side of Hanover Street, where they ignited the old Lindsay Block in which Ben Hirsh's Army-Navy store was located. The fire then traveled east, consuming the Suburban Gas building, Lewis Brothers Hardware, a wooden railroad bridge, Richard Courtemanche's barber shop, Tom's Toggery, and the Lamplighter Restaurant. The railroad tracks behind those buildings buckled from the heat.

Store employees and volunteers alike scrambled to remove as much inventory as they could. On the corner of Hanover and Court streets, Albert Healey was photographed as he relayed cans of paint up the line of a bucket brigade emptying out the Sherwin-Williams store in the Harrison Block. Tom's Toggery was heavily stocked for the upcoming Father's Day weekend and the Lebanon Days' sale. Owner Thomas Keane, Jr. remembers that "it happened so quick that you really didn't have an awful lot of time to think. The firemen were all telling us to get out, and the fire was coming in the back door as we were going out the front."

Across the street from Tom's, the fire also was raging at Fletcher's Paint Store on the south side of Hanover Street. It had made the jump from the blacksmith shop to a warehouse in the rear of the building, and then to the paint shop, producing explosions as the cans let loose. The headquarters of the local Odd Fellows group, located over the paint store, were also destroyed. From there the flames moved east up Hanover Street to the Custom Shop, a fabric store owned by Fred Cushing, Jr. and on to McNeill's Drug Store.

McNeill's had moved to that side of the street only within the past year. As the flames approached, Gordon Sargent recalled some advice from the store's namesake: "My grandfather (Charles) McNeill had always told my dad and me that if you ever have an emergency at the store—a fire or anything else—all you do is take your prescription files, your narcotics, your money, and get your employees out and lock up." He did, and then watched as the store was leveled.

Fire trucks were everywhere, it seemed, and nine firemen were hurt. Romeo Russell was with Fire Department Captain Harold Stone in an alley when both were stricken with heat exhaustion. "All at once I collapsed in the alleyway and I told him 'I got something wrong, I can't move.' He looked at me and said, 'You're getting pretty white. You better get out of here.' He started to follow me out and he dropped right there, too." Both men were treated at Alice Peck Day Memorial Hospital.

The fire consumes yet another structure as firefighters try to prevent its spread.

The blacksmith shop where the fire started goes up in flames.

Rubble from Mill Street crashes in the Mascoma as a firefighter hoses down the Bank Building.

The approaching flames and explosion of paint cans sends men running for cover.

The curious watch from the east end of Hanover Street in front of Currier's.

The New Hampshire Board of Underwriters concluded that

efforts of fire fighters were hampered by fallen electric wires, the involvement of a considerable quantity of flammable liquids in a paint store at 36 Hanover Street, and the rupture of several [liquid propane gas] tanks of varying capacity which were stored between the buildings at 27 and 31 Hanover Street. During the early stages, the fire spread was so rapid that apparatus had to reposition to escape destruction and, as a result, about 1,000' of . . . hose was lost. It was also reported that two fire fighters were forced to swim the Mascoma River to avoid entrapment."

Thousands of spectators came to town to view the rampage, and a half dozen reporters from the *Valley News* and *Free Press* scrambled to cover the conflagration. Eliot Page of WVTR (later WNHV) broadcast live bulletins from downtown, while his competition, WTSL, continued to air the Red Sox game.

The fire was declared "under control" at about eight o'clock, having been stopped at two fire walls—one at the western end of the new Woolworth's building, the other at the eastern end of the Pulsifer Block, which housed the Western Auto store.

The folly of rebuilding with wood after the 1887 fire was also pointed up in the report of the board of underwriters, which observed that "in every instance, these buildings were totally lacking in those structural features designed to prevent the spread of fire." The final toll: two men were dead, twenty businesses and twenty buildings were destroyed, one-hundred people were homeless, and damage was estimated at three-million-dollars.

Lebanon police were waiting for Albert Healey when he returned to his West Street home from a drive-in movie on the Sunday after the fire. Fingered for starting the blaze by his friend Joe Thibideau, Mr. Healey was charged with arson and murder for the deaths of George Lemay and Henry Leblond. The charges meant the possibility of a death sentence. On October 4, 1965—the day his trial was to have started—Mr. Healey pleaded guilty to two counts of arson and a pair of first-degree manslaughter charges, for which he was given a thirteen-to-twenty-five-year prison term. One of his lawyers, N. George Papademas, told the court that the city bore at least part of the responsibility for the tragedy: "There was a degree of lawlessness in Lebanon . . . There was permissive drinking in this blacksmith shed, and the police failed to put an end to the practice. Lawlessness was winked at in the neighborhood in which Mr. Healey grew up."

That latter was certainly true enough, for Mr. Healey grew up in the shadow of the tannery. High and West streets made up one of the city's toughest neighborhoods, a strictly working-class venue where the trappings of poverty were common. There was no shortage of alcoholics to patronize Tony's Cafe (KindleNook, 1994), a beer joint with cement floors where Pete and Rena Braley served customers who fancied shuffleboard and country music on the jukebox. Two doors down, Boze Heath's misnamed Friendly Market occupied the bottom floor of the shabby three-story Levesque Block; the much friendlier Bashaw's Market stood next door, and most summer Saturdays you could count on Lawrence Bashaw having the store's black and white television tuned to the Red Sox game. Mr. Bashaw delivered, which was more than you could say for the Sox. This was the neighborhood where Mr. Healey's grandparents did the best they could to raise him after his mother and father separated when he was young.

His other attorney, Alfred Catalfo of Dover, explained at the time that the guilty plea was entered to the manslaughter charges to eliminate the possibility of Mr. Healey being sentenced to hang. In arguing for a lenient sentence, Mr. Catalfo said, "We can save a good portion of this boy's life, and we should."

It appears that they did. Mr. Healey was released from prison in February 1973, and was on parole until 1981. His parole officer, Thomas Tarr, said Mr. Healey's record was one of "arrest-free behavior, steady employment, and conducting himself as a responsible citizen." Mr. Healey, who resettled in the Concord area, declined to be interviewed by the *Valley News* for a 1984 story about the fire. Said Mr. Tarr, "This time of year [early summer] is difficult for him. It's bothered him tremendously, what happened up there. He has to live with it all the time."

The Mall

Some merchants burned out made plans to rebuild immediately. Even as the fire was still raging, McNeill's Drug Store owner Francis Sargent made plans with the Trumbull-Nelson Construction Company for a new structure, and he also made hasty arrangements for temporary quarters. The latter plans, said Gordon Sargent, entailed an assist from the owner of Currier & Co. "Fred Cushing, whose dad had passed away the previous December and had been the owner of Lebanon Drug Store, came over and gave my dad the keys [to the Lebanon Drug store] and said, 'We'll get together later about rent.' "

That was the start of a hectic weekend for McNeill's employees, who cleaned, installed fixtures, and restocked shelves. However, on the Monday morning following Friday's fire, the store opened for business across the street from where it had been burned out. McNeill's also was the first store to celebrate a grand reopening in a new building—on March 1, 1965—and Tom's Toggery followed suit on April twenty-third. Those stores, along with Woolworth, Currier & Co., and C.H. Davis Jewelry, continued to anchor the downtown into the 1980s. Donald Taber reopened Lewis Brothers Hardware in a new building on the old site; and after Mr. Taber closed the store, the space was taken over by the Village Hearth restaurant in 1973. That business lasted three years, and then the Lewis Brothers building was taken over in 1978 by The Shoetorium, which Ralph McCoy had opened in the Commerce Building in 1970. The Commerce Building also housed Richard Courtemanche's relocated barber shop, and Richard Day's Colonial Bookshoppe, which later moved to the west end of the McNeill's building. Radio Shack also operated out of the rear of the Commerce Building for several years after first opening in the Commerce Building basement. Village Pizza has been a fixture on the mall since 1977.

Some merchants burned out in the fire moved out of downtown. Fletcher's Paint Store relocated to Campbell Street, while the Alafats reopened Landers' Restaurant on Route 120 in October 1965; Benjamin Hirsch, meanwhile, migrated up the street to the Harrison Block on the corner of Hanover and Court streets, before moving the store to its present Hough Square location (1994). Brown's Bike Shop reopened in White River Junction, but the Lamplighter, the Custom Shop, and a few other businesses did not reopen at all.

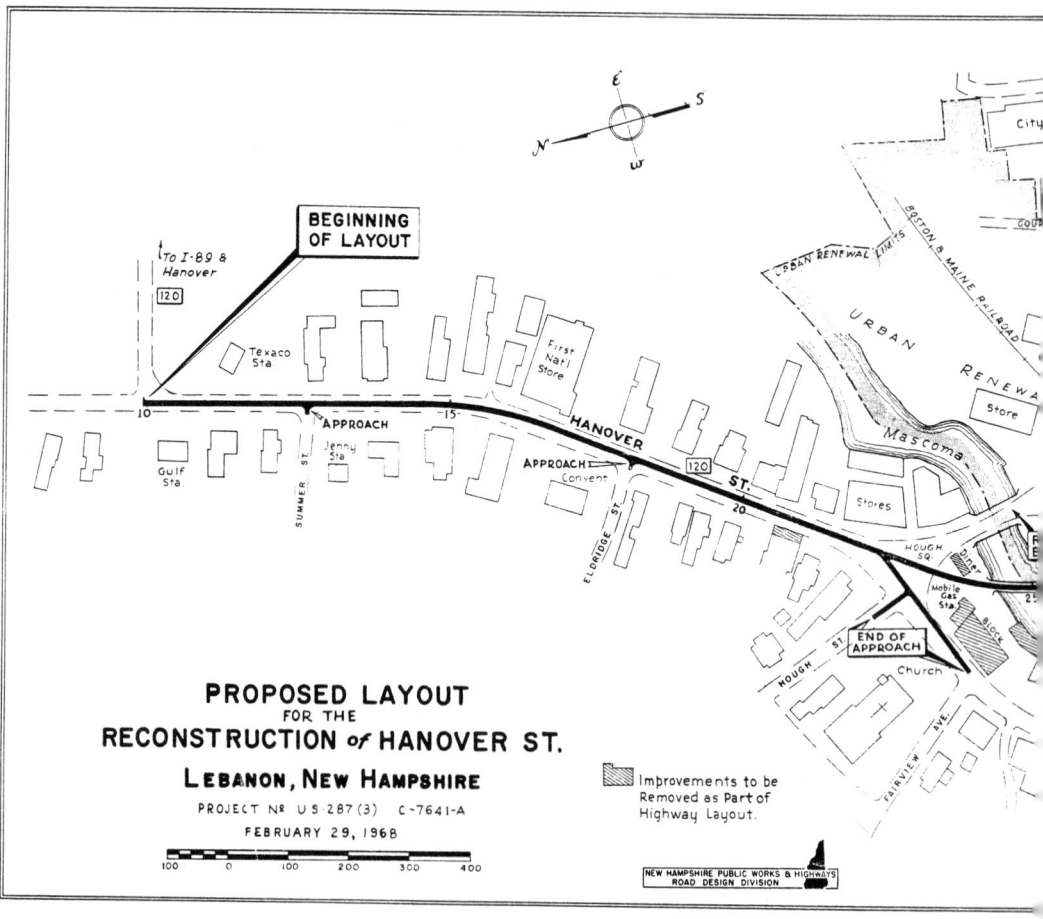

Lebanon was declared a federal disaster area after the fire, which made the city eligible for federal urban renewal money. That was the good news. It also, as it happened, turned out to be the bad news.

Several rebuilding plans were discussed, but the one that gathered the most momentum called for closing the burned-out section of Hanover Street to vehicular traffic and turning it into a pedestrian mall. It also proposed moving the bridge over the Mascoma River nearer to the Sacred Heart Church and diverting traffic to Colburn Park in front of the fire station.

The scheme was known as Urban Renewal Plan B-1, and most merchants supported it. Critics, however, wanted to keep Hanover Street open to promote traffic circulation through the core of the downtown area.

A lame-duck city council approved B-1 in December 1965, but the issue resurfaced in January with a new council in place. With 47 percent of the city's registered voters going to the polls in an advisory referendum on April 13, 1966, plan B-1 lost, 1,337 to 916. Many thought that vote meant an end to any plan to close upper Hanover Street. About a week later, however, an official with the U.S. Department of Housing and

Layout of Urban Renewal plan prepared by the New Hampshire Public Works and Highways Department in 1968 shows the proposed relocation of Route 120, buildings to be removed, and downtown landmarks. The plan was carried out almost exactly as shown here.

Urban Development met with the council and gave the city an ultimatum: Approve B-1 or go to the end of the line for receiving federal aid. The threat of losing $1.7 million in federal money was enough to make two councilors change their minds about the plan, and B-1 was adopted by a vote of 5-4.

The adoption of plan B-1 meant big changes for downtown Lebanon. Mascoma Street was moved south. No longer almost flush with the south end of the National Bank of Lebanon building, it veered off to enter South Park Street in front of the fire station and Congregational church. To make way for the new road, Fred King's gas station and Smith Auto Sales were closed. Mill Street was closed and buried beneath tons of earth needed to support a new bridge that bypassed Hanover Street and hooked up with Mascoma in front of the fire station. Mill Street businesses like Mike's Restaurant, the Lebanon Laundry, and the Feed and Grain were closed. Mr. King retired; Smith Auto moved to Mechanic Street until its new quarters were ready on Evans Drive; and Mike's moved to Mechanic Street into a building that had recently been vacated by Thermal Dynamics (occupied by the Legacy Restaurant, 1993-94).

Some landowners who resisted the city's effort to buy their property had their land

The Mall about 1970 with the Whipple, Pulsifer, McNeill's, and Commerce buildings on the left, Hildreth's and Woolworth's on the right. In the background are the Cummings tannery and the LaBombard Block.

taken by eminent domain. Finally, the mall was dedicated in August 1970 in a ceremony attended by Governor Walter Peterson. The final cost was $4 million, with about half that amount going for reconstruction of the buildings and the other portion paying the cost of relocating Route 120. The city's share was about $500,000. The reconstruction brought one important new look to the downtown. Instead of rebuilding with wood as was done after the 1887 fire, the federal government required all new construction in the area to be of brick.

The mall, however, did not meet with universal acclaim. The feeling among many of those who had voted against B-1 in the referendum was one of outright betrayal, and the mall vote was held up in 1981 by opponents of city government as an example of why the council-manager form of government was flawed. Fred Aldrich, one of those who advocated returning to town government, said in a 1981 *Valley News* interview, "It's still deep in the craw of all of those that were around at the time."

In fact, a few years after Mr. Aldrich's observation, City Councilor Robert Boisvert caustically offered to supply a bulldozer to reopen the street to vehicular traffic. His tone and body language suggested that he was not joking.

One of the goals of the redevelopment plan adopted after the fire was to create more parking in downtown Lebanon, an objective that was realized only too well. The theory behind the reconstruction—that people would park their cars in one of three spacious lots and shop in the quaint pedestrian mall—fizzled. What had once been a viable, highly visible shopping area was hampered by a new design that concealed most shops from the view of motorists. Instead of seeing storefronts as they passed by on routes

120 and 4, drivers were instead greeted by the brick backsides of the buildings that lined the south side of the mall.

The traffic pattern that emerged from the fire seemed to be designed to prove the old adage, "you can't get there from here." Motorists leaving the new IGA complex on Benton Hill bound for Hanover or Mechanic streets had to first turn in the opposite direction and circle the park. Even local residents who successfully mastered the intricacies of the downtown layout occasionally had to contend with bewildered visitors who turned down a one-way road or abruptly halted in the middle of a street to figure it all out.

III

White Collar City

The dome of city hall is silhouetted in one of the mirrors of the modern One Court Street building.

21

"If People Like It, We'll Build More"

Interstate 89

As convoluted as the post-fire traffic configuration was in the center village, it probably would not have mattered how the downtown was rebuilt after the fire. The village's days as a shopping destination were numbered. By the time the mall was dedicated, a group of new stores had opened amid the cornfields of Route 12A, just south of Exit 20 of Interstate 89.

The interstate altered traffic patterns that had channeled thousands of cars a day into and through the downtown area. Traffic between Concord and Burlington that used to travel through town on Route 4 now looped north of the village, past the high school, one of two routes the state had considered. The other, proposed for south of town, would have crossed LaPlante Road, Storrs Hill, Farnum Hill, and joined the Mascoma River just north of the airport. There also was another wrinkle that was considered but never built—the Campbell Street Extension. This plan would have allowed interstate traffic to leave the highway at Exit 18, cross the Mascoma River and enter downtown via Campbell Street, near the Gulf station then operated by Ray Lacoss. It was dropped when residents objected to the volume of congestion it would have brought to the downtown area, and to the destruction of Eldridge Park.

Instead of the Campbell Street Extension, all traffic from Exit 18 was diverted onto Route 120, which brought about the closing of the northern portion of Hanover Street between Barrows Street and the high school. Meanwhile, a footbridge was built over the highway to accommodate pedestrian traffic to and from the school. (Designers of the original footbridge, in their infinite wisdom, apparently did not foresee the possibility that children might toss rocks and snowballs onto passing cars below. However, when motorists started to complain about being pelted from above, a cage was added to the span in 1968 to stop the practice).

While the interstate diverted traffic around the center of the village, it also attracted new motorists who would have previously bypassed Lebanon altogether. A 1958 study by Northeast Planning Associates correctly forecast that:

> .... *traffic between Burlington, Vermont and Boston, Massachusetts now travels by way of Rutland, Bellows Falls, and Keene. Following completion of the Interstate facility, this traffic will travel via Montpelier, Lebanon and Concord.*
>
> *In addition to carrying induced traffic, the Interstate will handle diverted traffic, i.e., a component of traffic which has changed from its previous path of travel to another route without a change in origin or destination. Practically all existing through traffic from Routes 4 and 10 on the east to the Connecticut River bridge in West Lebanon will be diverted to the new facility.*

More than just a road, the interstate paved the way for Lebanon to become a city in more than name only.

Industrial Renaissance

The retooling of industrial Lebanon began even before the last of the textile mills had closed, when Dartmouth Engineering Professor James Browning started up a little company on East Wilder Road in West Lebanon, not far from the banks of the Connecticut River.

The year was 1957, and Thermal Dynamics was one of the world's first companies in the developing field of arc-plasma welding and cutting technology. Mr. Browning developed and manufactured hi-tech torches that utilized super-heated gas to conduct electricity for the cutting of stainless steel, aluminum, and other metals. The advantage of the new torches was their quicker, cleaner, and more precise cut than conventional acetylene torches.

As Thermal grew, it moved in 1959 to the Mechanic Street building once occupied by Split Ballbearing (Legacy Restaurant, 1994), and by 1960 the company employed forty people. Mr. Browning sold the business in 1968 to a group of investors and started up the Browning Engineering Company on the original Thermal site on East Wilder Road.

After the Mechanic Street building was heavily damaged by fire in 1968, Thermal moved to White River Junction for several months and then to new headquarters on Benning Street in West Lebanon, between the Mascoma River and Interstate 89. The new owners concentrated on the commercial plasma end of the business, becoming the town's second-largest industrial employer by the 1970s, with about 350 employees spread out over six buildings.

The January 1987 issue of the *Valley Business Journal* reported that Thermal had a twenty-five-person sales staff and sold its products worldwide. Its domestic customers included the Big Three automakers, steel companies, and virtually any other business involved in metal fabrication. Sales reached a reported $40 million in 1987.

Adding to the industrial base provided by Thermal and Split Ballbearing, the mid-1960s saw the startup of the forty-acre Etna Road industrial park on the old Chaloux farm. The New Jersey Machine Company became the park's first tenant in October 1965. "We opened the same day that Landers opened," recalled company president Linc Jepson. "They had twenty-five people and we had twelve people, and we spent many a lunch and evening over there." New Jersey Machine continues to manufacture packaging machinery and now employs more than 150 people. New Hampshire Industries was built at the same time as New Jersey Machine, and it continues to make pulleys for industrial use.

The park received more tenants through the seventies and eighties. Leonard Guaraldi, Sr., the founder of Bond Optics, moved the lensmaking shop there in 1971; Alpina Sports relocated its ski equipment distribution center from the Mount Support Road in 1978; the F.W. Webb plumbing and heating supply company built a warehouse and office building on the corner of Etna Road and Route 120 in 1979; and Loctite Luminescence joined the Etna Road neighborhood in 1979 after its founding by Edward Scheu, Jr. The company was one of the park's largest employers in 1994, with 150 people working to make specialty lighting systems for military and civilian aircraft.

An engineering research-and-development company called Creare also had an impact on the industrial park, although it did not locate there itself. Creare was founded in 1961 by Mr. Browning, former Thermal Dynamics research director Robert Dean, Jr., James J. Bailey, and Harvard professor Howard W. Emmons. Like Thermal Dynamics, the company started out on Mr. Browning's property on East Wilder Road, and according to *An Abbreviated History of the Creare Family of Companies*, "being by the river had its conveniences. We used to use the canoes to have private conferences. Bailey and Dean would go out at lunchtime in the middle of the river and there plan important policy matters—like how to keep from going over the financial dam."

Whatever strategies were conceived on the water apparently worked, as the company moved to Hanover at the end of 1961 and became so successful that it spawned more than a half-dozen related companies.

Three offshoots of Creare ended up in the Etna Road Industrial Park. In 1972 Creare geotechnical engineer Ivor Hawkes founded a company called IRAD GAGE, which developed mining instruments and was located on Parkhurst Street before moving in the late seventies to the Etna Road. It later merged with Creare Products, another spin-off of Creare, and the IRAD GAGE building was taken over by Verax Corporation, yet another Creare sibling.

Verax was established by Mr. Dean in 1978. The company, which developed technology used by pharmaceutical companies involved in bioengineering, moved to the Etna Road in 1984, and at its peak in the late eighties employed more than 120 people. It is now known as Creative BioMolecules.

Another Creare spin-off was Creonics, later known by the name of its billion-dollar parent company, Allen-Bradley Co., of Milwaukee. Started by Charles Hebble, Jr. in 1982, Creonics was located in the Rivermill complex at 85 Mechanic Street before moving to the Etna Road in 1985. The company employs about fifty people in the development of microprocessors and computer software for motion control systems used by industries.

New England Industries moved its metal shop from Bradford in 1985, and Unifirst Corporation relocated its industrial laundry to the Etna Road in 1990 after a prolonged regulatory battle with the city, which was well aware that Unifirst had been blamed for massive pollution problems in Williamstown, Vermont.

The eighties also added a mixture of offices to the Etna Road, as the Chiron Springs office building and Smith, Batchelder, & Rugg's accounting offices both located there during that decade.

The forty-acre parcel on the Etna Road was almost full by the mid-eighties, when the city's second major business park opened in West Lebanon.

With the airport about $60,000 in debt, the city opted to open up the surrounding land to industrial and commercial development, and the first parcel was sold in late 1983 to Trapper Brown, a Plymouth, New Hampshire, development company. Trapper Brown put up a building and leased it to sporting-goods distributor Technics/Donnay, which moved from the Mount Support Road to the airport in 1984.

That was the beginning of a flurry of construction that saw about twenty businesses move there over the next ten years, offering scores of jobs. The tenants ranged from the hi-tech to the low: Woodstock Soapstone Stoves, T-shirt printer TK Sportswear (the successor of Tom's Toggery), biotechnology companies like Creative BioMolecules and Medarex, McAullife Office Products, Imperial Printing, computer software company True Basic Inc., a distribution center for Refco Tools and Abrasives, North East Environmental Products Inc., and New England Engines.

Route 12A

Dartmouth graduate Daniel Rothenberg had a fondness for the Upper Valley and a house in Sunapee in the mid-1960s when the city asked him to consider a downtown Lebanon site as a possible location for a new shopping center. The Massachusetts developer made the visit, and although he does not recall its exact location, he remembers a tract with poor traffic circulation, no visibility, and "it wasn't nearly big enough," he said. "However, as a result of my doing that and looking around . . . I thought it would be a good idea to build a shopping center in Lebanon."

He chose a site on Route 12A in West Lebanon, just south of Interstate 89. Two prospective tenants with whom he had done business in the past agreed with him, and he announced plans in June 1968 to construct the Upper Valley Shopping Plaza in West Lebanon. He purchased twenty-two acres of land from farmer Paul Korpela and the plaza opened in November of that year anchored by a 50,000 square-foot Rich's department store at one end and a 20,000 square-foot Purity Supreme supermarket at the other (Sears, 1994). Between those two mainstays a group of smaller stores took up 15,000 square feet of space among them. There was parking for about seven-hundred cars.

"We're not saying we're building the Prudential Center," Mr. Rothenberg told a meeting of city officials gathered at Landers' Restaurant. "We're building the first part now, and if people like it, we'll build more."

People liked it. The junction of the interstates across the river provided easy access, and the stores became destination points for people from miles around. Purity's ability to buy in bulk from its suppliers meant savings that could be passed on to consumers who found it worth their while to drive thirty or forty miles. A visit to Rich's during the holiday season became like a trip to Mecca to many residents in outlying communities that lacked large discount department stores.

Other businesses quickly picked up the scent of money and migrated to the area.

The last harvest . . . a widely distributed photo of Route 12A which came to symbolize the encroachment of development upon some of the best farmland in the state.

True to his word, Mr. Rothenberg did build more. He added a new wing that housed the Valley Cinema I & II in 1969 (Cherry, Webb & Touraine, 1994), and the National Bank of Lebanon, The French Shop, and Fayva's shoe store in 1970. A W.T. Grant store was added to the north end of the wing in 1969 (replaced in 1977 by J.C. Penney).

McDonald's started the fast-food flood in 1971, and Burger King soon followed. Former Lebanon High School teacher and baseball coach Peter Johnson opened a huge hardware store in 1973 behind Purity Supreme. The K-Mart plaza—which also included a Grand Union grocery store—opened in 1976 on the north side of the interstate. Peanie Goodwin's Colonial Plaza also opened in 1976, and not long afterward Lebanon had its first Chinese restaurant since the thirties—the China Lite—and behind it the Sheraton North Country Inn, which welcomed guests in 1978 (Radisson, 1994).

Prior to construction of the Upper Valley Plaza the land south of the interstate was assessed at $20,000; it was more than $30 million by 1990, and Mr. Rothenberg's shopping center was the city's second largest taxpayer, trailing only Wilder Dam. By 1986, in fact, four of the city's top ten taxpayers—Mr. Rothenberg, the K-Mart Plaza, the Sheraton Inn, and the Colonial Plaza—were located along Route 12A, accounting for nearly 6 percent of the city's tax base. Developer Bayne Stevenson added the Powerhouse Mall to the mix later in 1986, and put up the Powerhouse Plaza in 1993. The result was several million square feet of retail space and thousands of jobs. Although many of the positions were low-paying clerkships, they combined to make the service sector an important cog in the Lebanon economy.

The size and variety of stores along the strip sucked shoppers from the city's other commercial areas, and from those throughout the region. In Lebanon, the downtown mall languished; the venerable Rockdale department store—which accurately billed

The early stages of Route 12A development before McDonalds. Rich's department store, Purity Supreme, and Grants occupy the first plaza at the top of photo, just south of Interstate 89. Brown's furniture had already relocated to the east side of Route 12A.

itself as catering to the working man—closed in the early 1970s, leaving a vacancy in the old Mascoma woolen mill building (Rivermill Complex, 1994); and the movie screen at the Lebanon Opera House went dark when the theaters opened in West Lebanon. Two grocery stores in the center village also closed after the shopping centers were built in West Lebanon: The A&P store on Campbell Street (Upper Valley Senior Citizens Center, 1994) was boarded up in 1975 after a ten-year run, and the First National Store on Hanover Street (U-Haul, 1994) shut down in February 1981 after thirty-one years in that location.

The Miracle Mile proved that a name does not a shopping center make. The grandiose moniker was attached to the stretch in the late fifties as a promotional gimmick; and in the years preceding the arrival of the interstate, the road was foreseen as the next big development center, anchored by JJJ Self-Service Discount Department Store, across from the Carter Country Club. By the early 1980s, however, vacancies were common on the strip. The Super Duper grocery store (Miracle Mile Plaza, 1994) survived long enough to be taken over by the P&C chain, which relocated to the old Giant department store building in 1984. The Giant store closed down in the mid-1970s and was replaced for a few years by King's, which went out of business in December 1982. The A&W moved to Route 12A after owner Henry Farr had a fire in his restaurant in the late sixties. Mr. Farr sold it to a partnership comprised of Ernest and Anita, and Bill and Pauline Gilman. Ernest and Bill were brothers, and they moved the restaurant to Route 12A and operated what was regarded as the most successful A&W in the northeast, including New York, New Jersey, and Pennsylvania. "It was just us and the Sunoco station," Anita Gilman recalled of the early years on the northern stretch of Route 12A. The relocation of the A&W left only the old Twin State Bowl on the lot across from Split Ballbearing, but the bowling alley closed in 1986 and reopened the following year as the Astro Bowl in White River Junction. Sears, which had opened on West Park Street in Lebanon in the early 1960s and then moved to the Miracle Mile beside the Super Duper, left an empty storefront when it relocated its catalog store to Route 12A in the late sevenites. Through it all, the Flanders & Patch Ford dealership, which moved there in 1948, and Bridgman's Furniture, which arrived in 1952, have anchored the Miracle Mile in good times and bad.

Downtown West Lebanon, meanwhile, carved out a strong niche in the field of home beautification, thanks in large part to Drew and Susan Tallman's Paint 'N Paper Barn, which took over in the old Dairy Queen building in 1980. They later brought in several complementary businesses and established the Decorator's Plaza. Another success story is that of Stateline Sports, opened on Bridge Street in 1983 by Robert Vanier and Jon Damren, two former Tom's Toggery employees. It started as a hole-in-the-wall operation and grew into the largest sporting-goods outlet in the region.

The 4 Aces Diner also continued as a West Lebanon landmark. Started by Roy Stewart in 1952 on the corner of Main and Dana streets, the restaurant was then run for more than twenty years by Phil and Dorothy Gomez, who sold it in 1986. Phil Mans and James Burnham then moved it to the corner of Bridge Street and Railroad Avenue in 1987, and it continues to be operated by the family of Frank and Fran Shorey (1994).

Meanwhile, Route 12A's success as a shopping hub was not without problems. Traffic worsened significantly at several intersections, especially on weekends when

Despite the presence of Route 12A just up the road, Main Street in West Lebanon continued to attract traffic. This 1980s photo of the southern end of Main Street shows Dunkin' Donuts, Voice and Vision, and the marquee of the Decorator's Plaza.

vehicles were usually bumper-to-bumper for most of the day. By 1984 zoning board members Robert Elliot and Kathy Schonberger suggested a building moratorium be imposed along the strip to give the city time to bring the road network in line with the traffic it was forced to bear. The city merely applied band-aids to the problem and waited for the state to take action and pay for most of the necessary multi-million-dollar improvements. The state, which held up the strip as a classic example of bad planning in the late seventies, let the city wallow in the mess, and not until about 1990 was Route 12A even added to the state's ten-year priority list. Unbridled development continued in the meantime, and the traffic issues seem to have climaxed with the 1994 applications of retailing giants Wal-Mart and Cosco, who proposed stores for the southern end of the road.

Shoppers were not the only ones to take advantage of the plaza's proximity to the interstate. Professional thieves also were attracted to the area on occasion, such as the robbers who entered the National Bank of Lebanon's West Lebanon branch on the weekend of July 28-29, 1973. They sawed a hole in the roof to gain entry and once inside rigged up batteries to the alarm system to keep the circuit intact. They then worked out of an enclosed office in the rear of the building to avoid detection, and it was professional work, indeed. A torch was used to cut a hole in the vault and the bandits entered the safe in precisely the area where the bulk of the bank's money was kept. Saturday had been a busy banking day at the plaza, and the thieves stole $82,980.24, and were never apprehended.

The two men who planned to hit the night-deposit box at the same West Lebanon bank in 1982 were not nearly as professional. Lebanon resident Errol Dodsworth notified police after he overheard the men planning the robbery on portable radios. When they made their move a week later one group of police was watching through binoculars from inside Brown's Furniture, while another posse listened to the heist from their hideout in the movie theater next to the bank. The bunglers were quickly arrested.

Lebanon's biggest bank heist, however, occurred on September 16, 1985, when armed robbers stuck up the LeBank branch of the Hanover Bank and Trust Co., in the K-Mart Plaza. The bank was an easy target, located as it was in the middle of a shopping plaza next to the interstate, with no security cameras and little other protection. The men made the hit, ditched their getaway car on the Glen Road in favor of another one they had hidden there, and made off with more than $100,000. They too were never caught.

22

Rock and Roll

The era of the interstate construction was one of profound change for the country, and Lebanon's social and demographic fabric received some new threads during that period.

"It was very unsettling for kids because the pros and cons of serving were heavy," recalls Raymond Plante. "Serving" meant going to war in Southeast Asia, and Mr. Plante's recollection of military recruiters during the Vietnam era was that "they were trying to clean the streets." Standards for entrance in the military were lower during that period than for any other he can recall in his twenty-nine years as a guidance counselor at the high school.

John Robinson graduated from Lebanon in 1968 and joined the navy. It was either enlist or be drafted. "People like myself who didn't have an affluent family and couldn't use college to beat it knew where we were going. We were going to war, and we knew some of us were probably going to die."

Charles Muzzy, Jr. wanted to serve, and the part-time cook at the Riverside Grill enlisted shortly after he graduated from high school in 1967. On January 19, 1968, just four days after he arrived in Vietnam he was shot to death while working on a Jeep. The city's other casualty was William Stanley Cutting, who was missing and declared dead on April 1, 1968.

While young men from Lebanon were fighting, the city itself experienced some of the turmoil common to the era. President Richard Nixon's mining of a North Vietnamese harbor in 1972 brought more than one-hundred people to the front of the Bank Building on May fifteenth. Most of the thirty-eight people arrested that day for laying down in front of a busload of draftees going to the Manchester induction center were connected with Dartmouth College. Five more were arrested the following day. The *Valley News* reported, "when the bus was ready to move, protestors joined hands in a human chain, encircling it. Police went to the front of the bus and began pushing their way through the mob. The chain was giving way until a few persons sat down on the pavement, the same tactic used yesterday to successfully stall the bus over an hour."

Police removed the demonstrators, and most of those arrested during the two days either paid one-hundred-dollar fines or chose to serve ten-day jail sentences. When one Dartmouth student told the Lebanon District Court judge that he could not afford the fine, the money was raised by passing a brown hat among courtroom spectators.

The era also begat changes in clothes, hair, and music and challenges to traditional icons of authority. There was, recalls Mr. Plante, a clash of values. "Blue-collar conservatism had always been a majority, but it became a smaller majority during that time," he says. "You had more pronounced positions."

That the Generation Gap was alive and well in Lebanon was apparent in September 1965, when the school board issued a new dress code for Lebanon High School. The edict mandated that:

Boys

1. Boys must wear shirts and they must be tucked in, no more than one button left open at the neck . . .

2. Tight trousers, dungarees, engineer or cowboy boots, and metal plates on shoes are not permissible.

3. T-shirts as an outer garment are not acceptable.

4. Long side burns, ducktail, beatle, or other extreme hair cuts will not be allowed.

Girls

1. Girls' dresses will be considered acceptable if they conform with the proper sense of modesty and good taste for school atmosphere. Shorts, slacks, or culottes are forbidden.

2. Stockings or socks must be worn, and boots, sandals, or other extreme footwear are forbidden.

3. Skirts should be within reasonable knee area.

4. Wigs, extreme hairdos, and excessive makeup are not allowed.

The board also adopted a policy that banned any girl who was pregnant from attending school.

It was the era of the mini-skirt, and some girls whose hemlines were deemed to be too high were sent home. The school board in 1967 suspended seventeen-year-old Brian Thompson of Meriden because his hair—which barely touched his collar—was too long. His family sued and sought an injunction while the case was pending.

Attorney William Baker, who represented the Thompsons, argued in Grafton County Superior Court that the school lacked the authority to regulate haircuts. Board attorney Robert Jones agreed that the young man had a right to wear his hair long, but countered that the question was "whether he has a constitutional right to attend school with a long haircut."

When the request for an injunction was denied, Mr. Thompson cut his hair and returned to school, but the fact that he had challenged it in the first place probably said as much about the times as the haircut rule itself. The U.S. Supreme Court, under Chief Justice Earl Warren, had placed a new emphasis on civil rights that went beyond just minorities. "Up until then if somebody pulled a fire alarm they didn't show up with their lawyer," said Mr. Plante.

By 1970, however, the cultural revolution that was sweeping the country had overtaken even the school board, which dropped the dress code.

The times were, indeed, a-changin'. The rock music once frowned upon as almost subversive was integrated into the curriculum, and students in the seventies took classes that used the lyrics of the Beatles and Bob Dylan to teach poetic methodology. Marijuana was readily available, and sometimes it was consumed in the area the school board had set aside for student cigarette smoking.

The town also could not completely ignore events taking place in the South, where African-Americans were fighting the repressive redneck establishment for the right to sit at the same lunch counters as whites. Lebanon was hardly a hotbed of social activity, but four-hundred marchers led by Mayor Robert Evans took to the streets in a March 1965 civil rights demonstration. It was amid this era of changing racial attitudes that the school board in 1968 agreed to participate in a program known as "A Better Chance," which allowed ten students from the inner city to attend Lebanon High School tuition-free.

The process that led to the establishment of the ABC program in Lebanon was not completely smooth, recalls Mr. Baker, the first president of the Lebanon chapter. "There certainly was a great deal of undertow about the fact that some or all of these kids were going to be black," he said. While the school board was receptive to the program, resistance surfaced at zoning board hearings held to approve the ABC house on Union Street. Mr. Baker recalls that when one opponent expressed doubt that ten teenagers living in one house would be controllable, Gilson Vanier rose from the audience and replied that he and his wife, Helen, had somehow managed the trick with their brood.

"That swung the meeting," said Mr. Baker. Thus, Lebanon High School became racially integrated, even if the ratio was seventy-to-one. The ABC students, mostly from New York and New Jersey, were exceptional scholars who went on to attend top-notch colleges and pursue successful careers until the program was phased out in 1977.

The era of social consciousness also saw the advent of a variety of cradle-to-coffin social services that augmented the traditional welfare roles of the town and its churches.

The Do-It Store across from the Dairy Queen on Main Street in West Lebanon was a center of local counterculture and consciousness-raising activity, recalls Jim Rubens of Hanover, one of scores of people who volunteered in the late 1960s. The Do-It Store featured a meeting room, recycling center, bulk food bin, and an alternative book library, among its many other functions. It stood out in the blue-collar conservative railroad village, but Mr. Rubens recalls many of the old-timers eventually accepted the hippies who worked there. "It did look odd to them, but quite quickly they'd come in and we'd make friends with them. They'd eat the cheese and find it not really all that alien."

One of the concepts to come out of discussions at the store, said Mr. Rubens, was the notion of a drug abuse hotline, which started on the Dartmouth campus in 1969 with a grant from Dartmouth College's Tucker Foundation. Headrest, as it was known, relocated to Lebanon in 1973 and settled on Church Street in 1978. One employee, Donlon Wade, became synonymous with Headrest as it expanded its services over the years to include a small emergency shelter and other programs. The organization was fielding over six-thousand phone calls a year by 1991, when it was recognized as one of President George Bush's 1,000 Points of Light.

Where wayward teenagers were once merely shipped off to reform school, the difficult transition from childhood to adulthood received more heed when Youth House, the forerunner of Upper Valley Youth Services, opened as a group home on Mechanic Street in 1972, providing temporary shelter for troubled adolescents.

Another of the major issues of the era was housing for elderly and low-income residents. In response to the former, the Rogers House was dedicated as an elderly housing facility by the Lebanon Housing Authority in 1971; and in 1973 the Upper Valley Senior Citizens Center opened in the Carter Community Building, offering rides, meals, and social activities for scores of elderly residents who might have otherwise found themselves isolated.

The CCB, however, was a less than ideal arrangement. For one thing, the seniors met on the second floor in a building with no elevator, and even then could only use the facility until 2 P.M. However, under the guidance of tireless and brash director Anna Pluhar, the group raised several-hundred-thousand-dollars and moved across the street in 1978 into the renovated A&P store. The facility at 10 Campbell Street featured ground-level access, automatic doors, and meant that participants could use the facility for the entire day.

Meanwhile, city officials who toured some of the city's grungiest tenements in May 1972 were shocked by numerous examples of substandard housing—exposed and unsafe wiring, a bathroom without a sink, and a man in a third-floor apartment whose only fire escape was a rope tied near a window. Many tenants said they had tried in vain to convince their landlords to fix the problems, and some faced eviction when they contacted the fire or health department about code violations. The city took months to answer complaints from tenants, who then had to endure additional months of appeals and delays while the city figured out which department was responsible for handling the problems. The *Valley News* concluded in a 1974 editorial that "the city's substandard housing ordinance is little more than a joke." That changed shortly after the editorial appeared, when the city council adopted a new housing code which required that body to respond to complaints within two weeks and to take a noncompliant landlord to court within thirty days.

At about the same time, William and Judy Gilbert began their own private urban-renewal campaign by purchasing and renovating several buildings on High Street that had fallen into disrepair.

The tour that led to changes in the housing ordinance was arranged by a group called Lebanon In Service To Each Neighbor (LISTEN), a low-income advocacy group formed in 1971 by River Street resident Marcia Boutin and New Hampshire Legal Assistance worker William Weismann. Mrs. Boutin ran LISTEN's thrift store and food pantry and coordinated social services, while Mr. Weismann operated the Organizing Project, the political arm of LISTEN that often battled the city over housing standards, tenants' rights, and other gains for low-income residents. They even tried, unsuccessfully, to wrest control of Wilder Dam away from New England Power.

There was a certain street-fighter's tenacity to LISTEN's early approach to problems, which was probably just what was needed to break the political apathy that prevailed at the time. However, the confrontational style favored by Mrs. Boutin and Mr. Weismann eventually alienated even some of the agency's supporters. Mrs. Boutin was forced out as director in 1978 and Mr. Weismann's Organizing Project was jettisoned. Musician Al Alessi was named executive director in 1978, an appointment that went a long way toward de-politicizing the agency. LISTEN then expanded to include everything from fuel assistance to budget counseling, and opened thrift stores in Enfield, Canaan, and White River Junction.

Another change that began in the 1970s and carried into the following decade was the formalization of child-care arrangements for working mothers. While the woolen mills and stitching shops had long employed women from lower-income families, child care had always been an informal affair. If there was supervision at all, it most likely came from a neighbor or nonworking family member. That began to change in 1971, however, when the Children's Center of the Upper Valley opened as the city's first official day-care center. When plans to put it in a carriage house on School Street were driven back by neighbors, the center opened in back of Mike's Restaurant on Mechanic Street in the same building that had once housed Split Ballbearing and Thermal Dynamics. The center then moved up the street after Peanie Goodwin purchased the building in order to evict restaurateur Mike Fontaine.

Peanie

Peanie Goodwin was a larger-than-life character who made, lost, and re-made millions of dollars during a four-decade career as an entrepreneur with a Midas touch. He did not, however, start out that way. If anything, the spoon in his mouth when he was born in 1927 on a farm near Poverty Lane was made of wood, befitting his early career as a teenage lumberjack. He graduated to his own logging operation while in his twenties, buying land, harvesting the timber, and often reselling the property for more than he had purchased it for in the first place. Former Mascoma Savings Bank president Reuben Cole, who oversaw many of Mr. Goodwin's transactions, figures that Mr. Goodwin probably owned most of the hillsides in Lebanon at one time or another.

By the 1960s Mr. Goodwin turned to real estate development, and it was here that he really left his mark, in Lebanon and elsewhere. "He never had the impediment of a formal education," said Mr. Cole. "He never learned in school what it was that he couldn't do." What he did do was build the Colonial Plaza on Route 12A; an antique automobile museum in Wells, Maine; the Timber Village antique mall in Quechee; the Tall Timbers mobile home park in Quechee, and a huge mobile home park near Vero Beach, Florida, that Mr. Goodwin's daughter, Sandy Player, recalls he sold for $3.65 million.

That was Peanie Goodwin's style—develop the vision and sell it. "He didn't want to be bothered to run things," said Mrs. Player. "He wanted to build and create."

He also had a strong interest in conservation which prompted him in 1974 to donate to the city of Lebanon 120 acres of prime forest land along Great Brook—the Goodwin Park exercise trail. In the mid-sixties, recalled Mr. Cole, he saved a handsome blue spruce tree that was targeted for destruction to make way for the interstate. He had workmen carefully remove the tree and—probably without asking anyone's permission—replanted it in Colburn Park, where it stands today (1994).

He also knew how to settle a score, as the original partners in the group that started the Sheraton North Country Inn in West Lebanon (Radisson, 1994) learned after they had a falling out with Mr. Goodwin, who sold them his share in the partnership before the hotel was built. As Mr. Cole recalls the deal, the remaining partners then found themselves in the awkward position of having to go back to Mr. Goodwin for an additional quarter-acre of land required to build the hotel out of the floodplain. He sold them the land all right—for a whopping $50,000. When asked why he drove such a hard bargain, Mr. Goodwin is said to have replied: "Half of that was for the value of the land. The other half is getting back the money that the other partners told everybody they had beaten me out of."

He also acquired Mike's Restaurant on Mechanic Street in a fit of pique. Mr. Goodwin and a group of friends were in the habit of meeting at Mike's each morning for breakfast and a discussion of their plans for the day. The restaurant featured a front area with a counter and tables, and a much larger dining area in the rear that was only open during lunch and dinner. One morning in 1976, however, the gang convened in the back dining area, which brought a rebuke from a restaurant employee who told them they would have to move to the front. As the story goes, an enraged Mr. Goodwin went up the street to a local real estate office and within hours was the new owner of the building. He then promptly evicted Mike's and eventually opened the Owl's Nest Restaurant, a completely remodeled establishment that was renowned for its antique stained glass and genuine Tiffany lamps, reflecting two of Mr. Goodwin's collecting interests.

"The Panic-Button School District"

When the price of a barrel of oil suddenly jumped by more than nine-dollars in response to the Arab oil embargo of 1973, Lebanonians quickly learned just how closely they were tied to the global marketplace.

The Densmore Brick Company, which dated to 1806 and was the oldest business in the city at the time, ceased production when the cost of running their oil-fired kilns became prohibitive. Ironically, they had switched over from coal in the mid-1960s.

Sunday drives in the family gas-guzzler became a thing of the past as gasoline doubled to more than sixty-cents. Cars lined up to fill up, and the state imposed a voluntary rationing program. President Richard Nixon reduced the interstate speed limit from seventy to fifty-five miles per hour, and an increasing number of full-service gas stations offered customers the opportunity to pump their own petrol at a reduced cost.

Thus began a trend away from the full-service corner service station and toward self-service convenience stores like the popular Colonial Deli on Hanover Street, Evans ExpressMart on the Miracle Mile, and the Foodstop in West Lebanon—places where you can pump your own gas and then go inside to buy everything from coffee to groceries and a lottery ticket.

At the same time, the old neighborhood store was falling by the wayside. Henry Staples' store on Colburn Street, Oscar's General Store on the Mount Support Road, and on High Street, Boze Heath's Friendly Market and Lawrence Bashaw's tiny grocery were all gone within ten years. Today, the Riverdale Store, The Little Store on School Street, and the Mascoma Village Store are the only of that ilk that remain.

The energy crisis also was felt in the schools, where the Lebanon and Mascoma

Not an uncommon sight in 1973 and 1979

school districts adopted a four-day week as an energy-conservation measure. The experiment lasted from January to March, and the school day was extended to make up for lost time, meaning that students boarded buses in the dark and sometimes returned home after sunset.

It was, at best, a case of taking from Peter to pay Paul. Many working parents had to pay a babysitter for an extra day that children otherwise would have spent in school, and the only member of the school board to oppose the change argued that using all of those televisions and stoves in hundreds of homes for an extra day would actually use more energy than if the children were in school. Jim Wechsler called Lebanon "the panic-button school district," during a story on the CBS Evening News with Walter Cronkite.

23

The Hanoverization of Lebanon

"Xenophobic Split"

WHEN DANIEL Whitaker was in the process of being fired by the SAU 32 school board in 1988, he told the *Valley News* that, "The whole city of Lebanon is undergoing tremendous changes and the estrangement of me and the board are sympathetic of those changes."

The changes could be traced to a period of federally-driven expansion at Dartmouth College in the sixties, seventies, and eighties. At the same time, Hanover became a popular retirement destination for wealthy Dartmouth alumni who had made their fortunes in the city. Their return helped push Hanover housing prices beyond the reach of many who filled new positions at the college, hospital, or the Cold Regions laboratory, and those newcomers moved to affordable Lebanon in increasing numbers.

Thus occurred between 1960 and 1990 the Hanoverization of Lebanon—a period when blue-collar workers were pushed out and Lebanon increasingly began to resemble its wealthier, better-educated neighbor to the north. It manifested itself in several ways:

> The educational background of the average Lebanon resident changed radically. According to the city's 1993 master plan, almost half of Lebanon's residents had no high school diploma in 1960, but only 26.6 percent in 1990 had failed to graduate. Likewise, only 16 percent of the town's population had been to college in 1960, but by 1990, 42 percent of residents could claim at least some college education.
>
> Although the number of manufacturing jobs in the city was greater than ever, it was smaller as a percentage of the whole, and those jobs were less likely to be filled by Lebanon residents. Instead, a large chunk of the city's blue-collar positions were filled by residents of the Mascoma Valley, which experienced a ripple effect from the Hanover housing crunch. That migration was well-established by

1980, when more than 30 percent of Enfield workers and 20 percent of those in Canaan commuted to jobs in Lebanon, making the city the leading employment destination for residents of the Mascoma Valley.

Professional jobs in fields such as health care, education, finance, and public administration accounted for 29 percent of the city's labor force. That led the field, and marked an abrupt departure from 1960, when only 18 percent of the city's workers held white-collar positions. That trend also was in place by 1980, when over 30 percent of the city's more learned work force commuted to jobs in Hanover and fewer than half worked in the city. At the same time, 12 percent of Lebanon's residents worked in the retail trade, the second-largest employment category. One barometer of this evolution could be found along Bank and School streets. By the mid-1980s many of the stately homes on those two streets had been converted to offices for lawyers, accountants, and other professionals.

Housing patterns also changed. While the total population rose 25 percent between 1970 and 1990, the number of housing units increased 61 percent, largely due to the construction of several apartment/condominium complexes. Rentals increased and home ownership declined as the region became more of a way station for young professionals starting a career.

While Lebanon continued to vote Republican in state and federal elections, the makeup of the school board and city council began to increasingly resemble the new professionals. It surfaced as early as 1979, when the city council became paralyzed over the selection of a city manager. Five councilors wanted to give the job to interim city manager Harry Henderson even though he lacked a college degree, while the other four wanted to hire a candidate from the Midwest who had better credentials. Six votes were needed to hire any candidate.

The *Valley News* correctly referred to it as an "xenophobic split." Supporting Mr. Henderson were five councilors who represented "Old Lebanon:" Francis Maville, Allen "Juggie" Monica, Donald Bromley, Harold Sanderson and Joseph Duggan. On the other side were Mayor Karen O. Wadsworth, Barbara Jones, John Wasson, and Stanley Brown, symbolizing the new breed of better-educated professionals with ties to the Dartmouth-Hitchcock apparatus.

Mr. Monica suggested the matter be put to the voters in a referendum, "and let the people decide if they want an outsider or a local person to run the city."

It never came to that. When the candidate from the Midwest withdrew his name, the council voted unanimously to hire John Wheeler. Even that, however, was not a complete solution, as Mr. Wheeler's own differences with the city's old guard ultimately led him to resign in frustration in 1982.

"Divisiveness, Deceit, and Dishonesty"

The dismissal of Daniel Whitaker marked the beginning of one of the most bitter and turbulent periods in the history of the Lebanon school district, which until that time had had a remarkable record for stable leadership.

The job of school superintendent in Lebanon had been filled by a local layman until 1903, when voters approved hiring a full-time professional for the job. Thomas Roberts of Madison, Maine, was chosen for the job in 1904, and he served until his death in 1918, when his wife, Charlotte, filled the job for the remainder of the school year. The position was then filled by H. Leslie Sawyer and Caleb Niles, who was succeeded by William English.

Mr. English held the job for the longest period of time. He became superintendent in 1925 and saw the district through the Depression and World War II before he was succeeded in 1951 by Hammond Young, still remembered as the man who closed West Lebanon High School. By the time Mr. Young moved on in 1961, the district had employed only five superintendents in fifty-eight years.

Mr. Young gave way to Gordon Tate in 1961, and the job then passed to William Merrill and, in 1973, to former Lebanon High School English teacher Daniel Whitaker.

In keeping with the changes that were taking place in and out of the community at the time, Mr. Whitaker presided over part of the most significant budget buildup in the district's history, which came at a time when enrollment dropped.

Like many communities, Lebanon began a period of educational self-examination in the wake of a 1983 report by a federal commission that pronounced the condition of the nation's schools as seriously deficient. (The commission also recognized the Lebanon Junior High School as one of the one-hundred best in the nation, and the school was honored with the others at a White House ceremony attended by Principal Robert Proulx. Mr. Proulx's fear of flying prompted him to make the journey by rail, and when he returned to the White River Junction station at 4:00 A.M., a student band was there to greet him, along with a few dozen parents and teachers.)

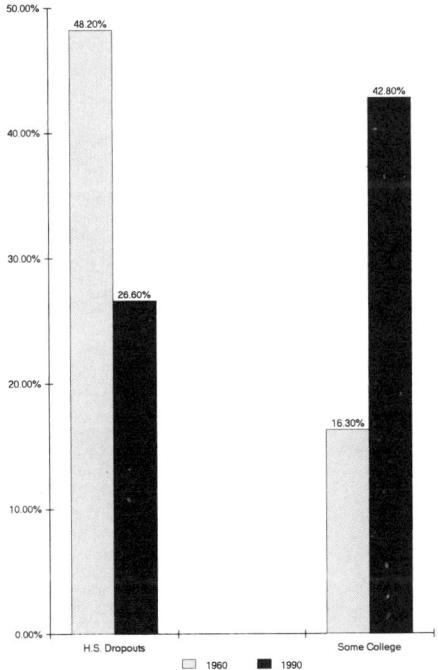

The education of Lebanon - a comparison

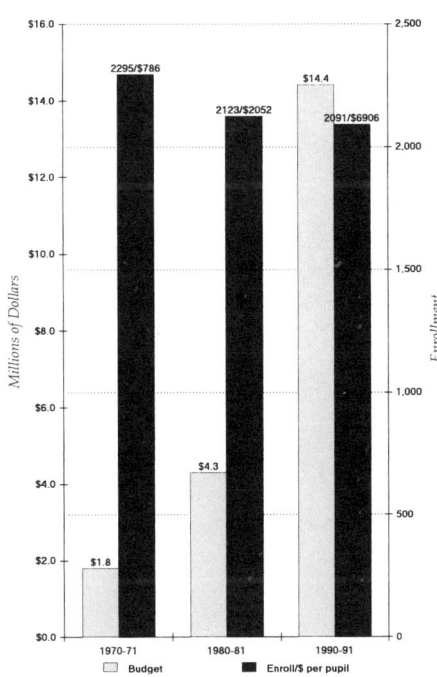

School spending-total cost and cost per pupil

The federal report, coming at a time when Lebanon was making the transition to a more literate population that placed a higher premium on education (as Hanover had for years), galvanized support for school improvement. When Lebanon scrutinized teacher salaries, it found they fell well below those of neighboring districts; voters approved a series of raises that finally paid teachers a competitive wage and placed them in the upper echelon of area schools. This increase in pay was just one factor behind the escalating price of education in Lebanon.

Other forces that drove the budget growth were inflation, the sophisticated and extremely expensive special-education services the district was obligated to provide, the escalating cost of health insurance for employees, and expensive equipment needed to teach students computer technology.

And then there is the case of Jerome Damren. When he retired in 1986 he was the director of school-community relations, the high-school attendance officer, and the transportation coordinator for the Lebanon School District, and he also did the athletic scheduling. Upon his retirement, however, the district hired three separate people to assume the responsibilities he had handled by himself. Although it is only an example, it is one that illustrates another reason for the spending explosion—the expansion in the number of nonteaching positions (aides, secretaries, etc.).

Mr. Whitaker oversaw this growth until 1988, when—in a move led by board members William Conner and Jon Stearns—he was fired. Mr. Conner, who was finishing his term on the board at about the same time that Mr. Whitaker was being shown the door, characterized the change as "my going-away present to the Lebanon School District."

As gifts go, it was not very well received. The community was deeply divided when the board voted to fire Mr. Whitaker on March 30, 1988, less than a month after school district elections were held. Although the superintendent's job performance and his employment status were being discussed by board members prior to the election, it was never publicly raised before the election—an omission some voters felt was an act of bad faith at best.

Board members who supported the firing characterized the superintendent as difficult to work with and not sufficiently responsive to their concerns about needed changes in the school district. Some also suggested that if Lebanon were a truly fine school system, more graduates would be going on to college, a criticism that seemed rooted in the Hanoverization of Lebanon.

The points raised by Mr. Whitaker's leading critics, however, were probably all secondary to the personality conflicts that he claimed were behind his dismissal. By his own admission the superintendent was a strong-willed, sometimes-abrasive personality, although that did not stop him from running the district with competence for fifteen years.

His departure marked the start of one of the most tumultuous periods in the history of the school system, a time of frequent administrative turnover and intense distrust of the school board, which usually held its most important discussions behind closed doors.

Assistant Superintendent Paul Rice served as interim superintendent until M. Ray Evans from Arizona was hired in 1989. When Mr. Evans left for medical reasons in the middle of the following year, Mr. Rice was appointed permanent superintendent. In this case, however, permanent proved very temporary. The board bought out Mr.

Rice's contract after only nine months on the job and refused to say why. The public had no right to know, board member John Dutille said.

Meeting behind closed doors and without a search, the board then filled the job with high-school principal Robert Coffill, Jr., who had no experience as either a superintendent or as an assistant. Only the day before he was hired, Mr. Coffill maintained that he had not been approached about taking the job. At the same time, Mr. Dutille was predicting that the votes were there to hire Mr. Coffill. In a pattern that residents would grow accustomed to over the next several months, somebody seemed not to be telling the truth.

The secretive process that led to Mr. Coffill's appointment was roundly criticized, and the events that followed did nothing to blunt the criticism. In fact, the dismissal of two individuals on the periphery of the school district resulted in a series of public meetings unrivaled in their venom since the debate over whether to close West Lebanon High School.

Shortly after Mr. Coffill became superintendent, respected physician Dr. Myric Wood was notified that he was being removed as the attending physician at Lebanon High School football games because he did not carry medical malpractice insurance. Dr. Wood, however, refused to go along with his dismissal from a volunteer position he had held for nearly thirty years, and showed up for the next game. Here, accounts vary. Dr. Wood maintained that he was met by officials of the school administration who threatened to involve the police if he attempted to continue as team physician. The administration initially denied that charge, although officials later acknowledged that they had, in fact, approached a police officer about the matter. Wisely, the cop refused to get involved.

The community was irate—not only at the way the affair was handled, but also at the way the administration's story kept changing.

At about the same time, Hank Tenney was informed that he would not be rehired as coach of the high-school girls' basketball team. Having twice taken the team to the finals, Mr. Tenney was an intense man who had his share of supporters and detractors. Even his critics, however, agreed that he deserved to be told the reason for his dismissal. Mr. Tenney insisted he had not been informed, while members of the school board and administration insisted that he had. Mr. Coffill maintained that the decision not to rehire Mr. Tenney was made by high-school principal Michael Healey. He, in turn, said it was a joint decision reached by members of a murky "administrative team" whose members he initially declined to disclose.

The public found the Healey-fired-Tenney explanation implausible. Mr. Healey had only arrived a few months before—the fourth high-school principal in as many years—and it was thought that it was much too soon for him to take such a controversial step. Public opinion suspected the superintendent.

Heated meetings were nothing new to the city, but residents had historically confined their passion to a discussion of the issues. That was not the case on the evening of October 24, 1991, when about four-hundred people turned out for a school board meeting in the high-school gym. It was evident from the beginning that the big issue was trust—or lack thereof—and the meeting turned into a three-hour bloodletting. The dismissal of Dr. Wood and Mr. Tenney was a vehicle for the anger, but the source of the community's fury was the feeling that they had been lied to by members of the board and administration. Dr. Wood captured the spirit of the group when he accused the superintendent and other school officials of being "filled with divisiveness, deceit, and dishonesty." The crowd exploded in raucous cheers when he called for the superintendent to resign. "You are destroying the confidence of the community," Mike Schonberger told Mr. Coffill.

Ultimately, Dr. Wood was reinstated as team physician, although Mr. Tenney was out as basketball coach.

Mr. Coffill was unfazed, and after the meeting assessed his own performance thusly: "I'm doing an outstanding job." The phrase became a widely repeated term of derision in the community, and at least fifteen-hundred people disagreed with him. They signed a petition suggesting that he either resign or be fired. The community abounded with rumors about Mr. Coffill's private life, and a sense of paranoia and low morale prevailed among school employees. Furthermore, the SAU 32 school board took the unprecedented step of establishing a special committee to receive complaints about the superintendent.

Still, the board refused to dismiss Mr. Coffill. The public did, however, dump board members John Dutille and Melinda Blodgett when they came up for reelection and elected Dr. Wood. Margaret Wheeler and James Goodrich did not seek re-election, and it was questionable that they would have won had they run.

Some semblance of normalcy finally returned to the district in 1993 when Mr. Coffill resigned to take a job in Connecticut, and John Fontana was chosen superintendent.

By then, however, the damage had been done. An accreditation team placed Lebanon High School on indefinite probation, citing not only problems with the school's physical plant, but also deficiencies in the school's social climate and in the area of communication between the faculty, administration, and school board.

Dr. Myric Wood on the offensive against Superintendent Robert Coffill and the school board

24

The Go-Go Eighties

"Up, Up, Up"

IN A 1989 supplement that reviewed some of the trends and characters of the 1980s, a *Valley News* columnist dubbed Philip Mans the Upper Valley's top "Mover and Shaker" of the decade.

No one else represents the go-go '80s quite like the Lebanon mayor, one of the most influential people in the Upper Valley. He tried to restore the town form of government and failed. A whole lot of his other projects succeeded. He bought the Four Acres diner, formerly a visual landmark, then encased it in a building. He bought car dealerships. He bought a mobile home park. He bought a radio station. He developed homes and condominiums, bought up open land. Mans saw the opportunities of the '80s and took 'em. . . . Mans fought the city over assessment of his unfinished condos, over sewage at his trailer park, and was connected to an illegal dump . . . He proved you could fight city hall. And run it, too.

It was, in some ways, an ironical choice. Mr. Mans hated the liberal paper and they despised him, too, for his conservative brand of politics, attacking him at every opportunity. On the other hand, it was a perfectly logical choice given the thousands of issues he had helped to sell by virtue of his position as the city's most controversial figure for two decades.

The *Valley News* was right in one respect, however. With the possible exception of Hartford, Vermont, auto dealer Charlie Kelton, nobody typified the eighties quite like Phil Mans, even though there were others who made and lost millions by speculating in real estate.

He had burst onto the scene in 1970 asking tough questions about the school budget and demanding that the school board provide him with a list of the salaries of specific teachers. When the board refused, Mr. Mans sued. The suit reached the New Hampshire Supreme Court, which in 1972 issued a landmark ruling in Mr. Mans's favor. The case,

Mans v. Lebanon School Board, remains a major piece of case law in the field of public access to information.

Mr. Mans began his career in elective politics by winning election to the school board in 1971, even as the suit over salaries was winding through the court system. Once on the board he demanded that meetings be held in a bigger place and that the administration provide facts to back up the numbers in the budget. Former superintendent Daniel Whitaker says Mr. Mans was "instrumental in making both the city government and the school government more accountable for what they were doing."

He also went after the budget with a vengeance. An effort to cut the 1970-1971 budget by more than $160,000 failed, but he led a successful 1980 revolt that lopped off more than $150,000 in spending and rejected state and federal money for a new regional vocational center.

He was a complex and enigmatic personality. For instance, after years of sometimes bitter battles with the teachers' union over salaries, it was Mr. Mans who made the motion for a multi-year, double-digit pay raise when a survey of area teacher salaries showed Lebanon lagging behind other districts.

He also sat on the planning board, where critics questioned whether his pro-growth philosophy was somehow tied to his position as manager of Dulac's Hardware, although a city legal opinion determined that he had no conflict of interest.

The 1980s began, ironically enough, with a recession as the double-digit inflation and interest rates of the Jimmy Carter era gave way to a nationwide double-digit unemployment problem under Ronald Reagan. The Upper Valley, however, was thought to be insulated from the brunt of the downturn by the presence of large institutional employers like Dartmouth College and the Dartmouth-Hitchcock Medical Center in Hanover,

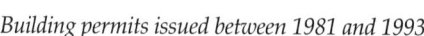

Building permits issued between 1981 and 1993

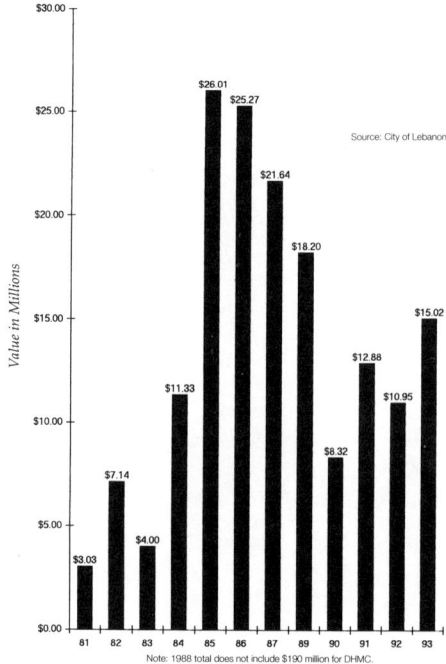

the Veterans Administration Hospital, and the U.S. Postal Service distribution center in White River Junction. As a result, when the national unemployment rate in 1983 stood at 9.6 percent, and the state was at 5.4 percent, only 4.1 percent of Lebanon residents were without jobs.

The nation's economic picture had brightened considerably by 1984, and nowhere was it brighter than in New Hampshire, with Lebanon one of the brightest stars in the state's constellation. The city experienced a frenzy of commercial and residential construction unrivaled since the 1870s. The planning board doubled and tripled their meeting schedule to keep up with the caseload, and still they fell behind.

The Boulders apartments and Wolf Run housing development off Route 120, the Terrace View apartments on Mechanic Street, the Renihan Meadows condominiums, The Powerhouse, Miracle Mile Plaza, North Country Plaza, and an assortment of other complexes went up during this period. So, too, did the value of property. Commercial expansion outpaced the labor supply and left many businesses—especially those in the now-dominant service industry—begging for help. Workers could choose from scores of jobs listed in the *Valley News'* classified advertising section.

Whereas the eighties had started with only two banks in town—the venerable National Bank of Lebanon and the Mascoma Savings Bank—by the end of the decade there were eight. Fleet Bank, Dartmouth Banking Company, and Connecticut River Bank all opened on West Lebanon's Main Street, and City Bank and Trust and BankEast opened on Route 12A on either side of Interstate 89. In the center of the city, meanwhile, the National Bank of Lebanon was taken over by First NH Bankcorp and remained in the Bank Building, the Mascoma Savings Bank kept its name and place of business, while Lake Sunapee Savings Bank opened on Heater Road. Landmark Bank joined the mix in 1991 in the middle of a recession.

The banks symbolized an era in which money was thrown around like confetti, a practice that not only met the legitimate credit needs of responsible borrowers, but one that also fueled a climate of rampant real estate speculation. Phil Mans started out in the former category, but finished in the latter:

I got caught up in the real estate boom of the eighties. I had been actively involved and had seen Lebanon grow since I started getting involved in Lebanon affairs in the early seventies, and real estate had done nothing but go up, up, up, and appreciate. Like a lot of other people I convinced myself that it was never going to end—that it was always going to be an upward spiral. I didn't think it would ever come to an end. I didn't have the benefit of growing up in the depression like my parents did. . . . I looked at the eighties as my opportunity to cash in on this real estate boom that I had spent so much of my last twenty years on the other side of, where I had been a resource for people who made all the money, being a public servant.

He quit his job as manager of Dulac's Hardware and purchased McNamara Motors in West Lebanon, later adding dealerships in Claremont and West Hartford; he also bought WTSL radio and added Oscar Laliberte's old mobile home park on Mount Support Road to his already-impressive collection of apartment buildings. Mr. Mans also was involved in the development of the Renihan Meadows condominium project on Mascoma Street Extension.

Phil Mans is the center of attention as he speaks during a school district meeting.

His election to the city council in 1986 led to some awkward moments, such as when the city sued him in 1989 over sewage that was leaking from his mobile home park on Mount Support Road. He also withheld property tax payments because he felt the city overassessed some unfinished condominiums in the Renihan Meadows development. Certainly some of his business dealings were an embarassment to the city, but there was never any evidence that he tried to line his pockets at the taxpayers' expense. Still, the *Valley News* made Mr. Mans out to be Mr. Conflict-of-Interest. "I'll let my voting record speak for itself," he says. "If people really believe that slop they wouldn't have voted for me. If people really believed that I was dealing in self-interest they wouldn't have voted for me. I can say to you honestly, looking you right in the eye, that I never voted, ever, out of self-interest."

His detractors attacked him on a variety of fronts, but they never claimed to be mystified about where he stood on any particular issue; and even with his in-your-face style of politics, the record says that he ran for elective office six times and—thanks largely to the backing of the Old Lebanon contingent—never lost.

He did, however, lose his empire when the bottom fell out of the real estate market in the late eighties. He once estimated his worth at $15 million, but the chink in his financial armor was that his real-estate empire was built on borrowed money. He accepts full responsibility for his problems:

> *I was a good salesman and I could go to the banks, and the banks were free and easy then, and I could convince them to highly leverage real estate buys of mine. Now, I could say that the*

bank's to blame for lending me the money. The bank's not to blame. I'm to blame for getting overleveraged. I got in a position where, when things went bust, I could not make the cash flow. Nobody's fault but my own.

He filed for corporate and personal bankruptcy protection in 1990 and lost not only the properties he had acquired in the eighties, but also the real estate he had purchased in the seventies. The Upper Valley's top Mover and Shaker then ended up where he had been when the boom started—back at the hardware store. Although no longer in politics, he did make an unsuccessful bid for the city manager's position when it opened in 1994, and was miffed when the council declined to grant him even an interview.

His demise, in many respects, mirrored that of the region itself, which found that it was not so recession-proof, after all. Dartmouth College reduced its work force, as did scores of other businesses. The once-plentiful *Valley News* ads seeking workers shrunk to but a few columns. Fleet Bank, BankEast, Valley Bank, and Dartmouth Banking Company all closed their branches in West Lebanon and Lebanon. The vacancy rate for housing units, once as low as 4.5 percent, topped 9 percent as people moved away in search of jobs. The city's building permit activity in 1990 was but a third of its 1985 peak.

WTSL gave out bumper stickers in 1989 that proclaimed they would not participate in the rumored recession. The station did, however, take part in the bankruptcy extravaganza that swept the region over the next few years.

25

Pastimes

L EBANON'S EARLIEST pastimes, like those of most settlers, probably revolved around work, with groups gathered to boil maple syrup, shuck corn, or share other labors with their neighbors. Wrestling was a popular early contest, and the successful grappler could make a fair name for himself. Circuses were a big attraction, too, dating to the early 1800s when the town was a regular stop on the circus circuit.

A. C. Hardy recalled that Colburn Park was a favorite after-school haunt of the boys of the 1840s who played an early version of baseball. Hide and seek was another favorite activity, as was "climbing the lightning rod and regulating the hands on the old town clock."

One nineteenth-century tradition was the annual muster of the town militia, of which the most prominent was the company of Shaw's Rifles, named after A. M. Shaw, who financed the group in 1878. The company opened a shooting gallery in 1885, and sponsored shooting contests to cover the overhead of the armory.

The Fourth of July was a big event in the old days. The *Whig* reported in 1848 that, "Every boy seemed to have something that could make a noise. Tin horns, shouts, crackers, pistols, guns, balls and cannon all mingled in the anthem." A modern variation of the Fourth of July tradition is the annual day-long festival of games, arts, and crafts, sponsored by the Lebanon Recreation Department, which caps the night off with a fireworks display that draws several-thousand spectators to the area around Lebanon High School.

The recreation department has also resurrected another old-time custom: Summer band concerts in the park. The community has a strong musical tradition dating back to Hough's Cornet Band and embodied today in the Lebanon High School marching band. The orchestra founded by Albyron Hough in 1859 anchored Lebanon's musical scene into the early twentieth century and once played before Queen Victoria in Montreal; the Lebanon High School band played at the inauguration of President John F. Kennedy in 1961, and under the direction of Ralph Bowie the band attended the Washington Cherry Blossom Festival four times, finishing third in 1972. The crisp

The side of this circus elephant carries a sign for Richardson & Emerson's store. A series of circuses have visited Lebanon since the early 1800s, usually holding the traditional opening parade to drum up interest.

sound and snappy visuals produced by the majorettes and flag drill team made the Lebanon band the envy of many a school.

Lebanon caught the bicycle fever and constructed a rink in the basement of the town hall in 1869, and also boasted a number of bicycle clubs through the latter part of the nineteenth century. Three companies of local bicyclists turned out for an 1896 parade in spanking new golden uniforms and torches in their helmets. In more recent times, the town hosted a professional bicycle race in 1982, sponsored by the Lebanon Chamber of Commerce and Tom Mowatt Cycles. Dozens of riders whizzed up Bank Street, onto Union, over to School Street, and then back to East Park Street for cash prizes.

The practice of "coasting" or sledding in the street was apparently enough of an irritant that voters at the 1877 town meeting passed a resolution that prohibited the practice without the permission of town selectmen. The state followed suit in 1883. In the early 1930s, however, selectmen restricted traffic on several streets so that children could slide.

Roller-skating caused quite a stir in 1885 when a rink opened on the site where Eldridge Park is located (1994). Parents seemed to place the rink in the same category as saloons, bowling alleys, and pool halls. "The devil has invented nothing worse in this generation," one reader wrote to the *Free Press*. "Thousands of girls have been ruined in them."

Less respectful children (in another time, perhaps) might have retorted that they were no worse off at the rink then the grownups were at the racetrack, of which

Lebanon had two. The town's first "trotting park" was opened in 1876 by C. D. Jewett on Mascoma Street Extension north of the Catholic cemetery (former Grafton County Fish and Game Club shooting range). The other was a half-mile track known as Riverdale Park, which opened in October 1897 with six races offering purses totaling $1,000. This track, which also hosted the occasional circus, had been dormant for several years when it was covered in the interstate construction.

Speaking of bowling, the 1848 town meeting approved a petition from West Lebanon resident Roswell Sartwell and others "in relation to the supression of bowling alleys." On the other hand, the *Free Press* of March 19, 1880, lamented the removal of "the Big L" from the Kendrick house on South Park Street. "No more playing tenpins there," the paper reported. There also was a bowling alley for many years in the basement of the Carter Community Building, and many persons earned their first "pin money" as pin-boys there.

Pool halls have come and gone in Lebanon. The *Free Press* reported in 1865 that "preparations are being made to open a billiard saloon in this village. This is a most fascinating game, with no possible beneficial result. On the contrary, we have learned from careful observation, and somewhat to our cost, that no man who frequents such a place is fit for business."

As in many small towns, much of Lebanon's social life before the advent of the television set revolved around competitive athletics at the high school and "town team" level. The following is a brief look at the history of some of the town's sports, and the people who played and coached them.

Football

The first Lebanon High School football team played in 1896, and the *Free Press* of that year reported that Lebanon defeated Hartford on Thanksgiving Day.

The 1907 team captained by Arthur Burnham won the state championship with a 20-0 thrashing of a Portsmouth squad that entered the final game having yielded no points. The team featured the brother-halfback combination of Guy and Roy Lewis and was coached by Dartmouth College student George H. "Dutch" Schildmiller who was himself an end on Walter Camp's 1908 All-American team.

The 1935 team went undefeated and untied and, recalls Edward Allard, Sr., "We were only scored upon once." The team was coached by Frederick Carver and it marked the beginning of the glory years for Lebanon football. The 1938-39 team was unblemished and yielded only seven points. Lebanon also went undefeated and untied in the autumns of 1938, 1939, 1943, 1947, and 1951.

Football fans then had to wait for the 1987 team coached by Jim Jette for another team to finish undefeated and untied. Playing in the Connecticut Valley League and ineligible under state rules to compete for the state title, the team cruised through its first seven games to set up a key Friday-night showdown with once-beaten Stevens High School in Claremont. With more than a thousand spectators looking on, Stevens took an 18-14 lead at the half. Then, a track meet broke out. Lebanon scored touchdowns on four of their next five offensive plays en route to a 48-36 victory.

Dozens of Lebanon players have competed in the prestigious Shrine Maple Sugar Bowl game featuring the best players from New Hampshire and Vermont, but only one

Lebanon High School's 1907 football champions. Front row: Harry Keniston, Charles Pulsifer, Arthur Burnham, Leonard Whipple, and Frank Ross; Middle row: Ralph Young, Elmer Bosworth, Dean Poland, Coach George Schildmiller, and Roy Lewis; Back row: John Lewis, Ralph Hough, Jay Griffin, Guy Lewis, and Prof. Crowell

has been named the game's outstanding player: Dave Faulkner caught eleven passes for 171 yards in 1967 (both records that still stand in 1994) and scored two touchdowns to lead his team to victory over Vermont.

Soccer

Although Lebanon High School did not adopt soccer as a varsity sport until the mid-1960s, the game that defined the sport's coming-of-age at the school came in 1985, when more than two-thousand spectators turned out for a playoff game in which Lebanon defeated perennial power Hanover, four-to-three. The team entered the finals against Keene undefeated, but Keene prevailed in a shootout, the most miserable way to lose. "As far as I'm concerned we weren't beaten all year," said coach Denis Reisch. "We won seventeen games, tied the championship, and lost a shootout." The school's soccer program finally reached the pinnacle in 1991, when Lebanon defeated Hanover for the state title.

Baseball

Baseball in the nineteenth century was a disreputable game, perceived in much the same light as pool. A group of women petitioned selectmen in 1868 to ban the sport from Colburn Park, and the game's local image was probably not enhanced much when the local newspaper reported twenty-five years later that, "Foley, who pitched for the Lebanons last season, is in the Hillsboro county jail for six months, convicted of larceny."

Still, the game overcame its image and flourished, and Lebanon has sent two men to the major leagues, both from West Lebanon. The first was Arlie Latham, known as "The Freshest Man on Earth." The acrobatic infielder was born in West Lebanon in 1859, and went on to play for several teams in the National League and American Association (then considered a major league). His father was a Lebanon Civil War veteran, but the Latham family moved away when Arlie was just a child, so he never competed locally and is not known to have ever returned to his native town.

After helping his high-school baseball team to the Class I championship in 1981 and the Lebanon Senior Babe Ruth team to the state title in 1979, pitcher Robert Woodward of West Lebanon was chosen in the third round of the 1981 draft by the Boston Red Sox. He made appearances with the Sox in 1985, 1986, and 1987, and owns a ring from the Red Sox 1986 American League Championship team. A fine all-around athlete, he was named to the New Hampshire Shrine Maple Sugar Bowl team (although his baseball career prevented him from playing), and was a key player on Lebanon's 1980 state championship basketball team.

Other Lebanonians who played professional minor-league baseball include Michael Walsh with the Braves organization in the fifties, Doug LaCoss with the Orioles in the sixties, and Troy Wessell with the Expos in the eighties.

Some residents remember the Lebanon Cardinals semi-pro teams that regularly filled Eldridge Park in the forties and won the state championship in 1948.

Lebanon High School has had its share of success, winning state titles in 1981 under coach Ted Andress and in 1986 under Charles Hunnewell.

No mention of local baseball would be complete without a word about the mighty West Lebanon Indians, the most dominant youth baseball team in Lebanon's history. They went unbeaten for almost three years until the West Lebanon Twins shut them down in 1968. Joe Romano's Indians then put together another twenty-six game win streak that lasted until 1970.

The Lebanon Senators

The best baseball team in the town's history was assembled in 1903 by a businessman-politician who brought together a "semi-pro" or town team the likes of which had never before been seen in the Northeast. It was, without question, the best team money could buy.

The politician was George E. Whitney, a state senator from Enfield and partner in the Lebanon woolen mills whose name was quickly attached to both the team and the park—now known as Eldridge Park, then Rogers and Whitney Park, as George Rogers was another major backer of the team—where the stars played their home games.

Of the starters who played for the Lebanon "Senators" during the 1903 season, seven had been or were shortly to be major leaguers. Crowds exceeding 1,000 regularly watched home games and special trains were chartered to carry fans to away games in Claremont, Concord, and other venues. The fans so enjoyed the season that they presented Mr. Whitney with an engraved, solid-silver loving cup at season's end.

The star of the team was Andy Coakley, one of several Senators with Holy Cross College connections. He had played the year before for Connie Mack's Philadelphia Athletics, and he returned to that team in the middle of the Lebanon season. To fill his spot in the Senators' pitching rotation, Mr. Whitney coaxed Wiley Platt away from the Boston Braves, where he had already won nine games and was second in the National League in strikeouts.

Other players of major league caliber included Ike Van Zandt, who later played for the St. Louis Browns before his tragic suicide (supposedly triggered by gambling losses) in Nashua in 1908; "Wert" Cannell, who married a local girl and went on to start in the Braves' outfield in 1904 and 1905; Pete Noonan, a catcher who followed Mr. Coakley to the A's and later started for the Cubs and Cardinals; a youngster named John Flynn, who started at first base for the Pirates and Washington Senators; and second baseman Tom Stankard, who made it briefly with the Pirates the year after wearing the Lebanon uniform. As for Mr. Coakley, he was the American League's leading pitcher in 1905, winning twenty games with a sparkling 1.84 earned run average.

Although Lebanon resident Herbert Tucker managed the team, there was no doubt that Mr. Whitney called the shots. In a laudatory post-season article in the *Boston Globe*, it was noted that Mr. Whitney "spared no expense to bring together a team which could give Lebanon the lead among the Independent New Hampshire teams." Such deep pockets even allowed him to insert himself into a couple of the team's games, and he scored three runs in a 23-0 drubbing of Windsor during which the regular first baseman, future major leaguer John Flynn, was unavailable.

Despite the tremendous crowds that turned out to watch the team, the experiment was not repeated after that 1903 season. Expenses far exceeded the income generated by the team, and despite the efforts of such local luminaries as Frank Fifield (who lost a reported $1,500) and Augustus Carter, the team was disbanded.

Girls' Basketball

"She is the Babe Ruth of girls' basketball in the Upper Valley," says longtime *Valley News* sports editor Don Mahler. "Her impact cannot be overstated."

Jayne Daigle was a 1982 graduate of Lebanon High School who led her team to that year's Class I championship before moving on to Dartmouth, where she was a four-time all-Ivy League performer and was the 1986 Ivy Player of the Year.

Of equal if not greater importance, however, was her impact upon the game itself. In the pre-Daigle era girls' basketball was a sleepy game played in the afternoon in front of a smattering of parents but summarily ignored by the community as a whole. Often, the same two officials who refereed the junior varsity game also worked the main event. Enter Jayne Daigle, six-feet-two with a range of skills honed under the tutelage of Dennis Fallon at the Carter Community Building and Bill Collishaw at the Lebanon Junior High School. She had speed, agility, the use of both hands, and a deadly jump shot. Her court awareness also made the players around her better.

Her freshman year also coincided with the first time that a full slate of girls' games was played at night, and the prime-time exposure made Lebanon girls' basketball impossible to ignore. Crowds filled the gym to watch the team, and younger girls with basketball aspirations finally had a role model who could do virtually everything that boys could do. Interest in the girls' game took off, and with it the quality of play.

Lebanon made the Class I finals in 1991, in the infamous "no clock" game in which the scoreboard at the University of New Hampshire failed to operate. The boneheaded NHIAA, however, insisted that the contest be played anyhow, with the score and time kept on the sidelines. Lebanon lost in overtime on a shot in the closing seconds. Several girls on that team, however, returned to the finals in 1993 and captured the Class I title under coach Tim Kehoe.

There was one other era in which Lebanon girls' basketball shone: The team in 1931 won a tournament billed as the "New England Championship." Actually, Northern New England would have been more accurate. The tourney was held in Windsor, and Lebanon defeated Barre, Vermont's Spaulding High School, Peterboro, and Windsor to claim the title.

Boys' Basketball

It was, said the *Valley News*, "your routine seven-overtime high school basketball game." *Scholastic Prep* magazine named it the high school "Game of the Year," and the contest between Lebanon and Laconia played on January 14, 1977 remains the longest in the annals of New Hampshire high school basketball. The game was finally decided by Richard Parker, Jr., one of the finest athletes in Lebanon history.

Mr. Parker won the state schoolboy golf championship in 1975, and was an all-state basketball player in both 1976 and 1977. He then took his considerable talent to Plymouth State College, where he excelled in golf, basketball, and baseball, and was elected to the school's Hall of Fame in 1993. As a professional golfer, he won the New England, New Hampshire, Maine, and Vermont open tournaments, and competed on the Ben Hogan/Nike tour (the minor league of professional golf), and also played in the U.S. Open in 1990.

With the score tied and time running out in the seventh overtime of the Laconia game, he drained a twenty-foot shot with three seconds remaining to give the Raiders a 63-61 victory. When wire services carried the game's results across the country, the team received letters of congratulations from Lebanon High School alumni as far away as Oregon and Alaska.

"I've never been through anything like that," a tearful coach Langdon Metcalf said after the game. Basketball was a decided family affair for the Metcalfs in 1976 and 1977. When Mr. Metcalf took his team on the road, his wife Beverly came along as cheerleading coach, daughter Terry was a cheerleader, while son Chip played for his father. Moreover, when the bus reached its destination, the occupants were invariably greeted by the First Fans of Lebanon Basketball, Mr. Metcalf's father and brother, Daniel, Sr., and Jr. They followed the team everywhere.

The program, however, was in something of a slump when Mr. Metcalf took over in 1965, although there had been fleeting moments of success. Lebanon won the 1944 Class B championship under the direction of Maurice "Pop" Taylor, and West Lebanon won state titles in 1948 under Roland Boucher and again in 1960 under Jerome Damren

Lebanon, 1761-1994 / 272

with a squad led by future UNH standout Skip Gale.

Coach Metcalf wasted no time establishing the school as a basketball power. His 1967 and 1980 teams won the Class I title, and five others made it to the finals including the 1970 team which had to play at Dartmouth after ice and snow caused the gym roof to cave in. It was a rare year when Lebanon did not make the tournament, and Mr. Metcalf's four-hundred-plus wins made him the most victorious active coach in the state by the early 1990s.

Track and Field

Probably the finest track participant in Lebanon High School history, Donald Burnham's 1940 school records in the 800- and 400-meter run have stood for fifty-four years. Dr. Burnham then went on to a fine track career at Dartmouth, winning the 1943 NCAA championship in the one-mile run with a time of 4:19.1.

In *Wearers of the Green*, a 1988 booklet about Dartmouth College's finest athletes, Elliot B. Noyes wrote that, "Don Burnham was Dartmouth's greatest runner across the board. He could run on a mile relay team, was a champion from 880 on up . . . I can't think of his ever being beaten after his second place in the IC4A indoor mile."

Two other school track records that have weathered the years include Leo Fafard's 1940 mark in the 1600-meter run, and Earl Jette's 1957 record in the long jump, which was equaled in 1988 by Chuck Callioris.

Dynasty

When the Lebanon High School ski team showed up for a meet in the 1920s, 30s, and 40s, everyone else was competing for second place. Such was the dominance of a ski program that was arguably the finest in the Eastern United States.

Lebanon's skiing roots go back to 1920, when the first winter carnival was held on the Hough Street hill behind the present Sacred Heart Church. The town boasted several makeshift ski jumps between 1920 and 1923: one near the old Sleeper farm on the road to West Lebanon, another near the old Flanders and Patch garage on Mechanic Street (near Rockdale); and a downhill run behind the Glenwood Cemetery that used the tomb as the takeoff point, to name a few.

Everything changed in 1923, when Norway native Erling Heistad arrived to teach mechanical arts at Lebanon High School. He established the first ski team featuring Bill Dunn, Clyde Barden, Clyde Briggs, Lane Dwinell, and Fred Hansen. It was the start of a dynasty in the days when there were four main events: downhill, cross-country, snowshoeing, and jumping.

New York Times ski writer Frank Elkins credited Mr. Heistad with doing more for skiing than perhaps any other person in the history of New England, and he noted the long list of topnotch skiers and coaches turned out under Mr. Heistad's tutelage: "The Hansens, Curtis', Tremblays, Dions, Gignacs, Densmores, Townsends (Paul, Ralphie, and Ira), Lacasses, Stones . . . It was said that any of the boys who made . . . Lebanon High School's first team would easily make any varsity college team. His Lebanon High ski teams for nine straight years won the coveted triple crown in eastern ski circles."

Jumping was the town specialty. Mr. Heistad, free of charge, designed and super-

Lebanon High School's first ski team coached by Erling Heistad in 1923-24. Left to right are Clyde Barden, William Dunn, Fred Hansen, Clyde (Tippy) Briggs, Lane Dwinell, and Coach Erling Heistad.

vised construction of thirteen ski jumps, including seven in Lebanon. The forty-meter steel jump on Storrs Hill is of his design and was dedicated to him when it was built in 1954 by the Lebanon Improvement Society.

He founded the Lebanon Outing Club and made it a regular stop on the northern New England skiing circuit, attracting countless Olympians to Storrs Hill. He also was a national ski-jumping judge and officiated at the 1960 Olympics in Squaw Valley, California. He was inducted into the National Ski Hall of Fame in 1966, and died in May of the following year.

Not long after Mr. Heistad retired as Lebanon High School ski coach, C. Allison Merrill came along in 1952 to continue the tradition. He coached the U.S. Olympic Nordic team in 1956, and the following year left Lebanon to become the first American-born head ski coach at Dartmouth. There, his teams never finished lower than fifth in the NCAA championships, winning the title in 1958, and finishing second three times.

His involvement at the Olympic level extended through 1980, when he saved the day as the supervisor of the cross-country course at the winter games in Lake Placid. Hanover physician David Bradley remembered that the cross-country meet "would have been reduced to water polo had not Al and Gary Allen insisted in 1979, and over all opposition, that snow-making equipment be ready and working for the jumping and cross-country events."

For his efforts on behalf of the sport, Mr. Merrill in 1976 became the second Lebanon resident to be inducted into the National Ski Hall of Fame.

He was but one of several men to go from the slopes of Lebanon to the head of a collegiate program. Ralph Townsend and his brother Paul both excelled in skiing at the University of New Hampshire in the late thirties and early forties, and then served together in World War II as part of the famed 10th Mountain Division ski outfit. After the war Ralph Townsend won the national Nordic ski championship in 1947 and 1949, and competed in the 1948 winter Olympics at St. Moritz, Switzerland. He took over as head ski coach at Williams College in 1950, and was the Dean of eastern ski coaches when he retired in 1972. He was inducted into the National Ski Hall of Fame in 1975.

Chip LaCasse, a 1963 Lebanon High School graduate, seems a sure bet for a similar induction. Since taking over the University of Vermont ski program in 1972, his teams have won five NCAA championships, finished second ten times, and never placed lower than fourth after his first season.

The fourth Lebanon resident to gain entry into the hall of fame surely would have been an Olympian but for World War II. Ernest Dion won the Eastern Interscholastic Ski Championships in both jumping and the combined events in 1935, won nineteen jumping titles in six states, and placed second at the Olympic jumping trials in 1938. His spot on the 1940 Olympic team seemed a lock, but the games were cancelled because of the war.

His career, however, was only beginning. In the 1940s he and Ralph Townsend formed the nucleus of the great LOC teams that beat, among others, the vaunted Dartmouth Outing Club. So potent was the contingent that Mr. Elkins of the *New York Times* recalled that, "... the Lebanon O.C. [Outing Club], permitted to compete in the Lake Placid College Week games, finished behind Dartmouth and Middlebury and might easily have won if the ski jump hadn't been called off."

Ski-hall-of-famer Ernest Dion, founder of the Whaleback Ski Area

Mr. Dion's contribution to skiing extended well beyond his competitive excellence, for the Dions brought renown to Lebanon as the town's First Family of Skiing. Mr. Dion's sons, Roger and Doug, and his nephew Bernie carried on the tradition in the fifties, and the family was featured in such magazines as *Collier's*, *Boys Life*, and in 1956 they appeared on Arthur Godfrey's "Winter Wonderland" special that was nationally televised from Lake Placid, New York. Roger Dion even filmed a television commercial for Prince Edward Tobacco, taking off from a jump with a pipe in his mouth.

Ernest Dion founded the Snowcrest (Whaleback) ski area in Enfield in 1957, and he started the "Ski Week" tradition in which more than 6,500 children took lessons over the years during February vacation. In 1972 Mr. Dion and an army of volunteers opened an upgraded Storrs Hill ski area, replacing the rope tow with a new poma lift and extending the trails onto land donated by Howard Townsend.

Mr. Dion was elected to the National Ski Hall of Fame in 1984.

"The Building"

"It was so new and so different from anything we did," Helen Smith said in a 1993 *Valley News* interview. "After school we'd go down to the building and they had this big Victrola in the front room there, and records, and we could dance."

"The building," as it is widely known, is the Carter Community Building, a fixture on the corner of Campbell and Parkhurst streets since 1917, and the center of recreational activity in the center village since its inception.

Actually, benefactor William S. Carter delayed the building's opening so that the local Red Cross could use the facility for its World War I headquarters (Mrs. Smith recalled bandages being rolled there) and because "the demands of the war have made it impossible to secure a suitable director," the *Free Press* reported in 1917.

The building finally opened in October 1919 under the direction of Maynard Carpenter, and dancing is but one of scores of activities that have since taken place in the brick and granite structure with the oak woodworking. It has hosted banquets, boxing, bowling, ballet, board games, cribbage, ping-pong, pool, riflery, kickball, and less formal events like the squirt-gun fights Robert Dagenais recalls from his childhood in the thirties. Basketball has long been the building's anchor and, as near as anyone can figure, the wooden backboards mounted on the brick walls of the tiny gym (1994) are the originals.

What remains long after the individual games are forgotten are the rules of fair play and good conduct instilled by the procession of directors who have served as the building's backbone. Maynard Carpenter, as mentioned, was the first, and others over the years have included W. E. D. Ward in the forties (the kids called him "Wednesday," but never to his face, recalls one former trustee); Clarence "Willie" Shelnutt in the fifties; and Patrick J. Walsh in the sixties and mid-seventies; Dennis Fallon through the late eighties.

One of the most revered directors was Patrick J. Walsh, a soft-spoken, white-haired man who seemed to live at the CCB. He opened the building at nine in the morning six days a week, closed it at five, and was back in the evenings. One year trustees had to order him not to work so that he could take his wife, Phyllis, shopping. In his spare time Mr. Walsh also served as the clerk and probation officer for the Lebanon District Court, a job he assumed full-time when he retired from the CCB in 1975.

Mr. Walsh also had a clever sense of humor that sent more than one youngster upstreet to the local hardware store on an earnest search for a mythical left-handed screwdriver or the equally imaginary key to the batter's box.

In addition to being a one-man recreation department, he also served as a de facto welfare officer. If a child needed shoes, a coat, or other clothing, Mr. Walsh saw that the youngster received them, but always in a quiet way so he or she would not feel stigmatized about his financial hardship. Sometimes the child might even be given a bag of clothes to take home to his siblings.

While it has served as an activity center, perhaps the CCBs biggest service to the community has been as a place for children to drop by after school and on weekends. "I think it kept a lot of kids out of trouble," says Frank Canillas, a CCB regular in the forties. That the building remains an attraction for scores of youngsters in the modern age of electronic diversion probably rests at least in part in the informality and traditions of the building, fashions now carried on under the supervision of Jim Vanier. As the *Valley News* reported in 1989:

A former CCB "gym rat" . . . Vanier has an intuitive rapport with children that observers say is uncanny. He is also steeped in the traditions of the CCB, a place where there seems to be no rules. But there are, and the kids know what they are, because they have somehow been handed down through the years from kid-to-kid, not unlike the oral traditions of an ancient civilization: Drop your pool cue and you lose the game; kick the ball in the basketball hoop during a game of kickball and you win a soda; no hitting; no swearing—common sense rules.

Pat Walsh, wearing his trademark smile and cardigan sweater, tosses up a jump ball in the gym of the old CCB.

Mr. Vanier, for his part, credits the children. "They take care of this place. They just watch after each other." Defacing the building has always seemed out of the question, since kids have long done much of the sweeping, polishing, and other cleaning. It was an honor to be asked to sweep the stairs. It also was a way for a child without a dime to earn a soda or candy bar.

Although William Carter left an operating endowment, it proved inadequate for late-twentieth-century economics, and the CCB traditionally operated on a shoestring budget made up mostly of donations and proceeds from the annual street fair. The building was so financially strapped in the late forties that trustees flirted with the idea of becoming a YMCA (the town actually had a "Y" in the 1870s).

The organization's financial struggle ended in 1979, when former trustee Carl Witherell died and left the CCB $3.5 million from the sale of his Twin State Cable TV business. That bequest, combined with more than a million dollars he left in trust to fund the Lebanon Outing Club and to send underprivileged children to summer camp, makes him the largest benefactor in Lebanon history.

Twin State Cable was founded in 1955 when Stanley Currier of Currier & Co., and former Dartmouth President Ernest Martin Hopkins backed a venture known as Twin State Television. They received permission from selectmen in Lebanon and a few other core towns to offer "piped in" television via cable, which dramatically improved the clarity of the product and also added a mix of Boston stations that would have been otherwise out of reach. Still, the company was hardly a gold mine when Mr. Witherell purchased it in 1963 at an auction of Bernard Goldfine properties. In fact, people thought the former educational consultant for the U.S. State Department had been snookered when he bought both the cable company and the Hotel Rogers in which it was housed.

The opposite turned out to be true. He sold the hotel to the federal government, which converted it to elderly housing, and the Upper Valley's status as an electronic backwater ultimately made cable a profitable venture. Even the Upper Valley's first television station turned into an on-again, off-again operation. Nelson Crawford, the owner of Voice & Vision on Main Street in West Lebanon, started WRLH in 1966 in a studio atop Craft's Hill, a location that required a tractor to reach in the winter. The station started as an 800-watt affair that remained on the air until 1969. After two years of dormancy it was resurrected at 12,000 watts by a group that included Lebanon attorneys William Baker and Ridler W. "Buzz" Page. The NBC affiliate was off the air again by 1977, but returned the following year as WMVW-TV in White River Junction. It was purchased in 1979 by Taft Communications of Houston, which changed the call letters to WNNE, the name it carried through the eighties and into the nineties.

Even with a station in the back yard, however, the quality of reception still depended largely on where you lived, further proof that the Upper Valley was tailor-made for cable. Carl Witherell capitalized on that situation, and when he died in July 1979 his will stipulated that 70 percent of the proceeds from the sale of Twin State Cable go to the CCB.

Actually, he was originally going to leave the money to Fitchburg State College, his alma mater, and some who served on the CCB board with Mr. Witherell have speculated that, had he lived six months longer, the CCB might never have seen the cable windfall. Mr. Witherell was a regular contributor to Fitchburg State and insisted that he be the one to decide how his money be spent. However, the college went ahead and built a television studio in his honor without his approval and the volatile alumnus wrote the school out of his will and penned in the CCB. He then left for a vacation in the Orient, where he suffered a heart attack. He returned home and was hospitalized, but died within a few months.

Twin State Cable was sold to Tele-Communications Incorporated of Denver, the nation's largest cable operator, and when CCB trustees took possession of Mr. Witherell's gift in the early eighties (after the out-of-town administrator of the estate was tried and convicted of embezzlement) the original bequest had reached more than $4 million, and there ensued a bitter fight over where (and, to a lesser extent, what) to build. Some trustees and corporation members wanted to add on to the existing building. Others, led by trustee chairman R. Peter Decato, pushed to build on the former N.P. Clough lumberyard property on Taylor Street, across the tracks from the original CCB.

The latter group ultimately prevailed and the $4 million Carter-Witherell Center was opened on Taylor Street in 1987 with a large gymnasium, a full line of exercise equipment, a swimming pool, and concerns that the bottom line would cause adult programming to eclipse the CCB's traditional kids-first role.

That last point—which made supporters of the new facility bristle—reflected the vast change in the scale and nature of the organization. What had been a two- or three-person operation with a $100,000 budget became a $600,000 business with fifty or sixty workers, including several trained in a variety of specialties. The new center meant that the organization was no longer the exclusive domain of children, because the new facility also served as a health spa for a more affluent, adult clientele representative of the New Lebanon. At the same time, the larger building and expanded programs attracted a more regional base of children and adults alike, and the CCB remains a focal point of recreation in the city. In fact, it is probably more of a true "community building" now than in the old days, when it catered almost exclusively to Lebanon youth and almost never saw children from West Lebanon.

26

New Town

THEY STARTED rolling at 5 A.M. on October 5, 1991, an army of ambulances and specially designed trucks fitted for taking patients on a three-mile journey from Mary Hitchcock Memorial Hospital in Hanover. One-month-old Kali Wunderlich was the first to go. She weighed all of a pound and a half and became part of Lebanon's history when she was checked in as the first patient at the new Dartmouth-Hitchcock Medical Center in Lebanon. Gordon Edwin Noyes III of Canaan, Vermont, claimed a spot next to Kali when he became the first baby born at the new hospital.

The Hanoverization of Lebanon that had been taking place since the 1960s seemed somehow more formalized on that day, when the Dartmouth-Hitchcock Medical Center, a quintessential Hanover institution, moved into a new $218 million complex in Lebanon. Built on 210-acres between Route 120 and Route 10 in Lebanon, the medical center was the largest construction project in the city's history—far eclipsing the $16 million spent to build Wilder Dam in 1950—and the second-largest in state history, behind only the Seabrook Nuclear Power Plant.

The groundwork for the move was actually laid in 1981, when Hanover construction executive Jack Nelson unveiled a plan to develop more than two-thousand acres of land he owned in the Route 120-Route 10 corridor. He called the tract Landmark, and he envisioned it as the next frontier of residential and commercial development in Lebanon. He abruptly sold the parcel to Dartmouth College a few years later, and college officials changed the name of the tract to the "Dartmouth-Lebanon property" (although that never really took and local residents continue to call it Landmark), and said they had no immediate plans for the land (a statement that was not quite accepted at face value).

It was not the first time that some of that land had been owned by Dartmouth. Many of Lebanon's earliest settlers had been members of Eleazar Wheelock's church in Lebanon, Connecticut, and he called upon them for a donation in 1769 when he was trying to establish the college in Hanover. Lebanon proprietors chipped in with a generous grant of 1,475 acres abutting the Hanover line, a donation conditioned on the

Aerial view of the new Dartmouth-Hitchcock Medical Center, looking west toward the Connecticut River

school's being built in Hanover, not in Lebanon. The proprietors' clerk, in fact, was instructed to withhold the deed from Mr. Wheelock until the school was constructed. Although the proprietors' records fail to state explicitly why they did not want the school in Lebanon, prejudice toward Indians was common and might have influenced their position.

Call it Wheelock's Revenge—or just plain irony—but some Lebanon residents have long since grumbled that enterprises which Hanover refuses to accept within its borders, such as low-income housing, always seem to end up in Lebanon. The 1991 relocation of the Dartmouth-Hitchcock Medical Center to Lebanon, which some residents welcomed, came only after Hanover officials refused to let the medical center expand in Hanover in 1984. When that happened, the medical center turned to a portion of the Landmark tract as the site for an entirely new facility.

After the state signed off on the plan, medical center officials sought approval from the city, a process that took fifteen months. The city council created a new medical-center zone, negotiated a $2 million payment from the medical center in lieu of taxes, and extracted an agreement that the medical center would adopt a Lebanon mailing address. The latter point was perceived as a matter of prestige for the city.

The negotiations between the city and hospital—held in public over the objections of both sides, because the law required them to do so—occasionally took on a harsh tone, and at one point the city dismissed the medical center's offer as "insulting." The city manager made noises about taxing the facility.

If Lebanon was not quite the company town that Hanover was, the fact that hun-

The main entrance to the Dartmouth-Hitchcock Medical Center just after completion

dreds of Lebanon residents depended upon the Dartmouth-Hitchcock conglomerate for their livelihood was not lost on the city's decision makers. The medical center alone spent more than $200 million on wages in fiscal year 1990-91, and as the *Valley News* noted in a 1991 article:

> *Lebanon's boards were populated with local residents who had friends and relatives associated with the center, be they full-time employees or part-time trustees and volunteers. Some Lebanon businessmen spoke out for the project on economic grounds: Having a major medical center in the area is a key drawing card for companies when they recruit employees. As one warned the state during its review, if the project were killed, "our local and regional economy would be dealt a blow from which it would never recover."*

The planning board, after devoting fifty hours and seventeen meetings to its review of the project, finally approved the plan on September 2, 1988, and ground was broken later that month.

Hundreds of laborers worked on the facility to build a complex featuring 400 beds, 1.1 million square-feet of floor space, a 200-yard mall topped by a three-story atrium, and parking for more than 2,500 cars. Initial projections called for 16,000 patients to be admitted each year, and 250,000 more to be treated on an outpatient basis.

Three years after construction began those ambulances and trucks arrived with the patients, and the place was in business.

One of the most obvious upshots of the move was the change it caused in the driving habits of hospital workers who lived along the Interstate 91 corridor. Where they had previously traveled to the Hanover facility via Norwich, after the relocation they drove to work on Interstate 89 and often arrived just in time to join up with the rush of parents dropping their students off at the schools on Hanover Street. It was not unusual for traffic on the southbound ramp of Exit 18 to be backed up nearly to the rest area.

Many observers theorized that the medical center would eventually act as a magnet to attract other medical-related developments on the land around the hospital and along Route 120. The key word was eventually. The most immediate and visible impact was the opening of Centerra in 1991, a joint venture between Dartmouth College and Lyme developer Bayne Stevenson that included plans for commercial, industrial, and office space spread over 140-acres on the east side of Route 120. (Their relationship later soured when Dartmouth vetoed a deal to have a Wal-Mart subsidiary open a retailing warehouse in the park, and Mr. Stevenson ultimately sold his interest in Centerra to the college.) The U.S. Postal Service was the first to locate there, and a company called Fluent, Inc. also did, but the development by 1994 had proved somewhat less ambitious than initial projections had forecast.

Yet to be seen is what Dartmouth will do with the rest of the Landmark property. Published reports indicate that the medical center relocation is but the first of a three-step plan hatched by consultants for the college. Part two, pegged to begin by the turn of the twenty-first century, calls for a 400-acre site to be constructed around a theme of research and high-technology businesses with supporting retail and commercial activity. The third component is the development of a 500-acre planned residential community to be started early in the twenty-first century. Dartmouth also hopes to expand its housing for graduate students and faculty by building on 250-acres east of the Sachem Village development.

That the college is in a position to dictate to a large degree what happens in that section of town brings to mind the old adage about "the more things change, the more they stay the same."

As far back as 1773 Dartmouth officials had petitioned the legislature to annex 1,400 acres of land on Lebanon's northern border, merge it with an abutting parcel in Hanover, and create a college-controlled town called Dresden. A majority of Lebanon voters had even supported the annexation, but eight homesteaders who lived in that part of town objected to it on the grounds that they would be deprived of hard-earned benefits they had won by settling a minister and building a meetinghouse and schools in Lebanon. They also argued that they would end up paying for the lion's share of the roads and other improvements that would have to be built to service the new town. Not only that, they reasoned, but the political deck would be stacked against them. ". . . [I]f such an incorporation should be made every vote would be carried according to the inclinations of the said [college] authority . . . who will always have a sufficient number of dependents, to assist them in carrying any point, whereby the situation of said resident owners would be exceedingly uncomfortable."

The Dresden plan was rejected by the legislature, but the concept of developing a "New Town" in the area was raised again almost two-hundred years later by a planning consultant hired by the city in 1970. Furthermore, a 1974 report commissioned by the town of Hanover for its Gile Tract property outlined six development options for the sector. Since the city owned much of the land around the Gile Tract, the report gives the appearance of Hanover doing the planning for Lebanon.

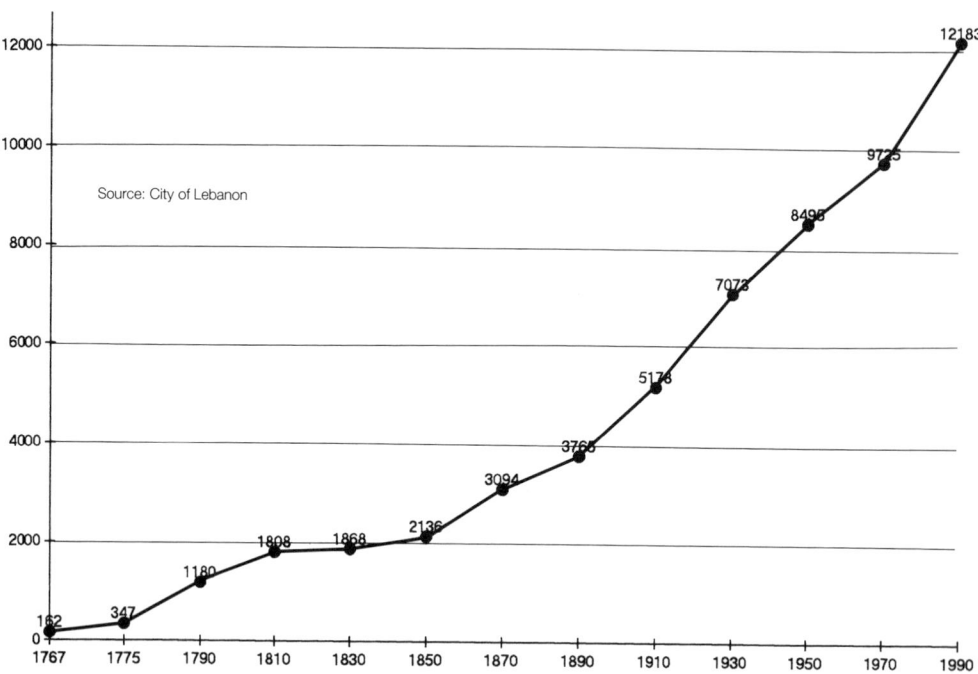

Population growth, 1767 through 1990. The relatively stable period from 1810 to 1840 was the era of westward migration, while the era from 1850 to 1880 coincided with the boom years that followed the arrival of the railroad. The 1890 to 1930 epoch was characterized by the heyday of the woolen mills and French-Canadian immigration. After that came the post-war boom and the arrival of the interstate highway, and a shift toward a more service-oriented economy marked by the development of Route 12A.

The key to any or all future growth in the area, however, may be the so-called Connector Road, a project so prickly that officials of a local planning agency refused to even discuss it at one point in the early 1990s. It is politically sensitive because college and hospital officials want to see the road built, but Lebanon voters are on the record in opposition to it. If there is to be another "xenophobic split" between Old Lebanon and New Lebanon it may well be over this issue.

From a strict planning standpoint the idea of an access road between the medical center and Interstate 91 in Wilder probably makes a lot of sense. It would help relieve traffic congestion at Exit 18 of Interstate 89, and also along West Lebanon's Main Street. It would also help alleviate some of Hanover's chronic traffic problems. That last reason, however, is probably reason enough for some Lebanon residents to oppose it *prima facie* and may help explain the vote taken in March 1991, when the connector-road concept was defeated in an advisory referendum.

Crystal Ball

While development of the Route 120 corridor seems a certainty, other questions about the future seem less clear. For instance:

Will the presence of the medical center transform Lebanon into a company town in much the same way that Hanover is dominated by Dartmouth? Perhaps the city's blue-collar heritage will mitigate against that to some extent, but the rising cost of housing may homogenize the population to the point where the prevailing attitude becomes "what's-good-for-the-hospital-is-good-for-Lebanon."

Will Route 12A development continue its northerly creep to obliterate the mostly residential section between the Glen Road and the bottom of Seminary Hill? Already some of the area has been converted to office use, and given the heavy volume of traffic passing through downtown West Lebanon, it does not seem unreasonable to believe that South Main Street will lose its residential identity to office or retail uses. In the end, the business district in West Lebanon may one day extend uninterrupted from Bridge Street to the Plainfield line.

On the other hand it seems unlikely that downtown Lebanon will ever return to the retail glory it enjoyed in the late nineteenth and early twentieth centuries. Although construction of the Courtyard Pavillion building in 1987 and One Court Street two years later filled longtime holes on either end of the mall, the present trend suggests that the future of the area around Colburn Park lies in office, rather than retail, uses.

In any event, Colburn Park sits like a jewel in the middle of the center village, affording a gathering place for events like the recreation department's summer concerts-in-the-park series, which gives Lebanon a small-town feel.

That coziness was recognized in 1993 when, after examining a variety of economic, demographic, and educational data, one book ranked Lebanon the fourth best small-town in America. The author heard no argument from us.

Appendices

Bibliography

Much of the source material listed below may be found in one or more of the following: Lebanon Historical Society; Lebanon Public Library; Baker Library, Dartmouth College; and the Dartmouth College archives.

Many of the items listed below are contained in the Lebanon Historical Society's archives, which also contain assorted ledgers from businesses dating to the eighteenth century; manuscripts (including the vast Leavitt collection); town and school district records; newspaper articles; and family histories that proved invaluable.

Much of the information about early corporations, as well as the early Northern Railroad records, are found in the State of New Hampshire archives, Concord. Reports of the New Hampshire Railroad Commission and journals of the House and Senate are located in the New Hampshire State Library, Concord.

Books

Akagi, Roy Hidemichi, *Town Proprietors of the New England Colonies*. Press of the University of Pennsylvania, Philadelphia, 1924.
Bogart, E.L., *Economic History of the American People*. Longmans, Green, and Co., New York, 1946.
Brault, Gerald J., *The French Canadian Heritage in New England*. University Press of New England; Hanover, N.H. McGill Queen's University Press, Montreal. 1986.
Champney, Benjamin, *Sixty Years' Memories of Art and Artists*. Wallace and Andrews, Woburn, Mass., 1900.
Chapman, Bernard F., *History in a Nutshell, A Brief History of Lebanon, New Hampshire, 1761-1961*. Lebanon Historical Society, 1972.
Child, Hamilton, compiler and publisher. *Gazetteer of Grafton County N.H., 1709-1886*. Syracuse Journal Company Printers, Syracuse, N.Y., 1886.
Cotton, Norris, *In the Senate, Amidst the Conflict and the Turmoil*. Dodd, Mead, New York, 1978.
Crampton, Norman, *The 100 Best Small Towns in America*. Prentice-Hall, New York, 1993.
Downs, Charles A., *History of Lebanon, 1761-1887*. Rumford Printing Co., Concord, N.H., 1908.
Fassett, James, *Colonial Life in New Hampshire*. Boston: Ginn and Company, 1899.
Guyol, Philip N., *Democracy Fights, A History of New Hampshire in World War II*. Dartmouth Publications, Hanover, 1951.
Hastings, Scott E., Jr., *Goodbye Highland Yankee*. Illustrated by Michael McCurdy. Chelsea Green Publishing Company, Chelsea, Vt., 1988.
Hill, Evan, *Beanstalk, The History of Miniature Precision Bearings, Inc., 1941-1966*.
Merrimack Valley Textile Museum, *Homespun to Factory Made: Woolen Textiles in America, 1776-1876*. Merrimack Valley Textile Museum, North Andover, Mass., 1977.
Millen, Ethel Rock, compiler, *Historical Sketches of Early Lebanon, New Hampshire*. Compiled for the Lebanon Historical Society. Reporter Press, Canaan, N.H., 1965.
Pease, Arthur S., compiler and editor, *Mountains, Mills, and Malls; Readings in New Hampshire History*. Courtesy, Arthur S. Pease.
Randall, Henry Stephens, *The Practical Shepherd; A Complete Treatise on the Breeding, Management and Diseases of Sheep*. Rochester, New York: DDT Moore; Philadelphia: Lippincott; 1863.
Richardson, Leon Burr, *History of Dartmouth College*. Hanover, N.H., Dartmouth College Publications, 1932. Two volumes.
Russell, Howard S., *A Long Deep Furrow; Three Centuries of Farming in New England*. University Press of New England, Hanover, N.H., 1976.
St. Croix, John, *Pictorial History of the Town of Hartford, Vt*. Equity Publishing Corporation, Orford, NH, 1963.
Smith, Lucy, *Biographical Sketches of Joseph Smith, the Prophet*. New York: Arno Press, 1969. Reprint of 1908 edition.
State Papers. Vols. VI, VII, VIII, XX, XXXIX, Lebanon Library Collection.
Tucker, W.H., *History of Hartford, Vt*. The Free Press Association, Burlington, 1889.
Wikoff, Jerold, *The Upper Valley: An Illustrated Tour Along the Connecticut River Before the Twentieth Century*. Chelsea Green Publishing, Chelsea, Vt., 1985.

Wilson, Harold F., *The Rise and Decline of the Sheep Industry in Northern New England*. [N.P.] 1935.
Wright, Harry Andrew, *Indian Deeds of Hampstead County*. Springfield, Mass., 1905. University of Vermont Library.

Newspapers, Periodicals, Periodical Articles

Boston Sunday Herald, March 12, 1916.
Claremont Daily Eagle.
Dartmouth Alumni Magazine, "Friends of Dartmouth Skiing." December 1983.
Frye, Harry A., "The Northern Road, A Brief History of the Northern Railroad." *The New England States Limited*, Vol. IV, No. 3. New England Rail Service, Keene, N.H., 1982.
Granite Monthly. Vol. XXXIX, No. 6. New Series, Vol. 2, No. 6. June 1907.
Granite State Architect. April 1967.
Granite State Free Press.
Hess, Wendell, "Enfield Shakers Welcomed the Railroad." *The Shaker Messenger*. Holland, Mich., Spring 1983.
Landmark, 1882-1952. White River Junction, Vermont.
The Lebanonian, courtesy Governor Lane Dwinell.
Manchester Union, December 8, 1941, October 29, 1922.
Manning's Lebanon, Hanover (New Hampshire), Hartford (White River Junction) Norwich (Vermont) Directory. H.A. Manning Company, Greenfield, Mass. ©1964 by H.A. Manning Co.
The Times-Picayune, New Orleans. September 2, 1950; November 11, 1955; November 14, 1955; November 22, 1955; November 26, 1956.
New York Times, February 23, 1944.
Skier Magazine, October 1967.
Squires, J. Duane, "Headlights and Highlights, The Northern Railroad, 1844-1848." New York: The Newcomen Society of England, American Branch, 1948.
Torbert, Edward N., "The Evolution of Land Utilization in Lebanon, New Hampshire." *Geographical Review*. The American Geographical Society, 1935. pp. 209-230.
Valentine, Donald B., Jr., "The Northern Awakens!" and "Riding the Northern." *The New England States Limited*, Vol. IV, No. 4. New England Rail Service, Westmoreland, N.H., 1982.
Valley News, 1952-1994.
Vermont Enquirer, Norwich; June 30, 1830.
Waterman, William R., "Locks and Canals at the White River Falls." *Historical New Hampshire*. Vol. 22, Autumn 1967. pp. 23-54.
Waterman, William R., "The Fourth New Hampshire Turnpike." *Historical New Hampshire*, November 1960.
Wirthlin, LeRoy S., "Joseph Smith's Boyhood Operation: An 1813 Surgical Success." Brigham Young University studies; Provo, Utah. 1980.

Manuscripts and Records

Allen, Diarca Howe, July Fourth, 1761: *An Historical Discourse in Commemoration of the One Hundredth Anniversary of the Charter of Lebanon, N.H., delivered July Fourth, 1861*. J.E. Farwell, Boston, 1862. Lebanon Historical Society.
Annual Report of the Bank Commissioner of the State of New Hampshire, Concord.
Annual Report of the Lebanon Historical Society, 1959-1976.
Annual Report of the Selectmen and Other Town Officers in Lebanon, 1850-1957.
Behrens, W.A.; Bennett, C.I.; Eaton, C.W.; *A Social Survey of Lebanon, New Hampshire*. Unpublished paper written by three Dartmouth College undergraduates. November 1924.
Civil War Records. Lebanon City Hall, Lebanon Historical Society.
Cook, Phineas. *Historical Recollections*: Asa McFarland, Concord, 1831. Lebanon Historical Society.
Cotton, William, monograph on life of Elisha Payne.
Downs, Allan B., Lebanon biographies, most taken from obituaries published in the *Granite State Free Press*. Baker Library, Dartmouth College.
1829-1979, 150 Years of Banking Service, The National Bank of Lebanon, Lebanon Library collection.
Federal Census Records.
Grafton County Registry of Deeds, North Haverhill, N.H.
Grafton County Superior Court records, North Haverhill, N.H.
Haddock, Charles B., *An Address Delivered Before the Railroad Convention at Lebanon, N.H., October 10, 1843*. Hanover: J.E. Hood, Printer, 1843.

Hardy, Julia Lovejoy diary; Lebanon Historical Society.
History of the Granite State Electric Company. Granite State Electric Company.
History of Sacred Heart Parish. 1976.
Hough, Christine; *A Chip of Granite.* Written in 1964 by Christine Hough, chronicling her life as a young girl on Hill View Farm, now Walhowdon Farm, Meriden Road, Lebanon, New Hampshire. Compiled and produced by Adele Patch, 1988. Illustrated by John Delandtsheer. Printed by Lebanon Graphics.
Lebanon Police Court records, Lebanon City Hall.
Lebanon school system records. Lebanon City Hall. Lebanon Historical Society, Lebanon Library, Lebanon School District.
Leno, Mark, *Lebanon in the Civil War.* Unpublished manuscript. Lebanon Historical Society.
Letters of Dr. Nathan Smith, Special Collections, Baker Library.
Marking the Spots: Addresses Delivered in Commemoration of Marking the Spots Connected With the Early Religious Life of Lebanon. Free Press, 1908. Lebanon Historical Society.
Mortgage books, Lebanon City Hall.
New England Telephone directories.
New Hampshire motor vehicle registrations, 1907-1915.
Rollins, Bruce Faye, *The History of West Lebanon High School. 1958.* Unpublished manuscript.
Storrs, Abel diary. Courtesy of Howard Townsend.
Tax Records, 1790-1994. Lebanon City Hall.

Miscellaneous

The 1964 Lebanon Fire: A Look Back. WTSL Radio program produced by Roger Carroll, 1984.
"Wearers of the Green." A souvenir program published on the occasion of a gala banquet honoring Dartmouth alumni who have excelled as Olympians, All-Americans, world and national champions, members of halls of fame, major league professionals. Dartmouth College Trustees, 1984.

Illustrations and Credits

The great majority of illustrations appearing in this volume were drawn from the archives of the Lebanon Historical Society and those from other sources are so noted in the chronological list below. The illustration used as background on the jacket is a line conversion of a photograph of the M. &. J. H. Buck machine works on High Street, and the small scratchboard drawing used on the jacket and decoratively throughout the book is of the original Mascoma Mill on Mechanic Street. The birdseye views of West Lebanon and Lebanon which embellish the endleaves were published in 1889 and 1884 respectively. The sketch of the Dana House which appears on page two is by Laurence Howard, Jr. and the graphs which appear throughout were prepared by the author.

Sketch of the Dana House, 2
Probable roads and settlements in 1767, 8
Probable roads and settlements in 1776, 9
Probable roads and farmhouses in the early 1800s, 10
Dr. Phineas Parkhurst, 15
1917 Sunday School convention poster, 20
The Congregational Church in the late 1800s, 23
House on South Main once occupied by Joseph Smith, 25
Mascoma Lake dam around 1888, 31
View of East Lebanon from Mt. Tug, 32
1860 map of East Lebanon, 34
Logging on the rapids above Wilder Dam, 39
1883 suspension bridge between Wilder and East Wilder, 40
Aerial view of the Densmore Brick Company, 45
West Park Street about 1865, 46
Major William Bliss, 47
Buck House, designed by Ammi Burnham Young, 49
Lebanon's first schoolhouse about 1870, 52
The School Street School, 56
The second Lebanon High School about 1910, 57
Rocky pasture on the Townsend farm / Courtesy Howard Townsend, 60
The Age of Sheep (graph), 61
Hugh Townsend plowing in 1915 / Courtesy Howard Townsend, 65
Cutting the railroad right-of-way about 1847, 70
The West Lebanon railroad yard in the 1950s / Courtesy Lebanon Public Library, 71
The Mascoma station in the early 1900s, 75
Thomas Waterman's saw and gristmill about 1910, 80
Auction at Nelson Johnson's stables about 1910, 81
1855 map of West Lebanon, 83
1860 map of West Lebanon, 85

Aerial view of West Lebanon's Main Street, 1950s / Courtesy Lebanon Public Library, 87
The Red Cross Pharmacy about 1910, 88
Looking north on West Lebanon's Main Street about 1910, 89
Laura Dana (Hinckley) at Tilden Female Seminary in 1870, 91
West Lebanon about 1866, 96
Lebanon Civil War veterans, 101
The former Frank Churchill home on Campbell Street, 108
Lower half of the Sturtevant woodworking shop, 112
The Sponge Factory, 114
Aerial view of the west end of Mahan Flat / Courtesy Lebanon Public Library, 121
Aerial view of the N.P. Clough lumberyard / Courtesy Lebanon Public Library, 122
Hanover Street after the blizzard of 1888, 125
1884 birdseye view of Lebanon showing landmarks, 127
North Park Street in 1904, 129
The west end of the Lebanon business district before the 1964 fire, 131
Aerial view of the American Excelsior Company / Courtesy Lebanon Public Library, 133
Looking east from Mechanic Street after the Great Fire of 1887, 140
Looking east from High Street after the fire, 141
Looking west from the top of the Whipple Block after the fire, 142
Colburn Park after the fire, 143
Map of the area destroyed by the fire, 146
The original "Mascoma Mill" built in 1882, 150
Interior of the Everett Knitting Works, 151
Postcard view of the old Sacred Heart Church on School Street, 156

291 / Appendices

The original Sacred Heart School building today, 157
The original National Bank of Lebanon building, 161
James Kendrick, 162
Hanover Street looking toward Colburn Park in 1922, 165
Last parking space for horses in the 1950s, 169
Float in Lebanon's World War I victory parade, 175
Croquet on the common before 1870, 177
Transients housed by the town during the Depression (graph), 182
The Park Hotel fire of 1931, 185
The Alice Peck Day homestead, 188
World War II observation tower, 195
The Lebanon airport in the mid-1960s / Courtesy Lebanon Airport, 199
Senator Norris Cotton makes a point, 203
Governor Lane Dwinell presides at an Executive Council meeting, 205
1938 campaign brochure of Joe Perley / Courtesy Philip Mans, 209
Governor Dwinell signs the bill establishing Lebanon as a city in 1957, 213
City expenditures 1960 through 1990 (graph), 215
The first West Lebanon High School, 218
Fire at the Seminary Hill School in 1940, 219
Buildings destroyed by the 1964 fire and subsequently removed in the urban renewal program, 225
Yet another structure consumed in the 1964 fire / Courtesy *Valley News*, 228
The blacksmith shop goes up in flames / Courtesy *Valley News*, 228
Rubble from Mill Street crashes into the Mascoma / Courtesy *Valley News*, 228
The approaching flames send men running for cover / Courtesy *Valley News*, 229

The curious watch from Hanover Street / Courtesy *Valley News*, 229
Layout of the 1968 Urban Renewal plan, 232-233
The mall about 1970, 234
The modern Court Street building, 238
The last harvest . . . symbol of encroaching development / Courtesy *Valley News*, 243
The early stages of Route 12A development / Courtesy *Valley News*, 244
West Lebanon's Main Street in the 1980s / Courtesy *Valley News*, 246
Sign of the times in 1973 and 1979 / Courtesy *Valley News*, 254
The education of Lebanon (graph), 257
School spending (graph), 257
Dr. Myric Wood on the offensive / Courtesy *Valley News*, 260
Building permits issued between 1981 and 1993 (graph), 262
Phil Mans speaks at a school district meeting / Courtesy *Valley News*, 264
Early circus parade, 267
Lebanon High School's 1907 football champions, 269
Lebanon High's first ski team in 1923-24, 274
Ski hall-of-famer Ernest Dion / Courtesy *Valley News*, 275
Pat Walsh tosses up a jump ball / Courtesy Phyllis Walsh, 277
General view of the new Dartmouth-Hitchcock Medical Center / Courtesy *Valley News*, 281
Main entrance to the new Center / Courtesy *Valley News*, 282
Population growth, 1767 through 1990 (graph), 284

Name Index

Abbott, Beriah, 35
Adams, Carl, 67
Adams family in Service, WWII, 196
Adams, Sherman, Governor, 221
Alafat, Michael and Beth, 226
Alafat, Michael Sr. and George, 227
Alden, Charles, 134
Aldrich, Clark, 30
Aldrich, Gerald, 65
Aldrich, Frederick, 216, 234
Alessi, Al, 252
Allard, Edward, Sr., 1935, 268
Allen, Al and Gary, 1979, 274
Allen, D. H., 19
Amsden, George, 111
Amsden, Uriah, 47, 81
Anderson, James, 4
Annuccilli, Harry, 130
Ash, Robert, 101
Ashey, Francis, 197
Ashley, Gerald, 208
Atherton, Sumner ("Cooney"), 198, 200, 219
Austin, Jim, 66
Austin, Sylvester and Charles, 1880, 86

Babineau, Leo and William, 125
Bacon, Abner, 84
Bacon, Charles, 96
Bacon, Theodore, 194
Bailey, Clifton and Hugh, 171
Bailey, Henry, 73
Bailey, James, Jr., 241
Baker, William, lawyer, 249, 250, 278
Balch, Charles, 102
Baldwin, Oscar, 126
Barber, J. W., Jr., Discount Store, 88
Barden, Clyde, 273
Barker, Rev. John, 183, 184
Barlow, E. Hubbard, 93
Barnes, Josiah, 30, 31, 38
Barron, William, 79, 86
Barrows, Samuel, 45
Bartlett, John H., Governor, 176
Bashaw, Lawrence, 230
Bassey, Harvey, 65
Baxter, C. M., 143
Baxter, Charles, 110, 120
Bean, Harvey, 104, 105
Bean, Pamela, 206, 216
Bedford, Frederick III, 118, 119
Beede, William, 135
Begin, Henry, 135
Bell, Frank U., 1910, 118
Bennett, Edward, 208
Bennett, George, 134
Bennett, John, 12

Benton, Colbee C., 43, 176
Benton, Howard, 135
Benton, William, 46
Bickford, Samuel, 84
Billings, Henry, 128, 144
Blair, Charles, 225
Blake, Lauris, 118
Blake, Thomas, 14
Bliss, John, 48
Bliss, Olive Hall Simons, 48
Bliss, William Wallace Smith, 47, 48
Blodgett, Harold, 128, 225
Blodgett, Melinda, 260
Blodgett, George and Seth, 128
Blood, Robert, 195
Bly, James, 109, 134
Boehner, Kenneth, 216
Bogle, Clarence, 86, 96
Bogle, T.F. and M.J., 86
Boisvert, Robert, 158, 234
Bond, Harold, 214
Bond, Paul, 171
Bordo, Leander ("Bumblebee"), 179, 180
Boucher, Roland, 272
Boutin family in Service, WWII, 196
Boutin, Marcia, 251
Bowen, Claire, 189
Bowie, Ralph, 266
Bradley, David, 274
Brady, Matthew F., 159
Braley, Pete and Rena, 230
Brewster, Amos A., 43
Bridges, Styles, 193, 194
Briggs, Clyde, 273
Brooks, M. P., 93
Brown, Channing, 206
Brown, Daniel, 214, 222, 224
Brown, James, 86
Brown, John, 211
Brown, Jonah, 81
Browning, James, 240, 241
Buck, Martin and James, 109
Bugbee, Amos, 47
Bugbee, Orrin, 110
Burby, Earl, 209
Burgin, Peter, 31
Burke, Earle, 155, 180, 211
Burke family in Service, WWII, 196, 197
Burnap, Oliver W., 82, 155
Burnham, Arthur, 187, 212, 268
Burnham, Donald, 273
Burnham, James, 245
Burton, William P., postmaster, etc., 84, 94, 95
Burton, Emily, 95
Burton, Maud, 94
Burton, William P., 84, 94, 95
Buswell, Carlos, 114, 179

Buswell, Paul, 43
Butler, Alan, 210
Butman, John, 79

Callioris, Chuck, 273
Cambridge, Philip, 43, 81
Campbell, Branch, 174
Campbell, Henry, 72, 115
Canillas, Frank, 277
Carlson, Albert, 224
Carver, Frederick, 268
Carignan, Pat, 174
Carlisle, Raymond, 174
Carpenter, Maynard, 276
Carter, Albert, 143, 148
Carter, Augustus and Frederick, 116
Carter, Frederick, 115
Carter, Henry Wood, 115, 116
Carter, Marion J., 51, 115
Carter, William S., 117, 136, 276
Case, Rufus, 84, 90
Catalfo, Alfred, 231
Chamberlain, Isreal, Jr., 176
Chamberlain, John and Erastus, 81
Champney, Benjamin, 47, 48, 53
Chellis, Andrew, 54
Cheney, Elias, 77
Cheney, Harry and Fred, 77, 201
Chrisofulli, Stephen, 118, 119
Church, Whitcomb, 86
Churchill, Frank C., 105, 117, 118, 136, 166
Clapp, Sumner, 47
Clapper, Harrison, "Red" and Bessie, 63, 95, 183
Clark, Arthur, 66, 85
Clark, Byron, 174
Clark, Darrel, 212
Clark, Erastus, 45
Clark, Vernon, 199, 200
Cleveland, Aaron, 30
Cleveland, J. W., 134
Clough, N. P., 279
Cobb, Charles, 22
Coffill, Robert, Jr., 259
Cohen, Gary, 212
Colburn, C.E., grocer, 144
Colburn, Robert, 19, 29
Colby, Anthony, 42, 43
Cole, Converse, 116
Cole, Ebenezer, 99
Cole, Forrest B., 36, 67
Cole, Reuben, 67, 166-167, 252-253
Cole, Solomon, 110
Coley, Charles, 86
Collins, Frank, 96
Collishaw, Bill, 271
Commings, Ferris, 84, 99
Cone, John, 223

Conner, William, 258
Converse, Mark, 1888, 130
Cook, Jesse, 31
Cook, Jesse, Jr., 30
Cook, Phineas, 82
Cooper, Charles E., 163
Copp, Leon, 178
Cornell, James, 100
Cory, Frank, 184
Cotting, Edward A., 100
Cotton, Norris, 194, 195, 199, 201, 221-222
Cotton, William, 28, 136
Couillard, R. J., 178, 210
Courtemanche, Richard, 227, 231
Coutermarsh, Ernest, 214
Coutermarsh, Herman, 226
Craft, Mrs. Charles, 95
Craig, Robert, 208
Cragin, Aaron, 99, 201-202
Crawford, Nelson, 214, 278
Creighton family in Service, WWII, 196
Crosby, Dixie, 33
Crowley, Frank J., 158
Cummings, Joseph, 22, 119
Currier, George, 195, 218, 220
Currier, Stanley, 126, 194, 278
Cushing, Frederick, Jr., 126, 227, 231
Cushing, Frederic, Sr., 126, 224
Cushman, F. A., 110, 115
Cushman, Joshua, 30
Cutler, Calvin, 19, 22
Cutting, William Stanley, 248

Dagenais, Robert, 276
Daigle, Jayne, 271
Damren, Jerome, 218, 258, 272
Damren, Jon, 245
Dana, Charles, 84, 90
Dana, Jonathan, 79
Dana, Laura, 95
Dana, William, 12
Davis, Charles, 150, 168
Davis, Deacon, 176, 177
Davis, Ferdinand, 103, 105
Davis, Irwin, 207
Davis, P. E., 140
Davis, William F., 113
Davison, Oliver, 7, 12, 81
Day, Alice Peck, 187
Day, Henry, 187
Day, Richard, 231
Dean, Michael Frank, 135
Dean, Robert, Jr., 241
Decato, Jimmy, 180
Decato, Leonard, 197
Decato, Norman, 4, 158, 193
Decato, R. Peter, 216, 279
Demag, Guy, 194
Demers, Mary, 216

Lebanon, 1761-1994 / 294

Densmore, Alfred, 194, 212
Densmore, Jason and family, 45, 147
Derrigo, Tony, 128
Dewey, Jesse, 98, 100-104, 135, 187
Dickenson, Ethan, 102
Dickenson, Gideon, 86, 90
Dickenson, Hiram, 80
Dion, Ernest, 275, 276
Dion, Roger and Doug, 276
Dodsworth, Errol, 247
Doucette, Joseph, 73
Downer, William & family, 9, 10
Downs, Charles A., 3
Drake, Charles, 86, 97
Dubuque, William, 194
Dudley, Charles, Jr., 224
Dudley, Terri, 211
Dulac, Edmond, 120
Dulac, Francis, 115
Dulac, Leon and Wilfred, 120
Dulac, Lillian, 151, 157
Dulac, Wilfred ("Bin"), 217
Dumelle, Jacob, city manager, 214
Dunbar, Joseph, 218
Duncan, James, 1793, 35
Dunn, Bill, 273
Durant, Edward J., 110
Durant, George, 111
Dutille, John, 259, 260
Dutille, Philip and Jude, 128
Dutton, Carroll P., 88, 208
Dwinell, Dean N., 118, 204
Dwinell, Elizabeth (Cushman), 204
Dwinell, Lane, 118, 168, 191, 194, 204-206, 208-209, 273
Dwinell, Ruth (Lane), 204
Dwyer, Thomas, 164

Eaton, Albert, 86
Edson, George, 87, 96, 207, 204, 214
Edson, Henry and Delia, 87
Ela, William, 73
Elkins, Frank, 273
Elliott, Robert, 246
Ellis, Henry, 105
Emerson, Albro, 119
Emerson, Albro, Frank, Elmer, 33
Emerson, D. B., 122
Emerson, Frederick, 126, 174
Emerson, Isa, 135
Emerson, Lloyd, 174
Emerson, Marion, 95
Emerson, Stuart B., 194
Emery, Robert, 157
Emmons, Howard W., 241
English, William, 185, 186, 212
Esquivel, Nancy, 216
Estabrook, Nehemiah, 13, 14, 28
Evans, M. Ray, 258

Evans, Robert, 214, 250
Ewing, James, 210

Fafard, Leo, 273
Fales, Henry, 86
Fallon, Dennis, 271, 276
Farley, James, 210
Farnham, Harry, 173
Fay, Barnabas, 35
Faulkner, Dave, 269
Fellows, Harvey, 208
Fenimore, Andy, 65
Flanagan, Patrick J., 155
Flanders, Daniel, 86
Flanders, George Langdon, 170
Flanders, William, 80
Fleetwood, Martha Atherton, 198
Flynn, Frank, 102
Fogg, Robert S., 198
Fontana, John, 207
Fontana, John, 260
Foord, John, 19, 22
Foster, Charles, 194
Freeman, Edmund, 53
Freeman, Jonathan, 36
Freeman, Russell, 36
French, Elmer, 94
French, Elmer and Blanche, 93
Fuchs, Dave, 66
Fuller, Benjamin, 27, 33

Gardner, Ray, 191
Garfield, E. C., 19
Gates, Charles, 61
Gendron, Odore, 158
George, Josiah, 84
Gerrish, Joseph, 79, 131
Gibbs, Lyman, 86
Gilbert, William and Judy, 251
Gillett, Lucian, 103
Gilman, John Taylor, 132
Goff, Comfort, 44
Goldfine, Bernard, 149, 151, 153, 210, 221, 223, 278
Gomez, Phil and Dorothy, 245
Goodell, Harold, 176
Goodman, Bennie and Anna, 196
Goodman, Richard, 196
Goodmans in Service, WWII, 196
Goodrich, James, 260
Goodwin, Alpheus, 111
Goodwin, Peanie, 252, 253
Gosselin Family, 223
Gottlieb, Ralph, 212
Gove, Ernest, 132
Grandy, L. Munro, 195
Granger, H. P., 144
Greeley family, 147

Greeley, G. N., 45
Greeley, George, 102
Green, Benjamin, 45
Green, Gloria, 188
Green, Henry, 84
Griggs, Benjamin, Jr., 197
Gunn, Robert, 89
Guyer, Arthur, 174
Guyer, Mrs. Ranile, 174

Haddock, Charles B., 69, 97
Hale, Samuel, 143, 148
Hall, Philander, 140
Hall, William, 102
Hall, Ziba, 15
Hambleton, Edward, 33
Hansen, Fred, 273
Hardy, A. C., 266
Hardy, Daniel, Hardy Hill, 42
Harrison, Fred and Frank, 124
Haseltine, John, 101
Haskell, William O., 33, 56
Hastings, Scott E., 87
Hathorn, Roy, 90, 208, 214
Hawkes, Ivor, 241
Healey, Albert, 224, 227, 230
Healey, Michael, 259
Heath, Boze, 230
Heath, Wilbur R., 100
Hebard, John, 53
Hebble, Charles, Jr., 241
Heistad, Erling, 273
Hemond, Jerry, 88
Herrin, Albert ("Gabby"), 226
Hewitt, David, 77
Hildreth, Charles Edward, 124
Hildreth, James, 99
Hildreth, James, Charles M., 124
Hill, Charles, 8, 12
Hill, Evan ("Beanstalk"), 189, 190
Hinkley, Daniel, 12
Hinkley, David, 12
Hinkley, Lewis, 128
Hirsch, Ben, 227
Hochberg, Steve, 125
Hoffman, William Henry, 102
Hogan, James, 155
Holt, Elias, 86
Honchuck, Dement, 135
Hopkins, Ernest Martin, 278
Hoskins, Jim, 89
Hough, Albyron, 266
Hough, Arthur, 67, 164
Hough, Asa, 124
Hough, Christine, 63
Hough, David, 29, 113, 167, 201
Hough, Enoch, 73, 130, 133

Hough, Frank, 208
Hough, Lemuel, 29, 35
Hough, Ralph Degnan, 204, 206
Hough, Thomas, 22
Hough, Willie B., 101
Houghton, George, 129
Houle, D. R., 212
House, Jerome, 103
Howe, Edward, 102
Howe, Henry, 84
Howe, James, 176
Hoyt, Florence W., 216
Hubbard, Billy, 182, 187
Hubbard, George, 81
Hubbard, James, 80
Hubbard, James and Sarah, 95
Hubbard, Oren, 81, 84, 90
Hull, Caroline Lowery, 135
Hunt, Ancil and Harold, 126
Huntington, Uriel, 44
Hutchins, Eva, 134
Hutchinson, Aaron, 40, 133
Hutchinson, Henry, 43
Hyatt, Belden, 93
Hyde, Silas, 35

Jackson, Frank, 116
Jackson, Harry, 116
Jackson, Stanley, 116
Jacobs, Rowland B., 149
Jepson, Linc, 240
Jette, Earl, 273
Jette, Jim, 268
Jette, Napoleon, 130
Jette, Robert and Bette, 88
Jewett, Nathaniel, 167
Johnson, Bruce, 128, 226
Johnson, Nelson, 80
Jones, Amos, 131
Jones, Fred, 172, 178, 201
Jones, Robert, 172, 178, 201

Keane, Thomas, Jr., 227
Kehoe, Tim, 272
Kelley, Edward, 80
Kelly, George, 135
Kelley, George H. and Richard H., 77
Kelton, Charlie, 261
Kendall, William, Jr., 78
Kendric, Stephen Timothy, 22, 31, 44, 123, 124
Kendrick, Clarissa, 134, 135
Kendrick, Edward James, 163
Kendrick, Edward and Sarah, 134, 135
Kendrick, Frank B., 114, 128, 148
Kendrick, George, 124
Kendrick, Henry L., 48
Kendrick, James, 134, 135, 163
Kendrick, Stephen, 123, 124
Kennedy, G. G., 148

Lebanon, 1761-1994 / 296

Kennerson, Elisher, 80
Kent, A. Atwater, 114
Kibling, George, 88
Kimball, Ebenezer, 81
Kimball, Mary, 168
Kimball, Richard, 81, 90
King, Alfred, 128
King, Frank, 86
Kinney, Austey, 70
Knapp, Henry, 76, 169
Korpela, Paul, 242
Kroner, David, 189

LaBombard, Stephen, 67
Lablonde, Henry, 226
La Casse, Chip, 275
La Coss, Doug, 270
Lafayette, General, 46
Laffan, James, 189
LaFlamme, Susan, 134
Lambert, Olivine, 151
Lamphere, Stephen, 138
Landers, John, 226
Landry family in Service, WWII, 197
Lane, Andrew, 103
Lang, Minnie, 187
Langlois, Maynard, 194
Langlois, Nelson, 126
Laplante, Moses, 155
Latham, Arlie, 270
Lathrop, Freda, 135
Lathrop, George, 113
Lathrop, S. H., 99
Lathrop, Samuel, 35
Laurie, Edward, 134
Laware, Kim, 200
Leah, Eddy, 135
Leavitt, Ernest, 118
Leavitt, George, 184
Leavitt, John, 80
Leavitt, John B. D., 110
Leavitt, Robert, 115
Leavitt, Sidney, 78
Leighton, George A., 149
Leighton, Levi, 102
Lemay, Anita, 135
Lemay, George, 226
Lemay, P. W., 144
Lessard, Aime, 88
Lewis, Roy E., 190
Lewis, Roy and John, 190, 268
Lincoln, Josiah E., 124, 136, 144
Lipton, Eric, 214
Liscomb, Charles, 102
Liscomb, Elija, 33
Liscomb, Elisha, 55
Longever, William, 176
Lopata, Theresa, 168
Low, Abel, Jr., 62

Lowe, Carrie, 1890, 129, 130
Lymon, George, 90

MacDonald, Edward J., 159
MacLeod, Lawrence, 132
Macy, Rowland H., Jr., 129
Maguire, Thomas, 80
Mahan, Clarence, 120
Mahler, Don, 271
Mann, Philip, Jr., 212
Mans, Philip, 89, 216, 245, 261-264
Mansell, Jean, 168
Manson, Harry, 211
Markham, Joshua, 133
Marston, C. E., 144
Marston, Thomas, 119, 144-145
Martin, O. S., 79
Mascommah, 4
Mason, John, 112, 146
Mason, Joseph, 22
Maxwell, John, 73
McArthur, Chester, 176
McCooey, James, 159
McCoy, Ralph, 231
McDonald, Larry, 213
McFee, W. P., 144
McGee, Edward, 86
McGonis family in Service, WWII, 196
McKinley, John, 22
McLaughland, Robert, 198
McNamara, Paul, 89, 159, 194, 208
McNamara, T. J., 178
McNeill, Charles, 125, 227
Mead, Owen, 112
Merrill, C. Allison, 274
Merrill, Shirley, mayor, 1970, 216
Messenger, Harry, 80
Mesropian, Robert, 189
Metcalf, Langdon, 272, 273
Millen, Ralph, 123
Miller, J. K., 173
Miller, William, 101
Mills, William, gunsmith, 1880, 86
Minard, Theodore, 214
Moore, George, 194
Moore, John, 33
Moore, Paul, 200
Moran, Geoffrey P., 49
Morgan, Frank, 194
Morse, Wareham, 46, 124
Moulton, Carl, 67
Moulton, Hutchins, 1887, 134
Mowatt, Tom, 267
Muchmore, Oramel, 113
Murch, Harvey, 179
Murray, Roger, 66
Muzzy, Charles, Jr., 248

Nelson, Jack, 280
Niles, Arthur, 190
Niles, Caleb, 58, 123
Nixon, Richard M., 202, 203
Noyes, Elliot B., 273
Noyes, Gordon Edwin III, 280

Olcott, Mills, 32, 40-41
Orcutt, Hiram, 91, 93
Osgood, William, 79, 90

Packard, Hershey, 65
Packard, Ichabod, 43
Packard, Thomas, 21
Page, Eliot, 213, 230
Page, Ridler W., 278
Paine, Walter, 210, 214
Panagopolous, John, 88
Papademas, N. George, 230
Parker, Mary, 92
Parker, Richard, Jr., 272
Parkhurst children, 16
Parkhurst, Phineas, 14, 24, 32, 43, 163
Partridge, Henry, 1848, 111
Partridge, Maynard, 111
Patch, Donald and Howard, 67
Patch, Robert and Edith, 170
Patch, Robert F. and Richard, 170
Paterson, J. N., 112
Payne, Elisha, 27, 28-30, 36
Peaslee, Edmund R., 54
Peck, Simeon and Eliel, 35, 43
Peck, Solon, teacher, 54, 104, 120, 132, 187
Penfield, Donald, 116
Percival, George, 102
Perkins, Joseph, 111
Perley, Isaac N., 125
Perley, Joseph ("Joe"), 183, 209-211, 221-222
Perley, William G., 31
Perry, James B., 102
Peterson, Turner, 44
Peterson, Walter, 234
Phelps, Howard, 43
Pierce, Lucy, 15
Pierce, N. W., 134
Pierce, Winslow, Jr. ("Bill"), 189, 190
Pingree, Mrs. Lucy, 97
Plamondon, Alfred J., 126
Plante, Raymond, 248, 249
Plastridge, Caleb, 30, 31
Player, Sandy, 252
Plummer, Elmore, Hugh, Gordon, 89
Plummer, William, 30
Polhemus, David, 21
Porter, Nathaniel, 23
Porter, Winnie, 134
Post, Andrew, 44

Post, Kate, 94
Potter, A. J., 128, 178
Potter, I., 17, 18, 19, 167
Powell, Wesley, 222
Powers, Mark W., 208
Powers, Thomas, 132
Primeau, Ernest J., 159
Pringle, Alexander, 65
Pringle, Daniel, 128
Proulx, Robert, 257
Pulsifer, C. E., 144
Purmort, Martin, 119, 136
Purmort, O. T., 144
Pushee, George A., 182
Putnam, John, 133
Putnam, Rose, 219, 220
Pyer, Nancy, 217, 220

Quigley, James, 133

Ralston, James, 30-31, 44
Ramsdell, J. Clayton, 118, 119
Randlett, Nathan, 99, 102
Rea, Thomas, 30, 31, 81
Reisch, Denis, 269
Reynolds, Milton, 23
Rice, Paul, 258
Richards, Carl, 128, 178, 204
Richardson, Clayton, 126
Richardson, Curtis, 276
Richardson, Daniel, 90
Richardson, David, 84
Rix, A. W., 111
Rix, George, 86
Rix, Herman, 134
Roane, Arthur, C., Jr., 211
Robb, Harlan, 135
Robb, Katherine, 135
Robinson, John, 248
Rock, Anthony, 144
Rockefeller, Lawrence, 200
Rogers, George, 136, 143, 148-150, 168, 270
Rohde, Dave, 212
Rothenberg, Daniel, 242
Rubens, Jim, 250
Russell, Romeo, 227
Rust, William, 212

Sabin, Elisha, 82
Sargent, Dennis, 82
Sargent, Francis A., 125, 187
Sargent, Francis and Mary, 125
Sargent, Gordon, 125, 227, 231
Sargent, M. H., 86
Sartwell, Roswell, 45, 79, 90
Savage, Harry, 214
Sawyer, J. B., 139
Sawyer, John, 22

Sayre, Frank, 180
Scheu, Edward, Jr., 241
Schildmiller, George H. ("Dutch"), 268
Schirra, Wally, 191
Schonberger, Kathy, 246
Schonberger, Mike, 260
Scott, Don, 143
Sessions, Horace, 109
Shaw, Robert Gould, 103
Shaw, William, 144
Shelnutt, Clarence ("Willie"), 276
Shepard, George, 113
Shields, Joseph, 159
Shorey, Frank and Fran, 245
Simons, Hiram A., 109
Slack, Volney & Barbara, 65
Slapp, John, 12
Slapp, Simon Peter, tailor, 30
Slayton, Stephen, 119
Sleeper, Clarence, 65
Sliney, John and Francis, 159
Smalley, Bertrand, 135
Smith, A. J., 86
Smith, Douglas, 170
Smith, Frank A., 170
Smith, Helen Kelley, 77, 276
Smith, Joseph, 24, 25, 26
Smith, Kenneth, 170, 187
Smith, Lucy Mack, 25
Smith, Nathan, 24, 25
Smith, Paul and Wade, 170
Smith, Stephen D., 103
Smith, Timothy D., 84
Smith, William and Helen, 77, 187
Snow, John W., 174
Snow, Robert Pease, 174, 175
Stearns, Nathan, 65, 90
Stearns, O. L., 82
Stearns, William, 86
Southworth, Edwin, 82
Spencer, William and Charles, 123
Stalter, Oliver, 78
Stebbins, Jack, Sr., 201
Stevens, Halsey R., 30, 31, 70
Stevenson, Bayne, 283
Stewart, Roy, 245
Stone, Harold, 227
Storrs, Abel, 60, 104
Storrs, Constant, 11, 12, 36, 167
Storrs, Mary Ann, 132
Storrs, Nathaniel, 11, 12, 167
Strong, F. W., 22
Sturtevant, Edward, 125
Sturtevant, Jesse, 111, 112, 113, 140, 145

Taber, Donald, 214, 231
Taber, Jack and Donald, 226
Tanguay, Jean-Paul, 193
Tallman, Drew and Susan, 245

Tarr, Thomas, 231
Tasker, Edward L., 101
Taylor, Ivory Elizabeth, 48
Taylor, Maurice ("Pop"), 272
Taylor, Steve, 210
Taylor, Zachary, 48
Tenney, Hank, 259
Terino, Clement, 89
Tesreau, Charles, 201
Therrien, Roger, 226
Thibideau, Joseph, 224, 230
Thompson, Brian, 249
Thompson, Elbridge, 128, 178
Thompson, Ira, 128
Thompson, John Milton, 128
Ticknor, James, 134
Ticknor, Oliver, 109
Tilden, Joel, 44
Tilden, William, 90
Tobey, Charles, 202
Took, Elias, 86
Torbert, Edward R., 38, 39, 62, 148
Towle, George, 77, 204
Townsend, Howard, 12, 214, 276
Townsend, Howard and Bruce, 66
Townsend, Madeline, 155
Townsend, Norman and Ruth, 67
Townsend, Philip, 65
Townsend, Ralph and Paul, 275
Townsend, Robert, Carolyn, Michael, Eric, 67
Trudel, Francis, 155
True, Osgood, 12, 43
Truxal, Andrew, 194
Tucker, Bill, 191
Tucker, Samuel, 81
Tyler, John, 84

Upton, Richard, 208

Van de Bogart, Carl, 220
Vanier, Gilson and Helen, 250
Vanier, Jim, 277, 278
Vanier, Robert, 245
Venetsanos, James, 184
Vittum, Donald, 134

Wade, Donlon, 250
Wadsworth, Karen, 206, 216
Wales, Rev., 17
Walker, C. N., 144
Walker, Haskell, 86
Walker, Ruel, 102
Walsh, Michael, 270
Walsh, Patrick J., 276, 277
Ward, Simon, Jr., 100
Ward, W. E. D., 276

Waterman, Thomas, 80, 164
Waters, Luther, 81
Watson, Charles, 88
Watson, Florence, 89
Watson, Richard, 198
Webster, Daniel, 70, 203, 217
Webster, Noble, 141, 142
Wechsler, James, 78, 208, 227, 254
Weismann, William, 251, 252
Welch, Lucius, 101
Wells, Alberta, 219
Wessell, Troy, 270
Wheatley, John, 19, 28, 29, 51
Wheatley, Submitt, 52
Wheeler, Glazier, 1783, 133
Wheeler, John, 217, 256
Wheeler, Margaret, 260
Wheelock, Eleazer, 280
Whipple, Gilman, 126, 136, 168
Whipple, Gladys, 208
Whipple, Lyman, 142
Whitaker, Daniel, 255, 258
Whitman, Steve, 223
Whitmore, Gordon, 40
Whitney, George E., 270
Whittier, Burton, 166, 167
Wilder, Charles, 41
Willard, Osmond, 32
Williams, Robert, 21
Willis, James, 31-33, 113
Willison, Sarah, 134, 135

Wills, Parmley, 198
Wilson, Harold F., 60
Winnek, John, 30
Winston, Jerry, 198
Witherell, Carl, 149, 278-279
Wolfe, Daniel, 126
Wood, Joseph, Jr., 79, 84, 90
Wood, Joseph, Sr., 10, 11, 12
Wood, Katherine, 115
Wood, Luther, 53
Wood, Moses, 84
Wood, Myric, 259, 260
Wood, Ralph, 114, 115
Wood, Richard, 224
Wood, Richard and Chester, 221
Wood, Roger, 115
Wood, Ross, 170
Wood, Samuel, 79
Wood, Thomas, 79, 80
Woodman, Milton, 86, 95
Woodward, Bazaleel, 28
Woodward, Robert, Jr., 270
Wooley, Neal, 134
Worthen, Arthur, 140
Worthen, George, 86, 124, 126, 140, 145
Wright, Alfred, 210
Wright, Clarence, 134, 185, 194
Wunderlich, Kali, 280

Young, A. Burnham, 22, 48, 160
Young, Hammond, 220

Subject Index

"A Better Chance" (ABC), 250
Abbott-Downing Company, 116
Adnabrown Garage, 178
Agency for International Development, 206
Air New England, 1972, 200
Airplane accidents, 200
Airplane crash on Moose Mountain, 1968, 197, 198
Airport, Lebanon, 197-200
Air Passenger, 1954, 199
Alcohol Rehabilitation Center, 1983, 188
Alcoholics Anonymous, 1951, 180
American Excelsior Company, 1915, 115, 132
American Legion Post, 197
American Patent Sponge Factory, 115, 141, 143, 148
American Red Cross, 183
American Woolen Company, 150, 151
Americanized names, 155
Antipathy, toward French-Canadians, 155
Apartments for the elderly, 150
Arab oil embargo, 1973, 253
Armory, 144
Army-Navy store, 88
Associated Charities, 1930, 183
Association Test, Lebanon, July 4, 1776, 13
Athletic Club, 144
Automobile dealers, 170, 184
Automobiles, 168-171
Ayer Cup, 213

Bailey Brothers, West Lebanon, 1932, 171
Bands
    Concerts in park, 266, 285; Hough's, 128, 175, 176, 266; Lebanon cornet, 104; Lebanon High School, 266
Banks
    Automatic teller service, 163; Annual report, 1830, 161-162; First NH, 140, 164, 263; Le Bank, robbery, 247; Mascoma Savings, 87, 124, 128, 137, 149, 166-167, 263; National Bank of Lebanon, aka Bank of Lebanon, first NH Bank, 89, 124, 149, 160-164, 246; Peoples Trust Company, 164-166
Baseball, 269-271
Basketball, 271-272
Baxter Machine Company (Baxter Court), 1888, 120
Beauty Shop Murder, 1939, 135
"Beer Vote Wins," 180
Bicycle Fever, 1869, 267
Blacksmiths, 44, 80, 144
Block
    Baldwin, 125-126, 144, 164; Bank, 1893, 128; Blodgett, 128, 166; Clark, 1869, 128; Densmore, 130; Harrison, 124, 227; Hickory, 226; Jette, 1922, 130; Johnson, 88; Jordan, 227; Kendrick, 128; LaBombard, 186; Lemay, 226, 227; Levesque, 230; Lincoln, 1895, 124; Lindsay, 227; North Park Street, 128; Perley, 125; Plamondon, 126, 130; Pringle and Hinkley, 1853, 128; Pulsifer, 126, 144, 230; Richards, 128; Thompson, 113, 128, 168, 178; Whipple, 46, 123, 126, 144; Worthen, 124
Boarding house, 1897, 149
Boston, Custom House, 49-50
Boston Lot, reservoir, 95
Bowling, 89, 126, 268
Brad & Co., 1994, 130
Brickmaking, 3, 44, 147
Bridges
    Hubbard, 8; Lower, rebuilt, 145; Lyman, 84; Mascoma Street, river, 143; Northern Railroad, 144; Railroad overpass, 227; Shaker, 71; Suspension, 41; Wilder iron, 41
British Royal Carriage Department, 110
Brooks
    Great, 43; Sawmill, 12; True's, 4
Browning Engineering Company, 1968, 240
Building boom, 1980s, 263
Business Inventory, 1855-1873, 123
Businesses, closed by 1964 fire, 231, 233
Businesses relocated, 233
"Butmanville," 1853, 79
Buttrick's Dairy, 64

CWA Project, 186
Cambridge Cloth Factory, 81
Camp Meadow, 7
Camp Whittier, 93
Canadians (see also French-Canadians), 70, 130
Carter & Churchill Company, 117-119, 153, 204
Carter Community Building, 1918, 115, 117, 251, 268, 271, 276-279
Carter Country Club, 1924, 115, 116
Carter, overalls factory, 115-117, 153
Carter-Witherell Center, 1987, 279
Catholic Daughters, 1928, 155
Cemeteries, 8-9, 268
Census, 1880, 62
Centerra development, 1991, 283
Chairmakers, 111
Changes, 1960s, 249-250
Charter, Lebanon, July 4, 1761, 4-6
Churches
    Animosity, 155; Assembly of God, 23; Baptist, Lebanon, 22; Baptist, Trinity, 23; Baptist, West Lebanon, 23; Christian Science Society, 23; Congregational, Lebanon, 17-19, 22, 49, 123, 126; Congregational, West Lebanon, 82, 84; Dartmouth Area Christian Fellowship, 23; Denominations listed, 1931, 156; East Lebanon Chapel, 1893, 34; Holy Redeemer, Catholic, 89, 159; Meeting House, history of first, 17, 18, 19, 22; Methodist, 21, 54, 102; Mormon, Church of Jesus Christ of Latter-day Saints, 24; New Believers Center, 24; Sabbath behavior, 18; Sacred Heart,

23, 35, 117, 154, 155, 157-158, 226; St. Anthony's, White River Jct., 97; Seventh-day Adventist, 23; Unitarian, 1866, 21, 177; Universalist, 21, 33, 55, 177

Cinema, West Lebanon, 179
Circus site, 268
Civil defense, 195
Civil rights movement, 250
Claremont, Industry, 210
Clubs
    Lebanon Rotary, 204; Lebanon Vega, 94; Lions, 187; "Sunset," 178
Colburn Park, 42, 99, 123, 139, 145, 177, 252, 266, 285
Colby and Company, 119
Colonial Plaza, 252
Commerce Building, 1970, 231
Committees of Safety, 13
Common, West Lebanon, 1880, 95
Cone-Bushway, auto-dealers, 90
Connecticut Valley Airways, 1946, 198
Conservation and Goodwin Park, 252
Constables, 1700, 133
Convents, 130, 155
Cotton, Tesereau & Stebbins, Lawyers, 222
Courtemanche, barber shop, 227, 231
Cow population, 1910, 64
Cowan Store, 126
Creamery, Lebanon, 63
Creamery, West Lebanon, 63
Creare Company, 241
Cummings Leather Company, 150, 194, 227

Dairy farms, 62-67
Dartmouth College, 3, 28, 49, 171, 199, 204, 224, 250, 280, 283
Dartmouth-Hitchcock Medical Center, 1991, 137, 192, 280-285
Dartmouth Lake Sunapee Region Association, 224
Dartmouth Medical School, 24
Dartmouth Mill observations, 152
Dartmouth students, 180, 249
Deeds, 28
DeFelice, Family furniture store, 1994, 88
Degnan, Hough & Co., 104
Densmore Brick Co., 3, 135, 253
Depression, 1870s, 112
Depression, Great, 1929, 150
Dewey Peck & Co., 104, 187
Diner, The 4 Aces, 1952, 245
Diner, White Owl, 130
Dresden town, 1773 story, 283
Drugstores
    Dr. William F. Davis, 113-114; Leo Desparte, 130; Drake and Woodman, 86; Foster's, 125; James Kilton, 1930, 86; Lebanon, 126, 224, 231; Joseph Lynch's, West Lebanon, 180; John McDonnell, Red Cross Pharmacy, 1905, 86; McNeill's, 125-126, 227, 231; I. N. Perley, Lebanon Center, 180; Red Cross Pharmacy, 1994, 86; F. H. Willard, Lebanon Center, 180; Woodman and Drake Pharmacy, 1877, 86

East Lebanon, 27-28, 30-34, 47
East Lebanon Endeavor Society, 34
Edson's Bakery Shop, 1890, 88
Electric iron, 136
Electric motors, 1900, 114
Electric service, 1890, 136
Electricity, Olcott Falls area, 1880s, 96
Electricity, West Lebanon, 1965, 137
English, night classes, 155
Everett Knitting Company, 146, 149, 183

Fair, Lebanon Annual Street, 278
Family-care physicians' center, 188
Farmer, migration, 42
Farms
    Ascutney View, 67; Bicentennial, 67; Dairy, 62, 67; Early, 10; Mergers, 42
Fast food, 243
Fellows Hill, 37
Ferry, 12
Fifield and Stearns, 128
Fire engines, 141
Fire Precinct, 140, 146
Fire Precinct pump, 140, 141, 142, 144
Fire Protection, 145
Fire Protection campaign, 139
Fire Station, 128
Fire Station, West Lebanon, 89
Firefighters, 142, 144
    Concord, 142; Enfield, 142
Firehouse, 95
Fires
    Army-Navy store, 184; East Lebanon, 1840, 33, 109; Economy Restaurant, 184; Free Press office, 184; Lebanon, 1887, 126, 138-148; Lebanon, 1904, 125-126, 130, 147, 214, 224-231; Lebanon, 1964, 125-126, 130, 147, 214, 224-231; Mahan foundry, 121; "Mechanics" factory, 1820, 44; Methodist Church, 1992, 21; Payne Mill, 1840, 28; Poor Farm, 1864, 113; Rockland, 1905, 94; Singer Sewing Machine agency, 184; Spencer Shops, 1920, 123; Town Hall, 1923, 128, 176-178; West Park Street, 1879, 128, 140; West Park Street, 1931, 128; Whipple Block, 1894, 125
Fletcher's Paint Store, 227
Football, 268
Fort Bliss, Texas, 48
Foundry
    William Cole, 1887, 122; Cole, Bugbee and Leavitt Co., 110; John Purmont, 1860, 110; Martin and James Buck, 110; Simon Durant and Co., 110
Fourth of July, noise, 266
Freight wagons, sleighs, 37, 38
French-Canadians, 132, 153-159

Lebanon, 1761-1994 / 302

French masses discontinued, 1950s, 158
Fund raising, wars, 173, 194

Garage, "Knights," 130
Gas lighting, 1882, 123
Gas Service Stations, 128, 171
General Ice Cream Plant, West Lebanon, 219
General Motors, 204
Glacial Period, 3
Gladding Corporation, 116
Glass Company, 66
Goldfine, Bernard Company, 222
Goodyear Rubber, 224
Goold and Holmes, grocers, 86
Grafton County Farm, 113
Grafton County Electric Light & Power Company, 137, 172
Grafton County Fish and Game Club shooting range, 268
Grafton County Superior Court, 118, 178, 220, 249
Granite Agricultural Works, 120, 122
Granite State Electric Company, 120, 128, 136-137, 166
Great Depression, 181
Great Elm tree, West Lebanon, 17
Gristmill, 140, 144

Hanoverization of Lebanon, 255-260, 285
Hapgood and Howard's store, 128
Hartford Water Company, 96
Hartford Woolen Mill, 1886, 96
Hat Factory, 44
"Headrest," Lebanon, 1973, 250
Health, Board of, Lebanon, 4, 26
Heavey's, Thomas, restaurant, 88
Herman's sporting goods chain, 119
Hildreth's Hardware store, 124
Hill
    Hardy, 21, 43; Hubbard, 91; Methodist, 21
Hippies, 250
Hirsch's, 1994, 130
Historical Society, Lebanon, 77, 95, 117, 163
History, Downs, 18, 21, 22, 69
Homicides, 134, 135
Honey Gardens, 65-66
Hospitals
    Alice Peck Day, 186-189, 227; Animal, 132; Dartmouth-Hitchcock Medical Center, 137, 192, 280-285; Donation Day, 187; Mary Hitchcock, 117, 171, 280; New brick, 187; State, 135; Veterans, 224
Hotels
    Coolidge, 137; Elm House, 180; Lafayette, 21, 38, 46, 99, 143-144; Mascoma House, 143; Park Hotel, 128; Rising Sun, 46; Rogers, 130, 137, 149, 178, 222, 278; Sargents, 82, 87, 180; Sheraton North Country Inn, (Raddison, 1994), 250, 253; West Lebanon House, 82
Hough Square, 130

Houghton's Pavillion store, 129, 149
House
    Dana, 15; Kendrick, 268; Wheatley-Colburn, 16
Housing charges, 1980s, 256

Immigrants, 153
Indenture of children, 124
Industrial Park, airport, 242
Industrial Park, Etna Road, 240-242
Ingram and Hildreth tin shop, 1855, 124
Inn, Amsden, 47
Inn, Hardy Hill, Stevens Road, 47
Insurance, 145, 146
Irish immigrants, 70
Irish population, 155

Jette's Quick Stop, 87
Jones, Fred and Robert, attorneys, 166
Juvenile cases, 134

K. & D. Company, 115
Kendrick, bank alarm system, 163
Kendrick & Davis Company, 1876, 111, 113, 114, 141, 143, 192
Kendrick Drugstore, 123, 124
Kendricks on South Park St., 123
Kindle Nook, 1994, 149
Kleen Laundry, 149, 223
Knights of Columbus, 1927, 155
Knapp Motor Car Company, 169

"L'Union St. Jean Baptiste," 154
Lake, Mascoma, 3, 27, 37, 70
Langlois and Sons, store, 126
Larson & Wells, architects, 178
Laws of Connecticut, 1780, 28
Lebanon
    Academy, 1835, 55; Budget Committee, 1932, 185, 204; Center growth, statistics, 109; Chamber of Commerce, 126, 165, 210, 267; conversion to city, 208-213; City charter debate and changes, 216; City Government, 1960, 215; College,1957, 224; Cotton & Woolen Company, 43, 44; District Court, 249, 277; District schools, 51; Downtown, 285; Economy, mills, 152; Electric Light and Power Company, 1890, 117, 136, 149; Families, losses in WWII, 197; First City Council, listed, 1957, 214; Graphics, 1994, 130; Improvement Society, 150, 178, 179, 274; Industrial Development Association, 191; Labor force diversified, 223; Land grant to Wheelock, 1769, 280, 281; Library, 105, 167, 168; Lion's Club, 1928, 126; Light and Power Co., 1890, 120; Machine Company, 123, 165; Manufacturing District, 139; Mall, 144; Mechanics Cotton and Woolen Factory, 43, 44; Men in service, 195; Municipal Court,

149, 204; Organ Company, 113; Outing Club, 274, 275, 278; Pharmacy, 125; Police Court, 179; Police Department, 1860, 133; Poor, 50; Public Library, 149; Radio Shop, 212; Recreation Department, 266; Retail establishments recorded, 1940, 193; Rotary Club, 124, 204; Savings Bank, 128; Soldiers' bodies returned, 1921, 176; Tax exemption for new business, 1881, 122; Textile industry decline, 1953-1962, 221; Town Hall, 1925, dedication, 178; Valuations, 1931, 184; War Observance, 1919, 176; Woolen Mill Corporation, 222; Workers from Mascoma Valley, 255, 256

Licenses, liquor, 44
Liquor raids, 1901, 180
LISTEN, 1971, 251
Livery stable, 143
Logan Insurance Agency, 35
Longacres, 1975-1987, 80
Lookout Tower, Prospect Hill, 195
"Lower City Hall," 217
Lumber trade, 41

Macy's, New York Dept. Store, 129
Magazines
  Boys Life, 276; *Colliers*, 276; *Factory*, 191; *Granite Monthly*, 81; *Granite State Architect*, 49; *Lebanonian*, 46, 82, 118; *Look*, 221-222; *New Hampshire Profiles*, 204; *Scholastic Prep*, 272
Mahan Flat, Lebanon center, 33, 120, 121
Mall, Lebanon, 130, 215, 232, 239, 285
  Opposition, 234; Dedicated, 234
Manufacturers, 145
Mascoma Edge Tool Company, 119
Mascoma Electric Light and Gas Company, 96, 137
Mascoma Light, Heat and Power Company, 1891, Story, 136
Mascoma Savings Bank, 87, 118, 124, 128, 137, 149, 166, 167, 263
Masonic Lodge, 97, 126
McDonald's, 1971, 243
McNamara, Automobile dealership, 1940s, 89
Mead-Mason Co., 1875, 112, 113, 140-144, 149
Meetinghouse, 16-19, 21-22, 35, 177
Mercury Spacecraft, 1962, 191
Military recruiters, 248
Militia musters, 266
Militia, Shaw's rifles, 140
Military service and high school boys, 195, 196
Mills
  Baltic, 224; Bobbin Co., 33; Butman sawmill, 79; Cambridge, mortgage and inventory of, 81-82; Carter & Rogers, 149, 151; Cloth, 8; Cloth-dressing, 43; Closed, 153; Cloverseed, 43; Dorr, 224; Early, 12; Everett-Norfolk, 149, 150, 153; Fulling Mill, Hinkley, 12; Grist and saw, J. Wood, Sr., 12; Gristmill, Lebanon center, 35, 79; Gristmill sold to Waterman, 80; Gristmill building, 227; Fulling, Lebanon center, 35; Labor problems, 152; Lebandale Mill, 151; Lebanon center, 35; Lebanon Woolen and Lebandale, 222; Lebanon Woolen Company, 149, 151; Lebanon woolen mills, 210, 222, 223; Linseed oil, Lebanon center, 35; Markham, Joshua, 90; Mascoma Flannel, 1883, 148, 150, 151, 154; Mascoma River, 132; Mascomy Manufacturing Company, 30; "Mill Street," Butmanville, 80; Owners, 43, 81; Packard's, 37; Parkhurst, 15; Payne's, 27; Pulp, East Olcott, 41; Ralston and Rea, 1790, 30; Riverside, 1899, 150, 151; Saw and Cloverseed Mill, Lebanon center, 35; "Shoddy," 148; Site, West Lebanon development (*Powerhouse Mall*), 1994, 79; Saw & Grist, 7, 12, 13, 27, 79; Textile mills close, 183, 222-223; War contracts, 194; Woolen, 148-152, 154, 194, 210; closing of, 221-224; Workers, 151, 152, 153, 223

"Miracle Mile," 67, 137, 245
Mock marriage story, 92
Money, 10, 13
Moody's furniture store, 130
MPB move to Keene in 1941, 190
Movie Theatre, Henry Edson operator, 89
Mules, 15, 16, 42
Murder-suicide, 1986, story, 135

Nabisco Warehouse, 1927, 123
Native Americans, 4
Neighborhood stores decline, 253
New England Electric System, 137
New England Nursery Company, 1869, 80
New England Power Co., 137
New Hampshire Bible Association, 156
New Hampshire House of Representatives, 204
New Hampshire Legislature, 149, 241
New Hampshire Manufacturers Association, 204
New Hampshire Mother of the Year, 1954, 196
New Hampshire Salt Manufacturing Company, 45
New Jersey Machine Company, 1965, 240, 241
New houses, 131
"New Town," 283
Newspapers
  Boston Sunday Herald, 169; *Canaan Reporter*, 145; *Claremont Daily Eagle*, 76, 210, 213; Connecticut Valley Publishing Company, 78; *Connecticut Valley Reporter*, 78; *Granite State Free Press*, 43, 56, 61, 73, 74, 76-78, 86, 93, 95, 103-104, 111-112, 115, 118, 122, 131, 132, 136, 138-139, 141, 144-145, 147, 150, 152-153, 164-165, 167, 168, 172-174, 176, 178-181, 183-187, 194, 204, 211, 230, 268, 276; history, 77-78; as *Granite State Gazette*, 77; as *Granite State Whig*, 55, 61, 68, 70, 77, 179, 266; name change to *Free Press*, 77; *Hanover Gazette*, 77; *Landmark*, 210; *Lebanon News*, 78; *Los Angeles Times*, 216; *Manchester Union*, 193; *Mascoma Week*, 78; *Montpelier Journal*, 92; *N.H. News Weekly*, 78; *New York Times*, 273; *Tri-Town Telegraph*, 78; *Valley Business Journal*, 240; Valley News, 78, 115, 198, 209, 211-214, 223-224, 226, 230-231, 234, 248, 251, 255-256,

261, 263-265, 271, 272, 276-277, 282; founded, 208-209; sold, 213
Niblocks, store, 128
Niles Machine Company, 190
Northeast Airlines, 1948, 198
Norfolk knitting mills, 1925, 149
Novelty Printing Company, 33
Nuns' lives, 157, 158

Odd Fellows, 97, 128, 140, 227
Opera House theatre, 179
Organ factory, 113
Osborne & Sexton, Machinery Co., 110, 111
Overseer of the Poor, 183

Paris Industries, 1984, 116
Park, Rogers and Whitney, (Eldrige Park, 1994), 176, 270
Park Theatre, 126, 178, 179
Pastimes, 266
Pearl Harbor, 193
Peck Homestead, 187, 189
Peoples Trust Company, 164, 165-166
Pest House, Storrs Hill, 24
Plazas - Malls, Route 12A, West Lebanon, 67
Police Court, 1875, 134
Police Department, 134, 185
Police Station, 89, 134, 178
Pool Hall, 144, 268
Poor Department, 183, 184
Poor Farm, 113
Population, Lebanon, 148
Post Office, first, Lebanon, center, 46
Post Office, West Lebanon, 1833, 79, 84
Priests, Irish and French, 155
Profile Skiwear, 117-119
Prohibition and Temperance, 179
Proprietors, Lebanon, 5, 6
Public building, first, 1768, 51
Public works jobs, 186
Pumping station, 141

Race track, 1897, 132
Radio Station, WLEB, 212
Radio Station, WVTR, (WNHV), 230
Radio Station, WTSL, 211, 212, 230, 265
Railroads, 68-78, 96, 111, 146, 180, 224, 227
    Boston and Maine; 34, 86, 171; decline, 76, 77; depots, 71, 76, 77; first train, November 17, 1847, 70; ice house, Mascoma Lake, 71; importance to West Lebanon, 72-73; locomotives with local names mentioned, 76; Northern, 69; Reaches Lebanon, 1847, 68; wrecks, 73-75, 77, 138-139
Rationing Board, 194
Real estate development, 252
Real estate speculation, 263
Repeal on alcohol, 1932, 180
Repeal of some blue laws, 1933, 180

Republican National Convention, 1952, 56, 68, 72, 206
Reservoir on Common, 141
Reservoir on hill, 1884, 141
Restaurants
    Lamplighter, 227; Landers, 226, 231, 240; Mike's, 253; Owl's Nest, 253; Riverside Grill, 248; Sargent's, 82; Village Hearth, 231
Retailing boom, 123
Richardson and Emerson, store, 1888, 126
Richardson & Langlois, store, 126
Richards shoe store, 128
Right-to-know suit, 261
Rivers
    Connecticut, 3, 13, 27, 36, 39-41; Mascoma, 3, 27, 35, 38, 43, 79, 82, 109, 137, 144, 148, 155, 227, 230; Mascomme, 27
"Riverdale," 1874, 132
Riverdale Park, 1897, 268
Riverdale Store, 132
"Rivermill," complex, 148
Rivermill Commercial Center, 1994, 223
Riverside Woolen Company, 1893, 149
Rix, Albert, machine shop, 144
Roads
    Cattle drives, 38; concrete slab, 1921, 170; Connector Road plan, 1991, 284; County, 13; Eastman Hill, 37, 38; East Wilder, 240; Enfield north of Mascoma River, 13; Fellows Hill, 38; Glen, 80; Heater, 38, 47; Horse, 7; Interstate 89, 132, 206, 239; Kings Highway, 11, 13, 56; Meriden, 43; Payne, 27; Podgum Lane, 10, 53; Poverty Lane, 10; River, 38; Riverside Drive, 37; Route 4, 37; Route 4A, 37; Route 12A, 79, 81, 130, 242, 243, 245, 246, 284-285; Route 120, 128, 284; Slayton Hill Road, (old Podgum Lane), 119; Sunset Rock, 21; Toll, 36
Roads, Turnpikes, 36, 37
    Croydon turnpike, 36, 39, 42, 47; 4th New Hampshire turnpike, 12, 36, 37, 38, 42
Rockdale store, 148, 223
Rogers House, 129, 150, 251
Roller-skating, 1885, 267
Rolston, W. B. and Co., Undertakers, 86
Romano Coal Company, 90
Running water, 1884, 141

Sandstone, East Lebanon, 33
Scannell's Cut Rate store, 130
School Buildings
    Bank Street, 58; East Lebanon, 34; Estabrook, 23; First, 51; Granite St., 157; Hanover St., 52; Lebanon High, 56, 58, 219; Main Street, 89; Sacred Heart, 157; School St., 56; Tilden Seminary 90-91
Schools
    Budget cuts, 185, 262; classes for French-Canadian mill workers, 58; conditions, 54, 56; discipline, 157; District-turbulent period, 256;

Districts, 1775-1784, 52; dress code, 249; Districts merge, 58; early construction, 53; early curriculum, 1847, 54; Estabrook, 23; four day week, 253, 254; High School, 57, 58, 224; High-School debate for Public High School, 56; High School District, 1876, 57; High School, merger, 219-220; High School, news, 219; High School, private, 1835, 54, 55; Lebanon Academy, Lebanon Liberal Institute, 90; Lebanon Liberal Institute, 1841, 55; *New Hampshire Military Academy*, 93; night classes, 1890s, Americanization, 158; Parochial, 1889, 157; Peck District, 120; private, 90; Prudential Committee, 53; religious education, 157; repairs, 54; Rockland Military Academy, 84, 86, 93-94, 198; rules, 55; Sacred Heart, 1909, 157; Sisters of Mercy, 157; ski teams, 273; State Aid for school building, 205; State industrial, 134; superintendents, 1903, some named, 256, 257; teachers, boarded out and demise of practice, 54; teachers' salaries, budget growth, 258; terms, studies, charges, 55; Tilden Seminary History, 90-93; trustees, 55; tuition, 157; West Lebanon High, 58, 196, 217-220; whispering problem, 53, 54
Schoolhouse, Hardy Hill, 21
Scytheville, 119-120
Sears, Roebuck & Co., 149
Secession, Lebanon to Vermont, 1778, 28
Self-Service gas and convenience stores, 253
Seminary Hill, West Lebanon, 86
Senator Cotton's influence on Lebanon, 202
Settlers, early, list of, 11
Shakers, 70
Shaw Rifles, 1878, 266
Sheep, 59
Shepard Organ Company, 1872, 113
Shops
    Ox handles, carriage spokes, 80; Box shop, 149; Brown's Bike Shop, 231; Courtemanche, barber, 227, 231; Custom Shop, fabrics, 227; joiners, 13; shoemakers, 13; woodworking, 144
Shopping Center, Powerhouse, 90
Ski area, Storrs Hill, 276
Ski Hall of Fame, National, 274
Ski jumps, 273, 274
Ski Week, 276
Slate factory, 33
Slaytonville, 131
Snow roller, 170
Soccer, 1960s, 269
Social changes, 1960s, 248
Soldiers Memorial Building, 105, 118, 123, 138
Spencer Woodworking shop, 123
Split Ballbearing Company, 189-192, 206, 224, 240
Stables, 80, 128
Stage line, 36, 38
State Liquor store, 166, 180
State Senate, president, 1952, 204
Steam heat, 1882, 123
Steam pump, 140

Stearns, George, meat market, 119
Stores
    A&P, 251; Bashaw's Market, 230; Bridgman's, 128, 245; Brown's Furniture, 130; John Butman's General, 80; William P. Burton and George Blood, 1860, 84; Cameo Creations, 1994, 87; Colonial Bookstore, 231; Currier Company, 126, 231; Currier & Langlois, 126; Dairy Queen, 250; Davis, C. H., jewelry, 231; Decorator Plaza, 245; "Do-It" Store, 250; Dulac Hardware and Building Supply, 110, 120, 262; Durant and Perkins, 110, 128, 140; Dutille's Jewelry, 128; Fifield & Stearns, 128; First National, 87, 130; Fletcher's Paint, 231; Friendly Market, 230; Goold & Holmes, 135; Elmore Plummer and Edwin Southworth hardware, 89; Hirsch's, 231; Howard Brothers, 130; Hunt's Department, 126; Lewis Brothers Hardware, 226, 227, 231; Radio Shack, 231; Sherwin-Williams paint, 227; Shoetorium, 1978, 231; Stateline Sports, 245; Tom's Toggery, 212, 227, 231; Village Pizza, 1977, 231; Voice and Vision, 278; Western Auto, 230; Woolworth's, 125, 126, 230, 231
Storage facility, 66
Street lights, 1890, 136
Streets
    Abbott, 222; Academy, 55; Allen, 132; Bank Street Extension, 47; Bridge, 89; Court, 144, 285; Court and Campbell, 128; East Park, 46, 149, 168; Eldridge, 132, 157; Elm, 132; Evans Drive, 170; Foundry, 109, 141, 143, 148; Guyer, 174; Hanover, 35, 44, 123, 126, 144, 239; Hanover and Mill, 144; High, 35, 120, 140, 141, 144, 149, 230; Howe, 128, 129, 134, 178; "Le Petit Canada," 153, 154; Main, West Lebanon, 12; Mascoma, 44, 46, 126, 128, 170, 189; Mascoma and Water, 143; Mechanic, 43, 120, 132, 143, 148, 170; Mill, 35, 143, 224; North Park, 166; Parkhurst, 132, 155, 169; School, 35, 46, 155; South (School Street), 54; South Main, West Lebanon, 24; South Park, 126; Spencer, Lebanon center, 33; Summer, 132; Taylor, 279; Valley, 143; Water, 44, 111, 141, 142, 143; Water and Church, 143; West, 144, 154, 230; West Park, 140
Sturtevant, J.C., & Co. furniture, 1852, 111
Substandard housing, 1972, 251
Suburban Gas, building, 227
Sun Life Assurance Company, 166
Supertest Dairy, 65
Supreme Court of N.H., 261
Surveyors, 7

Tadmor Farm, 67
Tanker, *Mascoma*, 4
Taverns
    Abbott's Beriah, 35; "Benton House," 38; "Benwood," Ephraim and Benjamin Wood, 47; Early, 11; Cook's, Jesse, 35; Dana, 12, 46, 79, 82, 86; Hough's, Thomas, 46
Tax exemptions to companies, 146

Teams, 12, 123
Telegraph, 142
Telephone, 135, 136, 142
Television stations, 278
Temperance Movement, 179
Tenements needed, 131
Thermal Dynamics Company, 240
Thibault, R., jewelry, 166
Thrift stores, 252
Timken Company, 1990, 191, 192
Toll charges, 37
Tony's Cafe, 230
Town Hall renovation, 1975, 178
Town Jail, 181
Town, "New Connecticut," proposed, 29
Town Team, 268
Township, Lebanon, 6
Tramps, 181
Transient Camp, Peabody Street, 182
Trapper Brown Company, 1983, 242
Trotting Parks, racetracks, 1876 and 1897, 267, 268
Trumbull-Nelson Construction Company, 231
Twin State Television and Cable, 1955, 278
Traffic patterns, 234, 235, 240, 282

Unemployed strike, 1933, 186
"Unemployment drive," 1932, 186
Unemployment rate, 1983, 263
Union of the Daughters of Temperance, 1848, 179
"Union Hall," East Lebanon, 32, 33
Union Hall, West Lebanon School, 84, 90, 93, 95
"Upper Valley," 210
Upper Valley Childrens Center, 1971, 252
Upper Valley Paintball, 1994, 110
Upper Valley Senior Citizens Center, 1973, 251
Upper Valley Shopping Plaza, West Lebanon, 1968, 242
Urban Renewal, 232, 233
U.S. Military Academy, 48
U.S. Olympic Nordic Team, 1956, 274
U.S. Postal Service, 283
U.S. Supreme Court, 249

Vermont
    Republic of, 28; State House, 49; Windsor Post Office, 50
Veterans of Foreign Wars, 130
Veterans return, 197

Wakema Dairy, 65
Walhowdon Farm, 67
Wars
    American Red Cross, 173, 174; Armistice, celebrations, parade, 175, 197; Civil, 22, 62, 73, 98-101; aid societies, 104; bounty, 99-100; casualties, 100; deserters, 100; Lebanon's debt, 99; POWs, 101; recruiting, 84; substitutes, 100; French & Indian, 13, 40, 52; Korean, 191, 197; Lebanon in the War, men and battles, 98; Liberty Bonds, 1917, 173; Mexican, 48; National Defense League, 172; personel in service, 372, 174; prisoners and dead, 174; Protest, 1972, 248; rationing, WWI, 172-173, WWII, 194; Registration Day Parade, 1917, 173; Revolutionary, 13, 29, 46, 52; Robert P. Snow Post Veterans of Foreign Wars, 175; Selective Service Act, 1917, 173; Soldiers in 1777, 14; Special Aid Societies, 174; Vietnam, 248; Victory Garden Campaign, 172; World War I, 66, 76, 95, 114, 172, 276; World War II, 4, 149, 152, 158, 186, 193-198, 275
Warehouse, 143
Watchmaker tools, surgical instruments, 114
Water power, "Mascoma Improvement Company," 33
Water rates, 146, 147
Water System, Lebanon, 139
Water Works, 85, 95, 96, 138, 145
Welfare, 1932, 181
Welfare Department employing seamstresses, 186
Well's Pool Hall, 88
West Lebanon, 37
    Boston Lot reservoir, 137; Civic Association, 207; Downtown, 245, 285; Economic changes, new names, 1855, 84; High School Alumni Association, 220; High School debate, 1957 and story, 217; High School moves to Rockland Academy building, 1915, 218; High School district merges with Lebanon center, 1927, 218; High School adds auditorium and gymnasium, 1934, 218; High School basketball team, 1948, 219; High School last class graduates, 220; High School merger meeting, 1957, 219; Library, 89, 93, 95; Main Street brick school, 1891, 218; Manufacturing Company, 79; Rural Development Society, 1884, 95; School becomes junior-high then elementary school, 220; School District, 1890, 218; secession considered, 1957, 207-208; social life, 84; ties to White River Junction, Vermont, 207; versus Lebanon center, 207; Village, 82
Wheelabrator-Frye, 1976, 191
Whipping Post, 133
Whipple Store, first, 126
White River Junction, ties to, 96
Whitman Press, 1994, 149, 223
Wilder Dam, 95, 137, 280
William Iselin & Company, 149
Winona Dairy, 65
Wool Tariffs, repealed, 1846, 62
Woodworking Industry, 111, 148
Woodworking to textiles, 146
Woolen manufacturing, 148

Youth House, 1972, 251

Designed by A. L. Morris,
the text of this volume was composed in Palatino
and printed by Knowlton & McLeary
in Farmington, Maine
on Cougar Opaque Vellum Text.
The jacket and endleaves
were printed on Curtis Tweedweave Text,
and the binding in Holliston Mills Roxite
was executed by New Hampshire Bindery
in Concord, New Hampshire.

Lebanon
1761 * 1994

*has been published in a first edition
of three thousand copies
of which two hundred and fifty
have been numbered and signed
by the author.
This is copy number*

and is here signed.